The View from Moscow:

Understanding Russia
and U.S.-Russia Relations

Natylie Baldwin

First Edition

Double Eagle Publishing LLC
Portland, Oregon

natyliesbaldwin.com

*Dedicated to the late **Robert Parry**,*
legendary journalist and founder of Consortium News

Acknowledgments

I want to express my appreciation to the following people for their support throughout my writing journey in general, and for this book in particular: Sharon Tennison, for her guidance and insights gleaned from decades of experience with the Soviet Union and Russia; Kermit Heartsong, for suggesting that I was knowledgeable and skilled enough to write a book; Rob Kall, for providing a platform at OpEdNews for my early articles on Russia; the editorial staff at Consortium News, for providing an even bigger platform for my articles on Russia and foreign policy; Rick Sterling, for getting me speaking engagements; Laura Dragonette, for copy editing the manuscript; Greg Maybury and Jeanne Burdoin, for beta reading the manuscript; James Chen, Bob Spies, Larry Sloan, and Gideon Anthony, for their financial support; my blog and Twitter followers, many of whom have been following my analyses for several years now; and my parents, for teaching me to be an independent thinker.

Any factual mistakes in the book are my responsibility.

Table of Contents

Introduction

Russia is the world's other nuclear superpower—the only country that has the ability to wipe the United States off the map within 30 minutes.

It is also the planet's largest country geographically and is the sixth largest economy in terms of purchasing power parity (1). The U.S. relationship with Russia, therefore, is incredibly important and delicate.

In order to conduct a rational foreign policy, we must understand the other country's point of view. It doesn't mean we must agree with it, but we must know how the other side perceives its own interests so we can determine what they may be willing to risk or sacrifice on behalf of those perceived interests. Furthermore, it's essential to determine areas of common cause and cooperation.

Understanding that viewpoint means understanding the other side's history, geography, and culture. The corporate media—and even some of our alternative media—have not provided this crucial service or provided a platform for those who can with respect to many of the nations with whom we've gone to war. The so-called experts they consult often have conflicts of interest, nefarious agendas, and lack an objective understanding of the nation about which they are writing or talking. This has certainly been the case when it comes to reporting on Russia, a country with which the stakes are potentially much higher. This book is an attempt to fill the void left by much of our media in understanding the Russian point of view.

A good starting point involves something that most Americans take for granted about our own country: geography.

America has an ocean on either side, friendly or benign neighbors to the north and south, and a nuclear arsenal, which makes an invasion from another country virtually impossible. But we still have the Monroe Doctrine, which grants us the whole Western Hemisphere as our security zone.

As one can see from the map at the front of this book, Russia has a very different geographical reality that has shaped its history and influenced Russians' mentality. They don't have oceans and mountain ranges as a natural form of protection, so Russians have a long history of invasions from many different directions: Vikings in the tenth century; Mongols twice in the thirteenth century (1223 and 1236); the Commonwealth of Poland/Lithuania in 1605; Sweden in 1707; France in 1812; and, Nazi Germany in 1941 (known as Operation Barbarossa).

The Soviet Union suffered 27 million deaths as a result of World War II, the most of any country during the war. This was mostly due to the Nazi invasion and included 17–19 million civilians. Around a third of the Soviet Union was destroyed. By comparison, the U.S. lost approximately 405,000 soldiers and saw no damage to its homeland.

It's fair to say that Americans likely cannot fathom this level of death and destruction. We haven't had a war on our soil since the 1860s, and the Civil War did not involve a foreign invasion. Americans have nothing comparable in living memory. On the other hand, many living Russians have grandparents and great-grandparents who have talked about their experiences of death and destruction in WWII, or the Great Patriotic War, as it's known in Russia. Victory Day—May 9—is an important holiday in Russia, and, according to polls, it is observed by Russians across the demographic and political spectrum.

I got a chance to see the Victory Day celebrations in Moscow when I was there in 2017. After the military parades, regular Russian citizens walked through the streets carrying photos of loved ones who served in or were casualties of the war. This is called the Immortal Regiment March.

This history has weighed heavily on all subsequent Russian leaders and played a role in Soviet President Mikhail Gorbachev's hesitancy to allow a reunified Germany into NATO in 1989. According to documents released by the National Security Archive in December 2017, there is no further debate. Western representatives, including then-Secretary of State, James

Baker, did in fact promise Gorbachev that there would be no further expansion of NATO eastward if he agreed to the reunification of Germany and its inclusion in NATO. (This is discussed in more detail in Chapter 7.)

After the Cold War, the French and German leadership believed that the best way to bring Russia into the Western fold and encourage its evolution as a democracy was through cooperation and gradual integration.

However, many in Washington developed a triumphalist attitude. Years of heavy lobbying by the U.S. arms industry and political groups including neoconservatives, imperialist ideologues, and members of Eastern European communities with an historical axe to grind against Russia, led by Zbigniew Brzezinski, ensued. This culminated in U.S. President Bill Clinton breaking the promise to Gorbachev when he allowed Poland, the Czech Republic and Hungary to be brought into NATO in 1999. This was followed by the entry of Romania, Bulgaria, Latvia, Lithuania, Estonia, Slovenia, and Slovakia in 2004 under the George W. Bush administration.

In the midst of this NATO expansion, the Bush administration also decided to unilaterally pull out of the Anti-Ballistic Missile (ABM) Treaty in 2002. This was seen as potentially jeopardizing the nuclear balance of power by leaving the United States free to pursue a first-strike capability with the eventual implementation of an anti-ballistic missile shield in Poland and Romania.

The Bush administration made these decisions despite the fact that Russian president Vladimir Putin was the first world leader to call him after 9/11 offering condolences and assistance in fighting terrorism, which included intelligence and logistical support and access to Russian military bases—the latter of which Putin did against the advice of his own national security team.

In early 2019, President Trump—whom we have been told is beholden to Putin—announced abrogation of the Intermediate-Range Nuclear Forces (INF) Treaty of 1987. This treaty had eliminated a whole class of nuclear weapons and protected Europe from being both a launching pad and a target in a nuclear exchange. According to Trump's then national security advisor, John Bolton, the New START Treaty will likely be allowed to sunset without renewal in 2021, leaving no meaningful nuclear arms treaties between the world's two nuclear superpowers who currently have 1,700 nuclear weapons combined on hair trigger alert (2).

Chapter 9 will discuss the Putin period of Russian governance in detail. Many facts will be presented that run counter to the narrative that many Americans have been given by corporate media and politicians. Putin is not a dictator and Russia is not an autocracy, but a transitional democracy.

Despite temporary setbacks with the financial crisis of 2008 and the recession of 2014–2016, the standard of living for Russians has improved drastically since 2000, including for Russians outside of Moscow and St. Petersburg. Putin laid out an ambitious plan for continued social and economic progress for Russia in his 2018 Address to the Federal Assembly, fully aware that Russians want to see better wages, improved health care, further investment in infrastructure, and more action to address corruption.

This is not to argue that Putin is a saint or a Boy Scout. Part of the point of this book is to get the reader to understand the perspective of Russia in general and Putin in particular as the leader of Russia and the pursuer of its interests both domestically and in the international arena. He does not shy away from using force if he thinks it is necessary to protect an important security interest for Russia. But, as will be shown with examples in the following pages, he has demonstrated a preference for resolving problems with diplomacy before they reach the level of potential military conflict, often getting rebuffed by the West for his efforts.

Although Washington has been in an economic and military position to dictate terms to the rest of the world since the fall of the Soviet Union, history shows that this position of supremacy by one power is not sustainable. We will eventually have to relearn the art of diplomacy. The most important country to start with is Russia.

Chapter 1: Tsarist Russia

The Princes of Kiev Rus and the Introduction of Orthodox Christianity

By the tenth century, Kiev was the center of the Rus territory and overlooked several rivers that connected the Byzantine Empire with the West. Having been settled by "warrior-traders" from the north (3), Kiev achieved relative stability and wealth due to its location as a flourishing trade hub. Its leader, Prince Vladimir, finally decided it was time to choose a religious faith for the territory.

In his quest, Vladimir received visitors who represented various religious traditions but wasn't quite satisfied with any of the options, including Islam and Catholicism. He then sent a small delegation on an expedition to learn about other faiths.

After the delegation's report of the beauty and profoundly moving spiritual experience they'd felt inside an Orthodox cathedral, Vladimir chose to adopt the Greek or Eastern Orthodox Christian faith. Orthodox Christianity was based in Constantinople, the center of the Byzantine Empire, also known as the Eastern Roman Empire, which encompassed "parts of Italy, the Balkan Peninsula, the Aegean archipelago and all of Asia Minor" (4).

As Western Europe was just beginning its ascent out of the Dark Ages, Constantinople and the Byzantine Empire, with its emphasis on the Greek language and literature, had served as a repository, preserving the ancient Greek and Roman arts, philosophy, and Christianity (4).

Russians incorporated their own traditional folk art, music, and pagan traditions into their adopted faith. These included "community and brotherly love," peace, and a reverence for beauty and nature. Religious art within the hundreds of churches that were built throughout the territory emphasized humility and human suffering (4). As Russians would not have a fully translated version of the New Testament for quite some time, they tended to focus on the essence of Christ—compassion and willingness to suffer—rather than his specific teachings (3).

The painters of the largely religious icon art of the next several centuries were not only responsible for the beauty and artistic execution of the paintings, but were also expected to convey the Holy Spirit in their subjects. To fulfill this obligation, artists engaged in deprivation, prayer, and the study of religious texts in addition to honing their creative skills. Of the several schools that each developed a specific technique, the Novgorod school became the most renowned (4).

Historian Suzanne Massie, in her book *Land of the Firebird: The Beauty of Old Russia*, describes the passion that Russians brought to their new faith during this period:

> So magnificent were the Russian churches with their decorated interiors, so mighty the music of Orthodox choirs, unaccompanied by any instruments, that many foreign ambassadors were awestruck upon setting foot in these palaces of God and . . . said that they felt they were in Heaven (4).

Vladimir softened his implementation of the Byzantine legal code by prohibiting torture and mutilation as forms of punishment and curtailing the death penalty. He also incorporated the traditional Slavic emphasis on social responsibility. During his periodic court feasts, Vladimir would have "wagons loaded with bread, meat, fish, vegetables and mead" wheeled out and distributed to the less fortunate throughout Kiev (4).

Vladimir's son, Prince Yaroslav the Wise, presided over the most peaceful and successful period for Kiev Rus. Devoted to the uniquely Russian form of Orthodoxy that had been adopted, Yaroslav oversaw the development of many schools and hospitals along with numerous churches and the Cathedral of the Holy Wisdom. The latter was partly a consequence of the flood of educated clergy from the Byzantine Empire. Art continued to thrive as well (4) (3).

Other cities in the territory, mostly a network of fortifications located along rivers that facilitated trade (3), developed similarly to Vladimir and Novgorod. Some cities even built roadways and constructed efficient drainage systems (4).

As the territory expanded during this period, it was mainly due to the spread of Orthodoxy. As historian James Billington explains in *The Icon and the Axe*:

> Kievan Russia received such unity as it attained essentially through waves of conversion—moving north from Kiev and out from the princely court in each city to ever wider sections of the surrounding populace. Conversion was apparently more important than colonization in unifying the region, and each new wave of converts tended to adopt not merely the Byzantine but the Kievan heritage as well. The Slavonic language became the uniform vehicle for writing and worship, slowly driving the Finno-Ugrian tongues which originally dominated much of northern Russia to peripheral regions. . . . The unity of Kievan Russia was above all that of a common religious faith. The forms of faith and worship were almost the only uniformities in this loosely structured civilization. Such economic strength and political cohesion as had existed began to break down with the internecine strife of the late twelfth century (3).

Kiev Rus had grown successful enough for members of its royal family to even begin marrying into other monarchies in Europe. But none of this success could compensate for the one major vulnerability of the general territory: its geographical lack of barriers to invasion from different directions. Indeed this vulnerability would underpin a major feature of the Russian mindset that still resonates today: patriotism and the high value placed on security.

The Mongols

By the time the Mongols first invaded in 1223, the Kiev Russian territory had degenerated into rivalries between princes who lorded over around "a dozen or so" independent areas, which had resulted in disorganized rule (5).

Subsequently, the Mongols were able to burn, sack, and massacre virtually all cities and towns of the territory in short order. Around two-thirds of the population perished, and many survivors retreated into the forests, taking solace in their Orthodox faith (4). They eventually migrated farther out to less vulnerable areas closer to Moscow.

The Mongols reigned over the land through the thirteenth and fourteenth centuries, forcing the surviving Russians into complete subjugation. They were able to impose their centralized and absolutist rule on the scattered Russians who had lost their complex Slavic tribal bonds in the process (5). Massie describes an important aspect of this rupture of bonds among the Slavs who'd constituted Kiev Rus:

> Earlier as the Slavs had expanded and absorbed the land, they had fallen into two natural divisions: the Great Russians in the north and the Little Russians in the south. After the Mongol invasion, the Little Russians were cut off from the Great Russians. While the Great Russians became vassals of the Mongols, the Little Russians, who were later known as Ukrainians, were taken over by the Poles and the Lithuanians (4).

The Mongols, for all of their viciousness, did have a sociopolitical ideology. It required absolute submission to the power of the Khan, who embodied the state. This Khan owned all of the land and had unqualified authority over his subjects. Land might be temporarily given to others to be overseen at the pleasure of the Khan, who could withdraw the privilege at any time. The overall objective was to create an empire that, after quick and dirty wars of conquest, would be ruled over by the Khan as a "worldwide social order based on justice and equality," living in eternal peace (5). The price for this security and justice was perfect submission.

The efficient rule of the Mongols, which lasted for almost 250 years, was achieved by reestablishing a form of national unity from the top, delegating responsibility at the local level for maintaining peace, collecting tribute, and enforcing the law to those princes and those among their entourage who showed trustworthiness. Faithfulness to the Khan (the state) was rewarded through a system of seniority among the princes (5).

The basic principles of Mongol rule—security and justice in exchange for submission to an absolute central authority—would influence Russian governance into the twentieth century.

The one city that was spared was Novgorod. Due to a combination of fortuitously bad weather that prevented the invaders from penetrating the city and the continual payment of tribute by its ruler, Alexander, Novgorod remained intact. Alexander also fought off a Swedish invasion instigated by an opportunistic pope who hoped to capture Novgorod and convert it to Catholicism (4).

As Russians fled from Kiev and the surrounding areas, Moscow—once considered a small and unimportant "trading post in the wilderness" (4)—gradually developed into a prominent city that was influenced by Mongol administration and Orthodox mysticism (3).

The princes of Moscow collected tribute from their subjects, which they, in turn, used to pay tribute to the Mongols. In exchange, the Mongols gave the local princes the liberty to administer their domain however they wished (4).

The Moscow princes expanded the city mostly through annexation, increasing its power and wealth. Its location between major river routes, which enabled communication, travel, and trade, contributed to its growing success (5). The leader of the Orthodox Church, called the metropolitan, moved from Vladimir to Moscow in 1326, adding to the city's importance (4). Moscow developed in a series of concentric rings around the center as churches and villages sprang up on the periphery.

The Moscow prince who founded the dynasty that would rule Russia after the Mongols and through the sixteenth century was Ivan I, also known as Kalita. Ivan was ruthless when it suited him to get rid of rivals and in the service of his Mongol bosses who rewarded his subservience with increased power and prestige within his fiefdom.

In 1327, the Mongols conferred upon Ivan the title of "Great Prince" (3). He was granted exclusive judicial authority and right of tax collection over all the other princes after he brutally put down a rebellion initiated by another prince attempting to overthrow Mongol rule (5).

Wars were a major feature of the next three centuries, including wars of aggression and expansion as well as wars of defense and of internal conflict. There were six wars with Sweden and twelve with Poland-Lithuania alone (5). Much of this martial conflict was driven, at least in part, by Russia's geographic situation between Europe and Asia.

When the Golden Horde's dominance eventually faded, the Tatars, based in the southwestern area of Crimea, terrorized Russia with constant raids on horseback that killed or captured Russians, selling the victims into slavery in surrounding territories. This only ended when Catherine the Great annexed the area in the latter eighteenth century.

Due to the Tatar aggression, Russian men were conscripted from spring through late autumn every year to defend against the violent incursions. This situation also forced Russia to focus its colonization efforts on the harsher areas to its north and east.

Ivan IV, also known as Ivan the Terrible (or "Ivan the Formidable" in Russian) finally defeated the last of the Mongol-controlled areas of Kazan, Astrakhan, and Siberia in the 1550s.

Ivan the Terrible

Ivan, who had lost both parents by the age of eight, spent his childhood watching rival factions in the royal court jockeying for power with unabashed violence. During this period he was reportedly often abused and neglected.

He also read voraciously, taking a particular interest in religion and the history of Russia, ancient Rome, and the Byzantine Empire.

At the age of sixteen, having nurtured his own ambitions for power, he had himself declared "Tsar and Autocrat," the first Russian leader to assume those official titles (4). He would go on to rule effectively for thirty-seven years, the longest ruler in Russian history.

Many historians recognize a distinction between a relatively "good" period under Ivan IV that coincided with the earlier years of his reign—when he was happier and healthier—and the well-known "terrible" period that came later.

In the early years, art, architecture, and music flourished in Moscow. However, it tended to be of a religious nature, as Ivan ultimately repressed most secular influences and emphasized the traditional, even to the point of micromanaging everyday aspects of life.

Ivan encouraged the completion of an extensive encyclopedia of world history in addition to volumes on Russian folklore and biographies of Russian rulers. He was even responsible for the first printing press being brought to Russia (4). The cathedrals of Kazan and St. Basil in Moscow were both constructed under Ivan's rule.

During this period Moscow was declared "the third Rome," since Constantinople had been captured by the Turks. As Billington states with regard to the interweaving of the religious and the political during Ivan's reign:

> Justification for his rule was rooted in the historical theology of Muscovy. The massive *Book of Degrees of the Imperial Genealogy*, drawn up by his monastic advisers, carried to new extremes the blending of sacred and secular history. Hagiography was applied wholesale to the descriptions of tsars, and imperial ancestries were traced to miracle-working saints as well as emperors of antiquity. . . . The Church code enacted in 1551 known as the hundred chapters was designed only to "confirm former tradition," and prescribed rules for everything from icon

painting to shaving and drinking. . . . Every aspect of
domestic activity was ritualized with semi-monastic rules
of conduct in the "Household Book" *(Domostroy)* (3).

Ivan's later violent purges were partly based on an exaggeration of perceived threats to his absolute rule in both the political and religious arenas.
Targets included the metropolitan of the Orthodox Church and any individuals or groups who were considered to have the potential for independent
influence.

During Ivan's reign, peasants—who only a few generations before had
enjoyed freedom of movement as long as they weren't indebted to a landlord—became bound to the land. This undermined any independent power
that landlords had begun to acquire through exploitation of the peasants'
increasing indebtedness due to poor lands and the inability to pay off loans.
In conditions of excess land and scarce labor with which to colonize it, landlords were forced to compete for peasant labor. Many prospective landlords
lured peasants away from their existing landlords by offering to pay off their
debt. However, the price for this repayment was the peasant relinquishing
his future freedom, as well as that of his descendants, in perpetuity to the
new landlord. Consequently, the landlords now effectively owned the peasants who served them (5).

This arrangement threatened the state's taxation system by the loss of
"free peasant" taxpayers and also limited the supply of men available for military service. By the middle of the century, landlords were understood to be
agents of their peasants, or serfs, being responsible for paying their serfs'
taxes, ensuring their serfs' good behavior, and conveying their serfs' grievances to the appropriate government officials.

Although landlords could legally try to punish their serfs—including
the use of torture, private imprisonment, and death—for insubordination
and other infractions, peasants also had a right to petition the tsar with complaints against the landlord (5). But it was impossible to predict whether such
a petition would have any beneficial effect, since there were no actual laws
regulating the relationship between a serf and his landlord and the results
were largely up to the caprice of the tsar.

Ivan's religious zeal, inculcated by his strident monastic tutors who emphasized the Old Testament in their teachings, prompted his initiation of the Livonian War in 1558. This war against the Baltic region of the West, which lasted 25 years, had religious and cultural overtones and was ultimately a failure for Russia (3).

Like the Mongols, Ivan the Terrible had a political ideology in which the ends justified the brutal means. He was the most responsible for synthesizing the despotism of the Mongols and the cultural influence of the Byzantine Empire into the Muscovite brand of autocratic rule that would reign for hundreds of years.

Ivan spelled out his views of governance in response to his former ally Prince Kurbsky's published condemnations of Ivan after he'd "defected" to Lithuania. Referring to his subjects as slaves and denying (dishonestly) that Russian rulers had ever governed any differently, Ivan maintained that he had absolute authority over all Russians and all lands within the territory (5).

Although the tsar's views were partly a reflection of his own personal love of unqualified power, they also were consistent with the views of church leaders and political writers of the time. Before their substance was articulated by Ivan the Terrible, Ivan Peresvetov, recognized as Russia's first political theorist, advocated the amalgamation of the Turkish political system with the Orthodox religion. He argued that the Turks had been able to conquer Constantinople because of their absolute authority and "use of terror," whereas the Byzantine emperor's authority had been too limited, which made him and his empire vulnerable (5).

Due to Russia's size and unwieldy nature (poor communication, rough terrain, and dubious social cohesion), it was further argued that the only way to achieve the obedience of its subjects and to govern effectively was for the people to be "kept in great dread" (5). Russia was perceived by its leadership to be in an existential struggle to survive as a unified entity. This would be a common theme throughout its history.

Ivan's gradual descent into greater savagery started 13 years into his reign, after the death of his beloved first wife, Anastasia. She was the one person who loved and accepted him and whom he trusted without reservation. He suspected that she was poisoned by political rivals in the court. Forensic analysis of her exhumed remains centuries later would confirm his suspicion of foul play (6).

An exhumation of Ivan's remains during the Soviet era confirmed that he himself suffered from mercury poisoning—a not uncommon side effect of which is psychosis. Many medicinal treatments at the time contained the toxic element, and it is believed he was poisoned as a result of the use of ointments for bone and joint problems he suffered in his later years that would have caused severe pain and limited mobility (7).

By the latter part of his reign, Ivan displayed increasing instability and paranoia, which would precipitate his calls for massacres carried out by a personal army of thousands known as the oprichniki. The most famous of his targets was approximately three thousand of the inhabitants of the independent city of Novgorod, who were murdered in the most barbaric manner because he had come to believe they were traitors.

In 1581, Ivan accidentally murdered his son and heir, striking him on the head with his wooden staff in a fit of rage. The scene is captured in Ilya Repin's famous painting in which an anguished Ivan is shown holding his dead son in his arms. Ivan himself died three years later at the age of 54.

In the Soviet era, Ivan the Terrible's rule was whitewashed (5) with Joseph Stalin and his advisors claiming that Ivan's cruelties were necessary in the context of the time and circumstances (8). But historians have pointed out that Ivan oversaw a powerful and unified state with no significant internal threats, only the usual dangers from the outside world (5).

Peter the Great

Our people are like children, who would never of their own accord decide to learn, who would never take up the alphabet without being compelled to do so by their teacher, who would at first feel despondent. But later, when they have finished their studies, they are grateful for having been made to go through them. This is evident

today: has not everything been achieved under con-
straint? Yet now one hears gratitude for much that has
already borne fruit.

—Peter the Great (5)

Like Ivan IV, Peter lost his father while still a young child. He, too, witnessed palace rivalries that resulted in massacres, including of family members and supporters of his mother, who was his father's second wife (4).

For many years of his youth, Peter, his mother, and his two sisters were exiled to a country village outside of Moscow. He soon befriended the village boys and excelled at numerous outdoor activities such as hunting, masonry, falconry, building construction, and shooting cannons. By his teen years, he was designing war games and had recruited hundreds of boys to play in them. These boys would later comprise the center of his royal guards and "elite units of the Russian army" (4).

He eventually grew to a full height of six feet eight inches. By adulthood, Peter had developed an insatiable curiosity, particularly about the mechanical arts, which he had a natural talent for. A particular passion was boats; he eventually learned shipbuilding under the tutelage of a Dutch expert during his extended trip to Europe in 1697. While there, he also learned papermaking and engraving (4).

When Peter assumed the throne, he took the title of emperor instead of tsar. Although his reign would see a flourishing of the arts, his emphasis was always on the practical, such as architecture, engineering, medicine, and manufacturing.

Based on his observations during his visit to Europe as well as his contact with various people of Dutch, Scotch, and German descent, from artisans to mercenaries, Peter concluded that Western culture and technology were superior. He consequently viewed the Mongol period of rule over Russia and the customs associated with it as backward (4). He therefore wanted to advance the country as quickly as possible to make up for it.

He started with changing customs of appearance in the royal court. Men were to shave their faces and wear English-style clothing, and women

were to remove veils from their hair and face. Forced marriages were prohibited (4).

He then turned toward modernizing the army and creating the first
Russian navy. He also founded schools specializing in subjects ranging from
math and science to philosophy and medicine. He oversaw the initiation of
the first Russian newspaper and encouraged the mass printing of books on
various topics. He introduced paper manufacturing and tapestry making,
and he sent Russian students to Europe to learn navigation and engineering
(4).

His most ambitious project came in 1703 when Peter decided that a
grand city would be built on a marsh facing Europe and the sea, a city
intended to rival the finest of the West in terms of art and architecture. The
city, now known as St. Petersburg, would be located along the Neva River,
which flows from Lake Ladoga and through a series of swampy islands into
the eastern Baltic Sea (3).

Most of the city's original 35,000 buildings were designed by the most
skilled Europeans who had contracted for years in Russia, some of whom
stayed on, since Westerners were welcomed into the area. However, these
Westerners often lived apart from the average native Russian (5).

The city was built in seven years. As Massie points out, this was an
amazing feat considering that the French, using the most modern materials
and methods, had taken 47 years to build Versailles (4).

But there was a dark side to Peter's advances. The human toll of making this magnificent city a reality is estimated to be in the thousands. Peter
meant to drag a lagging nation kicking and screaming into modernity – a
foreshadowing of his twentieth-century counterpart, Joseph Stalin (9).

St. Petersburg not only became an important naval base and center of
trade, but also became home to numerous learning institutions like the Academy of Sciences, as well as libraries, beautiful palaces, and ornate churches
with gardens, fountains, statues, and parks. A unique culture that synthesized
creative influences from the West and native Russia emerged in the city and
is still its trademark today.

Peter, however, prompted backlash from conservative merchants, religious traditionalists, and peasant rebels for his breakneck pace of Westernization. His reforms were perceived as a threat to Orthodoxy and traditional culture due to the influx of foreigners and "heretics" from the West. Peter's practice of subordinating the church and its leader into a state-controlled synod, along with declaring Russia an independent and secular state, caused particular offense. Peter also expanded tolerance of Catholics, allowing the first Catholic church to be built in Russia. But he also supported Galileo in his conflict with the church on behalf of science.

Peter was also the first Russian ruler to use political propaganda to spread his justifications for decision-making and ideology. He underscored a brand of secular nationalism as opposed to a religious one, and a foreign policy objective of maintaining a balance of power in Europe (3).

Peter ultimately repressed any forces that insisted on preservation of the traditional religious rituals as well as radical religious reformers. Although he did oversee the building of the last of the "great complex of monasteries," it's likely that he did so because he wanted St. Petersburg to be the equal of Kiev and Moscow, both of which were linked to such a complex (3).

In terms of the conditions for peasants, by the time of Peter's reign, the state showed very little interest in administering over them as long as the taxes were paid. This resulted in the landlords' increased control over them in all practical respects.

Peter had developed a belief in meritocracy during his teen years in the village outside of Moscow (4). As a result, meritocracy was incorporated into his program of military reforms, and some social mobility was established more broadly with the introduction of the Table of Ranks in 1722 (5).

Members of the nobility comprised most of the military, and the need to burnish the socioeconomic position of this group without actually granting them independence was recognized. Under the Table of Ranks, all Russian subjects were classified into ranks, also known as estates.

The lowest estate was occupied by the serfs, who were subdivided into two classes: state serfs and private serfs. The former consisted of those who were not under the bondage of private landholders and included low-level religious clergy, Siberian pioneers, and relatives of serfs who owned no land of their own. They were understood to be treated slightly better than private serfs, which created class envy. Peter declared the buying and selling of slaves to be illegal, but there was virtually no enforcement of the declaration, and the practice continued (5).

Merchants and traders comprised another rank, tied to trade. Nobles were tied directly to state service, either in the military or civil service. Massie describes the dynamic of this system:

> Everyone was recognized as belonging to one of these estates. Any educated person could apply to enter state service, regardless of background. Entering at rank four-teen and aspiring to rank one. As soon as a person reached the eighth rank, which corresponded to a colonel in the army or a captain in the navy, he automatically became a "noble." . . . There was a high degree of social mobility; one could move from one estate to the other, sometimes with alarming speed. . . . Serfs in the army could rise in two generations to noblemen. Dostoevsky, whose father was a modest doctor, was classified as a noble. Lenin's grand-father was a serf, but Lenin was born a nobleman because his father had achieved civil service ranking of hereditary major general (4).

Despite the many successes of Peter's rule, there were also many fail-ures and negative unintended consequences from his policies. For example, the majority of industries started under Peter failed. Sheer will alone could not paper over the fact that many of the elements that Western nations pos-sessed that facilitated the gradual development of manufacturing from crafts and cottage industries were absent in Russia (5). These included capital, entrepreneurs, workers, consumers, and the concept of supply and demand (3).

Historically, no wealth could accumulate, and no commerce could develop due to most cities and towns being little more than military outposts or fortresses with some basic trade. All people, whether they were peasants or landholders, were in bondage to the state to pay taxes and had no independence.

The state owned all resources and served as virtually the sole source of demand. It chose agents of the government to serve as industrialists. This led to a system that had no profit incentive and acquired workers by taking over villages and their serfs with the permission of the state. Convict labor was also used.

No competition existed to foster innovation or improvement, as demand was guaranteed along with monopoly status to the industry. Foreign companies were not allowed to compete, and private clients for industry were not allowed until 1809 with the advent of textile manufacturing (3). This resulted in poor-quality products.

Peter also changed the method of succession of the tsars, which led to instability for the next hundred years, as coups and murders followed the deaths of rulers. For approximately four centuries prior to Peter, the tsars had been chosen by male heredity. But Peter instituted the concept of choosing one's successor, which enabled the armed guards of the court to place an individual in power if they had curried favor with them. Since the guards came from the court nobility, this group effectively gained temporary influence until peasants were able to enter into the ranks around the turn of the eighteenth century (5).

Some historians have pointed to other negative aspects of Peter's legacy. First, it instilled the belief among future Russian reformist and revolutionary thinkers that change had to be forcibly imposed from above and rationalized the use of brutal methods on behalf of the goal. For all the beauty of the city he founded and the opening up of Russia to outside knowledge and modernity, Peter was ultimately a pragmatist who cared about results and not so much about what means were used to achieve them (5).

Second, his reforms resulted in a Europeanized court and nobility that had adopted the language and trappings of a culture foreign to the Russian masses, thereby widening the divisions between the two classes irrevocably (5). As Massie notes, "By exempting the clergy and the peasants from his

Westernizing reforms, he began a cultural schism between classes which had never existed, a schism never fully healed. For more than a century after him, for the upper classes what was Western became fashionable; what was Russian became lowly, unworthy, and plebian" (4).

This trend was reinforced by Catherine the Great and to a lesser degree by other subsequent tsars who considered Western-inspired reform.

Catherine the Great: Trying to Square the Circle

Peter's only son to have lived to adulthood, Alexis, died in prison in 1718 due to alleged participation in plots against his father. Consequently, Alexis's only son, Peter II, ruled Russia for a short time until he died and Anna, a niece of Peter the Great, was installed. After a few years, she fell into disfavor in the court and Peter the Great's daughter Elizabeth ascended the throne and ruled for two decades.

Elizabeth was a good-natured and generous pleasure-seeker who led an even greater expansion in the arts as well as openness to the West in facilitating that expansion. Although she oversaw two wars, she was not the pragmatist her father was and not much changed in terms of government or military reform during her reign.

Upon her death, an ambitious German princess whom Elizabeth had called over from Europe as an eventual wife for her teenage nephew, Peter III, had been gradually cultivating her own plans for power. The daughter of an indifferent father and an opportunistic mother, young Catherine realized quickly who to befriend and whose good side to stay on after she arrived in Russia. She also started to learn Russian and converted to Orthodoxy so she could further remain in the good graces of the right people in her adopted country. An intellectual who studied under private tutors, Catherine developed an interest in French culture and philosophy.

Catherine's sixteen-year marriage to Peter was an unhappy one spent mostly apart, as Peter soon took a mistress whom he later made clear would be declared empress after he took the throne. In consultation with her lover and royal court guard member, Grigory Orlov, she had her unpopular husband overthrown so she could become empress. Within a week of his abdication, he was dead under mysterious circumstances (10).

Unlike Elizabeth, Catherine took great interest in the administration of the country. As Massie wrote, "She pored over state papers and wrote not only her own laws but the arguments in their favor and philosophical commentaries on them" (4).

Catherine soon made French the official language of the court, and French culture was adopted by the nobility whose interests she championed throughout her rule. She acquired a prodigious number of paintings from Western Europe, particularly France, which later comprised the beginnings of the Hermitage collection (4).

Catherine's reign would see the introduction of vaccinations for smallpox, paper money, improved administration throughout the country, increased secularization, and the rebuilding of many cities—including St. Petersburg, whose population doubled.

She conducted a years-long correspondence with Voltaire and Diderot and had an interest in European Enlightenment-inspired reforms. But as we will see, the reform issue would ultimately pose a quandary for Catherine.

During this period, the number of books published—now mostly secular—skyrocketed from around 100 per year to 8,000. Secular education was allowed to spread into the farther reaches of the land in an effort to "transform provincial cities into imperial cultural and administrative centers" (5). This was enabled by the flood of private tutors into Russia from Western Europe and expeditions into the north and east of the country by Western scientists. These forays into the harshest parts of the country inevitably involved the locals, who served as guides and assistants (5).

Catherine founded a school for girls that accepted a significant number of students from families of moderate rank in addition to the nobility. It was the first girl's school in Europe to include science in the curriculum. This was in keeping with reforms started under Peter the Great that had improved the status of Russian women, who could now legally inherit and own land and money, able to exercise some independence if they had the means (4).

In another pioneering move for Europe, Catherine appointed a woman, Catherine Vorontsova-Dashkova, to head the Academy of Sciences in St. Petersburg. Dashkova was a highly educated and well-traveled widow who was devoted to the advancement of Russian scholarship and expanding the education of Russians. Under her leadership, a translation department was established to facilitate Russians' ability to learn from foreign academics. Russian literature and theater was encouraged as well as the establishment of Russian scientific journals. She also increased instructors' salaries and organized public lectures (4).

Catherine eventually wrote a treatise outlining her own philosophy, called "Instruction." It was not codified into law but was distributed widely throughout the non-peasant population of the country and became very influential to those who came in contact with it.

There were four major influencers on Catherine's thought: 1) Voltaire, who emphasized rationalism and skepticism; 2) Jeremy Bentham, an English philosopher who advocated utilitarianism; 3) Beccaria, an Italian philosopher who argued that crime was a product of ignorance and bad laws; and 4) the French philosopher Montesquieu, who inspired her desire to bring "rational order" to the political sphere (5).

Catherine, however, lost interest in reform after the French Revolution and its subsequent Reign of Terror. She was personal friends with Marie Antoinette and was upset by her execution.

Subsequently, she turned her focus to foreign policy and expanded the Russian territory through several wars, including the acquisition of Crimea, Poland, and parts of Turkey. She had many skilled military leaders at her disposal in this undertaking, including Grigory Potemkin, who would serve as a diplomat and reformer of the military as well as being the "great love" of Catherine's life (4).

As Billington notes, for all of Catherine's efforts in rebuilding major cities and expanding their artistic and architectural glory, these efforts ultimately revealed an emphasis on style over substance, as they did little to serve as the means of economic development and trade that still eluded the country compared to the lionized west (3). Instead they effectively served as grand cultural displays while no substantive changes occurred in the lives of the majority of the population, which consisted of serfs.

Serfs were still tied to the land under severe conditions, administered over by landlords who controlled all aspects of their lives (4). At this point, they had even lost the privilege of petitioning the tsar for any grievances. The nobility had been granted the right to exile serfs they were dissatisfied with to Siberia or into convict labor, and state serfs were regularly handed out to favored members of the royal court (5).

Catherine began her reign sympathetic to the idea of emancipating the serfs but ultimately did not go through with it. But she did issue the Charter of the Nobility in 1785, granting yet more rights to the aristocratic minority, who were now effectively "emancipated" from most of their state obligations. This privileged group was now free from taxation, compulsory service, conscription, and corporal punishment, and they enjoyed the right to a jury of one's peers if accused of a crime. Most of these perks would be reversed after Catherine's death, during the short reign of her despised son, Paul, whom she did not want to inherit the throne (5).

Catherine's legacy in connection with domestic reform was decidedly mixed. Billington mentions an important drawback to Catherine's focus on certain aspects of European Enlightenment philosophy that was ultimately not well thought out on practical grounds:

> From Catherine, aristocratic thinkers received only their inclination to look westward for answers. They learned to think in terms of sweeping reforms on abstract rationalistic grounds rather than piecemeal changes rooted in concrete conditions and traditions (3).

Furthermore, by using philosophy—as opposed to heredity or religion—as justification for her rule, Catherine unwittingly introduced the possibility of debate regarding legitimacy. And by expanding reform and education, she encouraged discussion of and rising expectations for further reform and progress. This would eventually undermine or at least call into question the continued viability of absolute rule by her or any tsar or emperor.

As Billington further points out, reform-minded rulers from Catherine to Alexander II all felt compelled to eventually put the brakes on reform and revert to authoritarianism to control forces that had been unleashed with unforeseen consequences (3).

When push came to shove, none of these rulers—with the possible exception of Alexander II—was ready to cede much if any of the omnipotence they enjoyed. Each was succeeded by a ruler who rejected reform. This led to a rise in the influence of more extreme elements demanding more profound changes, including those who advocated the complete destruction of the existing system.

Alexander I: The Leader Who Humbled Napoleon

Catherine's son Paul ruled for five years and then was murdered in a coup, which brought Alexander I, Catherine's grandson, to the throne. Alexander knew of the coup plot but had been promised that his father's life would be spared and was deeply upset at the news of the outcome.

Tutored by followers of the European Enlightenment, he also started out as an advocate for reform. But he would eventually follow the path of all such tsars and backpedal.

Alexander's education ended when he married at the age of sixteen, leaving him with high ideals but no real notion of how to effectively execute them. At the beginning of his reign, he surrounded himself with a contingent of advisors comprised of nobles and officials who shared his ideas for reform. One particularly influential advisor was a scholar and administrator named Mikhail Speransky, known for his abilities, honesty, and humble origins (5).

Together they implemented an impressive array of policies. Censorship was banned, landowners could voluntarily emancipate serfs, modern ministries were introduced, a wave of new schools and universities were built, and the mass publication of books took off (4) (3).

Alexander fraternized with average Russians and oversaw the construction on sixty bridges over the canals of St. Petersburg. He even corresponded with Thomas Jefferson regarding the idea of a constitution (4).

Speransky was an advocate for a constitutional monarchy. His practical background in civil administration led him to realize the need for better training of civil servants, establishing two schools for this purpose. These schools soon became hotbeds for more reform ideas.

Speransky had drafted a blueprint for even wider reforms, which included separation of powers: the establishment of a supreme judicial body and a legislative body. The latter would be composed of a network of "regional representative bodies." The tsar would still retain control over all of these institutions (3).

Speransky's papers were recovered in 1961, and his written commentaries on the conditions of Russia in the early nineteenth century are insightful and deserve to be quoted at some length:

> The fundamental principle of Russian government is the autocratic ruler who combines within his person all legislative and executive powers, and who disposes unconditionally of all the nation's resources. There are no physical limits to his power. . . . Under autocratic rule there can be no code of laws, for where no rights exist there can be no constant balance between them. What these governments call codes and laws are nothing but the arbitrary decisions of the sovereign authority, prescribing to the citizens their duties for a certain period of time, i.e. until the autocratic will chooses to change or otherwise circumscribe them. . . . Governments without political foundations can have no stability. . . . What is the use of laws assigning property to private individuals when property itself has no firm bases in any respect whatsoever? What is the use of civil laws, when their tablets can at any time be smashed upon the first rock of the arbitrary rule? People complain about the confusion of our finances. But how can finances be set in order in a country without public confidence, without any laws for regulating the financial system? (5)

But Alexander hesitated and ultimately decided against instituting these wider reforms. Consequently, Speransky—who was sympathetic to French liberalism—was exiled after Napoleon invaded in 1812. Alexander proceeded to crack down on what reforms he had implemented, imposing censorship and increasing police actions (5).

Ironically, Napoleon's invasion would not only inspire a rise in the trademark patriotism and tenacity of Russians that would lead to ultimate victory and new status as a great power in the world, it would also inspire additional demands for reform.

After the invasion, Russians of all ranks volunteered for service—even some in their seventies who reportedly fought with the same vigor as young men and donated whatever money and equipment they had (4).

Despite his best efforts, renowned General Mikhail Kutuzov wasn't able to keep the French from taking Moscow, which was captured within a week. What Napoleon encountered after this feat, however, amazed and flummoxed him. Alexander refused to surrender and negotiate a peace treaty. Instead, the Russians proceeded to burn Moscow to the ground, depriving the occupiers of much-needed resources. This would eventually enable them to turn the tables on the French.

An awestruck Napoleon had the following reaction:

> Such terrible tactics have no precedent in the history of civilization. . . . To burn one's own cities. . . . A demon inspires these people! What savage determination! What a people! What a people! (4)

The morale of the French forces, who were overstretched to begin with, plummeted as many of Napoleon's men fell ill or deserted and discipline broke down (11).

Five weeks later, after desecrating and robbing Uspenski Cathedral of tons of gold and silver, Napoleon and his men were forced to retreat through the Russian countryside where they faced a one-two punch of deprivation and bands of furious peasants and Cossacks who attacked them mercilessly:

A Russian account says that 36,000 French dead were found in the Berezina River alone. In all 125,000 men perished in battle; 132,000 succumbed to fatigue, hunger and cold; 193,000 were captured. Only 40,000 men returned alive from what was one of the greatest military catastrophes in history (4).

The Russian army eventually galloped into Paris, and Russian officers mingled with advocates of constitutional government and equality. After fighting alongside peasants to defend Mother Russia, some aristocrats and army officers were open to the French liberal ideas they were hearing and became more determined than ever to reform Russia (4).

After a failed military uprising that originated from one of his most trusted regiments, Alexander also became more repressive, purging educators, destroying books, expelling the liberal Jesuits, and abolishing all secret societies—including the Masons who had served as a far-reaching network of nobles who would meet to discuss politics and philosophy, among other topics. Their interests ranged from serious reform to mystical religion to relatively frivolous matters (3).

Following Alexander's death in 1825, the line of succession was unclear, since he had fathered no children. One of Alexander's brothers was likely to take the throne: Nicholas or Constantine. Reformers were hoping it would be Constantine, who was believed to be sympathetic to the cause of progressive change. However, by December, Nicholas took power after Constantine renounced, and a group of military officers, veterans of the war with France, protested in the capital and later led an uprising in Kiev (3). The insurrectionists would become known as the Decembrists.

As Billington points out, the Decembrists were united more by what they opposed than what they favored. They all opposed the arbitrariness and petty cruelties of the state as reflected by the actions of its bureaucratic officials (3).

They also seemed to agree that some form of constitutionalism was needed, but beyond that they were a motley crew, with some praising the historical independence of Novgorod while others had connections to and admired Poland's parliament or Lithuania's constitution. Still others desired a constitutional federation modeled on the United States. Some even eschewed nationalism altogether and wanted a pan-Slavic brotherhood (3).

Nicholas violently put down the uprising by publicly executing some of the leaders and imprisoning others or exiling them to Siberia. The regular soldiers—approximately 3,000 took part—were whipped and made the voyage to Siberia in chains as common criminals (12).

The leaders who were exiled to Siberia were well received by the indigenous Russian population of the area. They viewed the rebels as heroes, treated them with generosity, and were even known to facilitate communication among the Decembrists and with their friends and relatives.

Many of the Decembrists' wives went to Siberia to live with their husbands. For those who had the resources and wherewithal to survive the initial years of exile in the harsh hinterlands, many eventually became farmers and landowners, even choosing to stay on after their sentences were completed (13).

Nicholas quickly sent an unequivocal message to the reformists. He established a secret police that employed spies and informers throughout the country and emphasized the values of discipline, regimentation, and reverence for the military (5). The severe bureaucratic network was strengthened, increasingly made up of underpaid and corrupt officials.

Meanwhile, the influence of the nobility—associated in Nicholas's mind with the Decembrists—was neutralized. Class stratification was more strictly enforced, serfdom continued, and economic focus remained on agriculture rather than on the development of industry (3).

Philosophy was eventually outlawed in the later part of Nicholas's reign. Some refer to this period as the "anti-Enlightenment" in Russia. Before that, however, Russians had made great strides in the areas of math and astronomy. Russian intellectuals had turned their focus to German philosophers in their search for an as-yet undeveloped "systemic secular philosophy" (3).

With an abiding interest in history and their role in it, many Russians were attracted to the thinking of August Ludwig von Schlözer, an advocate of universal history in which Russians had a unique role to play. F.W. Schelling, who believed Russia was "fated to have a great destiny" within his more general belief in a world that was engaged in a meaningful process of evolution, was also popular (3).

Georg Hegel became another favorite among Russians from around 1838 to 1848. As Billington explains, "He offered the Russians a seemingly rational and all-encompassing philosophy of history and led the restless Westernizers—for the first time—to entertain serious thoughts of revolution" (3). The popularity of Hegel was facilitated by intellectual clubs that attracted young and enthusiastic followers, which included the literary critic Vissarion Belinsky as well as Mikhail Bakunin and Alexander Herzen (Belinsky, Bakunin, and Herzen will be discussed more in Chapter 2).

Hegel believed that rational sense and meaning could be derived from history and valued the objective over the subjective. His followers interpreted his views on destruction as a call to—or at the very least an allowance for—the destruction of the current state of affairs, including the institutions and individuals who kept it in place. His thinking was very influential to populists and anarchists, such as Bakunin. But Belinsky and Herzen eventually rejected Hegelianism to varying degrees (3).

Hegelian-derived ideas for social and political change suffered from the same problems that have been previously noted with respect to much of Western Enlightenment thought in Russia. Concerned with abstract and secular notions about history and philosophy, it lacked a practical program of reform rooted in moral imperatives that the majority of Russians could relate to.

The arts—namely poetry, music, and painting—and literary criticism became the main vehicles for the exploration of these philosophical ideas. Belinsky and poet Alexander Pushkin were probably the most famous examples of each. Belinsky summed up the period's blend of the rational, mystical, and creative in pursuit of existential truth and meaning: "For me, to think, feel, understand, and suffer are one and the same thing" (3).

Alexander II: No Good Deed Goes Unpunished

The new tsar had shown humanitarian and reformist inclinations before he ascended the throne, asking his father to grant a general amnesty to all prisoners as a wedding present. Nicholas wasn't amenable to this request but compromised by ordering the release of all incarcerated debtors and clearing their records (4).

When Alexander II came to power in 1855, he inherited the Crimean War with Britain, France, and the Ottomans. Recognizing that the war was unwinnable, he declared a truce, ending the three-year debacle. The defeat provided incentive for a renewed program of reform and development that looked more to France and England as influences rather than Prussia and Austria, which were viewed as failed allies (3).

Alexander also pardoned the Decembrists and cancelled all tax debts of the poor. By this point, the issue of serfdom had become more complicated. Some peasants were free, and those with good land had even prospered. Of those still under serfdom—which was the majority—not all had tyrannical landlords, though many did, and there was no form of legal redress. Furthermore, some serfs were domestics who did not work the land (4).

Comparisons have been made between American slavery and Russian serfdom. There were some significant differences, however. One was that Russian novelists never really talked about serfs in their literature, unlike American writers, since by rank their life experiences were far removed from those of serfs (3). Another difference is discussed by Massie:

> The fine distinction between Russian serf and American slave was that every serf family, other than house serfs, owned a piece of land where they could labor when the lord's needs had been satisfied and from which they could sell the surplus for their own profit. In principle, the serf was tied to the land, not the master, but in the late eighteenth century, Peter the Great established a tax bill on all the male population, which the landlords, not the peasants, were responsible for paying. Thereafter the tendency

was overwhelming to regard the serf as the landlord's property, to be bought and sold without the land, although later this was strictly against the law (4).

In 1861, Alexander freed the serfs. One reason why previous tsars who were sympathetic to emancipation eventually balked at going through with it was due to working out the aftereffects of such an act. Should land be granted to each serf as a means of future survival? If so, how would the landlords be compensated for the loss of both labor and a portion of land?

Alexander's emancipation decree did not include the granting of land to the released serfs; it contained provisions for each land-working serf to receive an allotment of land "similar to what they had cultivated in the past," but the allotment had to be purchased from the landowner. This provision, along with the fact that most landlords were only willing to sell off poor-quality land, effectively rendered most serfs landless (14).

Another complicating factor in this scheme was that much of the land was cultivated within the context of peasant communes (14).

The emancipation decree arguably left the serfs worse off than before in most practical respects. There is debate as to whether this was incidental or intentional as the country was finally focusing on the development of industry and the factories in major cities now needed a supply of labor.

From the year of emancipation on, Moscow became the industrial center of the country and grew at breakneck speed to catch up to the West. The city's population doubled between 1870 and 1912. A new class of rich industrialists emerged who became patrons of the arts, creating a rivalry between Moscow and St. Petersburg for recognizing and developing young artistic talent (4).

This rapid growth in industrialization and urbanization (3) and the mass of labor it required also had many negative and inhumane effects. These would come to a head in later years, enabled by the further expansion and liberalization of education and the press.

From 1870 to 1879, there were 326 strikes in factories and mills throughout the country. As during the industrial period in the West, workers were viewed as extensions of the machinery of production, to be used until run down and replaced. Shifts lasted 12–15 hours and included children, the sick, and the old (15).

Rural conditions were still very poor for many. Teachers in the provinces made below-subsistence wages and often slept on cots in the corner of their classrooms. There were occasional reports of teachers who died of starvation due to the authorities neglecting to pay the paltry wages they did earn for a month or more (15). There was also the high rate of indirect taxes on peasants in the scramble to build up the nation's financial reserves and fund its expansion (15).

In the meantime, Alexander continued to introduce more reforms. These included the establishment of units of self-governance in rural districts and large towns called zemstvos. The zemstvos consisted of local elected assemblies with limited rights of taxation (4). But they were not allowed in areas with a concentration of minority populations for fear of hostility toward the Russian state and the fostering of instability (16).

In the sphere of criminal justice, a package of reforms was introduced that included the rights to a public trial by jury, to a defense attorney, to question witnesses, and to "equality before the law" (14).

Formal university education was made available to all males (14), resulting in a major increase in students. Public lectures and debates became popular again, and newspapers and magazines proliferated along with professional and technical journals (4).

A part-time reformist educational program directed toward poor people emerged from 1859–1862 in the form of the "Sunday school movement." This was partly inspired by the romanticized idea of a peasant revolt, which the educators believed they were helping to spark by providing the education and consciousness-raising (3).

Billington underscores how this period of reform differed from previous ones in the sense that the modernization had now become irreversible as the changes were now affecting too many areas of the country. Railroads, which enabled quick travel over long distances, were being built, affecting the landscape and social relations. Former serfs who flooded into the cities were now coming into contact with reformist ideas that previously only nobles could access. Consequently, Russia would no longer be able to simply revert back to "self-imposed isolation" once disillusionment with change set in (3).

Populism arose as an independent political philosophy during this period. Its advocates included students who had come of age during the latter part of Nicholas's reign and hailed from different ranks like officials, professionals, and minorities. It included many from the "unsophisticated" provinces as well as seminary students who brought with them a strident zeal. The philosophy itself was heavily influenced by both utilitarianism and materialism, including nihilistic materialism (3).

Populists believed that revolution was inevitable, especially for Russia, and a moral necessity. They also revered science and believed that society could be administered in a cold and scientific manner. Seeing themselves as an elite cultural and political force, they were responsible for building this new society (3).

They idealized peasant communes as a model of egalitarianism and participated in the hippie-like movement in the summer of 1874 to live among the peasants and spread the "good news" of revolutionary change (3). But this project was largely a flop, as the peasants often saw them as interlopers and troublemakers, sometimes even reporting them to the authorities (4).

To the populists, Alexander's reforms were too slow and often were perceived to have been enacted in a sloppy manner that called into question the good intentions behind them. The prime example was the emancipation of the serfs without granting them land.

The first assassination attempt against Alexander occurred in April 1866. This ushered in a reactionary period through 1881. However, by the end of this period, Alexander had decided to give reform another try, working on a program that included a rapprochement between liberals and more moderate elements of the populist movement and incorporated reformers and the bourgeois into government structures modeled on the success of the network of zemstvos (3).

By March 1, 1881, Alexander had even drafted a decree, to be officially issued within the coming days, that would have set Russia on the road from an autocracy to a constitutional monarchy (17). But Ignaty Grinevitsky, the second in a trio of bombers from the revolutionary group Narodnaya Volya ("The Will of the People") who were lying in wait for the tsar as his carriage drove by, mortally wounded him as he stepped out to tend to those in his entourage who were wounded by the first bomber (17).

His son, Alexander III, made no pretense as to reform, so the idea of progress languished until the 1905 revolution when Tsar Nicholas II would cede some power to a parliament—if only on paper.

Nicholas II and the 1905 Revolution

Seen as an omen by some historical observers, the festivities surrounding Nicholas II's coronation were stained by the deaths of 2,000 people and the injury of thousands more who were trampled in Moscow as record crowds turned out for free beer and one of 400,000 specially made enamel mugs to celebrate the tsar.

Eyewitness reports at the scene described "piles of bodies, sometimes as many as fifty in a heap, a tangle of arms, legs, and heads, the people's clothing black with dirt and often torn from their bodies" (15).

Not only did this show disorganization resulting in serious loss of life and injury, it provided a glimpse into the tsar's attitude. After some members of his government suggested that the festivities should have been cancelled out of respect for the victims, Nicholas made it clear that while the day's events had been a tragic disaster, they should not be allowed to "darken the coronation holiday" (15).

The reign of Nicholas II was known as the Silver Age due to achievements in the arts, humanities, and sciences. More books on a wide range of topics were being sold than ever before. Numerous new art journals were established. Music societies, art exhibits, and theater all flourished (4). The creative community, which would have its share of revolutionaries and sympathizers within it, was also known for its decadence during this period (15).

In the latter part of the nineteenth century, railroads were laid all over the country—all of them, with the exception of the Trans-Siberian, built and run by private business entities. Moscow had nine rail stations and served as the railway hub for the empire (4).

By the dawn of the twentieth century, Russia was leading the West in economic growth. Between 1873 and 1913, oil output quadrupled, iron production levels increased by twelvefold, and coal production increased by twentyfold (4).

The new "independent dynasties of merchants" behind this growth gained great wealth and power. Like the Carnegies and Rockefellers of the Gilded Age in the United States, they were benefactors for the arts, hospitals, and schools (4).

But it wasn't enough to compensate for the yawning chasm between themselves and the workers who toiled in the factories or those who were barely surviving in the provinces. They inevitably became targets of anger and resentment by the intelligentsia—educated reformers and revolutionaries.

Indeed, the dark underside of this development had been growing. By 1902, labor unrest was breaking out more frequently in various parts of the empire. In Saratov province, a plot by teachers to carry out political assassinations was uncovered in 1903. The assassination of a minister of internal affairs who had been widely regarded as a reactionary also occurred around this time. Many in government obliquely acknowledged that it was an attack on the tsar himself and that support for the autocracy was "fragile" (16).

In August 1904, a wave of social upheaval was sparked by the "banquet campaign" pushed by the Union of Liberation. This underground organization called for a constitutional government with various socioeconomic reforms (16). The banquets were organized so that members, mostly from the educated classes, could air their grievances with current political and economic conditions. They also adopted resolutions advocating various liberal or radical reforms. Ironically, these banquets had to be approved by the government, which it reluctantly did in an attempt not to further antagonize the aggrieved (16).

Mass political meetings increased between 1904 and January 1905, demanding "civil liberties, amnesty for political prisoners, and a democratically elected constituent assembly" (16).

The tsarist government was facing a plethora of problems that were interrelated. A nationalist movement in Ukraine—which produced a large proportion of the empire's grain and sugar as well as 70 percent of its coal, 68 percent of its cast iron, and 58 percent of its steel—was also brewing (18).

Meanwhile, Russia was involved in a war with Japan that would ultimately end in humiliation. The tsar had chosen to listen to unofficial advisors who'd encouraged him to underestimate potential enemies and to take unnecessary risks (18).

Unfortunately, this was a pattern with Nicholas. The tsar was insulated and indecisive and did not always choose wise advisors who could help compensate for his ignorance and shortcomings. Occasionally, he did have farsighted advisors who recommended certain reforms to both stave off more pressure and improve Russians' lives, such as Sergei Witte and Pyotr Stolypin. But he often didn't listen. And if he did finally decide to implement a change, it was usually too little too late.

At this point, hard-pressed peasants and urban workers tended to resent the additional burdens of military service. Harrison Salisbury, a *New York Times* correspondent who covered the postwar Soviet era and author of *Black Night, White Snow: Russia's Revolutions 1905–1917*, described Khitrovka, Moscow's worst slum at the time, as comparable to the Haymarket slum in St. Petersburg:

> [It] was known as the foggiest place in Moscow. It was situated on low land, surrounded by old stone houses, paint peeling off, with peddlers and beggars huddled in rows on the pavement, cooking slumgullion in iron pots, frying sausage on charcoal fires, and boiling up messes which they called "dog's happiness." The smell of urine, manure, roasting mutton, frying onions, steaming horses, filled the air. Tens of thousands of human souls lived around this square, paying five kopecks a night for a place

to sprawl on a wooden shelf. Thousands of unemployed peasants and laborers gathered there each day, waiting for the labor brokers and shop bosses to pick them for manual work. If they were not hired by afternoon, they would sell a shirt or their shoes for a bite to eat and another night's lodging. At night, the place rang with drunken shouts and cries for help. But no one answered (15).

In an attempt to placate the increasing calls for major change, the government tried to co-opt peasant and urban reform movements in a more moderate direction.

Peasants comprised around 85 percent of the population but still owned only 37 percent of the land (15). Much of that peasant-owned land was via peasant communes. Therefore, the peasant commune was viewed by some as a possible bulwark against the excesses of early capitalist development and a stopgap against socialist revolutionary ideas (18). But others saw it as an inefficient method of farming in the long term (16).

Similarly, the government set up unions with the help of security forces and tried to serve as mediators between the demands of disgruntled workers and their employers. But these state co-opted unions backfired on the government, as illustrated by Father Gapon and the events leading up to Bloody Sunday, which kicked off the 1905 revolution (18).

Georgy Gapon was an Orthodox priest whose early work with the poor had made him sympathetic to their struggles. Starting out as a police shill, Gapon evolved into a genuine radical leader. Workers turned to him for leadership and advice, since other revolutionary movements were not as well organized at this point. He led labor demonstrations in St. Petersburg that were estimated to have as many as 120,000 participants. The growing calls for reform and the attendant increase in mass demonstrations throughout the empire over the previous year had reached fever pitch by January 1905 (15).

Referencing the historical right to petition the tsar for grievances, Gapon led the masses to Palace Square in St. Petersburg on Sunday, January 9, to demand an audience with the tsar or a suitable representative. As he'd stated in a letter sent to the tsar ahead of time, he wished to peacefully plead for the establishment of an eight-hour workday; higher wages; better working conditions; the right to strike; freedom of speech, press, and assembly; and an end to the Russo-Japanese war (15) (16). One of Gapon's followers exclaimed:

> We will go to the Father [Tsar] and tell him how we suffer.
> We will tell him—Father, forgive us. We have come to you.
> Help us, your children. We know you are happy to dedi-
> cate your life for us and to live only for us but you don't
> know how they beat and torture us; how we starve; how
> they treat us like cattle; how illiterate we all are (15).

In response to the demonstration, government troops ordered the crowd to disperse under threat of force. When the demonstrators didn't or couldn't, soldiers began charging into the crowds and shooting indiscriminately as well as using their sabers (15). Eyewitness accounts testify to the disbelief and shock expressed by many of the demonstrators at having actually been attacked:

> Direct fire at close range on people standing beside the
> garden and directed into the garden, on the curious, the
> passersby, the children at their games. The crowd stood
> frozen. No one believed these were real bullets. Then they
> saw. Bodies lay torn and bleeding around the square, in
> the gardens, against the iron railings, blood flowing over
> the white snow and the frozen ice (15).

By the time it was over, 130 were dead and around 300 wounded (16).

Though the tsar was not present in St. Petersburg at the time of the attack, anger and outrage were palpable among many different ranks of society. Since Gapon and his demonstrators were not revolutionaries calling for the overthrow of the autocracy, only for reforms and more humane conditions, the tsarist government's violent response gave new legitimacy to more extremist revolutionary thinking and action. Russian writer Maxim Gorky, a friend of Gapon who was with him during the march, cabled to the *New*

York Journal shortly after the massacre: "The Russian Revolution has begun"
(15).

By January 12, strikes had erupted in factories and railways and even
among white-collar workers throughout the empire, with a particularly large
one in Saratov province, echoing many of the demands made by Gapon and
his followers. These actions spread, renewing the motivation of revolutionary
leaders who'd previously been disorganized, and culminated in a general
strike that affected almost every major urban center in the country by October. It's estimated that around two million workers participated, bringing the
empire to a virtual standstill (16).

Paradoxically, it was difficult for the state to handle the unrest—despite
its repressive inclinations—due to the fact that, like so many other government officials, local police were woefully understaffed, underpaid, and poorly
equipped. It was not unusual for police to sometimes sympathize with the
strikers.

When the tsar ordered a crackdown on unrest in mid-October, this
time the army and police largely stood down (16).

The tsar was finally forced to realize that he needed to implement
reforms or at least give the pretense of doing so. Ministers and advisors
reported that, between continuing strikes throughout the country and the
deep divisions among the nobility that were literally paralyzing essential
government and commercial activity, complacency was no longer an option
(15).

The reformist faction of the tsar's government was led by Sergei Witte,
who formulated the October Manifesto, which granted freedom of con-
science, speech, assembly, and union as well as widespread suffrage. It also
established a cabinet of ministers (19) and a parliament, known as the Duma,
with the provision that no law would be enacted without its approval (16).

As a result, the number of newspapers multiplied tenfold with the press
freely publishing whatever they deemed newsworthy, and workers established a multitude of trade unions, consumer co-ops, clubs, and cultural
societies (16).

But the issuing of the October Manifesto also precipitated a backlash and ushered in much chaos. Right-wing interests violently attacked reformers and revolutionaries, pogroms erupted against Jews, and a faction of peasants looted and burned large estates and state-run liquor stores (16).

Along with the reforms, the tsar instituted a deadly retaliatory campaign against revolutionaries in the countryside over the next year (15).

The reforms of the October Manifesto were codified and known as the Fundamental Laws of 1906. The election of the first Duma that year involved the ranking of voters based on ownership of property and payment of taxes. The first group was landowners, followed by peasants, town dwellers, and workers. Each group chose electors who then selected Duma deputies.

The elections were boycotted by social democrats and the socialist revolutionaries (SR), which left the field open to other left-wing groups, who won the majority of seats (16).

It should be mentioned that right-wing populism would also become a significant force in the form of the Union of the Russian People party, which appeared in the period after the political opening provided by the October Manifesto. Its supporters often were involved in the vigilante Black Hundreds who took part in anti-Semitic pogroms and joined in state-sanctioned repressions of peasant and worker rebellions (19).

Although the tsar publicly recognized the Duma's legislative authority, he would proceed to try to sideline it as much as possible. He also maintained the right to veto any legislation, to declare martial law, and to issue commutations and pardons, and he still had sole decision-making authority when it came to the conduct of foreign policy and the overall administration of the empire (16). As part of his attempt to pacify the situation, the tsar appointed Pyotr Stolypin as prime minister and minister of internal affairs. He served in both positions from 1906 until his assassination in 1911. Having already spent years managing a large province, Stolypin had developed a program in response to social unrest that combined methods of soft repression and concrete reforms to improve living conditions.

Stolypin had grown up and lived in areas with minorities and was a relatively tolerant man. In his time as provincial governor, in both Grodno and Saratov, he'd acquired experience successfully negotiating with the leadership of rebelling groups to prevent escalation (16). He had also proposed policies to support public education, reform the credit system to assist modern agricultural schools, build fireproof structures to prevent the destruction of peasant homes, and prevent land seizures and horse theft (16).

He had also noted the generally better conditions enjoyed by workers and peasants in Russian plants and colonies controlled by Western Europeans. For example, workers in one French-owned plant were treated well with their own schools and hospitals on-site. Another example involved a German colony that had paved roads and stone houses with indoor plumbing (16). Stolypin wanted to replicate these improvements for Russian-controlled entities.

The centerpiece of Stolypin's envisioned transformation of Russia was agrarian reform. His package of reforms was designed to change peasants' mentality. He believed in the expansion of private ownership of land, which would enable the peasants to see themselves as stakeholders in a stable and orderly society. This, in turn, would confer to them a sense of citizenship based on being rational actors who could take the initiative to improve their lives, creating a sense of civic engagement and respect for the rule of law (16).

Stolypin pushed ahead with these policies even though he knew they would likely make the nobility feel threatened. He believed that if his reforms were successful, the nobility would eventually disappear as a class.

Stolypin viewed the peasant majority as the weakest segment of society at the time but also the segment with the most productive potential for Russia's future. He advocated a rudimentary form of state socialism to facilitate this transformation of the peasantry, as he stated in a 1907 speech:

> At the present time our state is ailing: the most ailing, the weakest part . . . is the peasantry. We must aid it. . . . The idea that all the forces of the state must come to the aid of the weakest part of it may be termed the principle of socialism; but if this is the principle of socialism, it is state socialism, which has been applied more than once in

Western Europe and has achieved real and substantial results (16).

Several sets of policies were enacted in 1906 to assist the peasants. The first set made more land available from the state to be sold to peasants and to make purchases easier with low interest rates on loans. Some interest was generated among the peasants, but not as much as hoped for because the peasants had expected the land to be granted for free rather than sold, and Stolypin had been unsuccessful in his attempts to persuade the tsar to give away the land (16).

A subsequent set of policies were implemented in October to expand the civil rights of the peasantry, allowing them to work as administrative officials, to be elected without limitation to zemstvos, and to freely attend school. It also permitted them to move from one region to another and to purchase land in other regions (16).

The third set of policies was enacted in November and involved methods for the voluntary transfer of allotments of land worked by peasants within communes to private ownership (16).

The radical left didn't like the reforms. Vladimir Lenin expressed his fear that it would lead to the creation of a large bourgeois class of peasants under a capitalist agrarian system that would soon be a fait accompli. The SR opposed the reforms as well (16).

Stolypin recognized that the reforms would take time to reach their full intended effects—up to a generation. But ultimately there were many obstacles to their success. These included peasants' hesitation to leave the communal structure, the fact that divided and privately owned plots did not necessarily have access to necessary infrastructure, peasants not wanting to separate from neighbors, and too few government officials to carry out the steps of implementation (e.g. surveyors). It also wasn't unusual for violent conflict to erupt between communal members who wanted to secede and those who didn't (16).

By 1914, around 20 percent of peasants had become private owners of their land, with those of average landholding showing the most motivation to take advantage of the new laws and benefitting the most from them. But the changes were ultimately too slow to prevent further upheaval.

In fact, Stolypin's historical reputation as a moderate reformer is often overshadowed by the cycle of violence and repression that continued during this period. The violence from 1905 through 1907 included some revolutionary groups who were using terrorist tactics such as killing police and other government officials. These groups often resorted to armed robberies to finance their activities. Between October 1905 and September 1906, 3,611 government workers were killed (16).

Stolypin ordered all local administrators to quell the unrest but emphasized that legal means had to be used, noting:

> The measures that are adopted must be characterized by firm, careful planning; therefore, indiscriminate repression must not be approved. Illegal and imprudent operations provoke bitterness instead of calm and are [therefore] unacceptable (16).

Based on his past experiences dealing with unrest as governor, he knew that this approach was a nuanced one that not all officials had the skill and patience to effectively execute. Consequently, he sent out a 20-page supplement to his order that outlined how to neutralize popular support for radical groups, such as implementing changes that enabled peasants to increase their land holdings by expediting loans. He also advised local officials to personally meet with peasants to discuss their grievances and protect them against abuses by landlords (16).

He made it clear that an immediate attempt was to be made to restore calm at the first sign of unrest by using means other than force. But if force was necessary, it was to be quick and decisive (16). He also advocated surveilling organizations that might be involved in anti-government activity as well as those in the press who might be encouraging it (16).

In August 1906, however, an assassination attempt was made on Stolypin at his summer home where he was conducting official meetings. Three members of the SR set off a bomb in a suicide mission. Although

Stolypin himself escaped unhurt because he was in another part of the house, 27 others were killed and 70 wounded, including two of his children.

Stolypin still believed that the use of overly repressive measures in response would backfire. But there was great pressure to clamp down further to combat the terror, including by the tsar himself. Some reactionaries were even calling for dictatorship.

A meeting of all cabinet members was convened to discuss the matter. All present except for Stolypin and the Minister of Justice agreed that an on-field courts-martial should be instituted. This would allow for suspicious civilians to be handed over, without investigation, to a field court consisting of five military officers. The field court would conclude all trials in private within 48 hours of arrest. Sentences, which were often severe and included the death penalty, were carried out within 24 hours (16).

Utilizing a loophole in the Fundamental Laws, the cabinet members enacted the decree when the Duma was not in session and no date had yet been set for when it would meet again. As a result, the law was in effect for a significant period of time before the parliament could act against it.

The field courts operated for eight months, with 1,102 executed and almost 800 sentenced to prison or hard labor. Around 71 were acquitted (16).

Though incidents of terror did decrease, the field courts were widely unpopular (16). Stolypin's association with this policy, which suspended the few elements of due process Russians had been granted, harmed his reputation and his objective of encouraging respect for the rule of law.

Chapter 2: 1917 Revolution

Overview of Revolutionary Thought Leading up to 1917

By the second half of the nineteenth century, a perfect storm was brewing for instability in Russia with the irreversible modernization campaign that had been undertaken. This campaign included the building of railroads that connected its vast territory and facilitated communication as well as a major industrial buildup. Subsequently, workers faced the same dehumanizing conditions as those in the West had endured. Peasants had their hopes raised and then dashed with the practical realities of the emancipation policy. All the while, a free press had opened up, and educational opportunities had expanded.

Philosophers and writers weighed in with their observations, concerns, and prescriptions. They had an eager audience of educated Russians who were trying to make sense of the changes and where they might be leading the country. The Western philosophers who had captured the imaginations of young students and disillusioned reformers in Russia included advocates of English utilitarianism as well as Hegel and Marx.

During the period from 1840 to 1917, there were different strands of thought among what came to be known as the intelligentsia: a class of Russians with some degree of education who largely opposed the autocratic system, with the exception of the Slavophiles who supported autocratic government. But what they all had in common was opposition to serfdom and the capitalist economic system with its nascent bourgeois culture.

The Slavophiles were a conservative group of thinkers who emerged around the middle of the nineteenth century. In response to what they saw as negative changes in Russia brought about by the infusion of Western ideas, they advocated a rejection or limitation of Western influence and an embrace of traditional customs and mores.

Slavophiles believed that Russia was a unique culture, distinguished by its "core Slavic ethnicity, Cyrillic language, Orthodox Christianity and Tsarist imperial history" (20). They believed that Russia had an historical experience different from that of the West that shaped it. Therefore, Russia should not be simply lumped in with Western European culture or expected to adopt the same policies that appealed to or were perceived to have worked for the West.

Some Slavophile philosophers were chauvinistic nationalists while some simply sought to place more emphasis on the traditional in terms of solving Russia's problems and finding its own path of development (20). The debate between Slavophiles and Westernizers has reemerged in the post-Soviet era as educated Russians have revisited many nineteenth- and early-twentieth-century Russian philosophers in their attempts to determine the best way forward for their country.

The Slavophiles were largely eclipsed in their own time, however, by Westernizers who would form the basis of the revolutionary movement.

The 1840s saw the first generation of revolutionary thinkers, which included Vissarion Belinsky and Alexander Herzen. This generation of writers emphasized the arts, mainly because it was the one relatively safe outlet through which political ideas could be expressed. Discussion of literature took place at literary salons that proliferated in Moscow and St. Petersburg (5).

Belinsky was a literary critic who believed that the writer of literature had a duty to serve as an instrument of social instruction and enlightenment. Literature was to be essentially weaponized on behalf of social struggle against the autocracy. He started out as a reformer but evolved into an advocate of revolutionary despotism, admiring Peter the Great's stern imposition of progressive change from above. He also believed that the masses didn't properly understand their own interests or how to achieve them, thus requiring an authoritarian system to pursue a better future for them—a common thread that would run through most of the revolutionary community (5).

Alexander Herzen was recognized as the most original and intellectual of the writers of this period. Having spent many years as an expatriate in London and Switzerland, he was the most well-traveled and well-read of his contemporaries, but ultimately he never fully embraced the West.

Motivated by opposition to serfdom and autocracy, he set out for France and Italy in 1848 to study revolutionary theory and practice. But after witnessing horrible poverty, exploitation, and a bourgeois culture he viewed as dull and mediocre, he came away with disillusionment of the West and a disdain for capitalism (5).

He subsequently used his writings to spread anti-capitalist ideas in Russia. He also began to recognize that Russia had a distinct historical experience as a nation straddling Europe and Asia, but never fitting firmly within either. As a result, he saw this as an opportunity for Russia to forge a fresh path, free of Europe's baggage. He married this strand of Slavophile thought with the potential for socialist revolution (5).

After Herzen heard about a German study sponsored by Nicholas I regarding the Russian peasant communes, he incorporated an idealization of this institution into his ideology as evidence of the appropriateness of socialism in Russia.

The fact that he and most other members of the intelligentsia had to learn about the everyday realities of Russian peasant life from a foreign study underscored their remoteness from the very people whose lives they were ultimately determined to run for the better. This isn't surprising, given that the intelligentsia were misfits in the sense of being a small minority that did not fit into either of the predominant classes in Russia of the time. They were too educated to be part of the peasantry and too alienated by ideology to be part of the traditional nobility.

This remoteness from the aggrieved group on whose behalf they were supposedly fighting represented another common thread that would run through the revolutionary movement.

Two of Herzen's colleagues who had more practical experience with the peasant village communes that were now being passed off as models of utopian socialism tried to disabuse Herzen of his mythology. One of the colleagues, Nikolai Ogarev, described the peasant commune as an "equality of servitude" (5).

Not long after Alexander II took the throne, Herzen started what would become a renowned political periodical called *The Bell*. For the next 10 years it was considered the most influential periodical in Russia, despite the fact that it was banned throughout the country. Even the tsar reportedly read it regularly to stay informed (5).

In his later years, Herzen expressed ambivalence about the use of violence on behalf of revolutionary change (5). The next generation, however, had few qualms about the role of violence and took some of the basic populism established by Herzen in a much more extreme direction. After publicly criticizing a segment of these more extreme revolutionaries, the nihilists, Herzen was attacked as being an out-of-touch aristocratic hypocrite.

Herzen was ultimately forced to rethink his ideology and how it had laid the groundwork for this extremism. He came to the following conclusions about the counterproductive direction the revolutionary movement had taken:

> Violence and terror are used to spread religions and policies, to found autocratic empires and indivisible republics; violence can destroy and clear the ground—but no more. . . . The popular masses themselves . . . are suspicious of the persons who advocate an aristocracy of science and issue calls to arms. And, mind you, these preachers come not from the people, but from the schools, books, literature, and a life spent in abstractions. These old students have moved further apart from the people than its enemies. . . . Great revolutions are not achieved by unleashing evil passions. . . . I do not trust the sincerity of men who prefer destruction and brute force to development and compromise. . . . A savage and unrestrained

explosion will spare nothing. . . . The rampant spirit of extermination will destroy, together with the boundary signs, all those landmarks of human progress that men have created since the beginning of civilization (5).

The 1863 novel *What Is to Be Done?* by Nikolai Chernyshevsky, though considered a work of low literary quality, inspired a segment of the revolutionary movement to embody the ideal social arrangements of a utopian future that included socialist cooperatives and equality between the sexes. It was also interpreted to have oblique references to the necessity of destruction and even suicide as methods of achieving the utopian goals (14).

One of those greatly influenced by Chernyshevsky was Mikhail Bakunin, an anarchist populist who believed in the "necessity of violence for suppressing the privileged classes" (14). A charismatic political rival of Marx and former friend of Herzen, Bakunin eventually teamed up with the nihilist Sergey Nechaev.

Nechaev was a fanatic who was known for his interpersonal manipulation and strident intolerance of those with differing views. He met Bakunin in Switzerland after having fled Russia the first time. He would later return to Russia and flee again after murdering a student follower, I. I. Ivanov, who had turned against him (14).

Bakunin and Nechaev collaborated in writing *Catechism for a Revolutionary,* which outlined the following requirements for revolutionaries to be successful: the forsaking of all other interests and attachments for the revolutionary project; the suppression of empathy and engagement in antisocial activity on behalf of opposing all established civil order, institutions, customs, and morality; the agreement that the only criteria for determining morality was whether something advanced the revolutionary project or not; the belief that the ends justified the means; the willingness to die and endure pain for the revolutionary project; and, in the service of expediting the revolution, the permitting of conditions to actively be worsened for its future beneficiaries (14).

Many revolutionary groups would utilize terrorism, including the SR, who were responsible for the bombing attempt on Pyotr Stolypin's life in

1906. The SR were more popular in the countryside and concerned themselves primarily with the peasants rather than industrial workers, but they had earned the fear of the tsarist government more than other groups (15).

The biggest achievement of this segment of terroristic revolutionaries would be the assassination of Alexander II in 1881, which was masterminded by Sofia Perovskaya, one of the leaders of Narodnaya Volya.

Perovskaya was ironically a descendant of Empress Elizabeth's husband Alexei Razum. A member of the nobility, her interest in revolutionary thought was first piqued around the age of 12 by her friend Varya Poggio, a granddaughter of one of the Decembrists. After participating in the failed peasant movement—the signature action of the Going to the People strategy espoused by Pyotr Lavrov in the 1870s—Perovskaya would become heavily influenced by Bakunin's writings (14).

Narodnaya Volya would play another pivotal role in the fate of Russia and its revolutionary future. A young student named Alexander Ulyanov soon fell under the group's sway and in 1887 was arrested for involvement in a plot to assassinate Tsar Alexander III. Refusing to ask for clemency, Alexander was hanged (15) (21).

Alexander Ulyanov was the older brother of Vladimir Ulyanov—later known as Vladimir Lenin. Vladimir and the rest of the family did not know of Alexander's revolutionary activities until his arrest. The death of Alexander deeply affected Vladimir, who up to that point had shown little interest in politics, much less revolution. As one chronicler of Lenin's path as a revolutionary stated:

> Some critics have tried to find cruelty, single-mindedness, egocentricity, or ultraism in the record of Vladimir's early years. It does not stand up in the objective evidence of those who knew him. This was no rebel, no iconoclast, no youthful messiah. Vladimir was by all accounts as normal and pleasant a youngster as any parents could have desired (15).

In fact, those who knew him later in life said that Lenin was not motivated by power but by genuine conviction. Combined with his boundless energy and "iron will," this gave him tremendous charisma. Compared to Leon Trotsky and Joseph Stalin, he was considered to have the least dictatorial personality—at least, in the beginning—taking the time to try to educate and persuade (21).

Vladimir and his siblings had grown up in a middle-class rural environment. Their father was educated in math and physics and enjoyed a career as a local school inspector. He was a liberal reformer who had supported Alexander II. He and his wife provided an intellectually stimulating environment for their children, encouraging reading and games, and instilling reformist values (15).

By all objective measures, the boys enjoyed a relatively stable and happy home life. Vladimir was known as a smart, rambunctious, and playful youngster who liked music and chess. His brother, on the other hand, was solemn, studious, and compassionate, but Vladimir idolized him, often seeking to emulate him.

Alexander eventually left home to go to university in St. Petersburg. His journey to radicalization was not uncommon for idealistic youths of the time. Having grown up rather insulated in the provinces, upon arriving in the big city, Alexander witnessed the deplorable conditions of workers as well as brutal crackdowns by the police on demonstrations. In fact, he had participated in a demonstration just weeks before his arrest that had been handled particularly violently by the authorities (15).

Vladimir was devastated by his brother's death and the sudden shunning of his family by others in their community (21). Witnesses describe a young man having trouble expressing his grief: "It was notable that in all the accounts no member of Vladimir's family, none of his friends, offers any remark or expression made by Vladimir in those days in Simbirsk. Change there was. Everyone noticed that. The gay, laughing boy, full of tease and jokes and high spirits, overnight became serious, thoughtful, gloomy" (15).

The effects were still visible four years later in 1891 when Vladimir went to St. Petersburg to take his law exams. While there, he looked up one of his brother's close friends, S. F. Oldenburg. "[Vladimir] asked many questions about his brother, especially his scientific work. Oldenburg remembered Vladimir as 'gloomy and silent,' and said he obviously suffered deeply over his brother's death" (15).

The lingering effects of Alexander's demise would be seen in Vladimir's now single-minded focus on revolutionary politics. By 1893, after practicing law successfully for about 18 months, he began immersing himself in revolutionary studies. He was already under surveillance and barred from government employment (21) (15). His mother disapproved and wanted him to become a farmer, but she would support him financially throughout his future exile and emigration (21).

As part of his revolutionary education, he repeatedly read *What Is to Be Done?* (15) and later acknowledged Chernyshevsky to be second only to Marx in influence (5). Lenin, however, rejected the use of terrorism at this point and instead advocated a strong centrally controlled movement of dedicated and professional revolutionaries who acted as secret conspirators.

Though never publicly lauded by Lenin, Pyotr Tkachev is seen as the philosophical bridge between the Chernyshevsky-inspired populists and the Bolsheviks. Tkachev was a radical journalist and agitator who served more than one stint in prison for his activities. He described himself as a Jacobin and briefly collaborated with Nechaev from 1868 to 1869. Although he was one of the few colleagues who apparently didn't fall under Nechaev's sinister spell, he also never repudiated Nechaev even after he fell out of favor when his killing of I. I. Ivanov was exposed.

Tkachev was one of the early Russian Marxists. He believed in historical determinism with economics as the prime factor, but strikingly he departed from Marxism regarding how revolution in Russia could realistically be achieved. He advocated the need for a secret "conspiratorial organization that would seize power by means of a coup d'état" (5).

Unlike Bakunin and other anarchists, Tkachev didn't believe that a spontaneous peasant rebellion would happen. Nor did he believe—like some other populists—that an isolated coup was plausible.

Tkachev laid out three central ideas necessary for achieving a revolution in Russia: 1) it would have to be established through an intellectually and morally developed revolutionary minority since the masses didn't understand their own interests and wouldn't be able to advance them—if they could, he argued, it would represent gradual evolution and would preclude the need for revolution; 2) the revolution was to be carried out as soon as possible, as conditions would become less favorable the more entrenched the capitalist system became in Russia; and 3) a revolutionary party was needed to execute the revolution.

That party would engage in organizing a unified and disciplined revolutionary entity, the dissemination of propaganda, using its own journal as the primary means, and incitement of the revolution itself (5).

Tkachev spelled out his blueprint for revolution in a pamphlet called "The Tasks of Revolutionary Propaganda in Russia." He engaged in a lengthy and hostile public debate with Pyotr Lavrov, who argued that revolution could only legitimately come from the masses themselves, and emphasis must therefore be placed on educating the masses toward this goal. Lavrov's approach would be largely discredited after his Going to the People campaign fizzled in the mid-1870s.

Tkachev reiterated to Lavrov and other critics, including Europeans such as Friedrich Engels, that since Russia had no well-developed industrial proletariat or representative bodies and no consistently free press, there was no way to win over the masses to a revolution in the foreseeable future. In Russia's conditions, in which all the power was vested in the state with no meaningful independent classes or institutions, the state was also vulnerable in terms of the universal resentment it elicited by its oppression and control of all. This, Tkachev argued, made the Russian state ripe for a "tight-knit, highly disciplined conspiratorial organization" to facilitate its overthrow (5).

Once power was seized by the revolutionary minority, it would rule as a dictatorship over the course of time needed to implement the economic, social, and legal changes required by a socialist system (5). Some of Lenin's writings would echo and build upon Tkachev's ideas and tactics, even using titles for his pieces that were strikingly similar to Tkachev's (5).

By 1895, Lenin had been exiled to Siberia for a year but was afforded enough freedom to continue his research and writing on revolution and even communicate with other revolutionaries. Upon his release, he visited Europe where he made many significant contacts, but most importantly, he met G. V. Plekhanov (21).

Plekhanov was a former populist who became one of the most well-known Marxists in Russia. He made considerable headway in getting Marxist socialism accepted as a meaningful alternative to populism. He advocated land redistribution and opposed the tactics of Narodnaya Volya, arguing that terrorism served as a pointless catalyst toward increased government repression (3).

Instead of issuing invectives at his philosophical opponents in the revolutionary movement, as was the common practice of the time, Plekhanov relied on the art of persuasion. He acknowledged the populists' desire to mix with the masses and work on behalf of their hoped-for political awakening, while explaining the practical shortcomings of this approach.

As a Marxist, Plekhanov was a strict materialist who believed in the possibility of "absolute objectivity." This undeniable objectivity would supposedly resolve the perennial tendency within the revolutionary movement toward splintering. Furthermore, unlike many other theorists, by 1884 Plekhanov was arguing that Russia was already in a condition of capitalism, albeit in the form of state capitalism. He saw this as evidence of the inevitability of a revolutionary clash between the social classes within Russia and the eventual triumph of the proletariat (3).

By this time, Plekhanov saw the peasant commune, held up as proof of a socialist legacy in Russia and a foundation for socialist revolution by the populists, as falling apart. As it turned out, Russia was not so unique that it could bypass the industrial capitalist stage on its road to socialist revolution. He saw an emerging bourgeois class as playing a major role in revolution and advocated fighting alongside the liberal bourgeois and opposing them after the revolution, if necessary (22).

Plekhanov would go on to have a complicated relationship with Lenin, whom he saw as a protégé and one who could ultimately execute his ideas

(22). It was later generally recognized that Lenin's overarching talent was indeed his ability to marry revolutionary political theory and practice.

Lenin mostly lived abroad from 1900 to 1917 (15). During the early years of this period he started a revolutionary journal called *Spark* and had begun using the surname he would become famous under (21). He, along with Plekhanov and Julius Martov—another Marxist—were the principal contributors to *Spark*.

In 1903, an official split occurred during the Second Congress of the Russian Social Democratic Labor Party. This party had formed in 1898 to unite the revolutionary movement in Russia. The split resulted in the Bolsheviks (meaning "majority" in Russian), led by Lenin, and the Mensheviks (meaning "minority" in Russian). Plekhanov would eventually side with the latter, headed by Martov (23).

The Mensheviks advocated a loosely organized structure that could exercise the option of allying with the liberal bourgeoisie, while the Bolsheviks wanted a centrally controlled and disciplined conspiratorial organization of full-time revolutionaries. The Bolshevik wing represented the ideas for spreading Marxism and inciting revolution among the working class that had been laid out in Lenin's 1902 pamphlet, *What Is to Be Done?* borrowing the title of Chernyshevsky's novel.

A fight over the editorial board of *Spark* also ensued, which the Mensheviks lost, leaving Lenin in virtual control of the publication. However, the organization's Foreign League convened in Geneva a few months later, at which time the Mensheviks prevailed and Lenin announced his resignation from *Spark* and the organization's party council (23).

This only turned out to be a minor setback for Lenin, who became noted among the intelligentsia for his knowledge of economic thought. In 1904, he started another journal, *Forward*. He also wrote an acclaimed book called *The Development of Capitalism in Russia,* which was in a second print run by 1905 (21).

Around this time, colleagues observed an increasing ideological rigidity and intolerance in Lenin. He had acquired the tactics of ignoring and insulting rather than refuting the arguments of other revolutionaries with whom he disagreed. This was not unknown in the revolutionary movement but it marked a transition toward behavior that was antithetical to those he was taught growing up. Moreover, he began acting more on the Machiavellian approach that had gained a foothold within the more extreme strands of the movement, rationalizing the use of individuals who engaged in dishonest and/or criminal behavior as long as it was perceived to be facilitating the goal of revolution (15).

Soon after the October Manifesto was issued after the 1905 revolution, Lenin returned to St. Petersburg. He had raised the issue of armed resistance publicly for the first time just prior to his return and continued a period of prolific writing.

In May 1906, he made his first speech in front of a mass rally in St. Petersburg, billed as a "leader of the Bolsheviks"—though he'd only just begun a meaningful association with the organized Russian Bolsheviks a few months before. He wouldn't make another appearance at a mass meeting until 1917.

Due to police pressure in response to his increased organized activities, he left Russia for Europe again in December 1907 (21), not to return until 1917 (22).

World War I Tips Russia into Revolution

A confluence of domestic factors, along with entry into World War I, would lead to the 1917 Revolution and the Bolshevik coup. In addition to the many personality traits of Nicholas II that were antithetical to being an effective leader, as historian Dominic Lieven acknowledges, the nature of tsarism—virtually total and unlimited power vested in one person—was a role that no human could fulfill effectively. This was particularly true during the period in which Nicholas II reigned, a period when all the challenges of modernity—arriving later to Russia than to the rest of the Western world—came to a head.

These challenges included industrialization, technological advances in communication and transportation that brought far-flung peoples closer together, expanded education, which resulted in increased nationalism and demands for social change, as well as competition with other imperial powers in Europe.

Nicholas had experienced several traumas during his formative years, including witnessing his grandfather Alexander II's death and surviving a train wreck from which his father had rescued the family (24). Upon ascending the throne in 1894 at the age of 26, he had not been properly groomed by his father, who denigrated him in private to others (15).

Aware of his inexperience, Nicholas kept his advisors and cabinet members at arm's length, fearing that they could exploit his weaknesses. He also was uncomfortable with confrontation, which led to passive-aggressive behavior. This created obstacles, as those working with him to solve problems had little confidence that they could trust what Nicholas told them during meetings due to his indecisiveness and tendency to flip-flop (18).

Unlike other European great powers, Russia did not have long-established supporting institutions like a council of advisors to assist in implementing policies on the wide range of issues that constituted the actual governing of the country. The vast and complicated Russian bureaucracy was cumbersome, and the tsar did not have anyone serving as a chief of staff to streamline information to him from the cabinet of ministers and other sources. The ministers themselves had historically resisted such a position being created out of fear of losing their individual influence with the tsar (18).

As detailed in the previous chapter, Russia only established a parliament in 1905—a reluctant concession made in the face of revolution. However, Nicholas was always attempting to defang the Duma, sidestep it, or order it out of session. Suffrage had already been limited by 1907, and only the educated classes—who also controlled the major media outlets and, thus, constituted "public opinion"—had representation (18).

These practical problems of governance, combined with Nicholas's insularity from average Russians, his personality flaws, and his primary interest in military and foreign affairs, contributed to his failure to be sufficiently responsive to domestic problems as they mushroomed into crises, especially after the onset of World War I.

On the foreign policy front, in the lead-up to 1914, Europe consisted of numerous imperial powers that had each expanded virtually as far as they could and were entangled in a system of alliances. There was the British Empire and the German/Prussian Empire, along with the French Empire, the Austro-Hungarian (Habsburg) Empire, and the Russian Empire in the east. The most powerful in terms of economic and military might were the British and German Empires. The French were allied with the British—who typically partnered with whichever continental power was weaker to balance out the stronger. The French were also allied with the Russians, while the Germans had allowed their previous nineteenth-century alliance with Russia to evaporate in order to ally with the Austro-Hungarians, whose power had been gradually waning.

As industrialization moved eastward across Europe, it was widely recognized that it was just a matter of time before Russia would become the continent's foremost power. This, along with a sense of cultural superiority over the Slavs, motivated Germany's growing hostility toward Russia, despite the fact that the two had a critical trade relationship (18).

With the Ottoman Empire also weakening, the one area where Austria-Hungary could expand was in the Balkans, a territory in southeastern Europe that formed the nexus of three major empires (Austro-Hungarian, Russian, and Ottoman) and bordered several important waterways, including the Mediterranean, Aegean, and Black Seas. The Balkans included Serbia, Bosnia-Herzegovina, Bulgaria, Greece, Montenegro, and Romania.

Though some of these states were ethnically Slavic and therefore considered to have kinship with Russia, their varied historical experiences of having been governed by different imperial powers over the recent centuries meant that their language, religion, and attitudes were sometimes very different. This, along with deep and long-running antipathy from Poland, undermined a true pan-Slavic force from emerging. Furthermore, as education expanded in these areas, nationalist sentiment increased, and many of these peoples did not hesitate to exploit larger imperial rivalries to advance their ambitions for national independence.

Those who served as government advisors, cabinet ministers, and military leaders in Russia from 1905 on had largely been educated to varying degrees in liberalism. However, Slavophile considerations still influenced some, leading to more support of the Balkan states than may have been justified based on romanticized notions of kinship. It also motivated some to contemplate the pursuit of a takeover of Constantinople, the capital of the Ottoman Empire and the historical heart of the Byzantine Empire and Christian Orthodoxy.

Those who leaned toward a Slavophile ideology were known as the "country faction," nationalists who believed that Russia was a country with a unique history and special destiny, expansionists who harkened back to the commercial value that had been obtained from historical acquisitions that occurred during reigns such as Catherine the Great's (18).

Their counterparts were the "court faction," comprised of moderate liberals who largely eschewed foreign adventures, believing instead that peace and stability were required for domestic development (18).

These public servants had generally been educated with an ideological foundation that subscribed to state-led programs of economic development, the idea of a balance of power in international relations that would temper nationalist tendencies toward competition and potential conflict, as well as increased trade leading to advancement of peace and international law (18).

Most of these men viewed themselves as professional civil servants with loyalty to the Russian state rather than the tsar or autocracy, with less of a tendency toward serving a leader with whom they had profound disagreements (18). This would later prove to be crucial in the collapse of tsarism.

In the period leading up to 1914, Russia had two foreign policy priorities. The first involved having unlimited access to the Turkish Straits to ensure uninterrupted trade, as well as addressing any vulnerability that could arise from Ottoman Turkey denying Russian warships access in any future conflict. The second involved dealing with the succession of crises that had engulfed the Balkan Peninsula.

According to archival Russian documents, secret meetings were held between representatives of Russia and Austria-Hungary in 1899 and 1900 in which the two powers agreed that the collapse of the Austrian Empire would be in no one's interests. Russia would derive little benefit while having the expense of administering new territory that would come with ethnic disputes (18). However, since Austria-Hungary's power had been waning since the 1870s, it was understood throughout Europe that it was becoming more subordinate to Germany's influence, and the only way to compensate for its shrinking dominance was to expand into the Balkans.

Russia attempted to maintain good relations with Austria-Hungary in the early years of the twentieth century in recognition of its own weakness due to the 1905 revolution and the Japanese defeat in the same year. But Germany's and Austria's attitudes of cultural superiority toward the Slavs irked both Russia and Serbia (18).

In October 1908, what became known as the Bosnian Crisis broke out. The Ottoman Empire would see the loss of two of its territories in the Balkans within 48 hours. Bulgaria declared independence on October 5, and Bosnia-Herzegovina was officially annexed by Austria-Hungary on October 6. Britain, France, Italy, and Russia wanted to resolve the crisis by convening a conference with all of the European powers in order to negotiate a formal change to the 1878 Treaty of Berlin, which had allowed for Austria-Hungary to occupy Bosnia-Herzegovina though it technically belonged to the Ottomans. But Germany opposed a conference, effectively giving Austria a green light to push the situation as far as it could.

Having been weakened in recent years, the Ottomans weren't able to stop the annexation militarily and advocated for an ultimately unsuccessful economic boycott of Austria.

Meanwhile, Serbian nationalists also had designs on Bosnia-Herzegovina as part of a future unified Serbian state and mobilized their army to counter Austria. Strident Slavophile opinion was prevalent in the Russian newspapers and civil society organizations at the time, mostly representing the educated minority in the country. This undermined a reasoned debate on how much responsibility Russia owed to the Balkan Slavs and whether it was worth a major war (18).

Russian intelligence soon discovered an Austrian military buildup near the border along with increased industrial production of war materials. Indeed, there was a significant "war party" within the Austrian government who believed that the time was ripe to take out Serbia as a growing threat before it could get any stronger and while Russia was still recovering from its revolution and loss to Japan. Their strategy was dependent upon a quick and decisive victory in the spring of 1909 (18).

Germany supported Austria's war plans. For its part, Germany enjoyed military superiority over Russia and wanted to put Russia in its place for supporting Britain over Germany since 1905. Together, Austria and Germany backed Russia into a corner, presenting demands for recognition of the annexation of Bosnia-Herzegovina with no compensation to Serbia (18).

Although public (media) opinion in Russia created pressure for the government to support the Serbs against Austria, the Russian leadership knew that it was currently in no position to win a war against a German-Austrian alliance, especially when France and Britain had made it clear that they would not use military force to defend Serbia or the principles of the Treaty of Berlin. Russia was ultimately forced to capitulate, but its humiliation would not be forgotten.

The incident incentivized Russia to refortify its military more quickly. It also resulted in a different attitude toward Germany, which it had heretofore viewed as a possible restraining influence should Austria become too aggressive. The Bosnian Crisis also resulted in more friendly relations between Germany and Ottoman Turkey, as the latter distrusted Russia's ambitions regarding the Turkish Straits and Germany had shown no historical aggression toward Turkey (18).

Russia and Germany continued to develop an important trade relationship in the period leading up to WWI, however, and reached an agreement in 1911 on access for each in northern Persia that would not threaten Russia's trade dominance in the region. That same year, after a favorable resolution to the Moroccan Crisis with Germany, France solidified its alliance with Russia.

It was now France's turn to consider striking while at its perceived peak of power in order to put a competitor in its place. The French signaled their newfound willingness to support Russia in the Balkans against Germany and Austria. Additionally, Russia had encouraged the formation of the Balkan League—an alliance between Bulgaria and Serbia that would later include Greece and Montenegro—which could counter any future advances into the Balkans by Austria (25).

Russia preferred trying to maintain the fragile stability in the Balkans for as long as possible, however. In recognition of the increasing tensions in Macedonia, which saw conflict among Slavs, Greeks, and Muslims, the Russians continued to engage in diplomatic negotiations with the Habsburgs. But this didn't keep the lid on for long.

The Ottomans had been weakened yet again, this time from war with Italy over Libya. An appeal was made to the Ottomans to grant autonomy to the various Balkan groups, but the Ottomans refused. Behind the scenes, Germany tended to believe that the Balkan peoples should put up or shut up and win their independence in a war. It was also confident of its military position in its alliance with Austria. Thus, Germany did not act as a force for peace (18).

With intensifying nationalist aspirations and the belief that they could "create facts on the ground" that would provide momentum toward their goals while manipulating imperial rivalries and domestic Slavophile sentiment in Russia, the Balkan League nations declared war on the Ottomans in October 1912 (18) and emerged victorious within eight months. In May 1919, the Treaty of London was signed between the Balkan League and the Ottomans, reducing the latter's territory in Europe to a mere shadow of what it had been (25).

Ultimately, Russia was unable to control its client states in the Balkans, and solidarity within the Balkan League soon fell apart as the nationalist ambitions of each member led to conflict over Macedonia. The Serbs were inclined to renege on their prior agreement with Bulgaria over how territory taken from the Ottomans was to be divided up, wanting to keep the larger territory they actually occupied. The Ottomans sought to exploit the rift in the hope of regaining Adrianople, a Turkish city south of modern-day Bulgaria (18).

In June 1913, the Serbs and Bulgarians participated in a failed mediation under Russian auspices. Bulgaria refused to compromise and attacked the Serbs and the Greeks at the end of the month. But Bulgaria's initial advances were defeated, leading to Romania's invasion of Bulgaria and the Ottomans' retaking of Adrianople. Bulgaria was forced to negotiate for peace. The resulting Treaty of Bucharest saw Serbia gaining territory large enough to equal Bulgaria (18).

By September, the Serbs were also eyeing Albania and used defense of its border as a pretext for incursions into Albanian territory, but they were forced to retreat after Austria threatened military action.

At this point, a split had emerged within the Serbian leadership. Some, including within the military, recognized that peace would benefit Serbia in terms of recovering from two wars in a row and assimilating its newly acquired territory and population. But there was also an extreme nationalist element that wasn't satisfied with the gains already made and actively schemed for more.

The latter group was emboldened by a belief that Russia would ultimately protect its "little brother" regardless of how reckless it became. Although it was false, this perception also existed in other parts of Europe, particularly in the British government (18).

The most influential organization representing this extreme nationalist element in Serbia was known as Black Hand. It was led by an intelligence officer, Colonel Dragutin Dimitrijević, nicknamed Apis. Its goal was the unification of all Serbs under the rule of Belgrade, especially Bosnia-Herzegovina, which was still under Austrian rule. The Serbian military was divided over Black Hand, with both supporters and detractors within its ranks. The leader of Serbia, Prime Minister Nikola Pašić, was not a supporter of Black Hand or its agenda but was ultimately ineffectual in keeping the group in check (18).

The Russian government was aware of Black Hand but viewed it as a threat to Serbian political stability, including Pašić, and thought it should form a party and participate in the political process rather than act as a conspiratorial organization. According to historian Dominic Lieven, there is no evidence to substantiate claims that Russia's military attaché, Colonel Viktor Artamonov, had any foreknowledge of, much less supported, the assassination of Archduke Franz Ferdinand—heir to the Austrian throne—in June 1914 (18).

The Assassination

The assassination itself, which occurred on June 28, 1914, involved eight conspirators—seven of whom were armed with bombs and/or guns and stationed along the route of the archduke's procession. When the time came, only two of the armed conspirators made any attempt to actually carry out the assassination. Some appear to have lost the will at the last moment. Others feared not being able to hit the intended target and either harming others or drawing attention with a botched attempt that would sabotage the opportunity of success for other participants. It was seemingly by dumb luck that the actual assassin, Gavrilo Princip, was able to pull off the regicide. According to historian Steven Sowards:

> On the day of the attack, Princip heard [co-conspirator] Čabrinović's bomb go off and assumed that the Archduke was dead. By the time he had heard what really happened, the cars had driven past him. By bad luck, a little later the returning procession missed a turn and stopped to back up at a corner just as Princip happened to walk by. Princip fired two shots: one killed the archduke, the other his wife. Princip was arrested before he could swallow his poison capsule or shoot himself (26).

All eight of the conspirators were born in Bosnia, with the majority ethnic Serbs and Orthodox Christians. Five of them, including Princip, were teenagers. In their testimony, none of the conspirators mentioned nationalism as a motive but instead spoke of particular grievances involving the conditions of life under Austrian imperial rule. Rather than incitement to war, the assassination was intended as a "symbolic act of protest" by those who carried it out (26).

Those who assert that Black Hand was behind the assassination believe that once these young men had been recognized as politically aggrieved with a willingness to engage in violent acts, they were steered toward specifically targeting the archduke by Apis and the Black Hand. Buttressing this theory is the fact that the conspirators also received supplies and important information that they would not otherwise have had access to in order to facilitate the assassination (26).

According to Russian government reports on the assassination, Austrian officials had botched the archduke's security and had a motive to blame a conspiracy. Due to the fact that Bosnia was generally stable and its population enjoying relative prosperity under Austrian rule, only a small extremist element sought to create provocations. The reports concluded, however, that Serbian military officers and border guards did have involvement in the plot (18).

In July, the Austrian government completed its own investigation into the assassination, which claimed the involvement of Serbian officials as well. This reinforced to hard-liners in the Austrian government, who were already alarmed at Serbia's growth as a result of the Balkan Wars, that Serbia represented a threat that could only be stopped by military means.

Austria felt that it was in a good position to act, as the morale and loyalty of its military was strong and it had negotiated compromises among rival ethnicities within its empire, although there was some concern that Russia was now courting Romania on the other side of the border (18). But, perhaps most critically, Kaiser Wilhelm II had agreed in a meeting with the Austrian ambassador on July 5 that Austria-Hungary would have the "faithful support" of Germany in whatever action it chose to take with respect to Serbia. This is historically known as Germany's "blank check" (27).

The Austrians refused to publicize the evidence from their investigation or share it privately with the Serbs or the Russians. Instead, on July 23, the Austrian government issued an ultimatum to Serbia, which was intentionally designed to be unacceptable. The ultimatum had two conditions: 1) Serbia was to conduct a judicial investigation into the assassination with the participation of Austrian officials, and 2) all "anti-Austrian propaganda" (i.e. Serbian nationalist writing) was to be removed from Serbian civil society, including the media and school textbooks. Furthermore, all civilian and military officials who'd ever advocated for such ideas were to be purged—with Austria providing a list of such officials (18).

The Serbs were given 48 hours to respond to the ultimatum or risk war.

The Austrians and Germans were hoping that Russia would follow its previous pattern of backing down, but given its past humiliations at the hands of its imperial rivals, Russia believed it could not capitulate again. Not only was the tsar's domestic political credibility at stake, but his international reputation of continually giving in was seen as likely to invite further aggression (18).

World War I Begins

During a meeting with his ministers on July 25 to discuss the ultimatum, Nicholas formally ordered the "army's supplies, plans and equipment" to be prepared for effective mobilization on July 26. This was due to the slow speed and farther distance that had to be traversed in order to mobilize sufficiently to the Austrian border in time to counter an Austrian attack that would aim to be quick and decisive. Russia also had to be ready to assist its French ally from a likely quick German attack.

Austria bombed Belgrade on July 29, which led to Russia mobilizing the four military districts facing Austria. However, it was not yet mobilizing the districts facing Germany, who advised Russia later that day that if Russia did not halt its mobilization, war would ensue.

Nicholas revised his order for a general mobilization to a partial one after receiving a telegram from the Kaiser—who was also his cousin—which he interpreted as a faint possibility of preventing war. After his military advisors insisted that a partial mobilization would be too dangerous, Nicholas changed it back, lamenting, "This means to send hundreds of thousands of Russian men to their deaths" (18).

On August 1, Germany declared war on Russia, then on France two days later. There had been uncertainty about what Britain would do. Anglo-Russian relations had been fraying, and Britain's leadership seemed inclined to leave Serbia and Russia to their fates. But Britain would not abandon France, and on August 4, Britain entered the war—the third nation in what would become the Triple Entente.

Ottoman Turkey—which had become essentially a military protectorate of Germany in a shrunken form—and Bulgaria joined Austria and Germany as the Central Powers. Austria and Germany both assumed that they could win a war quickly, but the latter's Schlieffen Plan was a failure and trench warfare soon commenced (28).

The Abdication of Nicholas II

The winter of 1916–1917 was particularly harsh for food shortages, high inflation, and low wages. Shortages of essential goods had also risen, since Russia had previously relied heavily on German imports, ranging from sewing machines and electrical switches to candle wax and medical supplies. Transportation within Russia had become slow and poorly organized, affecting the delivery of flour and coal as trains were often diverted for delivery of soldiers and war material (29). Fuel shortages led to freezing and the shutdown of industrial furnaces (15).

The number of labor strikes had grown, despite the fact that they were now punishable with hard labor or immediate transfer to the front. Many of the military regiments present in St. Petersburg consisted of recruits fresh out of training and those who'd been sent back from combat due to injury. These soldiers generally lived in poor conditions, with many hailing from the peasant class. In October 1916, a regiment was sent in to break up a strike in the city by force but ended up supporting the workers and firing on their officers instead (29).

There were a total of 243 strikes in St. Petersburg in 1916. By February 1917, there were more than a thousand (29) as desperate workers turned to the only recourse they had.

Meanwhile, Russian casualties were mounting at the front, totaling around 5 million by the end of 1916 (29). Anti-war sentiment spread as rural Russians saw around 10 million of their adult males sent to the front to potentially be sacrificed for a distant and questionable purpose. Moreover this lost manpower resulted in 25–30 percent less of the land being cultivated. It also affected industry, as around 60 percent of prewar workers in St. Petersburg were migrants from the provinces during the off-season (15).

Due to Russia's lack of industrial capacity for a drawn-out war, soldiers endured arms shortages, with only the first ranks at the front having guns while soldiers in the rear had to wait for those in front to fall to obtain their arms. Ammunition was also rationed, with the army barely able to hold on to positions currently held, much less make advances (29).

Anger at the tsar was reaching a boiling point as the Russian population increasingly held him personally responsible for the mess. In August 1915, Nicholas had taken over command of the military, overseeing the war while headquartered at a safe distance in Belarus, further removing him from domestic conditions and ultimately having little benefit on the war effort. By most accounts, he became aware of the food shortages and transport problems but was seemingly at a loss as to how to solve them (15).

By 1916, many of those serving in government could see that a revolution was likely; even Nicholas's mother and brother attempted to influence him in a more productive direction, but he remained indecisive, often listening to the ill-informed advice of his wife Alexandra, changing cabinet officers frequently, and appearing more preoccupied by the precarious health of his son than overseeing the empire he was responsible for (15).

On the eve of his abdication, it was noted by government officials that Nicholas had aged rapidly, looking haggard and thin, with dull eyes. A former prime minister who'd gone to visit the tsar around this time described him as being on the verge—if not in the middle—of a nervous breakdown (15).

Meanwhile, various members of the Duma—which was now composed of moderate liberals and a sprinkling of leftists since most socialists had been exiled—were turning against the tsar. The leader of the moderate

Kadet Party, Pavel Milyukov, publicly castigated Nicholas in a parliamentary speech, citing a long list of governing errors and dramatically inquiring after each, "What is this? Stupidity or treason?" (15)

By this time, a comprehensive report from the tsar's own secret police, the Okhrana, was finalized. Having infiltrated the political class, the city workers, the peasant fields, and even the war front, the Okhrana was able to ascertain the attitude of Russians across the board. The results, as delivered to Nicholas, confirmed that a revolution was imminent, but the tsar took no action (15).

On February 10, 1917, amidst talk from several quarters of the desirability of a coup, the leader of the Duma, Mikhail Rodzianko, made a last-ditch effort to persuade the tsar to immediately form a new government to take steps to solve the various crises. But Nicholas let his disdain for Rodzianko and the Duma cloud his judgment as he cut him off and sent him away (15).

By February 23, bakers, butchers, and candle sellers were running out of their paltry supplies even faster. The temperature was 40 below zero and firewood was becoming scarce. Police in some districts of St. Petersburg were reporting starvation among residents. Workers at Putilov Steelworks, the most important military and industrial factory, along with other workers had joined the Women's Day march. The demonstration grew as it traversed the industrial areas of the city, ballooning to approximately 300,000 by February 25.

The strikes, with students and professionals now having joined in, halted transportation and industry (29). Police, many of whom sympathized with the strikers, initially had orders from on high not to fire on the demonstrators in order to avoid any further negative press from Western Europe (15). However, when a contingent of mounted police officers began to aggress on the demonstrators, military forces fired on one of the officers. This marked a turning point, with the tsar's forces siding with the strikers.

The interior minister relayed the day's events to the tsar through an aide and implored him to return to St. Petersburg from his military headquarters in Belarus. The tsar refused and ordered his military commander for the capital, General Sergey Khabalov, to break up the demonstrations by force the next day.

On that same night, however, striking workers began to organize a worker's council—or Soviet—and were choosing delegates for service.

By the next afternoon, some Cossacks and a military regiment rebelled against orders to fire on demonstrators and attacked mounted police as multitudes of radicals were rounded up and arrested (29) (15). Other strikers came to the streets armed to defend themselves against police. Rodzianko made one final effort to get through to the tsar the direness of the situation, again pleading for the immediate appointment of a new government to address the crises of food, fuel, and transportation. But the tsar still refused to act (15).

On the morning of February 27, the soldiers of the Volynsky district were the first regiment to mutiny, vowing not to fire on the people and killing their commanding officer. Joining the demonstrators, they marched to Liteiny Prospekt where they raided an armory, taking 40,000 rifles and 30,000 pistols. The crowd then split up and attacked police stations, courthouses, and the notorious Kresty Prison, where they released recently rounded up radicals and long-imprisoned revolutionaries (15).

Liberal members of the Duma, who'd had good relations with many military leaders, met that morning in an attempt to preserve the monarchy with reforms. The parliament represented the only institution that was recognized, to some degree, by representatives of both the tsar and the strikers.

Alexander Kerensky, a colorful Duma member and one-time editor of a socialist revolutionary newspaper, had sent emissaries to the military barracks to encourage them to come out to Tauride Palace to protect the Duma from any possible attack by the tsar's forces. Within hours, tens of thousands of troops thronged the palace along with civilian strikers and recently released revolutionary prisoners. A provisional executive committee of the Petrograd Soviet was soon formed that included SRs, Mensheviks, and other radicals, but no Bolsheviks—they wouldn't arrive until later (15).

By the evening, most of the troops had joined the demonstrators, effectively dooming the tsar, who was finally on his way back from Belarus, still ignorant of his fate. At Tauride Palace, as the delegates of the Soviet attempted to organize efforts to provide food, fuel, and the restoration of services, Duma members became nervous as the reality of what was underway began to sink in.

The events of the past several days had taken on a life of their own, and the Duma wondered if the tsar would still be able to crush the revolt, leaving them to an ominous fate. But they seemed just as apprehensive of actually taking the wheel and governing. Some feared a military takeover (15). Others were stymied ideologically by events. Those sympathetic to Marxism believed that revolutionary change was supposed to happen in fixed stages, and Russia did not fit the mold for an actual revolution. What had just occurred seemed more appropriate to a transition to a parliamentary democracy, or the "bourgeois" phase (29).

By the next morning, however, a committee of Duma members reluctantly decided to take the irrevocable step of assuming power, accepting an offer of protection from one of the city's military regiment leaders (15).

In the early morning of March 1, the tsar's train was forced to stop outside of St. Petersburg because the next station was under the control of revolutionary soldiers. Nicholas then directed the train to turn back to Pskov, the nearest station with an operating telegraph. After back-and-forth communication and much rumination, the tsar finally agreed that evening to a constitutional monarchy.

But it was too late.

By the next morning, abdication was being demanded by the representatives of the Duma Committee who were dealing with masses of irate workers and soldiers.

On the afternoon of March 2, Nicholas agreed to step down. He showed little emotional reaction until he was informed that his son, Alexei, was to be his successor and placed under regency until he was old enough to rule. The tsar cried at the realization that he would be separated from his son. He illegally abdicated the throne on behalf of Alexei, requesting that Nicholas's brother, Mikhail, succeed him instead. However, Mikhail chose not to take power (15). Nicholas wrote the following in his diary:

[T]he situation in Petrograd [St. Petersburg] is such that
now the Ministers of the Duma would be helpless to do
anything since against them struggles the Social Democratic Party and members of the worker's committee. My
abdication is necessary. . . . The judgment is that in the
name of saving Russia and supporting the army at the
front in calmness it is necessary to decide on this step. I
agreed. From the headquarters was sent the project of a
manifesto. This evening [Aleksander] Guchkov [Chair-
man of the Central Industries War Committee] and
[Vasily] Shulgin [conservative ex-Duma member] arrived
from Petrograd with whom I conversed and gave them
the signed and completed manifesto at 1 a.m. I leave Pskov
with heavy heart. . . . I am surrounded by treason and
cowardice and fraud (15).

The Provisional Government

The provisional government was established on March 2, comprised of "an
assembly of upstanding citizens who could govern until elections could be
called and some more permanent regime agreed upon" (29). Prince Georgy
Lvov, a Moscow philanthropist, was first appointed as chairman of the provisional government while Kerensky, a lawyer, served as the justice
minister.

The tsar and his family were put under house arrest starting March 9.
An invitation for refuge was offered to the tsar and his family by his cousin,
King George V of England. But the offer was made with some hesitation as
the British royals were not keen to host the tsar's wife, who was German and
had a difficult personality. The offer was eventually rescinded after the provisional government delayed the invitation from being forwarded, fearing a
conflict with the Soviet. The family would later be moved to Siberia without
fanfare (15).

Many of the tsar's ministers and representatives were arrested by the
revolutionaries or gave themselves up. Anger and the desire for retribution

ran high among some of the revolutionary crowds, and Kerensky ran interference more than once to save the lives of those who'd served in the deposed
government (29).

Tension between the provisional government and the Soviet existed
from the beginning as members of the worker's committee of the Soviet had
demurred in terms of taking direct power, forcing the reluctant Duma members to do so. But it was well known that the provisional government had
little actual authority beyond what the Soviet allowed it to have, since the
Soviet, along with the Soldiers' Deputies, controlled "troops, railroads, the
post and telegraph" (29). While the representatives of the Soviet had the trust
of the people, they largely saw as their purpose the preparation for the next
phase of the revolution (29).

Kerensky soon announced the abolition of the death penalty, the freeing of all political prisoners, and the disbanding of the Okhrana. But it didn't
take long for observers to recognize the administrative incompetence of the
provisional government in general and Lvov in particular.

Although food distribution improved in the beginning, underlying
issues such as transportation were not solved, and most of the problems persisted. Industrial productivity fell. Moreover, the government's foreign minister, Pavel Milyukov, announced that Russia would remain in the war, citing
the duty to honor treaty obligations along with the expectation of acquiring
Constantinople and Galicia as allegedly promised by allies prior to entry into
the conflict. This decision led to divisions in the new government, particularly with a contingent of Mensheviks who'd gained influence in the Executive
Committee of the Soviet, which declared peace to be a primary principle of
the revolution (29).

It took weeks for news of the revolution to reach the hinterlands. Many
were leery of the new government, but a significant number of long-suffering
peasants saw an opening for waging retribution campaigns against large
landowners and merchants. Property seizures, looting, vandalism, arson,
and violence swept through large swathes of the countryside. Many of the
incidents of violence were touched off when peasants attempted to peacefully

negotiate land redistribution agreements and landowners refused to participate in the absence of a formal legal process (15).

By August, with Kerensky now leading the provisional government,
the country was suffering from severe inflation as well as plant closures that
had left approximately 100,000 out of work (15).

The war continued to be a disaster for Russia, as it was losing significant territory to the Germans. Morale among soldiers at the front had also
reached new lows, with 1.3 million deserting and regular reports of the killing of officers and outbreaks of disease (15).

Kerensky had several rivals for power by this time. The most dangerous was Lavr Kornilov, a Cossack military intelligence officer whom Kerensky had appointed as the commander in chief. Kornilov came to realize that
Kerensky's popularity was plummeting. He gained the support of several
bankers and industrialists to lead an uprising and become military dictator
(20) (15).

Steps taken to defeat Kornilov's uprising and any further counterrevolutionary actions would ultimately facilitate the Bolshevik coup in October
(15).

The October Coup

> The Bolsheviks were the only ones with a plan. It might
> not have been a good plan ultimately, but they had a plan.
>
> —Guide for the Russian Revolution Centennial exhibit at
> the State Central Museum of Contemporary History of
> Russia in Moscow, May 2017 (30)

The Bolsheviks had little involvement in the actual February revolution.
Other socialist parties, having access to a printing press—which the
Bolsheviks did not at the time—had leafleted relentlessly in the run-up to
the Women's Day march. When the Bolsheviks did arrive on the scene, they
tended to oppose the strikes as premature, lacking a strong revolutionary
goal, and having insufficient support from the military (29).

Due to funding shortages, government infiltration, and a lack of strong leaders, the Bolshevik organization had suffered. However, they had been perceived for some time among the revolutionaries in St. Petersburg as the most influential among the workers and the military, especially the navy (29).

As news of the revolution made its way to the eastern city of Achinsk, Joseph Stalin took the Trans-Siberian railway to the capital. Upon arrival he was granted only an advisory position on the Bolshevik Central Committee, which was scrambling to reorganize. His peripheral status was due to the poor personal image that many of his colleagues had of him.

On March 15, *Pravda* was relaunched by Vyacheslav Molotov, who advocated Leninist thought. Stalin became coeditor, along with Lev Kamenev. Ironically, Stalin advocated a more social democratic stance as editor and did not support withdrawing from the war as long as Russian troops were still on the German firing line. As a result, the Bolsheviks were actually considered to be moderates by the Soviet during this period (15).

Lenin was living in Switzerland when a fellow radical delivered news of the February Revolution to him. Having been far removed from on-the-ground conditions in his homeland for years, Lenin was taken aback at the turn of events.

He proceeded to pore over various newspapers in an attempt to wrap his mind around what had happened. He then began to theorize that it was only the first stage in an anti-imperialist revolution that would result in an international triumph of the proletariat. He would later elaborate on this idea in his April Theses (31). Lenin retained his maximalist position, reiterating opposition to unity coalitions and the new provisional government, which he condemned for supposedly wanting to reconcile with the tsar (15).

Lenin called for elections, an eight-hour workday, and immediate cessation of the war. He thought and wrote practically nonstop about the revolution and its portent for the future. But the product of some of this fleshing out of ideas in the interim was not well received by the editors of *Pravda,* who rejected or significantly chopped up some of his articles (15).

Lenin was also trying to work out how to get back to Russia. The main obstacle was figuring out how to cross through territory controlled by Russia's wartime enemy. The provisional government had announced that any Russian exiles accepting help from Germany would be arrested upon arrival at the Russian border (29).

Certain individuals in the German government, however, saw an opportunity to get Russia out of the war by facilitating Lenin's return (29). It was hoped that Lenin's activities would result in a takeover or destabilization of the Russian government, leading to a separate peace treaty. With Russia knocked out of the war, Germany could then focus on taking out the French on its Western front.

The German government was approached by Alexander Helphand-Parvus, a shady businessman from Belarus with socialist sympathies, who offered to serve as the middleman in funding and arranging the logistics needed to get Lenin to Russia. He had lived as an expatriate in both Switzerland and Germany and had connections with German socialists, often allowing his apartment to be used as a refuge for exiled revolutionaries (29).

Lenin eventually accepted German assistance to cross with the condition that the journey by train had to be nonstop with extraterritorial status, with no passengers being asked to leave the train or discriminated against for their political views (29).

Upon Lenin's arrival on March 3 at Beloostrov Station—the first stop in Russia—he was mobbed by Bolsheviks who carried him out of the train. He gave an unscripted speech in the station hall before returning to the train and continuing on to Finland Station, where he was greeted by workers lining the streets as well as soldiers, sailors, and a band. The Bolsheviks reportedly organized the large and raucous homecoming partly to drown out some of the negative press coverage regarding Lenin's reputed acceptance of German "hospitality" with some even accusing Lenin of treason.

These treasonous characterizations would escalate in the summer months, but for the moment Lenin was exploiting the revolutionary sentiment and muddled actions of the provisional government for his own agenda (29).

He climbed onto an armored vehicle that had been brought in by the Bolsheviks and gave an impromptu speech condemning compromise with the "bourgeois" provisional government and demanding expansion of the revolution.

At Bolshevik headquarters that night, Lenin lectured his comrades into the wee hours on their endorsement of the provisional government and its policy of remaining in the war. His most startling comments, however, involved his insistence on moving on to the "second stage" of the revolution, which required that power be placed "in the hands of the proletariat and the poorest sections of the peasantry" and said that working with the "bourgeois" in any way, including an end to the war, represented a betrayal of the revolution (29).

Lenin was also in disagreement again with his erstwhile friend Plekhanov, who himself had finally returned to Russia after almost 30 years abroad and was now almost forgotten among the revolutionary community (3). Plekhanov wanted to stay in the war, believing that it would be against Russia's long-term interests to allow Germany to win. His return was arranged by Britain, which wanted to keep Russia in the war, but the plan fell flat as Plekhanov received little support from Russians upon his arrival (29).

Lenin continued to vehemently repudiate any socialists who supported the national government in the war, arguing that the international conflict was an example of the capitalists getting the working class of one country to fight the working class of another for the benefit of the bourgeois. Furthermore, he insisted that any anti-war position that did not also demand simultaneous revolution was illegitimate.

This position had been hammered out at the Zimmerwald meeting in Switzerland in 1915, at which Lenin had created his own faction of the socialist internationalist movement, insisting that opposition to war had to be coupled with revolution: "An imperialist war cannot end otherwise than in an imperialist peace unless it is transformed into a civil war of the proletariat against the bourgeois for socialism" (29).

Lenin's ideas were not well received in the days after his return to Russia. Many socialists, of course, saw the coalitions and negotiations that Lenin condemned out of hand as leading to democracy and significant reforms.

They viewed the worker's revolution that Lenin demanded as unrealistic within Russia's current conditions.

But over the next couple of months, Lenin did gain supporters and eventually took control of the party from rivals, persuading the Bolsheviks at their annual spring conference in May to demand an end to the war and reject cooperation with the provisional government.

Lenin was able to achieve this due to a combination of factors. The first was publication of the April Theses, in which he outlined his program for revolution. Second, he engaged in relentless promotion of his ideas. Third, he was able to exploit the raised expectations of average workers for more immediate and concrete solutions to their problems in return for their efforts in removing the tsar. Additionally, more young and zealous revolutionaries had been making their way into St. Petersburg since February, demanding a more muscular approach than what the provisional government was offering (29).

However, the summer marked a setback for Lenin as rumors swirled about the extent of his connections to Germany amid renewed uprisings led by anarchists and disgruntled soldiers. Claims of documentation proving that Lenin was a German agent precipitated the need for bodyguards. Subsequently, Lenin was even forced into hiding for several months (29) (15).

It was around this time that Lenin decided that the only solution was for a Bolshevik-led "armed uprising" that would be carried out "not later than autumn" (15). He wrote prolifically while in hiding and had his pieces forwarded to *Pravda*. Interestingly, Stalin did not initially support Lenin's proposal for an armed uprising, though he would eventually assist in organizing it along with Leon Trotsky (15) (29).

Lenin was able to take advantage of the Kornilov mutiny in August. In response to the failed uprising, the St. Petersburg Soviet established a new Committee for Struggle Against the Counter-Revolution. The Bolsheviks took leadership of the committee, and the Soviet allowed arms to be distributed to tens of thousands of workers who formed armed battalions. Increasingly greater numbers of arms were extracted through this program, which would be funneled for use in the October coup (15).

Meanwhile, the Bolsheviks gained influence in both the St. Petersburg and Moscow Soviets as well as the Soviets in smaller nearby towns as disapproval of the Kerensky government grew by the day (15).

Lenin, however, had trouble getting his Bolshevik colleagues on the Central Committee of the Soviet to sign on to an armed uprising. Since the party now held the majority of seats in the St. Petersburg Soviet and would likely be voting to take over the government at their next meeting on October 20, an uprising was considered unnecessary. After Lenin threatened to resign and take his motion to the general membership, the Central Committee began to relent, with the members agreeing at a late night meeting on October 10 to pursue an armed coup. The logistics would be arranged by Lenin, Stalin, and Trotsky (15).

Plans were made for "troop disposals, seizures, communications, and arrests." The coup planners utilized 10,000 to 12,000 Red Guards, their influence among St. Petersburg's troops, and the Revolutionary Committee of the Soviet for arms and mobilization (15).

Though talk of the coup had spread throughout the city, Kerensky took little action. He was distracted by multiple crises during this period, including several trips to the war front. He also overestimated the loyalty of the military to the provisional government. He did finally issue a warrant for Lenin's arrest, but by this time Lenin was skulking around the city incognito and no orders were given for the arrest of any of his coconspirators (15).

The coup itself was carried out with no documented deaths on October 25–26. Phone and electricity lines at Winter Palace, where the government had resided since July, were cut. Telegraph and post offices were effectively under the control of Bolsheviks, as the workers were party supporters. Troops at key military installations were persuaded to either support the coup or take no action to prevent it, while nearby roads and bridges were taken over by Bolsheviks. As a result, the provisional government was left with insufficient protection, and Bolshevik forces, led by Vladimir Antonov-Ovseyenko, captured the palace. Government ministers were then arrested and sent to the Peter and Paul Fortress.

Kerensky was able to flee with the assistance of the U.S. Embassy, which loaned him one of their cars. He tried to organize a force to reinstate the provisional government but failed. He later took refuge in France and then the United States, where he died in 1970 (15).

Germany's gamble on facilitating Lenin's return to Russia paid off, but only in the short-term. The Treaty of Brest-Litovsk was signed on March 3, 1918. Though it staunched the bleeding for Russians, it was at a humiliating price (30) that was only agreed to after the German army had advanced toward St. Petersburg the month before (31). The treaty required the loss of Ukraine, Poland, Georgia, and the Baltics—approximately a third of the empire's cultivated land and population (32)—and prevented Russia from shaping Europe's interwar period at Versailles (18). It also did not stop Germany from ultimately losing the war or from experiencing blowback as Lenin's ideological fellow travelers attempted to incite revolution amongst German soldiers (15).

Counterrevolution Develops

There was cautious optimism among the peasants and soldiers who controlled the Soviet in the aftermath of the coup, but fractures soon emerged. After all, it was the inability of the provisional government to ensure a stable food supply and end the war rather than ardor for the Bolsheviks that tipped support or acquiescence for the coup over the edge.

The initial imprisonment of the provisional government ministers by the Bolsheviks was unpopular with the Soviet, and the ministers were eventually released into house arrest and kept under surveillance.

Lenin and Trotsky had also announced one-party rule, which prompted opposition by many, particularly the leadership of the railway workers' union. This resentment at the undemocratic nature of the Bolshevik government ultimately alienated other unions as well as the SRs, Mensheviks, and Kadet Party members (15). Armed resistance sprang up in both St. Petersburg and Moscow, which was now the capital with the government housed in the Kremlin. It's estimated that there were 200–400 murders resulting from pro-Bolshevik and anti-Bolshevik clashes within a week of the coup.

A contingent of workers from the Putilov factory in St. Petersburg barged into an October 31 meeting between Bolsheviks and oppositionists and castigated both sides for starting a civil war (15).

Lenin, now faced with evidence that perhaps colleagues who'd expressed concerns about the wisdom of a coup were right, responded with repression to preserve power. He abolished freedom of the press, representing a 180-degree turn from his pre-coup stance. He also prohibited unofficial political meetings and had nongovernment printing presses confiscated. Whatever democratic or quasi-democratic institutions remained from the revolutions that the Bolsheviks weren't able to take control of, Lenin dissolved, such as the Constituent Assembly and the city legislatures (15).

By the end of the year, Lenin would appoint Felix Dzerzhinsky to lead a secret police force, which would become known as the Cheka (15). Political opponents were to be tried before newly established revolutionary tribunals. But Dzerzhinsky soon began sidestepping the tribunals, carrying out extrajudicial executions that would eventually number in the thousands (31).

Lenin also had trouble getting military regiments to protect the Bolshevik government from armed rebellion, with soldiers either sticking to their "neutrality" agreement that had passively allowed the coup or ignoring requests to attack fellow Russians (15). Due to many former government servants' refusal to work with the Bolshevik regime, Lenin also faced a shortage of competent individuals to carry out policies, including those intended to help citizens.

Furthermore, rural communities and non-Russian areas of the empire were proving to be difficult to impose Bolshevik control over (31).

Execution of the Royal Family at Ipatiev House

Ipatiev House was the home of a local merchant in Yekaterinburg that had been hijacked by the Bolsheviks in April 1918 for the purpose of imprisoning Nicholas and his family. The Romanovs had just been moved from Siberia due to the advance of armed counterrevolutionaries in the area. The family, along with its doctor and servants, would eventually be murdered in the basement of the house in July.

Within weeks of the massacre, after a sloppy attempt at a cleanup, the house was returned to its owner, who later fled the country. In the following decades, Ipatiev House became a pilgrimage site for many, which embarrassed the Soviet government. As a result, the house was secretly razed in 1977 (33).

Former Australian ambassador to the Soviet Union Tony Kevin, on a return trip to Russia in 2015, visited the location where Ipatiev House once stood. In his memoir of the trip, he succinctly described the events of July 16–17, 1918 as follows:

> White [counter-revolutionary] forces were advancing on Yekaterinburg. Moscow feared that if the Whites rescued the Tsar, he might become a rallying point of invigorated resistance. Unwilling to risk moving the royal family again, Moscow ordered all of them killed in their house of imprisonment. They were secretly shot overnight by volunteer firing squad in a cellar, their bodies smuggled out in carts and hidden in unmarked country pits (20).

I recall, on my visit to the exhibit of the Russian Revolution Centennial at the State Central Museum of Contemporary History of Russia in Moscow in 2017, coming across a case full of artifacts that included one of the handguns used in the massacre of the tsar's family as well as a letter written by one of the participants. I asked our museum guide if any of the participants in the execution of the family ever expressed any remorse for the murders, particularly of the royal children. He replied "no" without hesitation. He explained that the participants believed they were doing the right thing on behalf of the revolution, much as Kevin explains their rationale above (30).

Trotsky is reported to have said that the decision to have the royal family killed was made to cement the Bolsheviks' power in the face of challenges from the Whites and to send a message that there was no turning back (31).

The Bolshevik Red Terror and the Civil War

In August 1918, Lenin was seriously wounded during an assassination attempt by an SR activist (31) as he gave a speech at a Moscow factory. The Bolshevik government responded by stepping up its repression, leading to what became known as the Red Terror.

The assassination attempt came on the heels of the murder of over 4,000 Soviet officials by armed oppositionists in the month of July alone (34). The Red Terror officially lasted for two months, starting at the beginning of September, though some historians use the term to cover all the Bolshevik repressions from 1918 through the end of the civil war (34).

The two-month-long terror campaign included the shooting of over 500 "representatives of the bourgeoisie and upper classes who were held hostage by the Bolsheviks" in St. Petersburg. Eighty were publicly executed on September 5 in Moscow, and 300 more were killed later in the month (34).

There was disagreement among the Bolshevik leadership about how widespread and long the repression should be, but as the civil war began to take off, brutal tactics of repression became more accepted (34).

The counterrevolutionary White forces received military support from the United States, Britain, and France during the civil war as the Soviet government's nationalization of industry and seizure of foreign assets threatened many Western business interests, which included $659 million worth of investments by U.S. corporate interests in trains, steel, and farming equipment (35).

The British sent 40,000 troops (32) to northern and eastern Russia to support the White army. After some initial hesitation, American president Woodrow Wilson sent around 10,000 (31). The United States and Britain threw support behind Admiral Aleksandr Kolchak, a volatile and reactionary Russian naval commander and explorer whom they hoped would lead an authoritarian government that would supplant the Bolsheviks (35).

Wilson did not have congressional authorization for the Russian action and created an executive body to facilitate arms to the White army. The State Department also manipulated humanitarian aid in favor of the Whites (35).

Due to the lack of an organized state and the patchwork nature of several right-wing counterrevolutionary militia groups, it is difficult to determine an accurate count of the crimes of those who fell under the umbrella of the Whites during the civil war. However, there is sufficient documentation to prove their brutality, with generally accepted estimates of between 20,000 and 100,000 victims of White Terror (36). Many of these atrocities were of an anti-Semitic nature (37) with pogroms carried out under the leadership of both Admiral Kolchak and General Anton Denikin. White crimes also included extrajudicial killings (35).

These crimes led to some episodes of mutiny among British, French, and American troops in early 1919 who questioned the purpose of their mission. Moreover, American General William Graves, who served in Russia at the time and had direct knowledge of these atrocities, turned against the project, recognizing its potential for backlash among the Russian population (35). Nonetheless, U.S. troops remained in Russia until 1920 (32), and Washington would refuse to recognize the Soviet government until 1933.

Although most in the West think of the Russian civil war as the Bolshevik government, or the Reds, against the Whites and their various foreign backers, there were actually more layers to the armed opposition during this period. As historian Walter G. Moss points out in the second volume of *A History of Russia*:

> Extensive anti-Bolshevik, as well as anti-White opposition existed among peasants, workers, and non-Russian nationalities, and this too was part of the civil war. Peasant, worker, and soldier/sailor resistance reached its height in early 1921, after the Whites had already been defeated. Only after the Communists overcame this final major challenge from below could the Civil War really be considered over (31).

Leftist opposition to the Bolsheviks consisted largely of the SRs, who were still popular in the countryside and in Siberia. There was also the Green movement—a combination of Red Army deserters and rebellious peasants who comprised scattered guerilla groups based in the forest (31).

In the midst of the war, some non-Russian nationalities took advantage of the early Bolshevik decree known as the Declaration of the Rights of the Peoples of Russia, which allowed for the right of self-determination "even to the point of separation and the formation of an independent state." In cases where it could effectively prevent secession, however, the Soviet government did, but during this period it was not always able to succeed. Lenin was forced to eventually recognize independent non-Soviet governments in Estonia, Latvia, Lithuania, and Finland (31).

By early 1921, strikes among workers, soldiers, and sailors were cropping up in major cities. Again, the people were suffering from food shortages, lack of heating, and transport problems. This culminated in the Kronstadt rebellion, in which sailors made a list of demands for better conditions for workers and peasants as well as themselves, including the restoration of civil liberties that the Bolshevik government had eliminated. When the government refused to even negotiate, the Kronstadt sailors stormed the nearby fortress. After 10 days, the Bolsheviks retook the fortress but only after suffering 10,000 casualties. The government finally relented on some of the harshest policies, including forced seizure and rationing of crops. This change would lead to implementation of the New Economic Policy (NEP). But change couldn't come soon enough to prevent a famine later that year, which resulted in even more hunger and death (31).

By the time the civil war concluded in 1922, millions had died from combat, disease, and starvation. In addition, Russia's economy was in shambles with a profoundly damaged transportation system, inflation levels that rendered the ruble worthless, industrial production at 20 percent and grain production at 66 percent of prewar levels, and only half the industrial workforce of 1917. Moreover, Russia suffered what would be termed today as "brain drain," with a significant number of educated elites among the 2 million émigrés during this period (31).

Lenin's Post–Civil War Rule until His Death

Between 1918 and 1922 Lenin had instituted what he referred to as "War Communism," whereby most industry was nationalized, and state centralization was increased with an "emphasis on industrial discipline and productivity" (31). Similar policies had been implemented in the Red Army (31).

These policies had helped to lead the Bolsheviks to victory over their scattershot enemies, but they also led to great suffering and more authoritarianism and rigidity. Even before the Kronstadt rebellion, Lenin recognized that the peasants needed incentive to produce enough crops to not only feed industrial cities but to produce surplus for export. He was also forced to acknowledge that the state could not produce and distribute needed goods sufficiently on its own. Consequently, at Lenin's behest, the Communist party finally began implementing the New Economic Policy (NEP), allowing some small-scale private enterprise and trade with state oversight, namely with respect to food, clothing, and household goods (31).

During the years that NEP was in effect, more space was also allowed for social and cultural diversity (38).

It wasn't until 1925 to 1927 that many areas of the Soviet Union began to see meaningful economic improvement, such as a return to prewar levels of industrial and agricultural output. Despite his lingering distrust of the bourgeois class, Lenin had come to realize that long-term economic stability and success was dependent upon specialized knowledge that most party members lacked. But certain policies were put in place to limit any potential privileged status that NEP businesspeople might be perceived to acquire. As historian Walter G. Moss stated:

> Lenin had already become convinced that Russia could not be run without the knowledge and skills of specialists—whether they be the tsarist military officers recruited by Trotsky or civilian specialists, such as economists, agronomists, engineers and professors. There were simply too few specialists among party members. Although "bourgeois" specialists and Nepmen might gain or regain economic and social status and often earn more than party officials, the party closely guarded its political pre-

rogatives. Nepmen, for example, were not allowed to vote or arrange meetings, and they had to pay more for rent and public services than the working class (31).

These attempted limits were not always successful, and the perceived downsides to NEP included the rise of a relatively wealthy "capitalist" class of peasants known as the kulaks and city merchants known as Nepmen. A stubbornly high unemployment rate among industrial workers was also seen under the program (39). NEP was eventually abolished in 1929 under Stalin (38). In its place, Stalin adopted the first of what would become the Five-Year Plans for industrial development and a "Socialist Offensive against the kulaks" in the countryside (39).

What Contemporary Russians Think of the Russian Revolution

According to a 2017 Levada poll, 57 percent of Russians believe Lenin played a positive role in Russia's history, a 17 percent increase from a decade before (40). Forty-nine percent of Russians thought the Bolshevik revolution had a positive effect on Russian history, while 30 percent thought it was negative (41).

Russians I spoke to that same year, mostly educated professionals from Moscow and St. Petersburg, thought that Lenin was a strong, organized leader with charisma and a stated program claiming to offer many Russians what they wanted at the time: food, control of the land, and an exit from the meat grinder of WWI. He was the antithesis of a weak and incompetent tsar and a successive government that was also perceived as ineffectual. But opinions were mixed on whether his ultimate legacy was good for Russia (42).

Some of Russia's historians say the provisional government that resulted from the February Revolution made the fatal error of "falling behind events" by wanting to take time to try to build democratic institutions. Those institutions, once established, would then solve the problems of war, hunger, and land. But these problems needed immediate attention (43), and the provisional government's dithering allowed the Bolsheviks to seize power on the promise of taking more decisive action without delay.

In a similar vein, my guide at the State Central Museum of Contemporary History of Russia in Moscow insisted that allowing the February Revolution more time would likely not have led to a more positive outcome, since the Kerensky government did not have a workable plan to solve the country's most pressing problems.

Boris Kolonitsky, an historian at the European University in St. Petersburg, noted the legacy of the Russian Revolution and the upheavals it paved the way for: "The majority of Russians will pay a big price to avoid revolution: they crave stability above all. We have overfilled our quota of revolutions" (43).

Chapter 3:
The Stalin Era and World War II

Lenin's Death and the Last Testament/Letters to the Congress

Despite constitutions drawn up in 1918 and 1924 that provided for some division of power among different branches of bureaucracy, the Communist Party effectively controlled the government, having exiled SR and Menshevik leaders and subordinated the local Soviets to its central authority. Lenin, as chairman of the Council of People's Commissars, was the de facto leader (31) (44).

But after years of being a workaholic, suffering a grave injury from the 1918 assassination attempt, and falling victim to a series of strokes, Lenin died on January 21, 1924.

Having been rendered incapacitated to varying degrees by strokes that began in 1922, Lenin often relied on his wife, Nadezhda Krupskaya, to serve as an intermediary between him and other Soviet officials. In the months leading up to his death, Lenin's relationship with Stalin, General Secretary of the Communist Party's Organizational Bureau, had become increasingly rocky. Lenin angrily demanded an apology from Stalin after the latter bullied Krupskaya into tears during a telephone conversation. Just days before this incident, Stalin had been granted authority by the Central Committee to oversee Lenin's medical treatment (31).

By that point, Stalin had taken the opportunity to fracture the unity of the Politburo, an organ of the Communist Party's Central Committee, which had acquired the authority to approve all significant government decrees, oversee foreign policy, and manage the secret police, prisons, labor camps, and the judiciary (31). Since 1922 the Politburo members had consisted of Lenin, Trotsky, Stalin, Lev Kamenev (who'd served with Stalin on the editorial board of *Pravda* in 1917), Grigory Zinoviev, Alexei Rykov, and Mikhail Tomsky (31). Once Lenin was no longer consistently healthy enough to counter it, Stalin created a "triumvirate" with Kamenev and Zinoviev against Trotsky (44).

Though they'd worked together relatively well in an earlier period, Lenin had come to distrust Stalin and his maneuvering. More specifically, Lenin did not think that Stalin had the proper temperament and judiciousness in terms of wielding power. In what became known as his Last Testament (aka Letters to the Congress), passed on to the Central Committee by Krupskaya after his death but repressed by Stalin from broader publication, Lenin stated:

> Comrade Stalin, having become Secretary-General, has unlimited authority concentrated in his hands, and I am not sure whether he will always be capable of using that authority with sufficient caution. . . . Stalin is too rude and this defect, although quite tolerable in our midst and in dealing among us Communists, becomes intolerable in a Secretary-General. That is why I suggest that the comrades think about a way of removing Stalin from that post and appointing another man in his stead who in all other respects differs from Comrade Stalin in having only one advantage, namely, that of being more tolerant, more loyal, more polite and more considerate to the comrades, less capricious, etc. (45).

Lenin also criticized Trotsky and—to a lesser degree—Nikolai Bukharin, who'd been considered a close student of Lenin's and an advocate of NEP-style liberalization.

By 1929, Stalin had turned against the NEP and began his Five-Year Plans, forcing collectivization campaigns in the countryside, which resulted in the death and imprisonment of millions (38). Moreover, Stalin stamped out any suggestion of an alternative to his harsh policies—which of course the NEP represented—along with the advocates of such alternatives (38).

Bukharin, along with all of the other members of the Politburo listed above, would later be executed during the purges of the 1930s. Stalin eliminated most of the original Bolshevik revolutionaries and was behind Trotsky's assassination years later in Mexico. Even Krupskaya would continue to be bullied and reportedly blackmailed by Stalin, though she was spared imprisonment and execution (29).

Stalin's Early Years

While it seems likely that Stalin had psychopathic tendencies, he was also very much a product of the revolutionary milieu of his time that believed the ends justified the means with regard to violence.

He was also a supreme opportunist, possessing an uncanny knack for knowing how and when to parlay circumstances to his advantage (19). Indeed, he had studied several well-known philosophers and practitioners of political cunning, including Machiavelli and Otto von Bismarck. The latter was particularly influential, as Stalin biographer Stephen Kotkin underscores:

> Bismarck had no master plan for German unity—his enterprise was an improvisation, driven partly by domestic political considerations (to tame the Liberals in Prussia's parliament). But he had constantly worked circumstances and luck to supreme advantage, breaking through structural limitations, creating new realities on the ground (19).

Stalin, who hailed from Georgia, was one of the few Bolshevik leaders who actually came from a poor background, as opposed to the professional middle-class origins of Lenin and Trotsky. He was the grandson of serfs (31) and the son of an alcoholic cobbler. His mother had ambitions for him and worked and connived to obtain the means to pay for his Orthodox seminary education. A victim of several childhood injuries and illnesses, Stalin was a resilient boy who liked to read. Having worked briefly alongside his father in a factory, he was resourceful and eventually found ways to help finance his own education (19).

Despite the strict environment of the seminary, it provided a space for study and debate of philosophical issues, which helped Stalin develop his not unimpressive intellect (19). Later, when he led the Soviet Union, many colleagues and diplomats would observe up close his remarkable memory and huge library of books on history and political philosophy—many filled with personal annotations in his own hand (46) (31).

Stalin behaved and performed well for most of his time at the seminary. It was here that he would meet his first political mentor, Vladimir "Lado" Ketskhoveli, a fellow student who introduced him to Marxism and encouraged his autodidact tendencies as well as his eventual role as a political agitator (19).

Nothing in Stalin's background indicates an abusive or violent childhood—certainly not for the place and time in which he grew up, where some corporal punishment was the norm, along with rough-and-tumble behavior for adolescent boys (19). In other words, there was little to portend a future tyrant who would often be compared to Hitler in terms of large-scale cruelty.

However, the domineering aspect of his personality had begun to emerge in his youth. A fellow student, who was later also part of a political circle that Stalin was in, recalled that in childhood "he was a good friend so long as one submitted to his imperious will" (19).

After becoming disillusioned and leaving the seminary, Stalin spent the summer of 1897 at a friend's village home, where he became aware of the life of the peasantry and gained sympathy with their cause (19). Stalin would later remark, "First one becomes convinced that existing conditions are wrong and unjust. Then one resolves to do the best one can to remedy them. Under the tsar's regime, any attempt genuinely to help the people put one outside the pale of the law; one found oneself hunted and hounded as a revolutionist" (19).

The following year, Lado and Stalin were reunited, and Stalin watched the charismatic Lado organize and fight on behalf of the socialist cause while defying authorities. Finally, at the age of 27, Lado was captured and jailed, where he died after a guard shot him for refusing an order.

By 1906, Stalin had become a Bolshevik in the Caucasus region. At the Fourth Congress of the Russian Social Democratic Workers' Party that April, Stalin opposed Lenin's proposal for land nationalization and instead advocated giving the land directly to the peasants. He also married for the first time later in the year.

His wife, Kato, was an educated seamstress who was already pregnant by the time of the wedding. She also appears to have been the great love of Stalin's life, as friends noted his tenderness and affection toward Kato, a major departure from his usual coarse behavior. But Stalin continued his revolutionary activities, including the establishment of a radical newspaper, leaving Kato for long stretches.

In 1907, Stalin masterminded a bank train robbery that netted 250,000 rubles from the State Bank. The operation, involving eight homemade bombs, killed about three dozen people and wounded another two dozen (19). He then made his way to Baku, the oil-refining capital of the Russian empire, where the hellish conditions of around 50,000 refinery workers provided an environment ripe for militant agitation. Kotkin describes his stint in Baku as follows:

> [Stalin's] Baku exploits included not just propagandizing and political organizing, but also hostage taking for ransom, protection rackets, piracy, and, perhaps, ordering a few assassinations of suspected provocateurs and turncoats (19).

Lenin was reportedly impressed with Stalin's loyalty to the cause and resourcefulness in "expropriating" needed funds, later making him a member of the Bolshevik Central Committee (19) (31).

But the move to Baku proved fatal to Kato's health, and she died from a gastrointestinal hemorrhage in December. Witnesses at her funeral claimed that Stalin tried to "throw himself into her grave." He later blamed himself for neglecting her (19), acknowledging that she was one of the few people he'd ever truly cared about: "This creature softened my heart of stone. She died and with her died my last warm feelings for people" (31).

Within a few months, Stalin was in jail and then sent into exile in the taiga forests of northern Russia. Around this time, suspicions circulated that Stalin was a police informant, as other revolutionaries were arrested soon after his exile. This was not the first time such an accusation had cropped up against Stalin, and it would not be the last (19).

From this point until 1917, Stalin would largely live a life of imprisonment and exile.

Stalin's Rise to Power

Though he acknowledged that movement toward more democracy and away from extreme bureaucracy was necessary, Lenin banned party factionalism in early 1921, insisting that the danger of counterrevolutionary elements taking advantage of such divisions was still too high. This would eventually help facilitate Stalin's consolidation of power throughout the 1920s (31).

In 1922, Stalin became secretary general, following four other members of the party in quick succession—with two years being the longest run for any of them. The job involved overwhelming responsibilities and likely contributed to the early death of its first occupant, Yakov Sverdlov, who was no incompetent (19). Not only did Stalin gradually learn how to efficiently handle the many requirements of the job, he built up a system that would build on and perpetuate his own power, putting to use his skills as a master manipulator. According to Stalin biographer Stephen Kotkin:

> [He] demonstrated surpassing organizational abilities, a mammoth appetite for work, a strategic mind, and unscrupulousness that recalled his master teacher, Lenin. Stalin proved capable of wielding the levers he inherited, and of inventing new ones. . . . What Trotsky and others missed or refused to acknowledge was that Stalin had a deft political touch: he recalled names and episodes of people's biographies, impressing them with his familiarity,

concern, and attentiveness, no matter where they stood in the hierarchy, even if they were just service staff (19).

After Lenin's death, Stalin used his triumvirate with Kamenev and Zinoviev to further weaken Trotsky, who was removed as war commissar in 1925. Within the next two years, Stalin had maneuvered to have all three of them expelled from the Communist Party, with Trotsky exiled to Kazakhstan in 1928. Stalin then filled the Politburo and other important organs with his own loyalists (31).

Stalin's "Revolution from Above"

As noted Russia scholar Stephen F. Cohen asserts, there are two aspects to Stalin's rule that Russians must attempt to reconcile: 1) the tremendous accomplishments of modernization and industrialization within a short time frame, and 2) the tremendous human cost of these accomplishments and the brutality that accompanied them (47).

Many Russians that I spoke to in 2017 acknowledged and lamented Stalin's brutality. However, they also acknowledged that if Stalin had not quickly and brutally dragged the Soviet Union into the industrial age, they would not have been able to defeat the Nazis. Given that Hitler had made it clear in *Mein Kampf* that he looked upon the Slavs as subhuman, a Nazi victory would have meant enslavement for most of the Soviet people at best and extermination at worst (19).

The following passage from historian Susan Butler's book *Roosevelt and Stalin: Portrait of a Partnership* provides an idea of what Stalin accomplished between 1928 and the start of WWII:

> [Stalin] had eliminated unemployment in the Soviet Union, provided food, shelter, education, and health care where there had been minimal or none before. He had presided over the top to bottom reorganization of Soviet society. His five-year plans had produced remarkable results, although at great cost, little comprehended at the time. The execution of these plans required great courage

and utter ruthlessness, according to [American diplomat] Joseph E. Davies. Stalin had turned the Soviet Union, a backwards society, into an industrial state that had to be reckoned with. Collectivizing the farms—involving the murder and deportation of millions of agricultural workers, the virtual extinction of the kulaks—in the end worked to change Russia forever. In 1928, the Soviet Union had produced 4.3 million tons of steel; by 1938 that figure had risen to more than 18 million tons. The production of trucks went from 700 per year to 182,000. In the space of ten years Soviet Russia, an agricultural society, had become an industrial society (46).

In 1928 and 1929, Stalin kicked off what he referred to as a "revolution from above" in order to address grain shortages, increased unemployment, strengthening of the military industrial complex, ideological concerns, and the cementing of his own power (31).

Though the factors contributing to the grain crisis were more complicated, Stalin blamed the kulaks, claiming they were withholding grain in an attempt to sabotage the government. In response, he confiscated their grain with the agreement of other Politburo members. Eventually, policies against peasants in general and the kulaks in particular went far beyond this, with Stalin requiring more farms to be consolidated and brought under state control (31). Mandatory requisitioning and quotas were instituted, along with punitive measures against peasants who were perceived to not be operating at maximum capacity. From 1928 to 1930, collectivized farms went from 3 percent of all farms to 58 percent (reaching 90 percent in 1936), and Stalin decreed that the kulaks should be "liquidated as a class." Any significant opposition to these policies from the peasants resulted in execution, deportation, or imprisonment in labor camps. In some areas, where peasants resorted to armed revolts against collectivization, military forces were brought in (31).

A partial rationalization for Stalin's brutal collectivization campaign involved financing his breakneck industrial development policy. The first

Five-Year Plan was initiated in autumn of 1928, outlining ambitious goals for industry—with an emphasis on heavy industry to support the military, agriculture, investment, and employment. A command economy was implemented with government officials determining what and how many goods would be produced (31).

While the first three Five-Year Plans did not achieve everything they'd set out to prior to the Nazi invasion in 1941, what they did accomplish in such a short time frame was remarkable. This included impressive increases in the production of metals, machinery, and chemical products as well as the introduction of new industries such as aircraft and agricultural and military machinery. The country had reduced its foreign dependence on strategic industrial products like machine tools to 10 percent, down from 80 percent. Indeed, Soviet industrial output was now second only to the United States, and the country had seen a sixfold increase in the number of those with engineering degrees since 1928 (31).

Conditions for women also changed. Although they held few leadership positions in the Soviet government and party apparatus (which partly protected them from the purges), far more women had joined the workforce. Though this was often motivated by financial need, women now constituted almost half of industrial workers and a majority of medical doctors (a poorly paid profession at the time), while female literacy shot up to around 80 percent (31).

Some historians have also asserted that Stalin's policies benefitted from the Great Depression in the capitalist west, without which the West would have had no incentive to sell technological products to the Soviet Union (19).

In any event, the human cost of Stalin's modernization program was staggering. In addition to the suffering of the peasants, the standard of living declined for many urban workers as shortages of food and other goods rose significantly while increased productivity rates were enforced with criminal penalties (31). Whether Stalin's method of achieving rapid modernization was the best or the only approach is very much debated.

Stalin's Terror and the Gulags

Soviet labor camps were first established in 1919 and housed aristocrats and former members of the provisional government (48). But the gulags, in which prisoners toiled in extreme weather conditions with insufficient provisions, were greatly expanded under Stalin's rule, swelling during the Great Terror of 1936–1938 when 1.5 million were arrested and approximately 750,000 were executed (48). A very high proportion of the arrestees were party officials, including military officers, party secretaries, and factory managers (49). By January 1938, it was already acknowledged within the Central Committee that the scale of the arrests was becoming counterproductive, as the fear they elicited among party officials was undermining job performance (49).

It is recognized that Stalin's head of the NKVD (political police and precursor to the KGB), Nikolai Yezhov, was largely responsible for carrying out the Great Terror of 1936–1938 as well as shaping Stalin's understanding of the alleged conspiracies to undermine the Soviet government. As James Harris explains in *The Great Fear: Stalin's Terror of the 1930s*:

> His commitment to break the conspiracies against the regime and root out enemies was doomed to fail because the conspiracies and enemies were largely chimaeric products of a misguided reading of flawed intelligence. Accelerating the patterns of arrests, interrogations, execution and exile deepened the appearance of conspiracy and enemy activity. Because the NKVD acted overwhelmingly on the content of denunciations or "confessions" obtained under torture, and not on physical evidence of counterrevolutionary conduct, they could never get to the "bottom" of conspiracy (49).

Yezhov was eventually hoisted by his own petard when a backlog of appeals against NKVD convictions mounted and compromising materials against him surfaced. This was compounded when an NKVD colleague stationed in Japan defected, which led to suspicions that Yezhov was going after innocent citizens while protecting real enemies in his midst. Stalin fired

Yezhov in November 1938, replacing him with Lavrentiy Beria, and used Yezhov as a scapegoat for the recent excesses, although Stalin himself had personally overseen and approved lists of citizens to be arrested and executed. By 1939, however, the number of arrests had tapered off (49).

It should be noted that the number of deaths that Stalin was purportedly responsible for during his long reign was greatly inflated during the Cold War era when Robert Conquest's 1968 book, *The Great Terror,* first estimated there had been 20 million deaths (50). Conquest, a former British intelligence officer, admitted that he was an unapologetic Cold Warrior who thought that the Soviet Union and Stalin could best be understood as a science fiction story world and character (51). Cold War propagandizing and caricaturized thinking likely played a role in this characterization of Stalin, as Conquest generalized from various sources, including claims by Soviet defectors (51).

Even popular historian Timothy Snyder, who shows little sympathy for Russia, estimates that Stalin is likely responsible for closer to 6–8 million deaths (52), based on research for his 2010 book *Bloodlands*. According to Snyder, with the exception of the war period from 1941–1945, the vast majority of prisoners left the gulags alive. The total number of Soviet citizens who died in the gulags for the entire Stalinist period is between 2 and 3 million, which is still an astounding number (52).

Snyder's overall figure includes estimates for the famines of 1930–1933, of which the famine that specifically took place in Ukraine, often referred to as the Holodomor, is estimated at 3.3 million out of the 5 million total famine deaths (52).

The Famine: Genocide or Bad Policy?

Perhaps the two most famous works attempting to argue that the famine that struck the Soviet Union in the early 1930s, hitting Ukraine particularly hard, was an intentional genocide on the part of Stalin against Ukraine are *The Harvest of Sorrow* by Robert Conquest and *Red Famine* by Anne Applebaum. As previously discussed, Conquest is a problematic chronicler of the Soviet Union. As for Applebaum—a neoconservative writer with a penchant for always depicting Russia in the worst possible light—historian Mark Tauger has detailed the many misrepresentations and twisted source interpretations that are contained in *Red Famine* (53).

Tauger has published a body of work on the Soviet famines that focuses on the role of climate conditions as a significant factor in the crop failures that led to the famines, arguing against intentionality on the part of the Soviet leadership. For example, Tauger points out that the rainfall received in Ukraine in 1932 was double or triple the norm and led to fungal infestations, which abated by 1933—the same year the famine began to subside (54). He also points out that there had been instances of crop failures preceding 1930, which likely contributed to the Soviet government's belief that the country's farming needed a modernization program (53).

Stephen Wheatcroft and R. W. Davies, two academics who specialize in Soviet history, have also published extensively on other factors that led to the famines that also undermine the argument for intentional genocide. The sources utilized by Wheatcroft and Davies include original archival material, previously unpublished records from the Politburo, and correspondence between Stalin and other officials about the agricultural policies (54).

Wheatcroft and Davies outline the main factors that contributed to the famine as largely involving mismanagement of grain shortages and related agricultural policies during this period (54), which reflected an attempt to implement ideological abstractions that had never been applied in the real world before. Furthermore, these policies were implemented at lightning speed and with completely unrealistic goals.

The overarching objective of the collectivization policy was to bring farming under centralized control of the state in order to modernize methods (e.g. increased mechanization) and increase productivity. As mentioned previously, increased productivity was intended to feed the growing industrial workforce in the cities and to be exported to finance or obtain advanced technology for further industrial and agricultural modernization. But things did not go according to plan.

Wheatcroft, who wrote his own critique of Applebaum's book in 2018, reiterated that many recent historians looking at the famine data often misunderstand how the harvesting of grain (the most important crop failure of the famine period) works, in addition to misunderstanding the different methods of measuring potential grain yields used by the Soviet government prior to 1934 and after. This leads to some historians, such as Applebaum, misunderstanding and/or misrepresenting crop comparisons, which leads to erroneous interpretations of what happened (55).

Wheatcroft goes on to explain the factors that contributed to low grain yields in 1931–32:

> The famine was associated with two years of harvest failure in 1931 and 1932. 1931 was a year of drought with demonstrably excessive temperatures and low rainfall in the early summer injuring the flowering and filling out of the grain. 1932 was a year in which the biological yield (prior to harvesting) was relatively normal, but in which harvest losses were excessively high as a result of damp weather during the harvest period, and a slow progression of the harvesting which greatly increased harvest losses (55).

He also explains the different stages of the harvesting process, particularly in Ukraine, and states that there were regular reports made at the time on the progress of the different stages of these harvests in 1931–32. The reports showed major delays in the harvesting process:

> This occurred for a variety of reasons, including unusually damp weather in Kiev Oblast and low levels of traction power [due to shortages of animals and machines]. Davies and I provide more detailed explanations of this in our 2004 *Years of Hunger: Soviet Agriculture 1929–1931*. . . . Our detailed, critical data analysis, however, estimates grain production in 1932–3 to have been 55 to 60 million tons, and that this was 15 to 17 million tons less than the following year when we estimate it to have grown to 70 to 77 million tons. It is this failure to understand that there really was a shortage of grain at this time that leads to the

conclusion that there was an easy solution to the problem, and that if Stalin failed to implement this easy solution, there must have been a political reason why he did. This is the reasoning for thinking that Stalin must have wanted to kill Ukrainians (55).

Wheatcroft also states that when he and Davies provided their evidence and arguments to Robert Conquest in 2003, he modified his views and no longer asserted that the famine was an intentional genocide but that Stalin abetted the famine by not prioritizing actions to immediately prevent or ameliorate its effects (55).

It should also be noted that it was not just Ukrainians who died in the famines of 1930–33 in the Soviet Union. Kazakhstan is estimated to have lost as many as 1.5 million people—or 1/3 of its population—to famine during this time, with some of the same issues contributing to the disaster, compounded by a drier and more soil-poor environment that underscored its formerly nomadic lifestyle. The Soviet government, building upon the Russian Empire's actions before it, attempted to force the pastoralist Kazakhs into a nation of settled farmers as part of its modernization campaign (56).

On several levels, the Stalin government mishandled agrarian policy and the grain shortages, which led to the famine. First, it set unrealistically high procurement quotas of grain that the farms were meant to fulfill, based on unrealistically high estimates of grain yields. Second, it underestimated the negative effects of peasant resistance to the collectivization/dekulakization drive, as various forms of sabotage were undertaken by resentful segments of the peasant population. Third, once evidence of a famine was apparent, it was publicly denied, which complicated attempts to resolve the problem, including the prevention of foreign food aid. Fourth, local officials often made incompetent decisions in addressing the problems in response to results not matching the ideological expectations set from above. Fifth, the lowering of procurement quotas and the provision of food aid to the hardest-hit areas were delayed with deadly results (55) (54).

Responsibility for these famine deaths, therefore, can still be laid at Stalin's doorstep as the result of the policies he imposed and the insufficient response once the crisis was underway. However, there's a difference between the side effects of a fanatical and badly executed policy and an intentional act undertaken with the aim of killing off a particular group of people based on their identity, as is required for a claim of genocide.

The Molotov-Ribbentrop Non-Aggression Pact

By 1939, President Franklin Roosevelt and some of his advisors had recognized the serious threat to world peace that Hitler's Germany posed. They also understood why Stalin signed the Molotov-Ribbentrop Pact with the Nazis, though FDR made a personal last-minute appeal to Stalin not to (46).

Stalin was well aware of Hitler's anti-Slavic views, as reflected in *Mein Kampf* and subsequent speeches by the German leader. Along with Jews, Slavs were considered subhuman. Shortly after taking power in Germany, Hitler's Nazi party implemented an anti-Soviet propaganda campaign and physically attacked Soviet diplomatic personnel and trade representatives in Germany (57).

Stalin knew that it was just a matter of time before Hitler would come gunning for the Soviet Union on behalf of Lebensraum ("living space" for the Aryans) and resources. He hoped to establish trade with the United States in order to obtain materials that might be useful in the event of war with Germany. But however sympathetic FDR might have been on the matter, he faced domestic obstacles that included strong isolationist sentiment and possible accusations of being a communist sympathizer.

The Bolshevik desire for trade and cordial relations with the United States to balance out anti-Russian dynamics in Europe and in the Pacific started with Lenin as early as 1919, despite Wilson's sending U.S. troops to assist the counterrevolutionary cause. Lenin still advocated for such a policy in 1921 (46). After Lenin's death in 1924, Stalin proceeded to seek official recognition of the Soviet government and only succeeded after Roosevelt took office in 1933.

After Hitler had taken Austria, Czechoslovakia, and the Sudetenland, Stalin vigorously sought a security pact with Britain and France to counter any further German aggression. But Prime Minister Neville Chamberlain continually rebuffed such offers. The fact that the British (58) and French elites tended to be fearful of communism and even sympathetic to fascism as a bulwark against it didn't help matters (59). Britain in particular actually enabled the early stages of Germany's aggression at several key points.

When in 1936 Hitler marched into the Rhineland—a neutral territory established by the Versailles Treaty as a buffer between Germany and France—Britain made it clear that it would not assist France in repelling the German invasion. Hitler later admitted that Germany would have had to retreat if the French had fought them in the Rhineland (60). Britain again declined to help the French in defending the Sudetenland, as France was obligated to do pursuant to its treaty with Czechoslovakia. The Soviet Union was intentionally left out of the infamous Munich Conference later in the year, where Czechoslovakia was divided up (60).

In terms of the Soviets being able to defend border countries, it was also a problem that the Polish leadership would not agree to Soviet troops on its soil even in the event of a German invasion (46).

Finally, at the end of July 1939, diplomats from France and Britain were sent to the Soviet Union, but Chamberlain intentionally placed them on a slow freighter. Upon arrival, the Soviets realized that the British diplomat did not have documents authorizing him to officially negotiate. Finally, after being told that Britain had minimal divisions available for potential military operations, the Soviets concluded that Britain was not acting in good faith (46) (59).

Some historians believe that the British leadership didn't foresee any potential for a pact between Germany and the Soviet Union and felt that the approaching autumn/winter weather would preclude any possibility of a German attack. Thus, the mere appearance of negotiations between Britain and the Soviet Union was thought to be a sufficient deterrent (46). Other historians say that the British leadership was hoping that Germany would eventually destroy the Soviet Union and its communist experiment (60).

Meanwhile, FDR saw the decision made by Britain and France to not ally with the Soviet Union to counter Germany as a grave miscalculation and figured a war was inevitable. Consequently, he "quietly" signed orders creating military infrastructure that could be utilized for action in the future. He also attempted to persuade key senators to repeal the American Neutrality Act so as to allow the transfer of weapons to vulnerable European nations, an idea based on diplomatic information from Belgium that such a move would make Hitler think twice about further aggression. But he was unsuccessful in those efforts.

Sensing the futility of his attempts to ally with Britain and France, Stalin fired the pro-British Maxim Litvinov as foreign minister and appointed Molotov, who was more sympathetic to Germany. Stalin also knew that as the Soviet official who was by far the closest to him, Molotov would give him more detailed reports of negotiations. Talks on trade with Germany were eventually begun, and those on political issues soon followed (46).

When Stalin signed the Nonaggression Pact with Germany on August 24, 1939, he believed that he was buying time to prepare for any invasion. He clung to the delusion that Germany would seek to take out Britain first, and Hitler intentionally gave that impression (46) (59).

Operation Barbarossa: The Nazi Invasion of the Soviet Union

Stalin's denial of an imminent German attack, in the face of continual warnings from his own generals and multiple intelligence and diplomatic sources, including information passed on to the Soviet ambassador from the U.S. State Department, which had surreptitiously obtained a copy of Hitler's directive for Operation Barbarossa, is simply mind-boggling.

Due to pressure from General Georgy Zhukov and Semyon Timoshenko, Stalin agreed to some modest defensive preparations. But he was so convinced that Germany would not yet attack the Soviet Union that he even granted a German request to search for bodies of German soldiers who'd died in WWI in Russia. Zhukov and Timoshenko were flabbergasted at this blatant attempt to survey Russian military positions and troop levels. Stalin's justification was that he was appeasing Germany to avoid giving it a pretext for an early attack (46).

Historian Susan Butler describes the consequences of these missteps, culminating in Operation Barbarossa, in which three million German soldiers invaded the Soviet Union from three directions (61), as follows:

> Because the Germans, using various pretexts, had been allowed to fly reconnaissance missions over the Russian border and had checked out the airfields, army bases, and command centers for the better part of a year, the Luftwaffe easily and quickly found its targets; the immediate devastation was huge: twelve hundred Soviet planes were lost the first day. The commander of the western front's air forces was so stunned he committed suicide. . . .
>
> In three days, the Wehrmacht advanced 150 miles. Within a week the Germans had captured 400,000 soldiers, damaged more than four thousand planes beyond repair, and penetrated 300 miles into Russia, capturing Minsk. Another 200,000 soldiers were captured the second week (46).

It took several days for the profound error in judgment Stalin had made to sink in, during which time he retreated to his dacha, drank heavily, and reportedly experienced a nervous breakdown. Molotov was forced to give the first post-invasion speech to the Soviet population.

When finally Molotov, Beria, and another Soviet official entered his dacha, Stalin feared they had come to arrest him. Upon realizing that they had not come to depose him but expected him to assume his duties as the Soviet leader, he managed to pull himself together (46).

Stalin proceeded to put in 18-hour days and got himself quickly up to speed on all relevant military and logistical matters. He immediately made efforts to reach out to the United States and Britain for an alliance.

By mid-September, however, Kiev had been captured and over 400,000 Soviet soldiers taken prisoner, after which they were held in open air fields where they were shot or allowed to starve or die from exposure (46). The Germans had also sent in death squads to systematically murder Jews, Soviet officials, intellectuals, and others. Ukrainian and Baltic nationalists were known to have collaborated in these massacres (62).

Most people have heard of the infamous siege of Leningrad, which lasted almost 900 days and killed around 800,000 Russians (61). However, in September 1941, the siege of Moscow began, which would kill 926,000 before ending.

> By October 5 three German fronts were close to encircling the city. Zhukov, ordered by Stalin to return to Moscow, arrived on October 8. On that day 600,000 Muscovites were mobilized to mine the main bridges and tunnels, build barricades, create obstacles, dig trenches, and destroy all remaining industrial sites. In all, 498 companies and 210,000 workers were packed up, put on rails, and transported to the east. (46)

By the middle of the month, Stalin was forced to order the evacuation of the city.

> October 16 was a day of terror in Moscow. The Moscow police had been sent to the front. The city closed down: there were no buses, no trolleys; the metro stopped running. The streets were jammed with panicked people—families, possessions, baggage—all trying to move out of the city, amid a rain of soot swirling overhead as office workers set their files on fire. (46)

The anniversary of the 1917 revolution was normally commemorated with an elaborate celebration in the capital. Stalin decided to hold the traditional march in Red Square with a military parade. Molotov and Beria were incredulous at the idea.

But Stalin ordered a fighter "umbrella" to protect the city from German bombers. He then gave a 30-minute speech, which was broadcast all over the Soviet Union. Ralph Parker, a reporter for *Overseas Press*, relayed the impact of the speech on heretofore despondent Muscovites: "[P]eople stood transfixed by their leader's voice and turned rapt faces towards Moscow whence it came" (46).

By November 23 things were looking extremely grim, as German soldiers were close enough to see the highest points of the capital city and Russian officials had asked British diplomats for help in destroying the oil wells in the Caucasus.

Then something fateful happened: the temperature dropped to −4° F (46).

German soldiers weren't prepared for the Russian winter, their leaders assuming they would have captured Moscow well before then. General Zhukov was finally able to mount a successful counterattack and go on the offensive. Moscow then handed the Wehrmacht a major defeat in December—the first such trouncing the Germans had yet received in the war, and at a point when most of the Western governments had figured the Soviets were down for the count (59).

Though Roosevelt understood the grave implications of Hitler succeeding in his conquest of the Soviet Union—gaining control of such vast territory, the oil of the Caucasus, and the agricultural resources of Ukraine—he had to deal with the deep anti-Russian sentiment that permeated much of the State Department. Indeed, the prejudice interfered with the foreign service staff's ability to perform its duties competently. With the staff comprised mostly of "conservative, wealthy socially prominent eastern establishment families that were bitterly anti–New Deal," their assessment of Stalin's proclivities on foreign affairs and willingness to cooperate with the United States turned out to be dead wrong (46).

FDR appointed Sumner Welles as Under Secretary of State to lead a reorganization of the department's staff. But the results were less than successful, and FDR was forced to find ways to circumvent the stonewalling he encountered within the State Department and other agencies when trying to implement policies to assist the Soviet Union.

For the time being, FDR had to work with Harry Hopkins to expand the Lend-Lease program to provide direct assistance as quickly as possible to the Soviet defense. Hopkins convinced FDR to let him go to Moscow immediately for a direct meeting with Soviet officials. Hopkins subsequently had a two-hour meeting with Stalin to coordinate assistance. During this meeting the Soviet leader said he would allow American troops to operate in any part of Russia under American command if they were willing to do so (46).

Roosevelt still encountered attempts to sabotage his robust efforts to supply the Soviet Union lower down the chain of his administration. Nevertheless, by the fall of 1942 as the Soviets battled the Germans at Stalingrad, the Lend-Lease program and the "Moscow Protocol" began providing "massive" supplies to the Soviet Union. The list of goods Roosevelt committed to sending the Soviets included large monthly quantities of airplanes, tanks, cars, trucks, weapons, diesel generators, radios, field telephones, combat boots, flour, sugar, and medical supplies (46).

Later, at the Tehran Conference of 1943, Stalin would acknowledge the critical contribution of Lend-Lease to the Soviet defense:

> I want to tell you, from the Russian point of view, what
> the President and the United States have done to win the
> war. The most important things in this war are machines.
> The United States has proven that it can turn out from
> 8,000 to 10,000 airplanes per month. Russia can only turn
> out, at most, 3,000 airplanes a month. England turns out
> 3,000 to 3,500, which are principally heavy bombers. The
> United States, therefore, is a country of machines. With-
> out the use of these machines, through Lend-Lease, we
> would lose this war. (46)

The Soviet Union's victory at Stalingrad turned the tide of the war in Europe against Germany. However, the victory had come at a tremendous price for the Soviets. General Dwight Eisenhower wrote in his memoirs of what he saw upon entering the Soviet Union in 1945:

> When we flew into Russia, in 1945, I did not see a house
> standing between the western borders of the country and
> the area around Moscow. Through this overrun region,

Marshal Zhukov told me, so many numbers of women,
children and old men had been killed that the Russian
Government would never be able to estimate the total
(63).

What Stalin had really wanted was for the United States and Allied
Powers to open up a Western front in France against Germany, which would
have taken some of the pressure off of Soviet forces in the east. In early 1942,
when the United States was fully committed to the war effort after the Pearl
Harbor attack, discussions were underway for opening up just such a front
with a cross-channel attack on Germany for 1943. The plan was known as
Operation Overlord and was supported by most of the American military
leadership, including Secretary of War Henry Stimson, General George Mar-
shall, and Dwight Eisenhower, who was then a colonel/brigadier general.
Eisenhower drafted the plan for spring of 1943. However, British cooperation
was necessary, and Churchill argued for delay of the plan as the Joint Chiefs
of Staff knew he would.

Churchill's main delaying tactic was to argue for a diversion of troops
to capture islands in the Mediterranean, a further push into Italy, and increasing supplies to "partisans" in the Balkans in the hope of provoking a Balkan
split from Germany, thereby pushing Turkey into the war. None of the other
allied political or military leaders were convinced of the feasibility of Churchill's plan, but his opposition to Overlord prevented its implementation at
that time (46).

Molotov later admitted that he knew the second-front plan was not
viable for the United States in early 1943, but public acknowledgment that
they were planning to do so served an important political purpose: "I
remained calm and realized this was a completely impossible operation for
them. But our demand was politically necessary. . . . I don't doubt that Stalin
too believed they would not carry it out" (46).

It has also been pointed out that all of the complicated logistics that
were required to carry out the Normandy invasion—which couldn't fail since
it would be a devastating blow to Allied morale and a boon to the Germans—

would not have been technologically feasible before it actually did occur, in June 1944 (64).

It was only at the Tehran Conference in December 1943 that Churchill begrudgingly agreed to Operation Overlord. By the time of the conference, indirect communications were being conducted regularly between Stalin and FDR, who had painstakingly begun a campaign to win Stalin's trust, as he realized that he would need Stalin's buy-in as the leader of the world's other emerging superpower to make his project for the United Nations (UN) successful. The nature of these contacts made Stalin realize that the Soviet Union was being viewed as an equal.

As a result of communicated concerns that would smooth the way for productive negotiations at Tehran and the basis for a quid pro quo relationship, Stalin began to allow for some freedom of religion in the Soviet Union, and he dissolved the Communist International (Comintern). The concession on religion was due to FDR's suggestion that to do so would quell domestic criticism about assisting the Soviet Union. Furthermore, Stalin was already inclined to dissolve the Comintern due to his belief that each nation should have its own communist party and it was not the Soviet Union's responsibility to export revolution. In addition, some of the duties of the Comintern could be reassigned to other Soviet agencies (46).

In order to pull off his charm offensive and build a rapport with Stalin, FDR deliberately began keeping Churchill at arm's length. Naturally, Churchill resented such treatment by the American president. In addition to the historical rivalry between the British and the Russians, Churchill and Stalin disliked each other personally. Churchill was also having trouble accepting that the sun would finally be setting on the British Empire and the Soviet Union was rising as a major world power.

Stalin's pursuit of a security zone to protect Russia from further invasions, totally justifiable in terms of its history of invasions in general and the specific costs of German aggression twice in the last 30 years, was ultimately acknowledged by Roosevelt and his administration.

It became clear to FDR during their conversations that Stalin had to be convinced of any postwar order being able to block the resurgence of Germany, which Stalin believed would be able to rebuild within a generation unless prevented from doing so. Stalin was not initially persuaded by FDR's idea of the UN being able to accomplish this.

During the third private meeting between FDR and Stalin at Tehran, the UN was discussed further, as were Poland and the Baltics. Roosevelt was willing to accept Soviet control of Poland as long as it was "peaceful and its institutions preserved." FDR and diplomat Averill Harriman acknowledged that the UK-recognized Polish government-in-exile was problematic in terms of its leaders' tendency to be strident and Russophobic, in addition to expecting the United States and United Kingdom to "restore their position and their landed properties, which were extensive, and prop up the feudalistic system that had existed in Poland earlier in the century" (46). Mindful of domestic politics in an upcoming election year, FDR did not discuss borders at the conference in order not to upset Polish-Americans. He did, however, show openness to the idea of ceding Polish territory in the east to the Soviets and adding German territory in the West as compensation.

As far as the Baltics, FDR initially wanted them to be independent but eventually gave up that request. In return for Soviet control of Poland and the Baltics, Roosevelt got Stalin to agree to the UN as a universal global organization rather than consisting of regional bodies.

By the time of the Yalta Conference in February 1945, the Polish question would be worked out in more detail. By then, the Red Army had pushed the Germans out of Poland and Stalin had established the Polish Committee of National Liberation (PCNL) to govern. At Yalta, Stalin and Churchill butted heads on the issue.

Still voicing support for the Polish government-in-exile with its Russophobic elements, Churchill stated his vision of a postwar Poland under such leadership: "The Poles have a home where they could organize their lives as they wished ... that Poland be mistress in its own house and captain of its own soul ..." (46)

Stalin responded with a lengthy counterargument on Russia's security: "It was a question of strategic security ... because throughout history Poland had been the corridor for attack on Russia ... During the past thirty years

Germany twice has passed through this corridor . . . Poland was weak. Russia wants a strong, independent and democratic Poland . . ." (46).

Of course, "independent" and "democratic" meant a Poland that was friendly toward the Soviet Union and did not contain elements within its leadership of the pre-1939 government that had harbored pro-German sympathies and actively spoke of "the next war against Russia" (46).

But this was largely theater, since Churchill had paved the way for Soviet control of Eastern Europe, including Poland, when he sent his foreign minister, Anthony Eden, to Moscow to propose a deal with Stalin the year before. In exchange for control of Eastern Europe, Britain would have control of Greece, an important geostrategic buffer for Churchill. Stalin was receptive, and Churchill flew to Moscow in October 1944 to seal the deal—months before Yalta (65).

FDR supported the removal of anti-Russian elements in any future Polish government and developed a rapport with the leader of the Polish Peasant Party, who favored amiable relations with the Soviet Union as a possible solution. But the leadership of the Polish Peasant Party was unable to secure significant support from the émigré community to agree to certain conditions. Consequently, the Party was unable to successfully work with the Soviet-sponsored PCNL, cementing FDR's resignation on Poland that it simply be allowed the outward trappings of "free and fair" elections.

Stalin's other top priority was the reconstruction of the Soviet Union, which had seen a third of its country destroyed by the war. He sought a major loan from the United States to help with this, although it never came to fruition. A peaceful postwar period was therefore in Stalin's interest in order to rebuild. He also believed it would facilitate Europe's evolution toward communism as a superior economic system. At the time, Stalin believed this was a real possibility in light of all that he was able to achieve in terms of the Soviet Union's industrial and social development prior to the Nazi invasion (46).

After the Allied victory in Europe, FDR and Stalin began working out how the Soviet Union would contribute to the war against Japan. Despite having been weakened by the spring of 1945, Japan still held significant parts of China and Manchuria (66).

U.S. military leaders were keen on getting Soviet assistance in order to decrease the number of American casualties in the planned invasion of Japan's main islands. Previous experience fighting the Japanese showed a 98 percent death rate for Japanese soldiers, who would fight to the death rather than surrender. In a series of memos from the Joint Chiefs of Staff to FDR on this subject, the JCOS suggested that Stalin be asked what steps should be taken to best facilitate quick and effective collaboration between the United States and the Soviet Union (46).

The joint military action to take out Japan, occurring after Truman's ascent to the presidency following FDR's death, was expected to be relatively quick, with Stalin offering the use of the largest army in the world. Indeed, the Soviet invasion of Japan would take place just three days after the dropping of the atomic bomb on Hiroshima and on the same day as the atomic bombing of Nagasaki. According to veteran war correspondent Eric Margolis:

> On 9 Aug, 1945, the Soviets unleashed one of the war's largest campaigns. Some 1.57 million Red Army troops in 89 divisions, backed by 27,000 guns, 5,500 tanks, and 3,721 warplanes stormed south in a giant, 2,500-km long arc from Outer Mongolia to Korea. Soviet tank armies raced across desert, mountain ranges and forests in a giant pincer movement that enveloped Japan's Manchuri-an-based 600,000-man, 25-division Kwantung Army.

> In only eleven days of blitzkrieg, the once-feared Kwan-tung Army—Japan's largest—was crushed. Soviet forces reached Port Arthur in northern China, much of Man-churia and right up to Korea's 38th parallel (66).

Allied intelligence had, in fact, revealed that the entry of the Soviet Union into the war against Japan would finally push the latter to surrender (67).

In return, Stalin wanted the Kuril Islands, which Russia had lost to Japan in 1875, and territory lost in the 1905 war, as well as control of a couple of ports. Return of the Kurils was eventually agreed upon, along with the southern portion of Sakhalin and an internationalized free warm-water port at Dairen, the use of which was to be shared with China.

The Cold War Begins

The United States emerged from World War II, which had left around 70 million dead and much of Europe and Asia in ruins, with its territory unscathed and its economy booming. As Cold War historian Peter Kuznick writes:

> Only the United States escaped such destruction. The U.S. economy was booming. GNP and exports more than doubled prewar levels. Industrial production soared, growing during the war at a record 15 percent annually. The United States held two-thirds of the world's gold reserves and three-quarters of its invested capital. It produced a phenomenal 50 percent of the world's goods and services. Yet businessmen and planners worried that the end of wartime spending augured a return to prewar depression conditions. They particularly feared the consequences should Europe adopt economic spheres close to American trade and investment (32).

Unfortunately, Harry Truman did not have FDR's understanding of the nuances of the international arena or the Soviet Union's security concerns, much less his diplomatic skills.

He also refused counsel from many more knowledgeable and wiser individuals who had been part of the Roosevelt administration. Instead, Truman was more comfortable taking advice from those who confirmed his own "gut" feelings on matters. He therefore listened to more conservative and anti-Russian voices, like Lieutenant General Leslie Groves, who, among other things, advised Truman not to share information about the atomic bomb with the Soviet Union, a decision others warned would increase distrust and lead to a dangerous arms race (32).

Truman had also been dismissive of Molotov during his first meeting with the Soviet foreign minister and made comments that seemed to indicate a backtracking of what had been agreed to at Yalta on the Polish issue.

During the inaugural UN conference in April, Hopkins had to fly to Moscow to assuage Stalin's growing concerns about the attitude of the new president after he ordered the immediate halt of Lend-Lease—an order he quickly reversed after being advised of its irresponsibility (46).

Stalin, for his part, was able to use the new hostility expressed by former wartime allies to continue justifying repression at home, especially against Jews and other "foreign influences." His paranoia did not abate with age. Before his death, Stalin had even begun demoting and degrading former close associates, such as Molotov, Beria, and Zhukov (31).

As 8.5 million veterans had to be reintegrated into civilian life, Stalin continued his economic policies consisting of Five-Year Plans that emphasized industrial development, particularly in the defense sector. Some estimates show that by 1950, 25 percent of the Soviet budget had been spent on the police and military (31). While very basic needs were provided for Soviet citizens—representing great material progress compared to prerevolutionary Russia—there were very few consumer goods or frills. Compared to the postwar environment of its superpower rival, life was austere and confined.

Between the end of the war and Stalin's death in 1953, industrial growth increased significantly, particularly in the areas of energy, iron, steel, chemicals, and machine production as workers were forced to toil for long hours, including convict and POW labor (31). Cheap housing went up quickly but was often of poor quality and still didn't keep up with demand. Again, peasants experienced harsh conditions in the form of a high tax burden, which prevented savings, and further consolidation of farms into yet larger units. Another major famine occurred in 1947, with government policies reflecting that Stalin had learned few constructive lessons from the 1930s (31).

What Contemporary Russians Think of Stalin

As alluded to earlier, Russians in general have a complicated view of Stalin's legacy. According to a 2017 Levada poll, 46 percent of Russians had a positive view of Stalin and 43 percent had a negative or indifferent view of him (68). The majority of respondents in a 2016 poll characterized Stalin as a tyrant and acknowledged that his repressions led to "millions of casualties among innocent Soviet citizens" (41).

Chapter 4: The Post-Stalin Soviet Era

The Death of Stalin and the Rise of Khrushchev

Sometime after Stalin went to bed in the early-morning hours of March 1, 1953, he suffered a major stroke that rendered him unconscious and paralyzed the right side of his body. He also began hemorrhaging from his stomach at some point. On the evening of March 5 he was officially declared dead. Stalin had had a heart attack in 1945 and suffered from high blood pressure and arteriosclerosis for years, so a fatal stroke at the age of 74 was not that shocking.

There are, however, questions surrounding Stalin's death, such as the long stretch of time between when Stalin was first discovered lying unresponsive on the floor of his bedroom and when a doctor was summoned. Modern doctors say that the type of stroke Stalin suffered could have been brought on by warfarin poisoning by someone in his inner circle (69), which included Nikita Khrushchev, Deputy Premier Georgy Malenkov, and Lavrentiy Beria, the sadistic former head of the security services who later oversaw the gulag prisons (70). If, in fact, Stalin was murdered, either Beria or Khrushchev are considered the likely suspects. Khrushchev claimed in his 1970 memoirs that Beria had admitted to killing Stalin. However, Beria was dead by the time Khrushchev made this public claim, with Khrushchev having played a key role in Beria's arrest and execution within months of Stalin's death (71).

Malenkov succeeded Stalin as Premier and State Secretariat for one week before he was elbowed out of the State Secretariat position due to its abolition. Other party officials were understandably loath to allow anyone else to possess the same dictatorial power as Stalin (69). Beria, meanwhile, had assumed the role of First Deputy Premier and was calling for a relaxation of communism. He'd amnestied around a million nonpolitical prisoners, announced reforms to the judicial system, and—most consequentially—advocated liberalization in Eastern Europe, particularly East Germany. In June, after East German government leaders announced reforms, critics protested for even greater changes. Subsequently, the Soviet military quelled the demonstrations (31). Though liberalization in the Eastern Bloc was initially supported by others as well, Khrushchev, Molotov, and Malenkov used the incident to circle the wagons against Beria, falsely accusing him of being an agent of the British. He was soon arrested, tried, and shot (69).

After eventually becoming leader of the Soviet Union, Khrushchev denounced Stalin's cult of personality, his terror campaign against members of the party, and his insufficient defensive preparations in the run-up to the Nazi invasion, during a "secret" speech to the Twentieth Congress of the Communist Party in February 1956. He also pointed out the irony of Stalin's cult of personality and abuse of power as he oversaw a system that was supposed to value the people collectively as opposed to the glorification of the individual (72).

But the speech didn't remain secret for long. Party leaders and Soviet citizens both reacted with shock and confusion (31).

Khrushchev gradually released all of the political prisoners, shutting down the gulags and implementing a program of reintegration.

One room of the Gulag Museum runs video interviews of some of those who were released from the gulags under Khrushchev. In these videos, the former prisoners discuss their ordeals in the camps as well as their feelings about what life was like after they were released, including the process of becoming "rehabilitated." Many mentioned being faced with possible ostracism for having once been imprisoned and the subsequent decision of whether to hide their past or not (48).

Khrushchev later admitted that he had much blood on his hands from the Stalin era, but that he and many others knew that if they'd resisted they likely would have also been executed (47).

Khrushchev's Background

Khrushchev was the son of a coal miner who worked in the Donbas region of eastern Ukraine. His mother, Ksenia, was a laundress who harbored an obvious rancor toward her husband for being a perceived failure, having been run out of the house by his more prosperous peasant father. Ksenia favored young Nikita over his sister and is said to have encouraged his ambition to compensate for his father's shortcomings (73).

Supported by a local village teacher—a rebel who secretly introduced him to his first illicit political literature—young Nikita showed promise in school. However, the pursuit of education occurred in fits and starts, as money was scarce and he eventually went to work in his early teen years.

He soon saw for himself the horrendous conditions in the mines, where sufficient housing and services were lacking for workers who lived in filthy conditions. As Khrushchev biographer William Taubman describes it:

> The primitive habits Khrushchev encountered in Yuzovka were bred by brutalizing conditions of labor. The workday stretched up to fourteen hours. Miners crawled through dark underground shafts dragging their picks and worked the entire shift lying down or crouching in waterlogged tunnels only three to four feet high. In the deeper shafts, where the temperature soared to thirty to thirty-five degrees (centigrade) [86–95 degrees Fahrenheit], they toiled naked in what they called Adam's costume. . . . Average pay for such work was a paltry one to one and a half rubles a day. Often miners were paid with coupons redeemable for high-priced, low-quality goods at the company store. In 1908, 274 men died from a gas explosion; another 118 died in 1912. There were 157 doctors in the whole Donbas region, and only 18 doctors, 23 doctor's assistants, and 5 nurses for 100,000 people in Yuzovka in 1916. Fierce epidemics swept through with frightening regularity (73).

What little money the workers earned in the isolated mining towns was often whittled away by petty fines imposed by the company and bribes demanded by police. While basic provisions were often scarce, alcohol was readily available, which often led to gruesome fights that would envelop entire streets. When workers attempted to take action for better treatment, they were publicly flogged. Political organizing had been weak, and there was no meaningful participation in the 1905 revolution in Yuzovka and only modest improvements afterward (73).

At the age of fifteen, Khrushchev worked his way into an apprenticeship to become a metal fitter, a more prestigious and better-compensated position than a miner.

By eighteen, he was reading radical periodicals and helping to raise money for strikers in another town, which caused him to be fired. He moved around to different jobs involving mining or equipment repair, gradually building up a reputation as a spokesman for workers when they wanted to request improvements with the owners. He also met and socialized with members of the "working-class intelligentsia" and became close to one member in particular, Ivan Pisarev, whose daughter, Yefrosinia, Khrushchev married in 1914 at the age of 20. Within three years, he would have two children and a four-room apartment. He admitted with embarrassment in his memoirs that he lived better during this period than the average worker during the Soviet era (73).

After receiving a work-related deferment during WWI, Khrushchev helped to lead a few wartime strikes and joined the Bolsheviks in 1918, serving in the Red Army during the civil war. Yefrosinia died of typhus during this period, and Nikita married Nina, a teacher of political economy at a local Communist school, in 1924 (31).

In the 1920s and '30s, Khrushchev served as a party leader throughout Ukraine and in Moscow. A loyal ally of Stalin, he became a member of the Central Committee in 1934 and the Politburo in 1939. He played a central role in overseeing the construction of various projects in Moscow during the mid-1930s, especially the new metro train station (31).

Khrushchev Attempts Reforms

In the years preceding Stalin's death, Khrushchev was part of the Secretariat in Moscow and had become a member of Stalin's inner circle, specializing in agricultural issues (31). Throughout this time, Khrushchev was an energetic and gregarious party functionary known for being a quick study, despite his limited formal education (73).

Khrushchev's denunciation of Stalin and the eventual publication of this in the West had unintended consequences. One of them was the triggering of protests that led to an attempted uprising in Hungary in the summer of 1956, which Khrushchev ultimately quashed with force (31).

This, along with Khrushchev's attempt to reshuffle economic decision-making from "central industrial ministries" to newly formed regional economic councils, the insertion of populist principles into Soviet governance, his mercurial temperament, and his increasing tendency to not seek the input of other members of the Presidium (formerly Politburo), would gradually alienate important segments of the party leadership (31) (74).

In the mid to late 1950s, however, Khrushchev did oversee some successful policies in agriculture and defense technology. The former included greater agricultural productivity that was partly a result of his "virgin lands" project, which utilized heretofore uncultivated lands in northern Kazakhstan, western Siberia, and the northern Caucasus for the planting of crops. Although there were problems and inefficiencies in the implementation of the virgin lands program, food production did rise.

Additionally, he implemented policies originally advocated by Malenkov such as "payment of higher procurement prices for agricultural products, relaxations on the peasant's personal plot, and higher investment which quadrupled between 1953 and 1964" (74).

The latter included the launch of a satellite into space and the successful testing of an intercontinental ballistic missile (ICBM). A housing boom and a modest increase in the production of consumer goods was also seen during this period, while general economic growth had reached a healthy rate from 1953 to 1957 (31) (74).

Censorship became less strict as some space opened up for literature and the arts. The country hosted the sixth annual youth festival in 1957, with young foreigners flocking to Moscow to participate in a cultural exchange that enabled them to see the Soviet Union's technological achievements (74).

A legal code was finally established in the country to prevent the arbitrary arrest and punishment of citizens. Most cases were decided by a judge and two "people's assessors"—the latter of whom were persons with no legal training. In practice, these assessors often served as a fig leaf of populism, since the judge's influence carried the most weight in the outcome. Judges did not necessarily make independent decisions either, as bribes were fairly common. In certain cases where party officials had a perceived interest, there was also "telephone justice," in which the desired verdict would be dictated by phone to the judge by a party official (31).

On several occasions Khrushchev manipulated the law to suit his desired outcome for particular accused criminals, including the retroactive application of the death penalty to two major currency dealers after their trial and original sentencing. Harsh penalties were still enforced against political dissidents, as relevant criminal codes had vague language that judges could easily use to justify their verdicts and sentencing (31).

Serious interest by the party leadership in further legal reforms would be absent until Gorbachev, a trained lawyer, took power in the 1980s (31).

By 1958, any successes from Khrushchev's reforms were petering out. Drought was occurring more frequently in much of the area that comprised the "virgin lands" project, eventually resulting in dust bowls. Despite some fiddling around the edges, the rigid command economy largely remained in place. Priority spending in the defense sector, which Khrushchev failed to effectively reduce, prevented the appropriate investment needed for agriculture and consumer goods. Economic growth soon retreated (31).

Khrushchev also became notorious for his rather grandiose—and often unworkable—policy schemes. An example was the idea of planting large amounts of corn in the Soviet Union after visiting the highly productive corn fields of the Midwest on his tour of the United States in 1959 (31).

By mid-1962, the economic situation had deteriorated to the point that Khrushchev felt the need to raise prices on meat and dairy during a period of lower industrial wages. This led to protests and work stoppages in various cities on June 1, with the largest action swelling to 10,000 by June 3 in the city of Novocherkassk in the northern Caucasus. The protesters had already beaten back a force of 200 police officers and a contingent of soldiers who arrived to quell the demonstration on June 2. On the morning of June 3, the marchers proceeded to Lenin Square, where authorities, including police, Red Army soldiers, and members of the KGB, had a presence. It remains unclear how the shooting started or who gave the orders, but 26 were dead and scores wounded by the time the demonstration was dispersed. Leaders of the strikes were subjected to show trials and sentenced to death or ten to fifteen years' imprisonment (73).

Khrushchev also cracked down on religion, closing some of the churches and other religious institutions that had been allowed to reopen during the WWII era (31). The Soviet government harassed Boris Pasternak from 1957 until his death in 1960 for allowing his novel *Doctor Zhivago* to be published in the West after it was rejected by domestic publishers. The writer was eventually hounded into renouncing the Nobel Prize for literature that he had been awarded (20).

To some degree, Khrushchev was facing the same quandary that had dogged other reform-minded Russian leaders before him. By opening up space for reform, the leader was inevitably setting in motion a process that he or she couldn't always control, as expectations were raised among certain constituencies who would press for more freedom and control than the leader was prepared to grant. Unintended consequences always followed.

It was around this time that Khrushchev's colleagues in the party leadership began to seriously chafe under his domineering style as he eschewed the collective decision-making of the Presidium, sowing the seeds for the coup against him in 1964 (74) (73).

The Cuban Missile Crisis and Its Aftermath

John Kennedy's first impression of Khrushchev during their first meeting, in Vienna in June 1961, where they agreed upon a neutral government for Laos, was unfavorable (75). Though Khrushchev was privately happy that Kennedy had defeated Nixon in the election, he took the opportunity to bully the young president, most prominently about the Berlin issue.

Tensions had been rising over Berlin, which had been split between the Soviet-controlled east and the democratic-capitalist west. Much of the tension was due to the high rate of East Germans fleeing to the West, causing serious labor shortages. This added to the economic problems of East Germany, as they were also seeing the wealthier West Germans buying up their low-priced products, which were government-subsidized for their own citizens. The economic problems the East Germans faced translated into more loans and aid needed from Moscow (31) (74).

The problem had dragged on for over two years, with the United States in no hurry to agree to a long-term resolution. But Khrushchev wanted recognition of East Germany as a sovereign government, codified in a treaty. He also sought a reduction of the threat posed by the U.S.-NATO presence in West Germany, which included nuclear weapons (31).

Going against the advice of those with more experience dealing with Khrushchev, Kennedy engaged in ideological debate with his Soviet counterpart in Vienna, which led nowhere (73). Khrushchev then sat stone-faced in response to Kennedy's stated concerns about the human cost of a possible nuclear war between their respective nations (75).

After a prickly two days of meetings, Khrushchev warned Kennedy before they departed that if Washington would not negotiate a resolution regarding Berlin by December, the Soviets would sign a separate treaty with East Germany and close off access to the West. Kennedy retorted that it would be a cold winter (73).

A few months later, in September, Khrushchev initiated a secret back channel correspondence with Kennedy. His first letter, which was 26 pages long, expressed regret at their inability to connect at the Vienna meeting due to distrust, which prevented them from working on more mutually beneficial goals.

Khrushchev likened their situation to "Noah's Ark where both the 'clean' and the 'unclean' found sanctuary. But regardless of who lists himself with the 'clean' and who is considered to be 'unclean,' they are all equally interested in one thing and that is that the Ark should successfully continue its cruise. And we have no other alternative; either we should live in peace and cooperation so that the Ark maintains its buoyancy, or else it sinks" (75).

Kennedy responded with a lengthy and receptive letter of his own in which he agreed with Khrushchev's analogy about their problem: "I like very much your analogy of Noah's Ark, with both the 'clean' and the 'unclean' determined that it stay afloat. Whatever our differences, our collaboration to keep the peace is as urgent—if not more urgent—than our collaboration to win the last world war" (75).

Thus began a delicate but crucial exchange between the world's two nuclear superpowers.

Khrushchev felt he had to keep the communication hidden from the Kremlin and the Soviet military establishment due to hard-liners in his government who would view such a project as alarming and weak. Kennedy would eventually learn that the very same dynamics were going on in his own government. By 1963, he would have to bypass his own State Department to continue his correspondence with Khrushchev (75).

By October 1961, Khrushchev had intuited enough about Kennedy to suspect that the crisis at the Berlin Wall was brought about by elements of the U.S. government without Kennedy's knowledge or approval. When Kennedy became aware of the intense standoff between American and Soviet tanks, he immediately utilized the back channel established with Khrushchev to work out a withdrawal plan (75).

Despite this successful negotiation to end a crisis that could have escalated out of control, the road ahead would be littered with regressions and dangerous behavior. Khrushchev continually pushed the envelope with Kennedy, believing that Kennedy's restraint regarding the Berlin issue meant that he could act boldly with few consequences.

In March 1962, Kennedy made a statement during an interview with *The Saturday Evening Post* that "Khrushchev must not be certain that, where its vital interests are threatened, the United States will never strike first. In some circumstances, we might have to take the initiative."

Khrushchev interpreted this as a first-strike threat, which resulted in a Soviet military alert. When Kennedy's press secretary tried to reassure Khrushchev during a visit to Moscow a couple of months later, the leader was not convinced and began to reexamine his military position (75).

Not long afterward, the United States conducted the largest Atlantic-Caribbean military maneuvers to date. Additionally, a rift had occurred between Fidel Castro and the pro-Soviet Communist Cuban leader Anibal Escalante. All of this increased Khrushchev's anxiety that the Soviets might lose their new Caribbean ally to Chinese Communist influence or even a return to the American orbit (73).

In many ways, Khrushchev was an insecure leader, particularly in the area of foreign policy. This insecurity, however, was not entirely unjustified. He was keenly aware that the Soviet Union was "surrounded by U.S. bases and missile sites from Western Europe to Japan and from Alaska to Turkey," which was on its southwestern border (31). The so-called "missile gap" touted during the 1960 U.S. presidential campaign turned out to actually favor the United States significantly (32). He was also presiding over a large country that was not as wealthy as its superpower rival, but Khrushchev wanted to open up more funds for domestic investment. In order to address both the security and the economic challenges, he focused on developing his strategic nuclear deterrence capability (31).

With an ideologically friendly government in power in Cuba at the moment, Khrushchev would have an opportunity to place Soviet nuclear missiles in the United States's backyard, achieving perceived nuclear parity while saving the money required for a higher quantity of ICBMs as an alternative approach. It would also serve to deter the invasion of an ally, as Castro was well aware of continued U.S. plans to invade, sabotage, or overthrow his government (31) (75).

In fact, since the failed Bay of Pigs fiasco, Castro had become increasingly convinced that Washington was set on invading and destroying the island. He therefore believed that Cuba's likely fate was to be martyred on behalf of its socialist revolution, which it would not renounce (76).

Khrushchev went ahead with the installation of the missiles. By October, a full-blown crisis would emerge that threatened a nuclear holocaust.

On October 14, U-2 spy planes captured images over Cuba that were analyzed by the CIA, which determined that the images included "[Soviet] construction of launch sites for ballistic missiles capable of striking the United States" (73). Kennedy, who had been out of town, was provided the images and briefed on the matter upon his return to Washington on the morning of October 16. For the next several days, Kennedy and his national security team tried to flesh out Khrushchev's motives for what they saw as a dangerously provocative act and to mull over what Washington's response should be. A military strike or a blockade were the main options considered (73).

On October 22, Kennedy gave a national televised address in which he informed the American public of the crisis and announced a blockade of Cuba.

Kennedy tended to believe that Khrushchev was looking for leverage in connection with the Berlin issue. He also believed that Khrushchev figured that the United States would soon find out about the missiles and must have had a ready plan of response. In fact, the mercurial Soviet leader appeared not to have thought the scheme through that far, having misjudged Kennedy. As a result, he improvised much of his response to the subsequent crisis (73).

Though Khrushchev wanted the operation to be secret until its completion with the missiles already fully in place, it was a large and cumbersome mission that begged being discovered. The plan called for the placement of 36 medium-range missiles and 24 intermediate-range missiles along with all of their launchers. In addition, a multitude of other weaponry was required to defend the missiles, along with tens of thousands of Soviet military personnel to implement and support the operation. Furthermore, all of the equipment and personnel had to be moved from the Soviet Union to Cuba in a camouflaged manner (73).

The most troubling aspect of the whole plan was that Khrushchev's original instructions—provided orally but not in writing—allowed for the firing of Luna missiles, or tactical nuclear weapons, without Moscow's further approval. These nukes were already in Cuba by October, unbeknownst to Washington. Khrushchev would revoke those orders by October 22, but General Anatoly Gribkov would reflect years later on just how dangerous the situation potentially was if the Americans had decided to invade Cuba:

> [W]ould the attackers have found and neutralized the bunkers where the nuclear charges for the Lunas and the cruise missiles were stored? Or would a desperate group of Soviet defenders, with or without an order from above, have been able to arm and fire even one Luna warhead— with a yield one-tenth that of the bomb dropped on Hiroshima—or one of the more powerful [cruise missile] charges? If such a rocket had hit U.S. troops or ships, if thousands of Americans had died in the atomic blast, would that have been the last shot of the Cuban crisis or the first of global nuclear war? (73).

The CIA had mistakenly concluded that Soviet nuclear warheads had not yet been delivered to Cuba, believing instead that they were on the Poltava, one of the Soviet ships that had stopped short of the U.S. blockade and turned back (76).

To complicate matters even further, Khrushchev assigned the experienced but elderly and quarrelsome General Issa Pliyev to head the operation. Pliyev did not get on well with Castro, which strained communications between the Cuban and Soviet leaders during the crisis (73).

On the morning of October 24, Washington's blockade went into effect. Officially, the United States referred to the action as a "quarantine" in order to avoid the martial language of "blockade" (76). U.S. naval ships were authorized to stop and search any Soviet ships for nuclear weapons or related cargo.

But it was soon realized that a Soviet nuclear submarine was escorting Soviet ships in the Caribbean.

Tensions mounted as the Soviets continued on their course.

The best insight into President Kennedy's reaction during this time, when nuclear war seemed imminent, comes from his brother, Attorney General Robert Kennedy: "His hand went up to his face and covered his mouth. He opened and closed his fist. His face seemed drawn, his eyes pained, almost gray. We stared at each other across the table. For a few fleeting seconds, it was almost as though no one else was there and he was no longer the president." Robert went on to explain that what most haunted the president was the fate of all the children who'd had no say in what was happening and would have no chance to grow up and make something of the world (75).

The miracle that ended the tension was Khrushchev's order for Soviet ships to stop dead in the water before breaching the blockade, thereby providing more time for negotiation. But other Soviet activities continued on the island, and nuclear-armed U.S. B-52 bombers remained in the air 24-7 near the Soviet border (76).

At this point, Castro believed that a U.S. invasion of Cuba was imminent. His attitude was that if Cuba was going down, then the United States should go down as well. He would ultimately encourage Khrushchev in an October 27 letter to avenge socialist Cuba with a nuclear strike on the United States if the United States invaded and destroyed the island (76).

The suggestion infuriated Khrushchev, who knew that a Soviet strike on the United States would trigger a retaliatory strike on the Soviet Union (76).

The crisis ended after a visit from Robert Kennedy to Soviet Ambassador Anatoly Dobrynin. Kennedy's message was that the president's military advisors were pressing for escalation and that things could spiral out of his control. Khrushchev agreed to remove the missiles in exchange for Kennedy's confirmation that there would be no invasion of Cuba. Kennedy also made a secret promise to remove U.S. nuclear missiles from Turkey on the Soviet border. Kennedy upheld his word on removal of the missiles within six months and never gloated about Khrushchev's "retreat" (75).

There is some debate about the extent of the spiraling threat that Robert Kennedy conveyed, but Khrushchev believed, as stated in his memoirs, that Kennedy feared the real possibility of a military overthrow (75).

When asked by journalist Norman Cousins in December 1962 how it had felt to have his finger so close to the nuclear trigger during the Missile Crisis, Khrushchev said:

> The Chinese say I was scared. Of course I was scared. It would have been insane not to have been scared. I was frightened about what could happen to my country—or your country and all the other countries that would be devastated by a nuclear war. If being frightened meant that I helped avert such insanity then I'm glad I was frightened. One of the problems in the world today is that not enough people are sufficiently frightened by the danger of nuclear war (75).

Historians James Blight and Janet Lang, two of the foremost experts on the Cuban Missile Crisis, have calculated that if the crisis were run 100 times with the same conditions, 95 times it would end in a nuclear war (76).

By 1963, Kennedy and Khrushchev had reached an impasse on the terms of a nuclear test-ban treaty over the number of inspections that would be allowed. The Soviets feared inspections were an opportunity for espionage and had reluctantly agreed to three. The Kennedy administration soon realized that Congress would not approve any treaty that required less than eight. Kennedy, however, sensed that most of the American public had drawn the same conclusion that he and Khrushchev had from the Cuban Missile Crisis—that of a need to turn toward peaceful coexistence, disarmament, and cooperation in whatever areas were possible.

Kennedy, however, had become increasingly aware of numerous factions in his own government that would undermine his peace policies. Partly in an effort to do an end run around these obstructionists, he enlisted advisor Theodore Sorenson to write an ambitious speech that would outline a vision of peaceful coexistence and disarmament. That speech was his American University Address (see Appendix I), in which he insisted that peace was possible if broken down into manageable and concrete steps, acknowledged the shared humanity of the Soviet people despite political differences, and encouraged Americans to self-reflect on their own attitudes that could impede progress toward peace (75).

Kennedy had gotten word to the Soviets ahead of time that he would be giving a significant speech. The Soviet Union's response to the speech was described as follows by historian James W. Douglass:

> The full text of the speech was published in the Soviet press. Still more striking was the fact that it was heard as well as read throughout the USSR. After fifteen years of almost uninterrupted jamming of Western broadcasts, by means of a network of over three thousand transmitters and at an annual cost of several hundred million dollars, the Soviets jammed only one paragraph of the speech when relayed by the Voice of America in Russian, then did not jam any of it upon rebroadcast—and then suddenly stopped jamming all Western broadcasts. Equally suddenly they agreed in Vienna to the principle of inspections by the International Atomic Energy Agency to make certain that Agency's reactors were used for peaceful purposes. And equally suddenly the outlook for some kind of test-ban agreement turned from hopeless to hopeful (75).

Furthermore, "Khrushchev was deeply moved. He told test-ban negotiator Averill Harriman that Kennedy had given 'the greatest speech by any American President since Roosevelt.'" He proposed the consideration of a treaty that would ban nuclear testing in the air, space, and water, obviating the need for inspections, as well as a non-aggression pact between NATO and the Warsaw Pact (75).

In the United States, however, the speech was largely ignored or greeted with skepticism.

Around this same time, Kennedy was contemplating a rapprochement with Castro in which he would acknowledge the revolution and Castro's government in exchange for a promise to not sponsor any more revolutions in the Western Hemisphere. Castro was prodded by Khrushchev to take the risk of trusting Kennedy enough to consider a dialogue with him. A back channel of communication was established by November in the form of Norman Cousins who, during a days-long interview of Castro, discussed with him the possibility of a negotiated peace with Kennedy on November 19, 1963. Castro's response, after several minutes of reflection, was incisive and prescient in terms of truly understanding Kennedy's predicament:

> I believe Kennedy is sincere. I also believe that today the expression of this sincerity could have political significance. . . . I haven't forgotten that Kennedy centered his electoral campaign against Nixon on the theme of firmness toward Cuba. I have not forgotten the Machiavellian tactics and the equivocation, the attempts at invasion, the pressures, the blackmail, the organization of counterrevolution, the blockade and, above everything, all the retaliatory measures which were imposed before, long before there was the pretext and alibi of Communism. But I feel that he inherited a difficult situation; I don't think a President of the United States is ever really free, and I believe Kennedy is at present feeling the impact of this lack of freedom. I also believe he now understands the extent to which he has been misled, especially, for example, on Cuban reaction at the time of the attempted Bay of Pigs invasion (75).

Another peace emissary, Jean Daniel, was present a few days later when a stunned Castro received the news of Kennedy's assassination and lamented: "Everything is changed. Everything is going to change" (75).

The Coup against Khrushchev

In October 1964, Khrushchev's colleagues in the Presidium—led by Leonid Brezhnev and KGB head V. F. Semichastny—were conspiring to oust him. Khrushchev's recklessness in his initiation and handling of the Cuban Missile Crisis was but one of the many grievances against him. As Khrushchev biographer William Taubman explains, the volatile leader had systematically alienated different sectors of the power structure:

> Three years after a new party program had pledged Communist abundance by 1980, food shortages had spread throughout the land. Party officials resented the loss of privileges and the job insecurity he had made their lot. For the military, deep cuts in troop strength and conventional weapons were the last straw. The liberal intelligentsia had lost faith, and rank-and-file workers and peasants too had turned against him (73).

Khrushchev's son, Sergei, had gotten wind of the conspiracy and tried to warn his father, who was dismissive of the revelation.

Lured back to Moscow during the start of what was to be a long-overdue two-week vacation, Khrushchev found himself in a conference room at the Kremlin being raked over the coals by his fellow party leaders—many of whom he had promoted. One by one, those in attendance went through a list of bungled policy decisions as well as professional snubs that had reflected his increasing authoritarianism and poor governance. Even Khrushchev's longtime friend and ally, Anastas Mikoyan, who was the only person present to offer any defense of Khrushchev, reluctantly supported the coup (73).

Recognizing his utter isolation, Khrushchev resigned himself to the inevitable and told Mikoyan in a phone call later that evening:

> Let them cope by themselves. I've done the main thing. Could anyone have dreamed of telling Stalin that he didn't suit us anymore and suggesting he retire? Not even a wet spot would have remained where he had been standing. Now everything is different. The fear is gone, and we can

talk as equals. That's my contribution. I won't put up a fight (73).

Khrushchev lived in a restricted but relatively comfortable retirement until his death in 1971. He and his son, Sergei, managed to smuggle out audiotapes of his dictated memoirs before the Soviet authorities could confiscate them. They were published in the West in 1970 (31).

What Russians Think of Khrushchev

During the Gorbachev era, public opinion of Khrushchev increased and reached its zenith during the mid to late 1990s (31). According to more recent opinion polls, Russians now feel mostly indifference toward him (77). In my conversations with Russians of different ages, Khrushchev was variously described as "weak," "strange," and "ineffective," but achievements in space technology were acknowledged (42).

The Brezhnev Era: Domestic Conditions

Leonid Brezhnev, like Khrushchev, was an engineer and an ethnic Russian who grew up in Ukraine. As secretary general, he would also be forced to deal with many of the same issues that Khrushchev did: negotiating the ebb and flow of tensions with the United States, confronting rebellion in Eastern Europe, and managing the split with China—which boiled over in 1969. But the similarities end there.

Brezhnev was more stable and politically cautious in his public life. He showed no interest in reform and brought investments in the military back up, which ultimately led to nuclear parity with the United States. He also generally worked in a more collaborative way with other high party officials, but less so toward the end of his rule (31).

He had modest ambitions of stability marked by gradual improvements in social welfare with the political bureaucracy to remain firmly entrenched. He did not advocate for a "revolution from above" like Stalin or for a populist mobilization from below like Khrushchev (78).

Alexei Kosygin, an engineer from St. Petersburg and veteran of the civil war, served as premier (the equivalent of prime minister in today's Russia) throughout most of Brezhnev's tenure. He had served in the Politburo from 1948 to 1952 and was appointed deputy premier in 1960. He advocated—not always successfully—for more investment in the civilian sector and encouraged Brezhnev toward detente with the United States.

Throughout most of Brezhnev's rule, living standards improved modestly. This was helped by the fact that between 1973 and 1981, fossil fuel prices were high, and the Soviet Union had increased its oil and gas production in Siberia. Investment in agriculture was raised, but the results were uneven and the government was forced to import grain during low harvest years (31).

As early as 1968, some Soviet officials recognized the need for long-term reform, particularly in the economic realm. Concerns included the overemphasis on the defense sector, waste, the poor quality of goods produced, increasing unemployment, and low wages for collective farmers (31). There was also recognition that, due to Brezhnev's consensus politics, he often acquiesced to investment in a multitude of sectors to avoid alienating party leaders. This resulted in a drain on resources, which Brezhnev sought to pay for—in part—with détente. Improved relations with the West would presumably lead to increased trade, credit, and technical assistance (78).

But whatever assistance came from the West wasn't enough to paper over the structural problems in the Soviet economy. Moreover, as we'll see later, the West could always use its economic relations to pressure the Soviets.

With the quashing of Czechoslovakia's reform movement by Soviet authorities in 1968, any narrow opening for change that may have existed closed. Since the economy had not reached a point of crisis, bureaucrats resisted the idea of structural reform, fearing loss of control and privileges (31).

The tacit social agreement between the Soviet government and its citizens during this period seemed to be that, in exchange for political control, the government would provide improved standards of living and a degree of limited personal autonomy (78). Even some private market space was begrudgingly allowed—such as private garden plots—to compensate for shortcomings in the provision of certain goods and services by the state. In the resulting gray economy, Soviet citizens bartered or sold surplus food products as well as various services such as tutoring and repairs (31).

A glimpse into how Soviet citizens navigated life during this period, often based on parlaying personal connections and exploiting the vagaries of the system, is provided by sociocultural anthropologist Michelle A. Parsons in her 2014 book *Dying Unneeded*:

> Work was the principle means by which Soviet citizens were ordered by the state. At work, Russians had personal connections and access to resources and services. Someone in the Soviet bureaucracy could arrange permission to build a dacha. A friendly butcher could set aside a good cut of meat. A test proctor could help a student pass an entrance examination. Collectively, people often circumvented the state, but they depended on the state to do that (79).

Parsons found that many Russians who'd lived under the Soviet system during the Brezhnev era reported experiencing it in ways that Americans may find surprising:

> For these elderly Muscovites, freedom was not always compromised by the Soviet state. In some cases the constraint of the Soviet state heightened a sense of freedom. As people, using their connections, collectively pushed against the limits of the state, and as those limits bent back or gave way, they experienced a sense of freedom (79).

Ultimately, however, economic performance deteriorated in the absence of meaningful structural reform, and the system had begun to seriously wither due to an aging leadership who couldn't or wouldn't implement changes.

Brezhnev's Foreign Policy:
Czechoslovakia, the Border War with China, and Détente

In the satellite countries of Eastern Europe, there were some administrative differences compared to the Soviet Union. Some of these countries, for example, did not have a strict command economy or allowed more religious freedom. However, there were certain boundaries that the Soviet leadership would not allow them to cross, viewing it as a threat to Soviet security and "socialist" cohesion.

These Soviet lines in the sand were reflected in how the Czechoslovakia crisis was handled in 1968. In January, reformist Alexander Dubček replaced hardline leader Antonín Novotný as head of the Czechoslovakian Communist Party. The ouster, tolerated by the Soviet government, was fueled by popular discontent with Novotný. But when popular mobilization, dubbed the "Prague Spring," extended to the granting of more freedom of expression and civil liberties, Soviet authorities—along with party leaders from other satellite countries such as Poland—feared that the Czechoslovakian government would cease to be able to control the reform demands. The Soviets also believed Western subversion was playing a role in the movement (31).

After failed attempts to convince the Czechoslovakian leadership to curtail reforms, a half million troops from the Soviet Union and other satellite countries invaded Czechoslovakia. The troops occupied the country, meeting no force, which resulted in minimal violence. Meanwhile the Kremlin pressured the Dubček government into acquiescence, eventually culminating in Dubček's resignation in April 1969 (31).

The Soviet government's justification for its actions in Czechoslovakia became known as the "Brezhnev Doctrine," which stated that each socialist country had an obligation to not undermine the larger socialist world (31).

At this point, there was actually little unity among the "socialist" countries, as a split had emerged between the Soviet Union and China earlier in the decade, which would soon come to a head.

As early as the late 1950s, visits between Khrushchev and Chinese leader Mao Zedong revealed personal dislike between them. But the actual schism occurred in 1960 over strategic and policy disagreements. More specifically, Khrushchev criticized Mao's "Great Leap Forward" program for the rapid attainment of communism. Mao, in turn, criticized Khrushchev's desire to engage diplomatically with the West. They also disagreed on the degree and nature of support for communism in the third world.

But more importantly, Mao wanted the renegotiation of tsarist-era treaties regarding borders between the two nations. In particular, the area around the Ussuri River, which had been designated as a border area by the 1860 Treaty of Peking, was in contention by the Chinese. The Chinese leadership had considered these treaties to have been agreed upon at China's expense during a period of weakness. Khrushchev refused to consider such a request, and the split led to the withdrawal of Soviet assistance to China (31) (80).

In the intervening years, relations continued to sour amid a Soviet military buildup and the unveiling of the Brezhnev Doctrine. Simultaneously, tensions increased on a group of small, uninhabited islands along the Ussuri River boundary, including Zhenbao Island. On March 2, 1969, Chinese troops ambushed a Soviet border outpost on Zhenbao, killing dozens and injuring many more (80) (81).

A Soviet memo to the East German government informing them of the incident described the brutality of the Chinese attack as follows:

> Based on the on-site inspection and the expert knowledge of the medical commission which examined the bodies of the dead Soviet border guards, it can be stated that the wounded were shot by the Chinese from close range [and/or] stabbed with bayonets and kni[v]es. The faces of some of the casualties were distorted beyond recognition, others had their uniforms and boots taken off by the Chinese (82).

On March 15, the Soviets took revenge, initiating a second clash between the two sides on Zhenbao, involving a larger number of troops and weapons. Several more outbreaks of fighting occurred on the border over the next several months (80).

The Chinese attack in early March was due to a combination of factors that they perceived as a major threat that needed to be deterred by demonstrating a willingness to use force. As Michael S. Gerson explained in his report "The Sino-Soviet Border Conflict: Deterrence, Escalation, and the Threat of Nuclear War in 1969":

> The sharp downturn in Sino-Soviet relations, a significant Soviet military buildup in the border region, and the Soviet invasion of Czechoslovakia in 1968 and subsequent announcement of the Brezhnev Doctrine all convinced Mao of the need to forcibly demonstrate China's courage, resolve, and strength in the face of what was perceived to be a looming Soviet threat. By initiating a limited attack, flexing some muscle, and killing a few Soviets, China sought to forcibly demonstrate that it could not be bullied, and that a future Soviet attack would be fiercely resisted. Mao, according to this view, wanted to teach Moscow a "bitter lesson" (80).

That bitter lesson, however, nearly provoked a nuclear response, as the Soviets viewed China's preemptive move as not only aggression, but evidence that the Chinese leadership was "insane" (81). As the Soviet Union enjoyed technological advantages in nuclear weapons, air power, and air defenses, the only cards the Chinese could play in a military conflict were the massive number of troops they could deploy and perhaps firing off a few of the rudimentary nukes they had at their disposal before they could be destroyed (81).

The Soviets did, in fact, consider a limited nuclear attack on China's nuclear facilities. They surreptitiously made contact with the United States to ascertain Washington's reaction to—and even possible participation in—such a strike. Though the reaction from Washington was unfavorable, it was also unlikely that the United States would take meaningful action to protect China in the event of a Soviet attack (81) (80).

When the CIA director, Richard Helms, publicly announced that the Soviets had made such inquiries to the United States, the recalcitrant Chinese leadership finally took the Soviet nuclear threat seriously and agreed to negotiations (80).

China's audacity did win it some respect in Washington, as certain officials considered ways to exploit the rift between the world's two largest communist countries, culminating in Richard Nixon's visit to China in 1972, officially opening diplomatic relations.

The pursuit of détente and arms control agreements was the focus of U.S.-Soviet relations during the late 1960s and early 1970s. As Washington was forced to recognize the Soviet Union's nuclear parity by 1967 via its buildup of ICBMs and the beginning of work on an antiballistic missile system that could deny a retaliatory attack, President Lyndon Johnson called for nuclear negotiations. These negotiations became known as the strategic arms limitation talks (SALT), which would be taken up by Johnson's successor, Richard Nixon, and would lead to the SALT I and Anti-Ballistic Missile (ABM) treaties of 1972. The treaties placed limits on the growth of offensive nuclear weapons and strategic missile defense systems, for both sides (83) (78).

A SALT II treaty was successfully negotiated by Brezhnev and President Jimmy Carter in 1979, which "limited the total of both nations' nuclear forces to 2,250 delivery vehicles and placed a variety of other restrictions on deployed strategic nuclear forces, including MIRVs [multiple independently targeted reentry vehicles]." However, SALT II was never ratified by the Senate due to various objections, but Washington and Moscow both agreed to abide by it until it expired on December 31, 1985 (83).

Détente eventually fell apart by the late 1970s due to differing expectations on both sides that largely went unfulfilled. The United States hoped that the Soviet Union would curb its support for nationalist and communist movements in the third world and expand civil-political rights domestically as reflected in the Helsinki Accords of 1975. The Soviet Union, in turn, hoped for a variety of economic benefits, such as favored nation trading status and low-cost credit, and less hostility in its backyard. It resented Washington's opening to China as well as what it perceived as interference and finger-wagging regarding its internal politics (78).

By May 1982, Brezhnev's health had seriously deteriorated and he suffered a stroke. He died in office six months later from a heart attack.

Mikhail Gorbachev

Gorbachev was promoted by Yuri Andropov—former head of the KGB—who led the Soviet Union for 15 months until his death in February 1984. Andropov reportedly wanted Gorbachev to be his successor, but the older men in the Politburo (formerly Presidium) weren't yet ready to hand the reins over to a young reformer (31). Instead Konstantin Chernenko became the new secretary general and lasted 13 months until he, too, died.

In 1985, Gorbachev finally became secretary general. He would quickly begin his reform program, as reflected at the 27th Party Congress of that same year, in which he laid out his ideas for glasnost—openness, democratization, and perestroika—restructuring. With this program, Gorbachev made it clear that he wasn't interested in simply making some superficial administrative changes.

The goal of his perestroika plan was to change the quality as well as the quantity of economic growth by increasing productivity, with more effective use of science and technology as well as better management of and incentives for workers (78).

Gorbachev believed that glasnost and democratization were needed to lay the foundation upon which the perestroika reforms would be built. More specifically, Gorbachev believed that a "psychological restructuring" was needed to transform society away from an autocratic Stalinist mindset and toward a humanist mindset that included personal initiative (78).

Born in 1931, at the dawn of Stalin's first Five-Year Plan, Gorbachev grew up in a family of peasants in a village near Stavropol in the northern Caucasus. Many residents of his village died during the tumultuous collectivization process, and several members of his family suffered due to the great famine as well as Stalin's purges (84).

After the Germans invaded in 1941, all able-bodied men were sent to fight, leaving only women, children, the sick, and the elderly to tend to the activities of survival. Mikhail, at the age of 11, took over the gardening as well as the physical labor required to maintain the land they lived on.

For four months in 1942, the Nazis occupied his village, appointing an elderly male resident to be a liaison. The old man served in this capacity reluctantly and did his best to protect the other residents, but that didn't stop the Stalinist government from later arresting him as a collaborator, despite the protestations of other villagers. He would eventually die in the gulags—an injustice that left an impression on Gorbachev.

When his father returned home from the front, he told Mikhail about some of his war experiences, including fighting with insufficient weaponry as well as episodes of savage and traumatizing hand-to-hand combat. Mikhail had witnessed some of the carnage himself, having stumbled upon the corpses of a group of Red Army soldiers outside of his village in the winter of 1943 (84).

Despite growing up in the shadow of poverty and war, Gorbachev eventually did well in school—having been encouraged to get an education by his family—and was optimistic and self-assured by the time he went to study law at Moscow State University in 1950. Some were put off, in fact, by how self-assured he was. Many would characterize Gorbachev throughout his life as overly confident (84).

Gorbachev met his future wife, Raisa, at Moscow State. While in college, he worked as an intern in the office of a procurator, whose function was to ensure adherence by local officials to the rules (in reality, many simply oversaw the execution of the party's orders). While serving in that position, he witnessed the young recently educated specialists who came into their posts eager to improve their society only to have their spirits crushed by the arrogance and condescension of the established bureaucrats (84).

After graduation, Gorbachev rejected several career possibilities, from work in the city prosecutor offices to administration of the state collective farms in the countryside. However, throughout the second half of the 1950s and the 1960s, he made his way up the ladder in the Komsomol (Communist

Party youth organization) and the Communist Party itself. His "erudition" and integrity made a positive impression on many along the way, despite the fact that he was sometimes perceived as lording his intellect and education over others (84).

As Gorbachev made his way up the Communist Party hierarchy, there was an increasing perception that reform would eventually be necessary, as many problems plagued the country, including corruption, incompetent officials, and increasing alcoholism (78).

One of the things Gorbachev did after he became leader of the Soviet Union was to use his training as a lawyer to strengthen the existing "constitutional procedures" to facilitate the country's evolution from an oligarchy to a nascent republic with judicial checks on the executive leadership, including on Gorbachev himself (38).

Gorbachev also systematically loosened the Communist Party's grip, intensifying a division in which conservative and social democratic wings emerged. However, he declined to officially split the organization into two parties that could compete in the democratic elections he pushed for, fearing a backlash from the security services, among other concerns.

Some believe this separation could have potentially saved Gorbachev's political vision and his career, as each of the new parties could have appealed to the respective poles developing within the larger society. Moreover, if negotiated effectively, each could have walked away with a sufficient segment of the party membership and political resources. Gorbachev would have then emerged from the "divorce" as the leader of the new social democratic party (38).

The Communist Party as it had existed for decades had roughly three levels of increasing authority. The lower level consisted of the rank-and-file who were motivated primarily by the career advances that membership offered. The next level up was the nomenklatura, or elite bureaucrats, who were appointed to their positions by a small group at the top level, known as the "apparat" (38).

By 1990, the top echelons of the party hierarchy had been effectively defanged while the powers of the Central Committee and Politburo had been transferred to a Soviet parliament and presidency. The nomenklatura remained, but a wide range of reactions to Gorbachev's reforms existed within its ranks. Many in the lower level had fled the party as advantages of membership dwindled (38).

In the economic realm, Gorbachev had introduced laws allowing state property to be privatized as well as establishing commercial banks and stock exchanges. At the close of the 1980s, around 200,000 co-ops had emerged in the Soviet Union, employing five million people and constituting 5–6 percent of GDP.

Not everyone was happy with Gorbachev's changes, however. Some liberal reformers had become invigorated to demand bigger changes more quickly, believing that Gorbachev was ultimately being too slow and too wishy-washy. Meanwhile, conservatives thought Gorbachev's reforms were leading to instability rather than a coherent transition toward anything viable on the horizon, in addition to their desire to protect the benefits they received from the established order.

But the vast majority of the population of the multiethnic Soviet Union, comprised of fifteen different republics spanning thirteen time zones, still believed in a unified fate for the country, as reflected in a referendum in March 1991 in which 76 percent of Soviet citizens voted to keep the country together. This was despite the very vocal desire of the Baltic states (Latvia, Lithuania, Estonia) and Georgia for independence, which Gorbachev ultimately did not suppress (38).

Gorbachev began negotiating for a new union comprised of Russia, Ukraine, Belorussia, Azerbaijan, Kazakhstan, Tajikistan, Turkmenistan, Kyrgyzstan, and Uzbekistan. The negotiations, which were taking place at Novo-Ogaryovo, would have provided for a national economy and military as well as a nationally elected president and parliament.

The agreement had been initialed by the leaders of all nine republics and was in the process of being finalized that August when Communist hard-liners attempted a coup (38). The coup failed in the short run but emboldened the ambitious leader of the Russian republic, Boris Yeltsin, with whom Gorbachev had had a years-long feud.

Yeltsin had started out as a local party chief and was the official who'd carried out the order to destroy Ipatiev House, the site of the murder of Nicholas II and his family, in 1977. Yeltsin was the same age as Gorbachev and was also from a peasant background with family members who'd suffered under the collectivization policies of the 1930s. Beyond that, they were as different as night and day (20).

In contrast to Gorbachev's intellectual and calculating nature, Yeltsin was a colorful and impulsive character. He was also ultimately driven by very different motives than Gorbachev in his political career. Though Gorbachev was sincere in his desire to reform the Soviet Union for the better (whether his campaign was ultimately good or bad is still very much debated among Russians), Yeltsin was adept at expressing populist rhetoric while desiring an accumulation of power.

As Russian studies professor emeritus Stephen F. Cohen observed, Gorbachev's tendency to cede power in his quest for democratic reform enabled Yeltsin's arrogation of power. Hence, the two foremost Russian personalities of the era would engage in a tragic dance that ended with the dissolution of the world's other superpower (38).

During a 1987 meeting, Yeltsin, then Moscow party chief, criticized Gorbachev's perestroika program as being too slow and ineffectual. He also accused Gorbachev of encouraging an incipient personality cult. Yeltsin was roundly condemned for his remarks and was removed from his position.

However, as word spread of his public confrontation with Gorbachev, his popularity rose. Eventually, he was elected to the Soviet Congress of People's Deputies, a new legislative body intended to decentralize the Communist Party and allow more local and popular control.

In 1990, he ran and won a seat in the Russian Republic's new parliament on a populist program that included popular election of the national president and the right for republics to secede. He eventually was elected as chairman, despite Gorbachev's attempts to convince the other members against it. In July, however, Yeltsin resigned the post in dramatic fashion, stating that he'd rather serve the people than the party (20).

Gorbachev viewed Yeltsin's nationalism and volatility as dangerous and his actions as grandstanding that would lead to a destabilizing split within the party. But in the face of an unimpressive economy and the inevitable disappointment that had set in after the high expectations Gorbachev had raised, Yeltsin was able to exploit the situation to his advantage. In June 1991, Yeltsin handily won popular election as the president of the Russian Republic (20).

People who knew Yeltsin said that he envisioned himself as a hero destined to rule. He also reportedly nursed a pathological hatred of Gorbachev. These factors likely motivated his Machiavellian flip-flopping on many issues over the course of his rise to the top. It also probably explains his conspiring with the leaders of Ukraine and Belorussia in December 1991 to dissolve the Soviet Union, rendering Gorbachev a president without a country, and forever changing the course of history (38).

Chapter 5: The End of the Cold War

By the time Mikhail Gorbachev took over leadership of the Soviet Union in 1985, the Cold War was in the midst of a deep freeze due to a period of poor diplomacy and major distrust between the superpowers. The economic effects of the Cold War and the arms race it necessitated was having negative consequences for both economies, but even more so for the Soviet Union, which was falling behind on economic growth and saw its technological development and modernization hobbled because of the heavy investment in militarization.

The Soviet Union was also in the midst of a guerilla war in Afghanistan, which added to the economic burden and reduced morale. Gorbachev recognized that negotiating an end to the Afghanistan war and the Cold War would enable him to implement reforms by transferring money invested in the arms race and militarization into civilian development as well as freeing the nation from the distraction of conflict. (38) (85)

However, as outlined in the previous chapter, the eventual dismantling of the Soviet Union was not only due to militarization. In terms of the Reagan administration's increased defense budgets, particularly in high-tech sectors, it would have been difficult for the Soviets to respond right away due to their 11th Five-Year Plan (1980–1985) that was already in place and would have required a lengthy undertaking to change. Alternatively, the 12th Five-Year Plan, beginning in 1986, did not reflect any of the changes one would expect in response to these U.S. defense policies. It does not appear that the USSR significantly changed economic policy in relation to military spending during this period. In fact, changes in defense spending were not seen until 1988, and then it was in the form of reductions (86) (87).

Another element that was important to the continued viability of the Soviet economic system was energy. As energy economics expert Douglas B. Reynolds explains, the Soviet economy up to that time had competed reasonably well with the West, despite its technological lag, lower productivity, and the absence of officially sanctioned markets. This is because it was largely cheap fossil fuel energy that had accounted for much of the world's postwar growth. Both the United States and the USSR had significant fossil fuel resources until each reached a peak in 1970 and 1988, respectively (86).

By 1977, the CIA had deduced that the Soviet Union was approaching a peak in their oil production capacity and predicted that the peak would occur by the early 1980s, leading to shortfalls for domestic needs as well as an inability to fulfill supply obligations to its Eastern European satellites and to maintain sales of oil and gas to the West, which provided 40 percent of the Soviet Union's hard currency earnings (88) (89).

CIA director William Casey, whom colleagues said viewed the Cold War rivalry with the Soviet Union as a continuation of the good versus evil fight against totalitarianism represented by Hitler's Germany, had presented Reagan in early 1981 with intelligence that reportedly detailed the economic vulnerabilities of the Soviet Union. The intelligence focused particularly on the vulnerabilities relating to oil and gas.

A program was formulated to use intensified covert operations and economic warfare to undermine the Soviet Union. The program included the following parts: 1) increased support for the Solidarity movement in Poland, 2) increased financial and military support to the Afghan mujahideen, 3) increased psychological operations, 4) blocking of Soviet access to advanced technology, and 5) reduction in Soviet hard currency earnings by driving down the price of oil in collusion with Saudi Arabia while limiting Soviet oil and natural gas exports to Western Europe.

The program was officially given the green light via the signing of several National Security Decision Directives (NSDD) by President Reagan throughout 1982.

However, Casey had already begun having meetings in 1981 with officials from Saudi Arabia, which accounted for 40 percent of OPEC's oil production at the time. A deal was gradually worked out with the Saudi royal family, who were strict anti-communists and feared growing Soviet influence in the region, whereby the United States would provide defense guarantees to the regime, including the sale of military weapons, in exchange for lower oil prices that would not only weaken the Soviet Union but would have the ancillary benefit of aiding the American economy. Defense Secretary Caspar Weinberger also played a significant role in bringing the deal to fruition (89).

Indeed, a sharp reduction in oil prices followed, from $66 per barrel in 1980 to $20 per barrel by 1986. It should be noted that, according to a 1983 Treasury Department study, $20 per barrel was viewed as the "optimum" oil price for the American economy. The drop in oil prices was due to a Saudi-induced oil glut. This, combined with diplomatic pressure exerted on Western European nations, such as France, to curb imports of Soviet oil and natural gas, created a budgetary crisis in the Soviet Union (90) (89).

As Reynolds (86) reiterates, American and Saudi policies did not cause the collapse of the Soviet Union but represented a conscious decision to exacerbate an already existing problem of energy depletion within a relatively closed and rigid system. This contributed to the economic and political downward spiral of the Soviet Union by ensuring that it could not procure better technology to alleviate the crisis, consequently creating hard currency and budgetary problems.

By 1987, pursuit of these policies had died off due to political pressures and divisions within the Reagan administration. Nonetheless, the administration was able to participate in the negotiation process with Gorbachev from a position of considerable strength (89).

Reagan and Gorbachev Rise to the Occasion

Although the Reagan administration presided over some unfortunate policies, Jack Matlock—who was Soviet affairs expert on Reagan's National Security Council and later ambassador to the Soviet Union—makes a convincing case that Reagan was sincere in his desire to significantly reduce nuclear weapons and to ultimately end the Cold War. However, due to the aforementioned policies during his first term, he understandably hit a brick wall with Soviet leaders Brezhnev, Andropov, and Chernenko (85).

Suzanne Massie, an author and professor who specializes in Russian cultural history and served as an advisor to Reagan during his second term, confirms Reagan's sincerity despite the nature of the implemented policies. Her path to advisor status began in the autumn of 1983 when a high-ranking Soviet official warned her during a visit, "You don't know how close war is." Alarmed, she became determined to get President Reagan's ear. She first had to go through National Security Advisor Robert MacFarlane, who was able to get the White House to agree to send Massie on a "back channel" mission in January 1984 to explore the Soviet leadership's willingness to negotiate on several key issues, utilizing her established rapport with some officials there (91) (92).

Reagan had already been briefed on information that had come through a Soviet spy working for MI6 that NATO's Able Archer exercise in early November—which "simulated an escalating conflict culminating in a nuclear attack on the Soviet Union"—was being interpreted by the Soviet leadership as preparation for an actual preemptive attack on the Soviet Union. This prompted Reagan to back off his pressure campaign and pursue diplomacy (93).

Massie's diplomatic mission was successful, and she became a regular at the White House from 1984 to 1988. During that time, she observed—and helped to facilitate—Reagan's evolution on how he viewed the Soviet Union and the Russian people. By educating the president on the cultural history of Russia and the nuances of Soviet life, she helped Reagan to gain enough wisdom by the time Gorbachev came to office to treat the new Soviet leader with respect, to keep an open mind while listening to a variety of views on the Soviet issue, and—despite his general loathing of communism and the Soviet system—to recognize Russia's contributions to the world and the fact that the Soviet Union had its own legitimate national interests.

By the time of his 1986 summit with Gorbachev in Iceland, Reagan confessed to Massie that his deepest wish for humanity was "to get rid of those damn nuclear weapons" (91) (92).

Nevertheless, Reagan and Gorbachev's initial meetings did not reflect a terribly auspicious beginning to bridging the chasm between the two nations. But a proposal by Gorbachev calling for complete nuclear disarmament by 1999 got Reagan's attention. Though there was suspicion that this proposal was more of a propaganda ploy on Gorbachev's part, it provided an opening between the two leaders. The subsequent Chernobyl catastrophe reinforced the danger of nuclear technology to the Soviet leader and represented another expensive disaster for which limited funds would have to be invested. This provided even more incentive toward a negotiated settlement.

According to Matlock, Reagan was very careful during negotiations with Gorbachev to allow him to come to the conclusion that many of the proposed changes were in the Soviet Union's interest due to the economic damage resulting from the military budget necessitated by the Cold War. If Gorbachev would not have been able to negotiate the Cold War's end and the need for allocation of massive resources toward the military, he would not have been able to implement the reforms needed for glasnost and perestroika (85).

Reagan also was careful never to frame the situation as a victory or defeat. Although George H. W. Bush apparently believed in private that Russia had been defeated, he followed Reagan's approach publicly until his reelection campaign when he declared to the American electorate: "We won the Cold War" (94).

The Peace Dividend That Wasn't

As the end of the Cold War beckoned in the late 1980s and, along with it, the potential for redirection of resources to improve the living standards of communities across America, Seymour Melman—an expert on the military industrial complex (MIC)—noted that 50 percent of the discretionary federal budget at that time went to the Pentagon (95). We are spending even more than that today: $989 billion out of a total discretionary budget of $1.4 trillion (FY 2020) is spent on the national security state, including the Pentagon budget, supplemental allocations for our Middle East wars, and supporting institutions of the government (96) (97). Meanwhile, the percentage of the discretionary budget allotted to "international affairs" (i.e. diplomacy, among other things) is in the single digits (96), which speaks volumes about our leaders' priorities and approach to international relations.

In comparison, Russia's recent defense allotments represent around 20 percent of its overall budget (98) with a decrease in 2018 and further decreases projected over the next few years (99). For further perspective, it should be kept in mind that Russia—as discussed earlier in this book—has a history of insecurity on its borders, including WWII, from which the memory of the loss of over 27 million of its people—17–19 million of them civilians—and the destruction of a significant portion of the country is still strong in the Russian consciousness. Meanwhile, the United States has not had a war on its soil for 150 years and is afforded extra protection by way of its geography.

What all that needless investment into militarism ultimately translates into is investment not made into the infrastructure for American citizens and their day-to-day needs. To illustrate this point, Melman also discusses the state of American domestic infrastructure by 1990 and how it had suffered from the diversion of resources into the MIC:

> The American ruling class, by 1990, has become a state/corporate managerial entity. Together they control the military-industrial complex. . . . The war economy, in the service of extending the decision power and wealth of America's state and corporate managers, has been consuming the US civilian infrastructure. Roads, bridges, the water supply, waste disposal systems, housing, medical care facilities, schools are in disrepair from coast to coast. (95)

Instead of seizing the opportunity provided by the end of the Cold War and investing in the improvement of Americans' lives, we have continued to feed the same amounts or more into the voracious military economy with our domestic infrastructure in worse shape than ever. The American Society of Civil Engineers Infrastructure Report Card for the United States in 2017 was a D+ (100); meanwhile, the federal government will be investing $1 trillion in modernizing our nuclear weapons arsenal over the next 30 years, using the confrontation with Russia over Ukraine as partial justification (101).

Melman observed the early stages of another negative trend with respect to the deindustrialization of the American economy, whereby the nation gradually loses the ability to produce essential goods and to repair the basic infrastructure needed to create and repair those essential goods. For example, in his 1990 and 2001 works, Melman describes how the United States was becoming dependent upon foreign production of basic machinery and tools that were no longer made in the country (95) (102). This deindustrialization leads to loss of living-wage jobs and loss of national independence and self-sufficiency in important areas of the economy. That trend has accelerated in the two to three decades since, and all of the social consequences one would likely expect are visible to all Americans, with the possible exception of the most wealthy and insulated.

One of the more pernicious consequences of this deindustrialization is that the lack of living-wage jobs that used to be available to those with little or no postsecondary education drives more youth into the professional military as they seek a stable income and educational opportunities, reinforcing the militarist feedback loop.

One of the strangest blind spots that American elites seem to have is what their own system has in common with some of the failed aspects of the Soviet Union, with its heavy burden of militarism and empire on its people and economy. They somehow seem to think they will avoid the same fate.

Chapter 6: Washington's Post–Cold War Ideology

The end of the Cold War provided an opening for a potential reorganization of the international order in a more peaceful and cooperative direction. This would have included a very different relationship with Russia as well. But there were several foreign policy influences in Washington that prevented this. There was, of course, the profit motive of the defense industry, which is covered in more detail in Chapters 5 and 7. Just as important, however, were the ideological influences. Three of the most consequential are discussed below.

Zbigniew Brzezinski's **Grand Chessboard**

Before getting into a deconstruction of *The Grand Chessboard*, it's important to first take a step back and provide some perspective on who the late Zbigniew Brzezinski was and why his worldview is particularly relevant to understand in terms of the 2013–2014 Ukraine crisis and the West's role in it. Brzezinski's view seemed to be partly derived from a deep-rooted and irrational antipathy toward Russia—irrational in the sense that it persisted despite what Russia actually was or did in objective reality.

Brzezinski was born in Warsaw, Poland, in 1928, but his paternal family originated from Galicia, which was once considered eastern Poland but is now part of western Ukraine. His father was a Polish diplomat who served in Germany from 1931 to 1935 and then served in the Soviet Union from 1936 to 1938 in the midst of Stalin's Great Terror. He was stationed in Canada when both Germany and the Soviet Union invaded Poland in 1939. With

Poland's subsequent placement in the Soviet sphere of influence at the conclusion of WWII, the Brzezinski family remained in Canada.

Brzezinski earned a master's degree from McGill University in Mon-
treal with a focus on the Soviet Union, followed by a PhD at Harvard with a
focus on the Russian Revolution and the leadership of Lenin and Stalin. He
became an academic at Harvard and then Columbia University, where he
taught and mentored Madeleine Albright. He served as an advisor to the
Kennedy presidential campaign and then was a member of the State Department's Council of Policy Planning from 1966–1968. In 1973, he helped establish the Trilateral Commission with David Rockefeller. Based on ideas
Brzezinski spelled out in an article he published in *Foreign Affairs* in 1970,
the Trilateral Commission was to be the organizational foundation of a club
of developed nations that included Japan, the United States, and countries
of Europe to balance world power away from the Soviet Union and China.
The club held annual meetings that included the elites of Europe, Japan, and
the United States, along with notables in world trade, international banking,
and the establishment media (103).

Throughout the Cold War, Brzezinski supported a policy of engagement with Eastern Europe, including dissidents, believing that divisions
within Eastern Europe would destabilize the Soviet Union and hasten its
breakup along national lines. He gave little to no support for any rapprochement with the Soviet Union and opposed Charles De Gaulle's vision of a
Eurasian project of "Europe from the Atlantic to the Urals."

Brzezinski eventually served as national security advisor in the Carter
administration. Touted as the Democratic Party's counterpoint to Henry
Kissinger (and implicitly Kissinger's détente approach toward the USSR), his
aggressive anti-Russian views often clashed with those of Carter's secretary
of state, Cyrus Vance, who was in the realist camp and opposed Brzezinski's
desire to strengthen ties to China while keeping the Soviet Union at a distance. He and others in the administration argued that such "triangulation"
could lead to dangerous and unnecessary perceptions of aggression toward
the Soviet Union (103). Due to Brzezinski's machinations behind Vance's
back to convince Carter to undertake the disastrous plan to rescue American

hostages in Iran instead of continuing to use diplomatic channels, Vance—who had come to oppose using military intervention to solve international problems—resigned. Upon leaving office, he characterized Brzezinski's aggression and Machiavellian tactics as "evil" (104).

During his tenure, Brzezinski was also the architect of the plan to goad the Soviet Union into its own "Vietnam" quagmire by arming and supporting Islamic mujahideen against the Soviet-backed government in Afghanistan. The plan, with the assistance of the Pakistan intelligence service, was put into place toward the end of Carter's presidency. In 1979, the Soviet Union responded as Brzezinski had hoped, embarking on a decade-long war in the nation that is not called the "graveyard of empires" for nothing.

When the French magazine *Le Nouvel Observateur* interviewed Brzezinski in 1998, he admitted that while he was national security advisor, he played a major role in setting the Afghanistan trap for the Soviet Union to get bogged down in a war. He also reiterated that he had no regrets about the policy, underscoring the fact that he did indeed see the nations and peoples of the world as pieces on a strategic game board, having no regard for the resulting deaths of a million Afghans and thousands of Soviets, the demolition of a country that at the time had minimal religious fanaticism and better conditions for women, or the blowback toward his own adopted country (105) (106). A pertinent excerpt of the exchange follows:

> *Le Nouvel Observateur*: Former CIA director, Robert Gates, says in his memoirs: the American secret services assisted Afghan mujahedeen six months before the Soviet invasion. By that time, you were President Carter's advisor and you played a key role on this. Do you confirm it?
>
> *Brzezinski*: Yes. According to the official version of the story, the CIA began to assist mujahedeen in the year 1980, that is, after the invasion of the Soviet army against Afghanistan on December 24, 1979. But the truth that remained secret until today is quite different: it was on July 3, 1979 that President Carter signed his first order on

the secret assistance to Kabul's pro-Soviet regime opponents. That day I wrote a memorandum to the President
in which I told him that that assistance would cause the
Soviet intervention (…) we did not force the Russian
intervention, we just, conscientiously, increased the intervention possibilities.

NO: When the Soviets justified their intervention by
affirming they were fighting against a secret American
interference nobody believed them, though they were
telling the truth. Don't you regret it?

B: Regret what? That secret operation was an excellent
idea. Its objective was to lead the Russians to the Afghan
trap, and you want me to regret it? The very same day the
Soviets crossed the Afghan border I wrote the following
to President Carter: "This is our chance to give Russia its
Viet Nam."

NO: Aren't you sorry either for favoring Islamic funda-
mentalism and providing weapons and consultancies to
future terrorists?

B: What is the most important thing when you look at
world history, the Taliban or the fall of the Soviet Empire?
Some excited Islamists or the liberation of Central Europe
and the end of the Cold War? (103)

Brzezinski also became active behind the scenes to use Islamic radicals
in Chechnya to destabilize Russia via the American Committee for Peace in
Chechnya (ACPC). ACPC was founded by Freedom House—a conservative
nonprofit that has historically been used as a front for CIA operations (107).
ACPC was an organization with a plethora of neoconservatives on its board
and in its membership (108). It has received up to 80 percent of its funding
from the notorious National Endowment for Democracy (NED), an organization funded by the U.S. Congress. NED was established in the early 1980s

in response to congressional hearings by the Church Committee that exposed the CIA's covert efforts to destabilize and overthrow foreign governments that were anathema to the U.S. political elite. Rather than cease these unpopular—and often violent and illegal—covert operations, they were simply transferred to another organization that obscured these nefarious activities under the guise of building civil society and democracy. Government officials who helped draft the legislation creating NED have admitted that NED now does much of what the CIA used to do in this arena (109) (110).

French journalist Arthur Lepic states in his 2004 article on Brzezinski's policies toward the Soviet Union and Russia, "The Outrageous Strategy to Destroy Russia," that Brzezinski was involved in a plan to pave the way for a pipeline deal that would undermine Russia's potential to gain from fossil fuel resources in the Caspian region:

> During the 90s he was the special envoy of the American president to promote the most important oil infrastructure project of the world: the Baku-Tbilisi-Ceyhan pipeline which was his best opportunity to prevent the resurgence of Russia. He has also been, since 1999, the president of the American Committee for Peace in Chechnya, whose headquarters are located at the Freedom House facility. This position allows him to intervene in peace negotiations between the Russian government and independence fighters led by Mashkadov. However, the truth behind these good will "democratic" activities [was] to assist independence followers to maintain a war in the area, like the Afghan one, to weaken Russia and to keep it away from the gains of the Caspian Sea. (103)

The Brzezinski calling card of goading Russia into a war or keeping it bogged down in one in order to weaken it has to be kept in mind in analyzing the Ukraine crisis, which erupted in late 2013.

With a negotiated end to the Cold War, a dissolved USSR, a Russian Federation that was firmly on the road toward an evolving version of capitalism, expanded economic ties with the EU, and cordial relations with Latin America and a lot of the developing world, Russia and most everyone else had moved on from the idea of Russia as "big bad bogeyman." But not an assortment of Russophobes in Washington, like Brzezinski, and those they influenced.

Brzezinski influenced both John Kerry and Barak Obama, having served as a foreign policy advisor, along with his son, Mark Brzezinski, to the 2004 Kerry presidential campaign and then to the 2008 Obama campaign. Although it is difficult to determine how often Brzezinski advised Obama, it is interesting to observe how hawks among both major political parties took their cue from Brzezinski when he compared Putin to Hitler in a March 3, 2014, op-ed for *The Washington Post* (111). Within two days, Hillary Clinton, John McCain, and Marco Rubio all repeated this absurd claim. It can, therefore, be deduced that Brzezinski still wielded considerable influence among the Washington elite at the time. As we will see later, U.S. actions in Ukraine since autumn 2013—the culmination of years of U.S. covert operations in that country (112)—are reminiscent of Brzezinski's previous policies and actions.

Brzezinski continued to offer advice to the president publicly on the crisis via another op-ed, this one published by *Politico* on May 2, 2014, in which he essentially restated his view that America is exceptional and has the right and duty to extract Ukraine away from the Russian sphere of influence into the U.S.-controlled Western sphere based on the premise outlined in his book: namely, that whoever rules Eurasia rules the world. This premise is based upon two assumptions: 1) that one country has the right to rule the world, and 2) that the United States is noble, or at least benign, and must be the one to do that ruling lest some other empire crop up and do it.

Or, as Terry Malloy said in *On the Waterfront*, "do it to him before he does it to you" (113).

It is clear from the opening pages of *The Grand Chessboard* that Brzezinski is obsessed with imperialism and cannot conceive of a world that is not organized under empire—whether it is the competing regional empires of old or the rise of one global empire as reflected by the United States after the

Soviet Union's exit from the world stage. He even repeats the common historical fallacy that "hegemony is as old as mankind." If he had even a cursory familiarity with anthropology or prerecorded history, he would know that throughout the vast majority of humanity's experience, mankind lived in small, relatively egalitarian units of hunter-gatherers. Empire and its attendant effects, such as hegemony, hierarchical social structure, and war, only emerged around 10–13,000 years ago, roughly coinciding with the widespread adoption of agricultural settlement. (114)

Brzezinski's Eurasian thesis appears to have been inspired by Nicholas Spykman's Eurasian Rimland concept, which was, in turn, built upon Halford Mackinder's Heartland Theory, first formulated in 1904. Spykman's Rimland emphasized the geostrategic importance of the densely populated coastal perimeter surrounding the Heartland of Eurasia. Spykman justified focus on the Rimland instead of the Heartland by arguing that the Rimland contained the majority of the world's people, a large swath of its resources, and an industrial base. Additionally, it served as an entryway to the seas, situated as a buffer zone between the Heartland (source of land power) and sea power (115). These two theories, like Brzezinski's Grand Chessboard, are widely acknowledged to represent an imperialistic offensive posture dressed up as a defense strategy (116).

In *The Grand Chessboard*, Brzezinski reiterates the factors cited by Spykman and Mackinder:

> About 75 percent of the world's people live in Eurasia, and most of the world's physical wealth is there as well, both in its enterprises and underneath its soil. Eurasia accounts for about 60 percent of the world's GNP and about three-fourths of the world's known energy resources (117).

He speaks throughout the book with a sense of entitlement on behalf of the United States that the American Empire should never cede control of these resources to those living near them who may strangely assume a claim to benefit from them.

He emphasizes the following two steps to achieve his imperialist objective of preserving U.S. world domination:

1.   Identify states in Eurasia that have the power to shift the international distribution of power or to be catalysts for doing so; and,

2.   Formulate specific U.S. policies to offset, co-opt and/or control the above so as to preserve and promote vital U.S. interests.

Brzezinski goes on to explain the role of Ukraine as a "pivot" state—in other words, a state that, if it remains under Russia's sphere of influence, allows Russia to project power into the rest of Eurasia due to its seaport, its major resources, and its role as a geographic defensive buffer—an important psychological factor for a nation that has been invaded from the West numerous times in its history via the Ukrainian corridor.

As explained in more detail in Chapter 9, what occurred in Kiev in early 2014 was a Western-backed coup that toppled a democratically elected leader in Ukraine in order to install a government that would implement an EU Association Agreement—a stepping stone to NATO membership. This led to Russia's countermove of reabsorbing Crimea to prevent its naval port from potentially being diverted into NATO's control, a move that would have compromised Russia's security and status as an independent nation.

Provocations to get Russia to invade Ukraine—where it would no doubt face a major insurgency in the western part of the country, supported by the United States and NATO—are a throwback to Brzezinski's plan to lure the Soviet Union into a quagmire in 1979, which contributed to that country's disintegration. It is an open secret that the neoconservatives and other Russophobes would consider the destabilization of Russia and the subsequent regime change ousting Putin to be the ultimate prize.

Their dubious assumption is not only that this would be possible to do in the first place without risk of a nuclear war, but that any successor to Putin would be weak and compliant—another Yeltsin who will allow them unfettered access to Russia's prodigious natural resources for exploitation—rather than a truly anti-Western hard-liner that would be far less accommodating than Putin.

Interestingly, Brzezinski's belief that whoever controls Eurasia controls the world does not necessarily rest on solid ground. As Matlock points out, history really only shows that whoever controls Eurasia controls Eurasia (85). Not that this wouldn't represent tremendous power and influence, especially economic, but there are other factors to consider in terms of world hegemony, such as control of the world's seas, which Russia is not likely to attain anytime soon even with firm control of Ukraine and a cemented alliance with China.

With this mindset and background, Brzezinski went on numerous media outlets, gave speeches, and testified before Congress with his talking points about the Ukraine crisis, asserting who was responsible and how it started, with Russia as the instigator and Putin as the archvillain described variously as Hitler, Stalin, a thug, and a Mafia gangster.

On June 16, 2014, while participating on a panel at the Wilson Center, Brzezinski continued flogging his theme of Russian imperialism, citing an obscure report by a Russian think tank and pushing the narrative that Russia violated Ukraine's sovereignty and Western actions in Ukraine are reactive and benign:

> What we are seeing in Ukraine, in my judgment, is not a pique but a symptom of a more basic problem; namely, the gradual but steady emergence in Russia over the last 6 or 7 years of a quasi-mythical chauvinism. . . . It follows from what I'm saying that the Ukrainian problem is a challenge that the West must address on three levels. We have to effectively deter the temptation facing the Russian leadership regarding the use of force.
>
> We have to, secondly, obtain the termination of Russia's deliberate efforts at the destabilization of parts of Ukraine. It's very hard to judge how ambitious these goals are, but it is not an accident that in that one single portion of Ukraine in which the Russians actually predominate, the

use of force has been sophisticated. The participants in the effort have been well armed, even with tanks, and certainly with effective anti-aircraft weaponry. All of that is something that even disagreeable, disaffected citizens of a country to which they feel they do not belong would not be storing somewhere in their attic or their basement. These are weapons provided, in effect, for the purpose of shaping formations capable of sustaining serious military engagements. It is a form of interstate aggression.

You can't call it anything else. How would we feel if all of a sudden, let's say, the drug-oriented gangs in the United States were armed from abroad, from our southern neighbor, by equipment which would promote violence on that scale on a continuing basis? So this is a serious challenge. So that is the second objective.

And the third objective is to promote and then discuss with the Russians a formula for an eventual compromise, assuming that in the first instance the use of force openly and on a large scale is deterred and the effort to destabilize is abandoned (118).

Not once does Brzezinski acknowledge the role the West played in the events that led to the ouster of a democratically elected president four months before, or the role played by neo-Nazi groups like Svoboda and Right Sector in the violence that took control of the Maidan protests and facilitated the coup. What's never mentioned is how John McCain and other American politicians egged on the protestors on Maidan Square, regardless of their dubious affiliations. The intercepted phone call between U.S. assistant secretary for European and Eurasian Affairs Victoria Nuland and American Ambassador to Ukraine Geoffrey Pyatt in which they discuss the United States's favored candidate to replace Yanukovych—the candidate that did subsequently replace him—is never acknowledged (see Appendix 2) (119). Nor is the intercepted conversation between Estonian Foreign Minister

Urmas Paet and then-EU High Representative Catherine Ashton, wherein it is admitted that, according to eyewitness and forensic medical evidence, it appears that individuals from the Maidan protestor–controlled buildings were responsible for fatally shooting protestors and police officers, not Yanukovych's forces (see Appendix 3) (120). This is all despite the fact that the aforementioned information was readily available to anyone with an internet connection at the time of Brzezinski's speech.

Moreover, whatever military assistance being provided by Russia to the rebels in Eastern Ukraine at that time—which would be in reaction to Western-fomented instability on their border, not due to some unprovoked imperialistic aggression—was a matter of conjecture and had not been proven with any concrete and verified evidence. Much of the military hardware that Brzezinski refers to was available either from Ukrainian military depots that the rebels had access to or gained control of, Ukrainian soldiers who switched sides in the early stages of the conflict, or in later stages, Ukrainian soldiers that deserted and left behind their hardware (121) (122).

Furthermore, as University of Rhode Island Professor of Politics Nicolai Petro, who had just returned from a year spent in Ukraine, pointed out in a September 3, 2014, article in *The National Interest*, there were several credible reports that the numerous pronouncements in the summer of 2014 of Russian troops and heavy weapons crossing into Ukraine were false:

> This version of official Russian complicity has been challenged by some Western reporters on the scene, most notably, Mark Franchetti who wrote a remarkable piece for the *London Sunday Times* after spending several weeks embedded with rebel forces. His assessment is backed by the UN High Commissioner for Human Rights and the OSCE observer mission that has been deployed to the border region since the end of July. Both say they have seen no evidence of weapons or military personnel crossing from Russia into Ukraine during this time, even as U.S. and NATO officials say the exact opposite. Moreover, between April and July of 2014, as Russian Ministry of

Defense likes to point out, eighteen international inspection teams visited the border region and found "no evidence of undeclared military activity" (123).

Brzezinski's false framing of events, which had also been consistently echoed by the White House and the State Department, also suggested that the rebellion in the southeastern parts of Ukraine, which considers itself to be ethnically, culturally, and linguistically Russian, had no indigenous support but was instead contrived through Russian interference. However, Petro cited the results of sociological surveys taken in Ukraine in April, May, and June 2014 that contradict this:

> Three-quarters of the populations in Ukraine's eastern cities regard the Euromaidan protests as illegal. Specifically, two-thirds of Donbas residents consider the Maidan to have been "an armed overthrow of the government, organized by the opposition, with the assistance of the West." A similar percentage believes that the Right Sector is "a prominent military formation that is politically influential and poses a threat to the citizens and national unity." That may explain why most people in the eastern and southern regions of Ukraine (62 percent) blame the loss of Crimea on Kiev, rather than on Crimean separatists (24 percent), or on Russia (19 percent).

> Majorities in Donbas (60 percent in Donetsk and 52 percent in Luhansk) disagree with the view that Russia is organizing the rebels and guiding their actions. Moreover, if a referendum were held today (April 2014), only 25 percent would want to join EU, compared to 47 percent wanting to join the Eurasian Customs Union (123).

Chapter 9 lays out more detailed evidence about the Maidan coup and the subsequent rebellion in the Donbas, which further supports the above points.

During testimony before the Senate Foreign Relations Committee on July 7, 2014, Brzezinski continued with his misrepresentation of the events in Ukraine:

> [Russia must] accommodate with Ukraine by terminating the assault on Ukrainian sovereignty and economic well-being. . . . At the same time, it would be made clear that Russia no longer expects Ukraine to become part of the "Eurasian Union," a designation which is a transparent cover for the recreation of something approximating the former Soviet Union or the Tsarist Empire. . . . Putin's second choice is to continue the effort to destabilize Ukraine by sponsoring thinly veiled military intervention designed to disrupt normal life in portions of Ukraine. . . . In brief, the obvious choice for everyone concerned is to find a formula for international accommodation, and that has to involve the abandonment of the use of force against Ukraine by Russia (124).

In addition to repeating the false narrative already begun in previous articles and interviews, Brzezinski now added in the implicit accusation of Russia attempting to force Ukraine to become a member of the Eurasian Union, which is mischaracterized as some nefarious imperial project. In reality, the Eurasian Economic Union (aka the Eurasian Union or Customs Union) is a voluntary common market, similar to the EU, currently comprised of Russia, Belarus, Kazakhstan, Armenia, and Kyrgyzstan, that has free trade agreements with other Eurasian countries such as Iran, Vietnam, and Singapore. Brzezinski provided no explanation as to why Ukrainians would not have the right to decide for themselves whether to join such an economic union, as he makes explicit they have the right to do in connection with the EU. Nor did Brzezinski ever characterize the EU as some Western European neo-imperialist project.

Brzezinski followed this up with an interview with CNN's Fareed Zakaria in which he stated that "I would say that we're not starting the Cold War. He (Putin) has started it." He once again reiterated the false narrative that the Ukraine crisis came about at Russia's instigation and shrieked about Russian imperial ambitions, "What is the alternative? To let war break out in Europe? To let Russia go on to the Baltic States from Ukraine? To let such acts simply be ignored? Is that the choice? Is that the test of leadership?" (125)

Either Brzezinski was incredibly ill-informed (which is not very plausible) or he was lying on behalf of his own anti-Russia agenda.

Furthermore, his talking points on the Ukraine crisis were almost identical to his talking points to the media about the war between Russia and Georgia in 2008. For example, Brzezinski said the following during an interview with *Huffington Post*'s Nathan Gardels regarding hostilities between those two nations:

> The question the international community now confronts is how to respond to a Russia that engages in the blatant use of force with larger imperial designs in mind: to reintegrate the former Soviet space under the Kremlin's control and to cut western access to the Caspian Sea and Central Asia by gaining control over the Baku-Ceyhan pipeline that runs through Georgia (126).

Brzezinski also made sure to compare Putin to both Hitler and Stalin, comparing the Russian "invasion" of Georgia to Hitler's invasion of the Sudetenland and to Stalin's attack on Finland. Apparently, Brzezinski failed to realize that Dmitry Medvedev was the Russian president and commander-in-chief at that time, and there is no dispute that he gave the military orders while Prime Minister Putin was at the Olympics in Beijing.

So, how did Brzezinski's hysteria-laced analysis of the Russian-Georgian conflict hold up to the facts?

According to the EU's "Independent International Fact-Finding Mission on the Conflict in Georgia," issued in September 2009, it was the Georgian armed forces that initiated the conflict, not Russia (127). Georgia's president at the time, Mikheil Saakashvili, was a Western-backed leader who, based on the observations of several world leaders and diplomats, exhibited behavior that indicated he may have been psychologically unbalanced.

Saakashvili was apparently operating under the delusion that he could militarily take on Russia and that the United States had his back (128) (129).

As for wanting to seize control of the Baku-Ceyhan pipeline, the Russians could have done that easily in the midst of the armed conflict in Georgia but made no attempt to do so.

So, Brzezinski was either woefully misinformed about that conflict or he was lying on behalf of his anti-Russia agenda then, too. It is troubling that in spite of his incompetence and/or mendacity, he was still being given credibility to comment on the Ukrainian conflict by mainstream media outlets and the U.S. Congress, as well as being invited to the White House for a meeting with the president as a foreign policy "expert" in early September 2014.

And with respect to his oft-repeated claim that Putin is an incipient Hitler or Stalin, in the intervening five and a half years between the Georgia conflict and the Ukraine crisis, Russia did not engage in or threaten any military conflicts with its neighbors. As Russia expert Thomas Graham writes:

> Russian territorial ambitions beyond its traditional geopolitical zone have been quite limited historically. In this regard, the Soviet period stands out as an anomaly, born of the unique conditions of the mid to late 20th century: the power vacuum in the center of Europe created by the total collapse of Nazi Germany and the subsequent bitter ideological divide and revolutionary upheaval that produced a global competition between the Soviet Union and the United States. Those conditions no longer prevail, and Russia has reverted to its historical policy of creating a suitable balance of power on the European continent that takes into account the interests of the other great European powers (130).

Brzezinski never missed an opportunity to accuse Putin of being an imperialist and wanting to revive the Soviet Union—an accusation that was dutifully repeated by other demagogues like John McCain, Hillary Clinton, and Marco Rubio. This accusation is largely based on a sentence plucked out of a 2005 speech given by Putin and used as Exhibit A of his imperial ambitions. Let's take a look at what Putin actually said:

> Above all, we should acknowledge that the collapse of the Soviet Union was a major geopolitical disaster of the century. As for the Russian nation, it became a genuine drama. Tens of millions of our co-citizens and compatriots found themselves outside Russian territory. Moreover, the epidemic of disintegration infected Russia itself. Individual savings were depreciated, and old ideals destroyed. Many institutions were disbanded or reformed carelessly. Terrorist intervention and the Khasavyurt capitulation that followed damaged the country's integrity. Oligarchic groups—possessing absolute control over information channels—served exclusively their own corporate interests. Mass poverty began to be seen as the norm. And all this was happening against the backdrop of a dramatic economic downturn, unstable finances, and the paralysis of the social sphere.

> Many thought or seemed to think at the time that our young democracy was not a continuation of Russian statehood, but its ultimate collapse, the prolonged agony of the Soviet system.

> But they were mistaken.

> That was precisely the period when the significant developments took place in Russia. Our society was generating not only the energy of self-preservation, but also the will for a new and free life. In those difficult years, the people of Russia had to both uphold their state sovereignty and make an unerring choice in selecting a new vector of development in the thousand years of their history. They had to accomplish the most difficult task: how to safeguard their own values, not to squander undeniable

achievements, and confirm the viability of Russian democracy. We had to find our own path in order to build a democratic, free and just society and state.

When speaking of justice, I am not of course referring to the notorious "take away and divide by all" formula, but extensive and equal opportunities for everybody to develop.

Success for everyone. A better life for all.

—Annual Address to the Federal Assembly of the Russian Federation, April 25, 2005 (131)

This excerpt of Putin's speech—correctly translated and in context—where he discusses the conditions of post-Soviet Russia in the 1990s (which we will explore in detail in Chapter 8) speaks for itself and shows the willingness of Western politicians and pundits to perpetuate misinformation on behalf of an agenda.

It is clear that Brzezinski's psyche was frozen in another era—when his fellow Poles were under subjugation from the Soviet Union. This kind of anachronistic and narrow thinking, based on the unresolved emotional wounds of one small segment of the American population who are émigrés or descended from émigrés of former Soviet bloc countries, along with a preoccupation with imperialism, is dangerous if it overtakes U.S. foreign policy, which it appears to have done, considering the influence Brzezinski has had in Washington.

The real issue is whether there will be a multipolar world or whether the United States will insist on continuing its role as the lone hegemon, which will necessitate resorting to more desperate and more brutal measures to maintain. Brzezinski came out firmly in favor of the latter.

It should be stressed that Brzezinski's reckless Grand Chessboard gambit had little traction with the American people. According to a Pew poll conducted in April 2014, Americans strongly opposed sending military aid to Ukraine and believed, just as strongly, that what happened in Ukraine has little to do with America's vital interests (132).

The Neoconservatives

> These people are crazy, they're frightening. Believe me, I rubbed up close and personal with them for four years. I can tell you how frightening they are. I sat in the Pentagon and listened to a briefing where Iraq was just the start, then we're going to Syria, then we're going to Iran. You know, these people are nuts. . . . Their long-term plan is American hegemony—now, tomorrow and forever. And when I say hegemony I don't just mean America rules as in Pax Americana. I mean America has its way wherever it goes, whenever it goes and however it wants that way. And this is commercial, financial and economic as much as it is geopolitical.
>
> —Col. Lawrence Wilkerson, former Chief of Staff to Secretary of State Colin Powell (133)

The Philosophy

The godfather of neoconservative philosophy was Leo Strauss. A one-time friend and fellow traveler in philosophical circles with German Nazi philosopher and jurist Carl Schmitt, Strauss developed what would become his ideology in response to a newly dominant post-WWII America that he perceived as crass, materialistic, and devoid of a meaningful sense of community.

According to the well-received 2004 BBC documentary *The Power of Nightmares*, Strauss was an enigmatic figure who never appeared in the media but "devoted his time to creating a loyal band of students." Some of those students went on to hold major positions of power within the George W. Bush (Bush II) administration, though some of them had been influential before then. Paul Wolfowitz, Elliot Abrams, Irving and William Kristol, and Michael Ledeen were all greatly influenced by the teachings of Strauss. Ironically, all were former leftists to varying degrees who had become disillusioned with what they perceived to be the failings of liberalism in the midst of the social tumult of the 1960s and '70s.

The basic idea behind Strauss's teaching was that liberalism and individualism would eventually destroy the fabric of the national community. That community, according to Strauss, seemed only to have a meaningful and coherent identity in relation to an outside "other." This "other," by its very nature, represents a threat that must be fought via a full-scale mobilization of society. Only within this focused and unified fight against an outside "evil" foe can the members of society reinforce their common ties and have a satisfying moral purpose as those on the "good" side of an epic life-and-death struggle.

Underscoring this whole scheme was the need for myths, which Strauss conceded did not need to be based in reality and that the leaders themselves did not have to believe, harkening back to the concept of the "noble lie" in political philosophy. A successful society would be led by those wise enough to know how to pull the levers behind the curtain to keep society unified and stable (134).

These ideas are reflected in Schmitt's political theology as Strauss himself summed them up in a 1932 letter to Schmitt: "Because man is by nature evil, he therefore needs dominion. But dominion can be established, that is, men can be unified only in a unity against - against other men" (135).

It is this need for a mythology that paints America as the force for good against an evil foe that has motivated neoconservatives to opportunistically ally with other elements that, at first glance, may seem unlikely, such as fundamentalist Christians during Bush II's administration and the Responsibility to Protect (R2P) crowd as we will see later.

Having been largely shunned in the academic community, the neoconservatives entered think tanks and public service as a way to spread their influence. The first politicians they successfully latched on to were Donald Rumsfeld and Dick Cheney, who served as the secretary of defense and chief of staff, respectively, under President Gerald Ford. Together they put into place the first attack on realist Henry Kissinger's détente policy with the

Soviet Union by accusing the Soviets of violating the nuclear arms treaties the Nixon administration had negotiated. These allegations were completely baseless, but it didn't stop Rumsfeld from persuading Ford to set up Team B, which would be headed by Paul Wolfowitz, to investigate.

An illustration of the neocons' tendency to be impervious to arguments or evidence that was contrary to their views comes from Dr. Anne Cahn, who worked with the Arms Control and Disarmament Agency during this time. According to Cahn, the neocons would sift through data that the intelligence community had already analyzed and come up with conclusions that did not match reality but instead their own preconceived fantasies:

> I would say that all of it was fantasy. I mean, they looked at radars out in Krasnoyarsk and said, "This is a laser beam weapon," when in fact it was nothing of the sort. They even took a Russian military manual, which the correct translation of is "The Art of Winning." And when they translated it and put it into Team B, they called it "The Art of Conquest." Well, there's a difference between "conquest" and "winning." And if you go through most of Team B's specific allegations about weapons systems, and you just examine them one by one, they were all wrong (134).

But that didn't stop them from creating the Committee on the Present Danger, a lobbying group that sought to publicize the bogus "findings" of Team B. One of the politicians who bought into this group's fairy tales was future president Ronald Reagan.

The neocons gained more influence during the Reagan administration. In fact, many members of the Bush II administration would be recycled from the Reagan era. As Jack Matlock (85) noted in his book *Superpower Illusions*, although many intelligence professionals and diplomats had known for some time that the USSR was experiencing significant internal challenges, they were drowned out by the neocons' Cold War rhetoric of an evil empire that was voracious in its ambitions to take over the world and threaten America. According to *The Power of Nightmares*:

> They would set out to recreate the myth of America as a
> unique nation whose destiny was to battle against an evil
> in the world. And in this project, the source of evil would
> be America's Cold War enemy: the Soviet Union. And by
> doing this, they believed that they would not only give
> new meaning and purpose to people's lives, but they
> would spread the good of democracy around the world
> (134).

Consequently, defense spending was greatly increased with no regard for deficits, and military aid was provided to dictators who said the magic words "I'm fighting evil communists." Appeals to religious mythology were incorporated into public debate to obfuscate the real issues (134).

Reagan himself did not fully embrace neoconservative ideology, but some key people around him were greatly influenced by the neoconservative woo-woo. Reagan's CIA director, William Casey, was one such person. He was convinced by then-Special Advisor to the Secretary of State Michael Ledeen that "terrorist" groups throughout the world, such as the PLO, the Provisional IRA, and Baader-Meinhof in Germany, were part of a terrorist network overseen by the Soviet Union instead of local groups that had emerged to fight various grievances specific to each group. Ledeen was using a book called *The Terror Network* as the basis for this belief. CIA specialists at the time tried to disabuse Casey of this fallacy—namely due to the fact that much of what was in *The Terror Network* was black propaganda that the CIA itself had invented to smear the Soviet Union. Melvin Goodman, who served as Head of Soviet Affairs for the CIA from 1976 to 1987, stated:

> When we looked through the book, we found very clear
> episodes where CIA black propaganda—clandestine
> information that was designed under a covert action plan
> to be planted in European newspapers—were picked up
> and put in this book. A lot of it was made up. It was made
> up out of whole cloth. We told him that, point blank. And
> we even had the operations people to tell Bill Casey this.
> I thought maybe this might have an impact, but we were

all dismissed. Casey had made up his mind. Lies became reality (134).

This was another example of the neoconservative pattern of not letting facts get in their way. Ledeen's depth of thinking, or lack thereof, was revealed by the following response he gave to the episode:

> The CIA denied it. They tried to convince people we were really crazy. I mean, they never believed that the Soviet Union was a driving force in the international terror network. They always wanted to believe that terrorist organizations were just what they said they were: local groups trying to avenge terrible evils done to them, or trying to rectify terrible social conditions, and things like that. And the CIA really did buy into that rhetoric. I don't know what their motive was. I don't know what people's motives are, hardly ever. And I don't much worry about motives (134).

Supposedly, Casey was able to find an academic to produce a document showing that the "terror network" did exist. With this in hand, Casey was finally able to put enough pressure on Reagan to convince him to sign a confidential document to allow funding for covert wars to counter this threat from the Soviet Union (134).

When the Soviet Union's own internal problems came to a head, and Reagan followed his better instincts to engage the new leadership in Moscow to negotiate a peaceful and mutually beneficial path out of the Cold War, the neocons claimed a victory for their aggressive policies based on more dangerous mythology (85).

When the people controlling foreign policy in America believe that one cannot have a substantive or meaningful identity without something or someone to oppose—in other words, when an enemy disappears, as was the case after the end of the Cold War—an existential crisis ensues. As many analysts observed during the height of the Global War on Terror, if one just substituted the word "terrorist" for "communist" in all the lines of the script, the movie remained pretty much the same.

The profit motive of the military-industrial complex (MIC), of course, also plays into this interest of keeping conflicts going throughout the world in order to guarantee markets and profits. What were all those powerful arms manufacturers going to do when the Cold War ended? As we will see in Chapter 7, the peace dividend was not going to be allowed to happen.

Military Strategy

Though Leo Strauss gets much of the credit and attention for influencing the group that would become known as the neoconservatives, a lesser-known inspiration was a RAND Corporation researcher and Pentagon advisor named Albert Wohlstetter. Wohlstetter found the contemporary nuclear policy of mutually assured destruction (MAD) to be immoral and ineffective due to the fact that it would be so destructive to the civilian population if acted on and therefore no American leader would choose "reciprocal suicide" (apparently, he believed it was plausible that a Soviet leader might). According to authors Alain Frachon and Daniel Vernet in their article, "The Strategist and the Philosopher":

> To the contrary, Wohlstetter proposed "staggered deterrence," i.e. accepting limited wars that would eventually use tactical nuclear weapons with high-precision "smart" bombs capable of striking at the enemy's military apparatus.
>
> He criticized the joint nuclear weapons control policy with Moscow. According to him, it amounted to bridling U.S. technological creativity in order to maintain an artificial balance with the USSR.

It was purportedly Wohlstetter's influence that led Reagan to pursue his "Star Wars" shield, which was the precursor to the missile defense shield pursued during the Bush II administration and was the reason behind Bush's unilateral withdrawal from the ABM Treaty (136).

The Wolfowitz Doctrine

Paul Wolfowitz, a former student of both Strauss and Wohlstetter at the University of Chicago, wrote a draft version of a document called the Defense Planning Guidance for 1994–1999 in his capacity as Under Secretary of Defense in the Bush I administration. The draft was leaked to *The New York Times* on March 7, 1992, which led to public outcry about its imperialist overtones, moving official policy from one of "containment" to one of unilateralism and preventing the emergence of any potential rival to the United States's hegemony as one of its tenets. The document was subsequently revised by Secretary of Defense Dick Cheney and Chairman of the Joint Chiefs of Staff Colin Powell and was officially released the following month. The original draft became known as the Wolfowitz Doctrine, and its precepts re-emerged during the Bush II administration for which Wolfowitz served as deputy secretary of defense (137). Some of the controversial language of the doctrine that is most germane to the subject of this book includes the following, under Section 1.B:

> Our first objective is to prevent the reemergence of a new rival, either on the territory of the former Soviet Union or elsewhere, that poses a threat on the order of that posed formerly by the Soviet Union. This is a dominant consideration underlying the new regional defense strategy and requires that we endeavor to prevent any hostile power from dominating a region whose resources would, under consolidated control, be sufficient to generate global power. These regions include Western Europe, East Asia, the territory of the former Soviet Union, and Southeast Asia. . . .
>
> Finally, we must maintain mechanisms for deterring potential competitors from even aspiring to a larger regional or global role (138).

Other disturbing sections of the doctrine that pertain to pushing ideological hegemony and the implicit potential for interfering in the internal relations of other nations include part of Section 1.A:

> We will seek to promote those positive trends which serve to support and reinforce our national interests, principally, promotion, establishment and expansion of democracy and free market institutions worldwide (138).

And Section 7.B:

> To deterring and, when necessary, defending against threats to our security, and interests; and to exercising the leadership needed, including the decisive use of military forces when necessary, to maintain a world environment where societies with shared values can flourish (138).

Basically, this doctrine gives the United States government permission to decide that any other nation on the planet may be subject to its definition of democracy, free-market institutions, and an environment where "shared values can flourish." If the U.S. government determines that a nation does not meet these criteria, its rights to sovereignty and to self-determination as enshrined in international law can potentially be overruled, with unilateral military force. In other words, those controlling U.S. government policy ultimately get to decide what form of political government and economic arrangement is best for another nation anywhere in the world, not the people living there and not the recognized leaders of the nation in question.

President Obama, with his frequent citing of America's exceptionalism, never repudiated this doctrine.

A Clean Break

The concrete policy of regime change has been traced back, according to the late investigative journalist Robert Parry, to the work of several of the above named neocon politicians on behalf of Israeli hard-liner Benjamin Netanyahu's 1996 campaign to become prime minister. As advisors to

Netanyahu, they formulated a strategy published under the name *A Clean Break: A New Strategy for Securing the Realm.*

The idea behind this strategy was to undermine good faith negotiations, whereby the Palestinians may secure anything resembling a functioning and sovereign state, by destroying the leadership of countries sympathetic to and supportive of Hamas or Hezbollah by way of regime change interventions. The nations included Iraq (then led by Saddam Hussein), Syria under the Assads, and Iran.

While the overt intervention in Iraq and the covert intervention in Syria have resulted in chaos and suffering for the people living there, that chaos has benefitted Israel, as Parry points out:

> In the end, the regional chaos has helped Prime Minister Netanyahu starve the Palestinians of the financial support they once had, supposedly making them more susceptible to whatever demands the Israelis choose to make. And it has given Netanyahu a freer hand to engage in periodic slaughters of Gazan militants, a process the Israelis call "mowing the grass" (139).

The neocons' unequivocal support for Israel has been observed by others, some even suggesting that there is such a blurred line among neocons between the Israeli government's interests and the United States's interests that the two are often conflated.

Former CIA analysts Kathleen and Bill Christison, in their 2002 *CounterPunch* article, "A Rose by Another Name: The Bush Administration's Dual Loyalties," noted that from the 1990s onward, there was an increasing trend toward not even making any pretense of balance on the Israel-Palestine issue.

> In the Clinton administration, the three most serious State Department officials dealing with the Palestinian-Israel peace process were all partisans of Israel to one degree or another. . . . [But] the link between active promoters of Israeli interests and policy-making circles is stronger by several orders of magnitude in the Bush administration,

which is peppered with people who have long records of
activism on behalf of Israel in the United States, of policy
advocacy in Israel, and of promoting an agenda for Israel
often at odds with existing U.S. policy (140).

Douglas Feith, who helped develop the Clean Break strategy for Netanyahu, later contributed to the fabrications that enabled the invasion of Iraq
in 2003 by setting up the Office of Special Plans in the Defense Department
through which he funneled his own "unverified" intelligence, reminiscent
of the fantasies and falsehoods churned out by the neocons for Team B during
the Ford administration (140).

Robert Kagan and Victoria Nuland

Robert Kagan, a neoconservative writer and historian, is not a direct disciple
of Strauss, but he buys into the basic neocon myths about the end of the Cold
War; the good-versus-evil political framework of international politics, and
that America always represents the good and, hence, has a duty to intervene
on behalf of remaking the world in its own image via regime change.

Kagan is perhaps most infamous for cofounding, along with William
Kristol, the think tank Project for a New American Century (PNAC) in 1997.
One of PNAC's main projects was to encourage a policy of regime change in
Iraq via publication of policy papers and political lobbying. It wasn't until
Bush II occupied the White House that they would find a receptive audience.

Kagan's views developed while he served as a policy staffer in the State
Department in the Reagan administration, where he later became a speech
writer for Secretary of State George Schultz. His thinking and experience
culminated in an article published by *Foreign Affairs* magazine in 1996 in
which he lamented "America's reduced role in a post-Cold War world." Instead
he suggested that America should serve as a "benevolent global hegemon."

Despite the fact that, by any reasonable standard—such as the reality
that most of his predictions about regime change and war in Iraq have proven
to be completely wrong—his basic ideas have not fundamentally changed,
they have not ceased to be taken seriously in Washington.

Kagan still believes the United States has a legitimate duty to expand its power and dominion throughout the world in pursuit of "common universal values," which is still code for our definition of democracy and free-market institutions (141).

With new opportunities for the spreading of chaos and destabilization via regime change having temporarily exhausted themselves in the Middle East by 2008, Kagan began transposing his theme of bringing good old American "democracy" by force to a different geographic area: Eurasia.

As he told Peter Beaumont of *The Observer* that year, "Democracies need to be working together to promote their fundamental values in the new confrontation with the globe's newly confident autocracies" (141).

Those "newly confident autocracies" he was referring to were Russia and China.

Around this same time, Kagan served as a foreign policy advisor to John McCain, who had consistently expressed public hostility toward Russia.

Subsequently, Kagan continued spreading his interventionist ideology in media outlets such as *The New Republic* and *The Washington Post*. The latter published a column in July 2014 in which Kagan made the following comment:

> In my view the willingness of the United States to use force
> and to threaten to use force to defend its interests and the
> liberal world order has been an essential and unavoidable
> part of sustaining that world order since the end of WWII
> (142).

Apparently, Kagan missed the history lesson on U.S. interventions since WWII that have removed democratically elected leaders and replaced them with brutal dictators (e.g. Iran in 1953 and Chile in 1973) and the American provision of support for brutal paramilitaries who slaughtered anyone suspected of opposing their agenda (e.g. Central America in the 1980s) (143). As a reputed historian, he also seems to have missed the fact that there is no historical evidence that a functioning democracy can be imposed by an outside force. Furthermore, the theory of democratic peace that he implicitly believes in has been shown to be erroneous. There is no guarantee that two nations that both have some form of democratic government will not go to war. A cursory search on Wikipedia of "wars between democratic nations" demonstrates that.

In response to Kagan's essay in the May 2014 issue of *The New Republic*, "Superpowers Don't Get to Retire," Obama said he wanted to have lunch with Kagan to compare worldviews.

Kagan eventually began to distance himself from the term "neoconservative" and has publicly stated that he prefers to be called a "liberal interventionist." Moreover, he maintained bipartisan connections by serving on a civilian advisory board for Hillary Clinton during her tenure as secretary of state. He even intimated that he would support her if she ran for president in 2016:

> I feel comfortable with her on foreign policy. If she pursues a policy which we think she will pursue, it's something that might have been called neocon, but clearly her supporters are not going to call it that; they are going to call it something else (142).

In regard to the Ukraine crisis, he has pushed the standard line of misinformation and distortion and used it as a pretext to justify a more muscular and interventionist policy in Eurasia:

> When Vladimir Putin failed to achieve his goals in Ukraine through political and economic means, he turned to force, because he believed that he could. What might China do were it not hemmed in by a ring of powerful nations backed by the United States? (142)

In this case, Kagan's distortions are particularly egregious and willful because he knows full well the role his wife played in fomenting the chaos in Ukraine.

Victoria Nuland, a former chief foreign policy advisor to Dick Cheney in the Bush II administration and later ambassador to NATO, served as a spokesperson for the Obama State Department prior to her gig as assistant secretary for European and Eurasian Affairs. She is one of the neocons who found a place in the Obama administration—part of the new tactic that many neocons had embarked on by 2008, which was to embed themselves within the broader Washington establishment, according to former neocon Jacob Heilbrunn, now an editor at the realist publication *The National Interest*:

> Whether it's the Foundation for the Defense of Democ-
> racies or the National Endowment for Democracy, the
> *Weekly Standard* or the *New York Sun*, the neoconserva-
> tives are battle-hardened fighters who have created a per-
> manent base for themselves. They will not disappear
> (144).

Heilbrunn provides unique insight into the neocon mindset by describing what amounts to an internalized case of post-traumatic stress disorder in connection with the Jewish Holocaust, which makes for an eternal vigilance about the failures of German and European liberal democrats in standing up to Hitler and the Nazis as well as communism. "Neoconservatives see Munichs everywhere and anywhere. [They] have shaped a romantic narrative for themselves in which they are the new Churchills staring down the forces of evil" (144).

This is the kind of mindset that can find within a leader like Russian President Putin, who is a pragmatic moderate within the Russian political landscape and seeks to maintain Russia's independence on the world stage, a new Hitler.

After greasing the wheels via the funding of numerous political and media organizations in Ukraine by the National Endowment for Democracy (NED), led by its neocon president Carl Gershman, Nuland actively encouraged the protests at Maidan Square along with neocon Senator John McCain, who was photographed with leaders of Svoboda in front of their neo-Nazi banner (145).

Responsibility to Protect (aka R2P, or Liberal Intervention)

> War is essentially an evil thing. Its consequences are not confined to the belligerent states alone, but affect the whole world. To initiate a war of aggression, therefore, is not only an international crime, it is the supreme international crime differing only from other war crimes in that it contains within itself the accumulated evil of the whole.
>
> —Judgment of the Nuremberg Tribunal, 1945–1946

John Horgan, in his book *The End of War*, scientifically analyzes war throughout human history via anthropological, historical, and psychological and sociological studies of warfare and atrocities. One of his conclusions is that the old cliché about justice being a prerequisite for peace is wrong. Actually, the opposite is true—peace is a prerequisite for justice and for the pursuit of other noble goals. By the very nature of war and the conditions it produces, justice, democracy, and physical well-being cannot flourish (146) (147).

Those who believe that war can be the means for bringing peace, democracy, and human rights to an area in conflict or breakdown are required to delude themselves with notions of "short, clean, surgical" wars that have no basis in reality. To believe such is to be actually or willfully ignorant of what modern war is: soldiers who have typically undergone training that has been refined over the past 70 years to produce higher kill rates through operant conditioning, the use of weapons and munitions that are guaranteed to be nondiscriminatory due to their awesome power of destruction or continuing danger after the cessation of hostilities, and theaters of operation that do not have clearly delineated lines separating the battlefield from the non-battlefield (148) (149).

"Humanitarian interventions" based on the theoretical promotion of human rights and democracy are a modern variation of the crusader mindset that has been used to justify colonialism in the past, including Christian missionary work, "civilizing" the pagans and savages, and the "white man's burden." It has also proved a very successful way to get traditionally anti-war and anti-imperialist segments of the left to support such wars even though there is little reason to believe that "great powers," like the United States, are suddenly pursuing something different than what they have in the past when they choose to intervene militarily or otherwise embed themselves by force in another country: economic gain and geopolitical advantage (150).

As alluded to earlier, one need only look at the United States's documented record of military interventions and covert operations in other countries since the end of WWII to realize that a country's human rights record or functional democratic institutions are not the criteria by which the United States determines what leaders or governments it will support, install, prop up, or ally with. A more consistently recognizable pattern involves receptivity to U.S. corporations and geostrategic advantage against perceived competitors on the world stage (143).

Diana Johnstone, author of *Fools' Crusade: Yugoslavia, NATO and Western Delusions* and a critic of R2P, points out that genocide and ethnic cleansing actually tend to occur within the context of or as the result of wars. The Jewish Holocaust and the Khmer Rouge genocide are obvious examples. The Rwandan genocide happened during a civil war that took place from 1990–1994 (151).

Another example, although less clear to the American public due to the dominant portrayal offered by the U.S. government and establishment media, is the Serbian genocide of the Milosevic government against Kosovo Albanians immediately following the initiation of the US/NATO military intervention—a humanitarian catastrophe that NATO expected as a result of its actions, according to international law expert Francis Boyle, who represented the Republic of Bosnia and Herzegovina in proceedings at the International Court of Justice (152). Moreover, a July 2014 report by the chief prosecutor of the Special Investigative Task Force, set up by the EU to conduct a criminal investigation into allegations of war crimes by the US/NATO-installed Kosovo Liberation Army (KLA), found that a criminal indictment is justified against senior officials of the KLA. This finding was based on sanctioned actions that constitute ethnic cleansing and crimes against humanity against large portions of the Serb and Roma populations, as well as violent persecution of political opponents within the community of Kosovo Albanians (153).

The UN was established to protect the concept of national sovereignty with the understanding that in order to save future generations from war, it was necessary to highlight the sanctity of national borders from violation by more powerful and belligerent nations. Johnstone argues that advocates of the R2P doctrine seek to undermine this legal concept of national sovereignty:

> In fact, Hitler initiated World War II precisely in *violation* of the national sovereignty of Czechoslovakia and Poland partly in order, he claimed, to stop human rights violations that those governments allegedly perpetrated against ethnic Germans who lived there. It was to invalidate this pretext, and "save succeeding generations from the scourge of war," that the United Nations was founded on the basis of respect for national sovereignty.

> In practice this [R2P] can give the dominant powers carte blanche to intervene militarily in weaker countries in order to support whatever armed rebellions they favor. Once this doctrine seems to be accepted, it can even serve as an incitement to opposition groups to provoke government repression in order to call for "protection" (151).

Furthermore, R2P campaigns are often undertaken in order to address problems that were created by imperialist or colonialist powers to begin with. This dynamic played out in 2014 when then-President Barack Obama ordered military air strikes and an increase in forces to protect the northern Iraqi city of Erbil from advances by Islamic State of Iraq and Syria (ISIS) fighters and to help the thousands of people belonging to the Yazidi religious sect that were reportedly stranded on a mountain in the middle of hostilities (154). It should be noted, however, that the Kurdish territory in which Erbil is situated is home to 25 percent of Iraq's oil reserves (155). For those who argue that this is a cynical statement about the United States's true motives, one can rest assured that the United States "incidentally" ensured some kind of direct or indirect control of those nearby oil resources.

By invoking the R2P doctrine, Obama was ostensibly addressing a problem that resulted from the U.S. government's invasion and occupation of Iraq, which created the conditions of a civil war in the first place, in addition to providing support to an armed rebellion in Syria next door in the hopes of overthrowing the Assad government. A segment of those same rebels eventually became the radicals who joined Islamic State of Iraq (ISI)—a splinter group of Al Qaeda in Iraq—to become Islamic State of Iraq and Syria (ISIS) (156).

Considering the fact that Israel had just finished a military campaign that resulted in the deaths of over 2,000 Gazans—the vast majority of which were civilians—as well as the demolition of what little civil infrastructure was left in the area, all without any substantive concern expressed by the U.S. government, much less the invocation of R2P, it is apparent that the United States picks and chooses which violations of humanitarian laws deserve action. This is all the more pronounced in the case of Israel since the invocation of R2P in Gaza would not require direct military intervention and the costs associated with it, but only the withholding of the annual $3 billion plus in aid the United States provides Israel each year on the condition that Israel stop violating international law. Additionally, the United States could decide not to continue using its veto power at the UN to shield an increasingly defiant Israel from the consequences of its actions. Neither of these approaches would cost the United States blood or treasure.

Origins of R2P

The Responsibility to Protect doctrine was inspired, in large part, by the failure of the international community to stop the genocide in Rwanda in 1994 and controversy over NATO's "humanitarian" actions in the Balkans in that same decade. Subsequently, then-Secretary General of the UN Kofi Annan sought guidance and clarification on when the international community should intervene for humanitarian purposes.

R2P later emerged from the report of the International Commission on Intervention and State Sovereignty (ICISS) in December 2001. The commission had a thorny issue to deal with involving the principle of state sovereignty and when it may presumably be breached for humanitarian reasons, namely genocide. It is recognized that the Iraq War of 2003 dealt a setback to R2P, as a partial justification proffered for that war was humanitarian intervention. Subsequent humanitarian disasters in Darfur, however, kept interest in R2P alive, and attempts were made to revise and clarify the doctrine.

What emerged by 2005 at the World Summit was an agreement by the heads of states and governments to three general ideas. Those three ideas evolved into the Three Pillars of the Responsibility to Protect doctrine and were unveiled by Secretary General of the UN Ban Ki-Moon in his 2009 report, "Implementing the Responsibility to Protect":

Pillar One: States have the primary responsibility to protect their populations from genocide, war crimes, ethnic cleansing, and crimes against humanity;

Pillar Two: Addresses the commitment of the international community to provide assistance to states in building capacity to protect their populations from genocide, war crimes, ethnic cleansing, and crimes against humanity and to assisting those which are under stress before crises and conflicts break out; and,

Pillar Three: Focuses on the responsibility of the international community to timely and decisive action to prevent and halt genocide, ethnic cleansing, war crimes, and crimes against humanity when a state is manifestly failing to protect its populations.

A resolution of the UN General Assembly was introduced in September 2009, and it was agreed by that body to continue consideration of R2P. Informal interactive dialogues on the issue have continued since 2010 (157).

Libya: An Abuse of R2P

Despite the noble intentions of most of those behind this doctrine, which is still in the process of becoming a customary norm and is not enshrined in any legally binding treaty, it is not without serious problems and criticisms.

International law expert Marjorie Cohn has expressed concern with the possibilities for abuse of the doctrine by powerful actors, citing its invocation in Libya:

> Security Council Resolution 1973 begins with the call for "the immediate establishment of a ceasefire." It reiterates "the responsibility of the Libyan authorities to protect the Libyan population" and reaffirms that "parties to armed conflicts bear the primary responsibility to take all feasible steps to ensure the protection of civilians. The resolution authorizes UN Member States "to take all necessary measures . . . to protect civilians and civilian populated areas."
>
> But instead of pursuing an immediate ceasefire, immediate military action was taken instead. The military force exceeds all bounds of the "all necessary measures" authorization. "All necessary measures" should first have been peaceful measures to settle the conflict. Yet peaceful means were not exhausted before the military invasion began. . . . After passage of the resolution, Libya immediately offered to accept international monitors and Qaddafi offered to step down and leave Libya. These offers were immediately rejected by the opposition (158).

Moreover, Obama, along with then-President Nicolas Sarkozy of France and British PM David Cameron, admitted in a *New York Times* op-ed that NATO would continue its military campaign in Libya until Qaddafi was gone—in other words, the R2P invocation in the UN Resolution was used as a cover for regime change:

> However, so long as Qaddafi is in power, NATO must
> maintain its operations so that civilians remain protected
> and the pressure on the regime builds. Then a genuine
> transition from dictatorship to an inclusive constitutional
> process can really begin, led by a new generation of lead-
> ers. In order for that transition to succeed, Qaddafi must
> go and go for good (159).

Eventually, Qaddafi was captured by rebel forces, tortured, and murdered. Then-Secretary of State Hillary Clinton was caught on camera gloat-
ing at the news of this blatant violation of international law, exclaiming, "We
came, we saw, he died" (160). Since then, the country has degenerated into
tribal conflict, is a haven for terrorists, and has an open slave trade (161).

Robert Parry describes the Libyan intervention, instigated by White
House R2P advocates Samantha Power and Susan Rice, as a war that "the
Neocons and the R2Pers teamed up for" (162). Indeed, it seems to have been
the beginning of a strange partnership in which the neocons do their part to
destabilize and bust up a state—to paraphrase Wolfowitz—by taking a
minority opposition and arming it in the target country so that it attracts
increasingly nuttier elements, thereby setting up the nation for an intervention with an R2P pretext as the leadership of the target country predictably
reacts to the armed rebels with force.

A September 2013 report by the Belfer Center for Science and International Affairs of the Harvard Kennedy School found that the U.S. government's narrative about the events in Libya that supposedly required a
"humanitarian intervention"—repeated by the mainstream media—was
wrong. In fact, the uprising in Libya was armed and violent from the beginning and Qaddafi's military response did not target civilians or use indis-
criminate force (163).

A subsequent inquiry and report on the Libya intervention by the UK
parliament in 2015–2016 confirmed that the intervention was based on false
pretenses, that the French government's motives for initiating the intervention were political and economic (not humanitarian), that Qaddafi was not
threatening to massacre civilians, that the rebellion was violent and contained

significant Islamist elements, and that the intervention had resulted in plung-
ing the formerly most prosperous nation in Africa into anarchy. Moreover,
it was concluded that the British government did not perform sufficient due
diligence before making its decision to go along with the action (164).

A similar process was attempted in Syria but was thwarted by a combination of Russian diplomacy and elements of Obama's military leadership
being weary of a full-fledged military engagement on the erroneous assertion
of Assad's responsibility for a sarin gas attack (165) (166).

Parry cites a Washington insider as confessing that these two ideologies "now represent the dominant foreign policy establishment in Official
Washington." The source went on to observe that "the Neocons are motivated
by two things, love of Israel and hatred of Russia. Meanwhile, the R2Pers are
easily enamored of idealistic young people in street protests" (162).

Putin, educated in international law, publicly expressed grave concern
at the pattern of intervention being established by both Bush and Obama. At
the outset of intervention in Libya, Putin said the following to international
journalists:

> About the UN resolution, which gives grounds for the
> present military intervention—this resolution is defective.
> If we look at what is written there, it becomes obvious that
> it allows anyone to take any action against a sovereign
> state. It reminds me of the medieval call for a crusade.
> When countries call on each other to go out and liberate
> something.
>
> But, you know, I don't worry more about this military
> intervention—there are a lot of military conflicts going
> on and, unfortunately, will unfold in the future. I'm more
> worried about the ease with which decisions are being
> made to use force in international affairs nowadays. For
> example, it has become a steady trend in U.S. policy.
> During Clinton's era, they bombed Yugoslavia and Bel-
> grade. Bush invaded Afghanistan. Iraq was invaded under

> far-fetched false pretenses, liquidating an entire admin-
> istration, including Saddam's children. And now it's Lib-
> ya's turn. It opens with a pretext to defend civilians, but
> it's the civilians who die under the bombs during air-
> strikes. Where is the logic and conscience here? Both are
> absent. There are already victims among the civilians
> (167).

The R2P doctrine still has traction among mainstream Western commentators, however, as Jean Bricmont observes in his book *Humanitarian
Imperialism: Using Human Rights to Sell War*: those who exercise power typically utilize an ideology that is meant to convince those on the receiving end
that the power being exercised over them is for their own good. Such language was found among Hitler's supporters in Germany and renowned
American commentators during the Vietnam War.

He goes on to explain that ideology is the most important in "open"
and "democratic" societies, where it constitutes the main form of social control by marginalizing debate outside of a narrow set of parameters. These
methods are arguably much more effective than the control by fear that autocratic societies utilize:

> Today's secular priesthood is made up of opinion makers,
> media stars of all kinds, and a considerable number of
> academics and journalists. They largely monopolize pub-
> lic debate, channeling it in certain directions and setting
> the limits on what can be said, while giving the impression
> of a free exchange of ideas. One of the most common
> ideological reinforcement mechanisms is to focus debate
> on the means employed to achieve the supposedly altru-
> istic ends claimed by those in power, instead of asking
> whether the proclaimed aims are the real ones, or whether
> those pursuing them have the right to do so (150).

Hence, respectable debate in our so-called open and "liberal" media
in the United States is focused on the effectiveness of means and tactics of

the policy and not the legitimacy of the aims or the policy itself. In contrast to an autocratic society, the purveyors of propaganda among the secular priesthood in open societies typically believe the distortions and obfuscations they peddle. (Chapter 10 will go into more detail on the problem of the media.)

Based on what transpired in the Balkans and in Libya after US/NATO intervention, as well as what turned out to be faulty evidence or outright mendacity regarding the reasons for the interventions in both areas in the first place, along with the near intervention in Syria following the same pattern, the argument that US/NATO military interventions is the way to stop or prevent genocide, ethnic cleansing, and other crimes against humanity is refuted.

On September 1, 2014, when French and Russian diplomats and parliamentarians convened a dialogue on the Ukraine crisis, the participants stated that these abuses had degraded the efficacy of international law:

> The Ukrainian crisis is in fact a product of the destruction of the framework of international law that we have experienced since the middle of the 1990s and which manifested itself around the subjects of Kosovo (1998–99), of Iraq (2003)—the magnitude of whose consequences are today being measured—and, more recently, of Libya. Today we are tasting the bitter fruits of this destruction of the rules of international law; a destruction for which the United States and NATO bear the responsibility. It is not possible to find a framework for resolving this crisis without rules that are acknowledged by all. International law is still based on two rules, which are profoundly contradictory: respect for the sovereignty of states AND the right of peoples to determine for themselves. Mediation between these two principles has been dramatically and permanently weakened by the actions of NATO states and the United States since the end of the 1990s. It is these mediations that we must rebuild (168).

No further movement seems to be imminent to get the R2P doctrine incorporated into an international treaty, and its evolution into an eventual customary norm has hit some snags among countries in the global south. In fact, during the UN General Assembly's "High-Level Meeting on the Rule of Law at the National and International Levels" in September 2012, the resulting declaration expressed no further support or even mention of the R2P doctrine (152).

Cohn points out that during General Assembly discussions on the issue back in 2009, the Cuban delegation raised some prescient and thought-provoking issues that are worth quoting here:

> Who is to decide if there is an urgent need for an intervention in a given State, according to what criteria, in what framework, and on the basis of what conditions? Who decides it is evident the authorities of a State do not protect their people, and how is it decided? Who determines peaceful means are not adequate in a certain situation, and on what criteria? Do small states have also the right and the actual prospect of interfering in the affairs of larger states? Would any developed country allow, either in principle or in practice, humanitarian intervention in its own territory? How and where do we draw the line between an intervention under the Responsibility to Protect and an intervention for political or strategic purposes, and when do political considerations prevail over humanitarian concerns? (158)

Chapter 7: NATO Expansion and American Empire

Expanding NATO would be the most fateful error of American policy in the entire post-Cold-War era. Such a decision may be expected to inflame the nationalistic, anti-Western and militaristic tendencies in Russian opinion; to have an adverse effect on the development of Russian democracy; to restore the atmosphere of the Cold War to East-West relations, and to impel Russian foreign policy in directions decidedly not to our liking.

Russians are little impressed with American assurances that it reflects no hostile intentions. They would see their prestige (always uppermost in the Russian mind) and their security interests as adversely affected.

—George F. Kennan, author of U.S. "containment" policy for the Soviet Union (169)

They probably rubbed their hands rejoicing at having played a trick on the Russians.

—Mikhail Gorbachev in a 2009 interview with Germany's *Bild* newspaper on the West's broken promise not to extend NATO east in return for German reunification (170)

In December 1989, a few weeks after the fall of the Berlin Wall, President George H. W. Bush (Bush I) participated in a summit with Mikhail Gorbachev in Malta. During that summit, Washington promised that it would not "take advantage" of the political upheaval taking place in Eastern Europe in light of Gorbachev's decision not to use force to maintain control in the region (171).

Subsequently, on February 9, 1990, Bush's Secretary of State James Baker negotiated a gentleman's agreement with Gorbachev that, in exchange for allowing a reunified Germany as a NATO member, NATO would not be expanded any further east. The following day, West German Chancellor Helmut Kohl reiterated this same offer, which is when Gorbachev actually accepted it. Due to the Soviet Union's history of having been invaded twice by Germany during the twentieth century, Gorbachev was understandably hesitant to allow reunification. However, Baker had explained that it would be better to have a unified Germany in NATO, where it was implied that any contemplated military actions would be kept in check, than to have an independent Germany. Gorbachev ultimately agreed with this reasoning but made a grave error in not demanding that the agreement be put in writing, which has provided U.S. leaders with plausible deniability when it suited them (172).

In December 2017, documents were released by the National Security Archive (NSA) at George Washington University proving once and for all that such a promise was, in fact, made to Gorbachev by Baker and other Western officials. An excerpt from the NSA's write-up that accompanied the release reads:

> The documents show that multiple national leaders were considering and rejecting Central and Eastern European membership in NATO as of early 1990 and through 1991, that discussions of NATO in the context of German unification negotiations in 1990 were not at all narrowly limited to the status of East German territory, and that subsequent Soviet and Russian complaints about being misled about NATO expansion were founded in written contemporaneous memcons and telcons at the highest levels. . . .

... Not once, but three times, Baker tried out the "not one
inch eastward" formula with Gorbachev in the February
9, 1990, meeting. He agreed with Gorbachev's statement
in response to the assurances that "NATO expansion is
unacceptable." Baker assured Gorbachev that "neither the
President nor I intend to extract any unilateral advantages
from the processes that are taking place," and that the
Americans understood that "not only for the Soviet Union
but for other European countries as well it is important
to have guarantees that if the United States keeps its presence in Germany within the framework of NATO, not an
inch of NATO's present military jurisdiction will spread
in an eastern direction" (see Document 6) (173).

NATO Secretary General Manfred Woerner reflected Gorbachev's
understanding of the agreement in a speech three months later in Brussels
where he stated, "the fact that we are ready not to place a NATO army outside
of German territory gives the Soviet Union a firm security guarantee" (174).

That "firm security guarantee" translated into a total of thirteen new
members, all from Central and Eastern Europe, that have joined NATO since
the end of the Cold War, with North Macedonia in the process of becoming
a member and overtures also being made toward Kazakhstan and Azerbaijan
(116).

The agreement was first broken by Clinton, who encouraged the entry
of Hungary, Poland, and the Czech Republic. This followed both an intensive
lobbying effort by the arms industry, which needed a mission to justify its
continued share of public largesse after the Cold War, and a political battle
between Clinton and Bob Dole for the Polish-American vote during that
year's presidential campaign (175) (176). Later, Bush II actively lobbied for
the entry of seven more Eastern European nations into the alliance, including the three Baltic states of Estonia, Latvia, and Lithuania on Russia's border.

Jack Matlock, who served as U.S. ambassador to the Soviet Union in
the Bush I administration, explains that when Clinton was advised by Russian representatives and Soviet/Russia experts, some of whom had partici-

pated in the negotiated end of the Cold War, that he was about to make a serious geopolitical blunder in encouraging NATO expansion, he did it anyway.

> [One of two decisions] turned Russian public opinion during the years of the Clinton administration from strongly pro-American to vigorous opposition to American policies abroad. The first was the decision to extend the NATO military structure into countries that had previously been members of the Warsaw Pact. There was no need to expand NATO to ensure the security of the newly independent countries of Eastern Europe. There were other ways those countries could have been reassured and protected without seeming to redivide Europe to Russia's disadvantage. . . . Combined with rhetoric claiming "victory" in the Cold War, expanding NATO suggested to the Russian public that throwing off communism and breaking up the Soviet Union had probably been a bad idea. Instead of getting credit for voluntarily joining the West, they were being treated as if they had been defeated and were not worthy to be allies (85).

The obvious question to ask is why we needed to keep NATO if the reason for its existence had disappeared and the Warsaw Pact, its Soviet-era counterpart, had been disbanded. Alexey Pushkov, Russian legislator and former professor at the Moscow State Institute of International Relations, recalls that this question was indeed put to the West over the years: "The standard response to the arguments against NATO's eastward expansion was that Russia's neighbors felt unsafe. . . . [But] neither Warsaw nor Prague could point to any signs that Russia had aggressive designs towards Eastern Europe" (174).

Pushkov states that proposals were offered to guarantee security for the countries of Eastern Europe that did not require the expansion of NATO, as Matlock suggests above, but such offers were rejected in Washington and

Brussels. He goes on to describe his experiences over the years in trying to explain Russia's concerns about NATO expansion to the West:

> Throughout the 1990s, I often made the point that by expanding NATO eastward, Russia would be pushed out of the Euro-Atlantic community. From the geopolitical point of view it is as if the West were saying to Russia, "From now on, your security is of no interest to us. You are on your own." The answers I was repeatedly getting were amazing and extremely short-sighted: "What can you do to oppose the expansion? Move your troops to your Western borders? What practical measures can you take?" As for the guarantees given in 1989 and 1990, I was told that none of them had been codified in any formal treaty or agreement and that, even if Western leaders such as Helmut Kohl or John Major reiterated what Baker or Woerner had said, they were now of no consequence" (174).

Despite warm personal relations between Bush II and Putin at the start of the new millennium, Russia's security concerns ultimately did not fare any better with the new administration.

According to retired CIA analyst and Russia specialist George Beebe, on September 9, 2001, Putin called Bush and personally warned him about an impending attack that was being planned out of Afghanistan and had been picked up by Russian intelligence (177). Another more general warning from Putin about terrorists in the region who were being funded by Saudi Arabia and enabled by Pakistani intelligence was confirmed by Condoleezza Rice in her 2011 memoir, *No Higher Honor*. But she admitted that the warning was dismissed as Russian bitterness about Pakistan's role in the Soviet Union's humiliating defeat in Afghanistan (178).

Putin was the first world leader to call Bush after the attacks, seeing it as an opening for cooperation (85). After supporting the U.S. War on Terror, including logistical and intelligence assistance, as well as providing access for what were to be temporary military bases to conduct the war in Afghanistan—a decision Putin had to persuade naysayers among his defense and security chiefs to agree to—Putin undoubtedly thought there would be some meaningful reciprocity. However, he eventually was forced to realize that little would be forthcoming (128).

In October 2001, Putin met NATO Secretary General George Robertson in Brussels and boldly inquired as to when Russia would be invited to join NATO. Robertson told him that he'd have to apply for membership, go through a vetting process, and then an invitation would be issued. Putin shrugged this off with a dismissive comment to the effect that Russia would not wait in line with smaller, less important countries (128).

As a way to placate Russia, British Prime Minister Tony Blair came up with a plan in 2002 to create the NATO-Russia Council, a measure "stopping well short of membership but at least giving them a sense of belonging to the club." Russia would have a permanent ambassador to NATO and would participate in NATO discussions. But problems soon arose, including complaints from Russia that they were often excluded from informal discussions prior to official meetings and would consequently face a coordinated bloc. These effects, combined with Blair's underlying attitude in creating the plan—as stated by one of his aides (128)—that "even if they [Russia] weren't really a superpower anymore, you had to pretend they were," created the impression that the West was merely being condescending. This is particularly striking when one reads Putin's words at the signing ceremony about his desire for Russia's needs to be heard and to be respected:

> The problem for our country was that for a very long time, it was Russia on one side, and on the other practically the whole rest of the world. And we gained nothing good from this confrontation with the rest of the world. The overwhelming majority of our citizens understand this all too well. Russia is returning to the family of civilized nations. And she needs nothing more than for her voice to be heard and for her national interests to be taken into account (128).

Bush II's Senior Director for Russia on the National Security Council Thomas Graham admitted to *Reuters* in an April 2014 interview that an alternative, which was not pursued by the United States, was to dissolve NATO and create a new pact that reflected new global realities and eventually included Russia (179).

The unwillingness to allow Russia into NATO or to negotiate an alternative security architecture that could be in everyone's interest represented a lost opportunity that would prove to have fateful consequences. Putin's cooperation and stated yearning to be accepted into the Western world not only did not get him a meaningful chance at NATO membership, but it didn't stop Bush's insistence on unilaterally pulling out of the ABM Treaty to pursue a missile defense shield—a move that basically tells Russia that the United States reserves the right to a nuclear first strike without retaliation.

According to Soviet/Russia expert Patrick Armstrong, the West's mentality toward post-Soviet Russia has been one of either condescension or hostility or a strange combination of both. The condescension justifies having economic advisors go in and induce "shock therapy" on the nation in the 1990s, as well as lambasting it when convenient for not being a full-fledged liberal democracy after barely three decades of attempts following 1,000 years of authoritarian rule.

The aforementioned NATO membership charade was preceded by Bill Clinton, his amiable relations with his Russian counterpart notwithstanding. Clinton made the following patronizing statement to a departing Boris Yeltsin, over whose objections he began NATO expansion, which led to one of the few times Yeltsin briefly lashed out at the United States:

> Boris, you've got democracy in your heart, you've got the trust of the people in your bones, you've got the fire in your belly of a real democrat and reformer. I'm not sure Putin has that. You'll have to keep an eye on him and use your influence to make sure that he stays on the right path. Putin needs you, Boris. Russia needs you. . . . You changed Russia. Russia was lucky to have you. The world was lucky you were where you were. I was lucky to have you. We did

a lot of stuff together, you and I. . . . We did some good
things. They'll last. It took guts on your part. A lot of that
stuff was harder for you than it was for me. I know that
(128).

As will be discussed in Chapter 8, rather than being the flaming democrat that American politicians and mainstream media hailed at the time,
Yeltsin was personally corrupt, utterly compliant to the United States's desires,
and more authoritarian in many respects than Putin. He was also deeply
unpopular among his own people by the time he left office (128) (180).

In a candid conversation with his deputy secretary of state, Strobe Tal-
bott, in 2006, Bill Clinton made an admission that reflected the American
political elite's attitude toward post-Soviet Russia, saying, "We keep telling
Ol' Boris, 'Okay, now here's what you've got to do next—here's some more
shit for your face'" (181).

The hostility is exemplified by NATO expansion, missile defense
shields, unilateral abrogation of nuclear treaties, and accusations that Russia
has imperial ambitions if it asserts its political and economic independence
or insists that it also has legitimate interests in its own backyard.

This evaluation, however, really only tells the story of the mindset of
the politicians and advisors around the presidents who have had the most
influence from Clinton to the present. Another attitude does exist among
some leaders and advisors, but it has been overruled by the assortment of
Russophobes and neo-imperialists represented by neoconservatives, humanitarian interventionists, or Brzezinski advocates of the Grand Chessboard
idea previously discussed.

As a case in point, in the Bush II administration, there was a split about
the proper approach to Russia. There were, according to former *BBC* Moscow correspondent Angus Roxburgh, the "Russophiles," led by Secretary of
State Colin Powell, who believed in trying to understand Russia's concerns
and their legitimate right to consideration of their interests. This perspective
was more in line with some of Western Europe at the time, particularly France
and Germany. In addition to trade and economic ties, they had the view that
Russia was like a prodigal son that should be welcomed home due to a sense

of shared history and culture. It was also believed that this approach was the best way to strengthen democracy in Russia (128). As some independent analysts have pointed out, had the West made a good faith attempt to integrate post-Soviet Russia into the European community, there would have been no "civilizational" clash for countries like Ukraine to be caught in the middle of (123).

The other camp within the administration was led by the neoconservatives, who adhered to the belief that the United States "won" the Cold War and that Russia should accept its position as a vanquished nation that would have little say over anything the United States did, even in its own border regions, no matter how myopic or reckless it turned out to be. Jack Matlock has publicly denounced this dangerous rewriting of history:

> Reagan normally rejected [the neoconservatives'] advice if it involved refusing to talk to adversaries. But when his policies actually worked, instead of conceding that Reagan was right and they were wrong, they have sought explanations for the end of the Cold War that bolster the myths that have plagued us. Thus the idea is perpetuated that it was U.S. force and threats, rather than negotiation, that ended the Cold War, and also that Reagan's rhetoric "conquered" communism, and that the collapse of the Soviet Union was the equivalent of a military victory. These claims are all distortions, all incorrect, all misleading, and all dangerous to the safety and future prosperity of the American people (85).

By 2002, seven more nations of Eastern Europe were invited to join NATO (they were admitted in 2004), creating another strain in the American relationship with Russia. By March 2003, further problems emerged as Russia, correctly recognizing that Saddam Hussein had nothing to do with Al-Qaeda or terrorism, made a last-minute, behind-the-scenes diplomatic push to avert the war. When that failed, Russia partnered with France and Germany to oppose the invasion at the UN (128).

Two months later, Bush made a stop in Poland—a country whose political class has historically had Russophobic tendencies and who had supported the U.S. invasion of Iraq, like all of the new post–Cold War members of NATO—before heading to St. Petersburg for its 300th Anniversary celebrations. This insult was the nail in the coffin for Putin's attempts to establish a mutually respectful and beneficial relationship with the United States. He was later overheard telling French Prime Minister Jacques Chirac at the event, "My priorities were the following: first a relationship with America, second with China, third with Europe. Now it's the other way around—first Europe, then China, then America" (128) (116) (182).

As we shall see later, it was the successful results of that revised program of prioritizing a relationship with Europe and China that the United States later viewed as a threat.

NATO: From Cold War Defense to Global Power Projection

The refusal in Washington to give up the Cold War mentality was foreshadowed as early as 1989, as Russia scholar Stephen F. Cohen relates in describing his debate at the invitation of the White House with Cold War professor Richard Pipes before the Bush I administration over the possibility of a U.S.-Soviet strategic partnership: "Declarations alone could not terminate decades of warfare mentality. . . . Many of the top level officials present clearly shared my opponent's views, though the President did not" (38).

This residual Cold War mentality, along with the profit motive of the military-industrial complex and the ideological mix of neoconservatives, humanitarian interventionists, and Grand Chessboard advocates who wielded influence, doomed the possibility of a true rapprochement between the United States and Russia as well as a more cooperative international framework. Indeed, Brzezinski himself had stated publicly in the 1990s that the fate of NATO was either to expand or to become obsolete. In 1997, he went further by claiming that NATO preservation was "vital" to keeping the U.S. relationship with Europe to the United States's advantage on the Eurasian "chessboard" (117).

NATO in the 1990s: Laying the Groundwork for Expansion

> If we treat Russia as irredeemably hostile, then we will initiate a self-fulfilling prophecy . . . we must engage Russia instead with a clear determination to foster security cooperation. As we approach the 21st century, the main task of Europe is to find a place for Russia. This was done for Germany in the post–Second World War period. If they can't for Russia, Central Europe will return to being what it was during the interwar period, the chessboard of European powers.
>
> —NATO Secretary General Willy Claes, Munich Security Conference, 1995 (183)

In 1991, President George H. W. Bush was determined to "kick the Vietnam Syndrome." In other words, he wanted the American public to get over its apprehension toward military intervention overseas that had resulted from the long, brutal, and increasingly dubious war in Vietnam. On behalf of that goal, Bush rejected proposals for Iraq's withdrawal from Kuwait, including one brokered by Gorbachev and supported by U.S. military leaders, after a destructive coalition bombing campaign. Bush saw a ground war as an opportunity for a cheap and easy victory against weakened Iraqi forces (184).

NATO had quietly participated in military operations during Gulf War I in early 1991, which motivated military leaders in both the Pentagon and NATO to consider expanding its use in other geographic and operations areas outside of its stated jurisdiction.

Meanwhile, certain political insiders were already angling for NATO expansion. For example, an ethnic lobbying group called the Polish American Congress (PAC) called for Poland's entry into NATO at their National Directors meeting in June 1991, six months before the dissolution of the Soviet Union. In September, they also called for the entry of Hungary and Czechoslovakia—also known as the Visegrad Group of nations (Poland, Hungary, and Czechoslovakia, or later the Czech Republic and Slovakia). One of PAC's most prominent members and a major advocate of NATO expansion was Jan Nowak, who had worked for years for Radio Free Europe until it was outed in the 1970s as a CIA propaganda outlet. After leaving Radio Free Europe, he went on to serve as an advisor to the Carter administration, which included his friend Zbigniew Brzezinski (185) (186) (187).

In autumn 1993, PAC stepped up its advocacy for NATO enlargement by adopting a resolution to push the U.S. government to facilitate Poland's entry into the alliance as soon as possible. A strongly worded letter enclosing a copy of the resolution was sent to President Clinton on October 28 (185).

The following month, an article appeared in *The Washington Post* about the contents of another article written by a history doctoral candidate named William Larsh. Larsh's obscure piece, published in an academic journal, was critical of WWII-era diplomat Averell Harriman, asserting that Harriman was naïve about Stalin and facilitated a deal to replace the previously recognized government of Poland with Stalin's puppet leaders in the days when the war was winding down. This was followed up by another article in *The Washington Post* ten days later, "Ghost of Yalta," in which the authors reiterate the theme of the sellout of Poland by the Roosevelt administration during the resolution of allied boundaries at the close of the war in Europe (185). As discussed in Chapter 3, how Poland ended up in the Soviet sphere was more complicated than this narrative.

Meanwhile, these articles helped to gain traction for the "not another Yalta" meme that would follow, which had its genesis among members of the political class that emerged from post-Soviet Central and Eastern European nations, such as Václav Havel, who was a Czech dissident playwright. While Poland and Czechoslovakia both had a long history of being carved up and subjugated among various empires, unlike in the aftermath of WWI or WWII when the victors drew up borders based on their own interests, the USSR/ Russia peacefully withdrew all its troops from East Germany and the other satellite countries of Central/Eastern Europe under voluntary agreement at the end of the Cold War. Therefore, to compare the release of the Central/ Eastern European nations from Soviet control to the Yalta conference of WWII is problematic—even more so as time goes on, when every Russian leader since Gorbachev has stated that they wanted to be part of the West—albeit as a partner, not a vassal.

Furthermore, Havel's views did not represent a monolithic opinion about how to best secure the futures of Poland, Czechoslovakia, and Hungary among Soviet-era dissidents in these countries. For example, some wanted to strengthen the Organization for Security and Co-operation in Europe (OSCE) in the hopes of eventually creating a pan-European arrangement that included Russia (the USSR was already a member, as would be its successor state, the Russian Federation), replacing both NATO and the Warsaw Pact. But the approach advocated by Havel to enlarge NATO to include these three nations, which would conveniently maintain the United States's dominant role in European security, quickly won the day among the new leadership of these countries.

The Clinton administration, taking the helm at the beginning of 1993, did not jump at this proposal to enlarge NATO; in fact, only National Security Advisor Anthony Lake really supported the idea in the beginning. People in both the State Department and the Pentagon were initially leery of taking on the added burden of providing security for the Central/Eastern European states. Also, it was recognized that NATO enlargement would complicate Clinton's foreign policy priority of assisting post-Soviet Russia in its transition to a market democracy.

Eventually, Havel of the Czech Republic, Lech Wałęsa of Poland, and Árpád Göncz of Hungary played on Clinton's neo-Wilsonian philosophy of the need to facilitate the spread of "democracy" and sold the president on the convoluted belief that inclusion of their respective nations in NATO would prove their credentials as Western market democracies and would encourage Russia on its own path toward democracy. Clinton subsequently expressed openness toward eventually allowing these nations into the alliance. The narrative of NATO's purpose also began to change from that of a Cold War defensive alliance to that of "an inclusive alliance protecting the democratic states and open societies of the continent" (188) (189).

When the Clinton administration would actually put this enlargement idea into practice, however, was another matter. The Partnership for Peace program—a voluntary and somewhat vague program connected to NATO in which the various parties tended to project what they wanted onto it—was established and soon became a vehicle for the possibility of NATO membership for those nations, who eventually joined. The Clinton administration saw it as a means to eventually enlarge NATO, but at a gradual pace to placate Russia for the time being and to address the reservations of other NATO members in Europe.

That summer saw a controversial conference and public communique between Wałęsa and Russian President Boris Yeltsin in which it appeared that Yeltsin had allowed Wałęsa to talk him into allowing Polish entry into NATO—a meeting that observers noted was later beset with yelling matches among Yeltsin and his advisors, who demanded that he withdraw such language from the communique. Russian Foreign Minister Andrei Kozyrev later clarified to U.S. Ambassador Tom Pickering Russia's position that it did not oppose NATO enlargement as long as it could be the first post–Cold War nation to join. Yeltsin subsequently moderated his view in a letter stating that NATO enlargement was interpreted as only a theoretical possibility at the time and suggested that both NATO and Russia could provide reciprocal security guarantees to the Central/Eastern nations in question. In November, the head of the FSB (one of the successor agencies to the KGB) presented its own report on the possibility of NATO enlargement and concluded that it was a threat to Russia's security and would require a reset of the nations' defense policy (188).

In December, Brzezinski made a personal appeal to National Security Advisor Anthony Lake for the entry of Poland, Hungary, and the Czech Republic into NATO. Lake was, of course, sympathetic, but the administration was still holding back (188).

The results of the midterm elections in November 1994 provided a shot in the arm to NATO expansion, as the Republicans used the administration's slow pace and cautious public wording to argue that the Democrats were pussyfooting around on an enlargement commitment and were too quick to appease Russia. NATO enlargement became one of the few foreign policy provisions of the Contract with America, calling on the United States to reaffirm its commitment to enlargement and to include the democracies of Central/Eastern Europe. It also contained a goal for the entry of Poland, Hungary, and the Czech Republic into NATO by January 1999 (188).

By this time, Poland had already been subjected to "shock therapy" to prepare it as a proper market democracy and, hence, for entry into NATO. When the heroes of the Solidarity movement were able to take power in Poland in 1988, they faced an economic mess due to years of Communist Party mismanagement, and the movement's leaders were looking toward the kind of system that Gorbachev initially had in mind for Russia: a gradual move toward a mixed economy with a strong public sector modeled on the Scandinavian countries. But before they could implement the reforms necessary to do this, they needed debt relief and initial aid money.

With Western economic elites licking their chops at the possibility of opening up state-controlled assets in Central/Eastern Europe to privatized foreign investment, the International Monetary Fund (IMF) allowed Poland's debt and inflation levels to deepen in order to increase desperation and the subsequent acceptance of austerity and privatization conditions for receipt of loans. Harvard economics wunderkind Jeffrey Sachs (who will make another appearance in Chapter 8), along with international speculator George Soros, went to Poland in 1989. Without wasting any time, Sachs introduced a program that included the sudden elimination of price controls and subsidies as well as the sell-off of public resources to private entities. Sachs convinced the reluctant leadership of Solidarity—a movement that had arisen in response to price increases imposed by the communist government in Moscow and had advocated direct worker ownership—to make these painful sacrifices that would hurt their rank and file on the promise that it would be for the best in the long run (180).

1996: The Turning Point

> Far from promoting democracy in Eastern Europe, Washington is promoting a system of political and military control not unlike the one practiced by the Soviet Union. Unlike that empire, which collapsed because the center

> was weaker than the periphery, the new NATO is both a
> mechanism for extracting Danegeld [tribute levied to
> support Danish invaders in medieval England] from new
> member states for the benefit of the US arms industry and
> an instrument for getting others to protect US interests
> around the world, including the supply of primary
> resources such as oil.
>
> —John Laughland, trustee of British Helsinki Human
> Rights Group (190)

The turning point for entry of Poland, Hungary, and the Czech Republic into NATO occurred as Clinton was pressured by presidential election rival Bob Dole's campaign to acknowledge that Poland should join the alliance in order to court the Polish-American vote. Moreover, this was around the time that intense lobbying by the military industrial complex to enlarge NATO as a new market for arms-related sales started yielding results.

The U.S. Committee to Expand NATO (aka U.S. Committee on NATO) was a lobbying group founded in 1996 by Bruce P. Jackson, director of global development for Lockheed Martin, and Ronald Asmus, a former Rand analyst who worked with the future leadership of the Visegrad states as soon as the Cold War ended. Asmus became known as the intellectual architect behind the idea of NATO enlargement and how to frame the idea in a publicly acceptable way. The Committee's board membership during its active years reads like a neocon all-star list: Robert Kagan, Richard Perle, Paul Wolfowitz, Stephen Hadley, Condoleezza Rice, and John McCain. But Democratic hawks were also deeply involved in the group and its mission, including Brzezinski disciple Madeleine Albright, a Czech American (191) (192).

The Committee regularly wined and dined U.S. senators as well as politicians from Poland, Hungary, and the Czech Republic, in addition to conducting free "defense planning seminars." Maps used during these presentations to the Poles reportedly showed arrows pointing from Russia as the origin of a hypothetical attack. Not exactly a subtle message.

They also coordinated their lobbying efforts with the Hungarian American Foundation and the Polish American Congress. In fact, the legislative director for PAC at the time admitted that PAC was working with the Committee in their effort to win NATO membership for Poland. Arms manufacturers also provided funding for various relevant ethnic lobbying groups like American Friends of the Czech Republic and the Romanian-American community (175).

It would be unfair, however, to suggest that the Committee and the arms dealers and political influencers it represented had to carry the entire burden of lobbying for NATO expansion and the arms sales it would portend. They got significant help during the Clinton administration from many sectors of the federal government, such as the State Department. As darkly comical as it may sound, our department of diplomacy at Foggy Bottom promoted the sale of American-made instruments of warfare via the Office of Defense Trade Controls, which advised the Merchants of Death on how to "cut red tape" and facilitate faster and easier approval of arms sales. According to defense spending expert William Hartung's March 1998 report, "The Hidden Costs of NATO Expansion," "State Department personnel posted overseas are graded for promotion based in part on how helpful they are to US defense firms in marketing military equipment in the host country" (175).

U.S. ambassadors to Poland, Hungary, Romania, and the Czech Republic were encouraged to push strenuously for the sale of American attack helicopters, fighter planes, and missiles to ostensibly prepare their militaries for NATO membership readiness.

The Commerce Department also made it a priority to pitch for arms export sales during the secretaries' overseas trade missions, including air shows and weapons exhibitions. And, of course, the Pentagon promotes arms sales through the Defense Security Cooperation Agency, which administers the Foreign Military Sales program.

This lobbying blitz from 1996 to 1998 meant that two-thirds of countries receiving the Pentagon's largest direct subsidy program for weapons exports, the Foreign Military Financing program, came from the Central/ Eastern European area. Each of these nations, including Poland, Hungary, and the Czech Republic, as well as Bulgaria, Romania, and the three Baltic states (all part of the second wave of new NATO entries in 2004), received at least S155 million per year during this period to facilitate preparation for NATO membership and "acquisition of NATO compatible equipment." Taxpayer-subsidized loans worth $647.5 million from the Pentagon's Central European Defense Loan Fund were provided to "assist in the gradual enlargement of NATO by providing loans to creditworthy Central European and Baltic States for acquisition of NATO-compatible equipment" (175). Another Pentagon loan program, known as Defense Export Loan Guarantee (DELG), provided up to $15 billion in loans for the export of U.S. arms and military paraphernalia to 39 nations—a quarter of which targeted Central/Eastern European nations. A spokesperson for the DELG program admitted that a "disproportionate interest" in the $2.4 billion worth of requests they had received came from the Central/Eastern European nations. These subsidized loan programs have a history of simply writing off billions of dollars owed, which increases the burden on U.S. taxpayers.

Another racket of the Pentagon that benefits nations receiving arms exports is the regular practice of giving away what they label as "surplus" quantities of military equipment and then ordering brand-new equipment to replace it. Not only are American taxpayers getting ripped off by giving away equipment that has been paid for, they are then hit up for the cost of more expensive replacements. The Excess Defense Articles grant program authorized 12 Central/Eastern European nations to receive free U.S. weaponry in fiscal year 1998—11 of which gained entry into NATO by 2009.

Finally, there were the Export Import Bank loans, which were allowed to fund military exports again in the 1990s after a period of prohibition following abuses during the Vietnam War. The largest loan by this bank for military equipment during this period was for $90 million to Romania to finance the purchase of five Lockheed Martin radar systems.

In all, $1.2 billion was estimated to have been spent on grants and loans to begin NATO enlargement between 1996 and 1998 (175).

By 1998, the U.S. Senate had voted in favor of accession of Poland, Hungary, and the Czech Republic into NATO. Senators William Roth and

Barbara Mikulski held a press conference in Warsaw on November 16 (185) on American support of NATO expansion. Senator Roth stated in his remarks that "NATO is a threat to no one. It is a defensive alliance, and all we seek is peace, security and stability for all of Europe." This echoes Brzezinski's comments at a Senate Foreign Relations Committee hearing the year before wherein he advocated NATO enlargement and responded to criticisms of the project by denying that the project was anti-Russia or a moral crusade of retribution for historical wrongs against Eastern Europeans. However, neither Roth nor Brzezinski stated who or what was the actual threat to Europe that was so grave that it required not only that NATO continue on, despite the fact that no opposing military alliance existed anymore, but must be enlarged. Both admitted that Russia was not a threat at the time. Indeed, the Polish Defense Minister, Janusz Onyszkiewicz, had stated by the middle of the decade that the motivation to join NATO was "not to defend against a Russian attack. We see that attack as a virtual impossibility." This is buttressed by the fact that the Central/Eastern European nations, including Poland and the Czech Republic, had all decreased their defense budgets, shortened terms of military conscription, and disbanded many of their army divisions by 1995. Not exactly the actions of nations terrified of the bear next door (193) (183).

It appears at this point that the U.S. political class had no intention of using the historic opportunity provided by the end of the Cold War to incorporate Russia into the West as an equal and respected partner, but instead to subdue it through political co-optation and economic exploitation (as we'll see in Chapter 8), and—if that didn't work—to view it as a future enemy. Either way, money would be made and power would be maintained by those sitting at the top of the American food chain.

NATO in the 2000s

When three of the four Visegrad states were formally inducted into NATO at its Washington summit in 1999, no new nations were extended official invitations, but the Membership Action Plan (MAP) was soon introduced, which provided a procedural framework for the vetting process and objective criteria for the future membership of any nation—at least, in theory. The MAP procedure was different from the first wave of post–Cold War enlargement that had occurred on the unilateral initiative of the United States. Nine countries were named for the initial MAP process: Albania, Bulgaria, Estonia, Latvia, Lithuania, Macedonia, Romania, Slovakia, and Slovenia.

In May 2000, a conference was held in Vilnius, Lithuania, attended by the foreign ministers of the nine MAP countries. The representatives agreed to work cooperatively toward NATO admission for all. They became known as the Vilnius Group and would add Croatia as a member the following year, making it the Vilnius 10.

Four successive summits of the Vilnius Group were held over the next two and a half years: at Bratislava, Sofia, Bucharest, and Riga.

Their cause was bolstered by a letter signed by 17 U.S. senators to President Bush in April 2001, urging further NATO enlargement. Two months later, Bush gave a speech in Warsaw in which he announced strong support for all the democracies of Europe to be included as full members of the alliance (194).

The public focus on this latest round of NATO enlargement was on the commitment and capability of the candidates. The Vilnius 10 nations implemented economic, military, and judicial reforms to prepare for accession.

The terrorist attacks of 9/11 created an additional rationale for the more rapid expansion of NATO both in terms of membership and geographic reach.

In 2002, NATO invited Romania, Bulgaria, Slovenia, Slovakia, and the three Baltic states of Latvia, Lithuania, and Estonia to join the alliance at its summit in Prague. Bruce Jackson—the Lockheed Martin executive, cofounder of the U.S. Committee to Expand NATO, PNAC board member, and a chum of neocon Vice President Dick Cheney—called the plan to get the Vilnius 10 into NATO the "Big Bang." During his testimony before Congress in April 2003 advocating for NATO enlargement to include seven of the Vilnius 10, he used the now-established rationale that NATO enlargement represented the inclusion of these nations into an innocuous club of peaceful democracies. He cited the words of both Brzezinski and neoconservative politicians to underscore this dubious claim (195) (196).

Seven of the Vilnius 10 would be admitted in 2004 and two more in 2009. Membership for the 10th candidate, Macedonia, was initially vetoed by Greece. However, Greece withdrew its opposition after Macedonia changed its name to North Macedonia, assuaging any Greek concern of possible designs on its own territory, which includes an area called Macedonia. As of 2020, North Macedonia was undergoing the admission process to NATO.

Meanwhile, Article 5 of the NATO Treaty had been invoked to use NATO in the Global War on Terror and specifically in Afghanistan, where it eventually took over military operations via control of the International Security Assistance Force (ISAF) in 2003. NATO was also involved in air operations during the invasion of Iraq that same year and participated in the occupation of the country from 2004 to 2011 under the "NATO Training Mission - Iraq" (116).

All of the new NATO members and future members would eventually participate in the Iraq War in some capacity, prompting Donald Rumsfeld's quip about "Old Europe" as opposed to a newly developing focus on the Eastern nations.

According to Mahdi Darius Nazemroaya, author of *The Globalization of NATO*, the Global War on Terrorism, viewed as an example of Samuel Huntington's "Clash of Civilizations" theory, enabled EU and NATO power to be projected into Eurasia's surrounding areas from two different fronts: from the Western Front in Europe and from the Eastern/Southern Front via Japan, South Korea, the Arabian Peninsula, and Afghanistan—which are now littered with U.S. military bases as well as ties to NATO and three branches of the global missile shield system.

By 2009, not only had NATO greatly expanded in terms of membership by twelve new nations in Central and Eastern Europe, its mandate had also expanded to include peacekeeping, international policing, and counterterrorism activities—a far cry from its start as a defensive alliance to protect Western Europe from invasion by the long-dead Soviet Union (116).

Around this time, former UN Assistant Secretary-General and UN Humanitarian Coordinator for Iraq Hans von Sponeck wrote an article published in a Swiss journal in which he expressed deep concern for the direction NATO had been taking since the 1990s. He believed that the United Nations was at a crossroads, reflected in its relationship with NATO:

> The world of the 192 UN member states has come to a fork in the road. One way leads to a world focused on the well being of society, conflict resolution and peace, i.e. to a life of dignity and human security with social and economic progress for all, wherever they may be—as stated in the United Nations Charter. Down the other road is where the nineteenth century "Great Game" for power will be further played out, a course which, in the twenty-first century, will become more extensive and dangerously more aggressive than ever. This road supposedly leads to democracy, but in truth it is all about power, control and exploitation (197).

In those two preceding decades, he argued, NATO had been attempting to usurp the UN's authority on the "monopoly of the use of force" by greatly expanding its objectives as well as its geographic reach, first by trying to cast itself in the role of military arm of the UN, including invocation of what would evolve into the Responsibility to Protect doctrine in the Balkans. Then it went further, serving as an occupation force in Iraq (197).

In 1999, NATO acknowledged that it was moving beyond the mandate of a defensive alliance to include "the protection of the vital resources" needs of its members. Besides the defense of member states' borders, it set itself new purposes such as assured access to energy resources and the right to intervene in "movements of large numbers of persons" and in "conflicts far from the borders of NATO countries."

In his article, von Sponeck asked how NATO's now-broadened mission could be reconciled with international law, particularly with the UN charter. In this vein, he was particularly worried by an accord signed between the

UN and NATO in September 2008, which did not consult the Security Council. He believed that an accord between the two institutions undermined the UN's neutrality if three members of the Security Council are members of NATO, have a hostile posture toward the other two Security Council members, and aim to assert power interests by use of force. Additionally, NATO is a "military alliance with nuclear weapons," and Article 2 of the UN Charter "requires that conflicts be resolved by peaceful means" (197).

In 2011, the troubling trends of NATO continued when the alliance blatantly breached the UN mandate to implement a no-fly zone in Libya (116).

More recently, NATO continues to conduct provocative military exercises near Russia's borders. In 2020, the alliance, which outspends the Russian military by 11 to 1 and has four times as many soldiers (198), oversaw troops from 17 member states when it conducted the "largest military deployment in Europe in 25 years" (199). The exercise, known as "Defender 2020," entailed a simulated war with Russia and included around 37,000 soldiers as well as tanks and other war equipment. The United States, Germany, and Poland had the most prominent roles (199).

The EU-NATO Dance

To understand the mechanisms that facilitate NATO expansion, the purpose behind it, and the underlying rivalries that could one day possibly undermine it, one must understand the role of the European Union, the dynamics within it, and its relationship to the United States.

Within the European Union (EU) there are two recognized axes of power and influence, which are also recognized axes within NATO. The first axis is the Anglo-American (also known as Atlanticist) partnership, which arose from the relationship between Britain and the United States after Britain's post-WWII decline and coincided with the United States's ascent. This axis has more power in NATO, with its military might supported by 48 percent of the world's total military expenditures (198). And although the United States is not an actual member of the EU, Britain was largely recognized as its proxy across the pond. This likely explains why then-President Obama openly encouraged British voters in 2016 to vote against Brexit (BBC 2016). Moreover, the United States invests significantly in the European Central Bank (ECB) as well as throughout the EU in general.

The second axis is the Franco-German axis, which was cemented between France and West Germany after WWII, partly to put a check on the first axis. But a rivalry between the continental powers with Britain had much longer historical roots, as Britain had periodically shifted its alliance to whichever continental power seemed weaker to counterbalance the stronger one (116). The unification of Germany after the Cold War strengthened the Franco-German axis, which has also historically tended to lean toward a Pan-Europeanism or even a Eurasian partnership. With Germany as the strongest economy in the EU, this axis has more influence and power within that entity (116).

The Washington Treaty, which created NATO, requires a potential member to be European, so it should be pointed out that Europe is not truly a continent unto itself but part of the Eurasian landmass, which includes diverse cultures and politics, including in the UK, France, Germany, Scandinavia, Greece, Italy, Russia, and, arguably, Turkey. This is important when considering the definition of "European," as it relates to both the European Union's assumption that it solely represents some "European" interest and NATO's pushing the boundaries of that definition when it is advantageous to its expansion (116).

Interestingly, French President Emmanuel Macron has talked up the idea of a European army (200), and German Chancellor Angela Merkel publicly supported the idea (201). The two countries signed a friendship treaty in January 2019. *AFP* described the agreement:

> In the new accord, meant as a follow-up to the 1963 Élysée Treaty, both France and Germany pledge to stand shoulder to shoulder in case of a military attack against either of them, reaffirming a commitment already written into EU and NATO treaties.

Paris and Berlin will also create a new joint Defence and Security Council and seek to harmonise rules for military equipment procurement (202).

So far, the development is being billed, particularly by Merkel, as a complement to NATO. However, Macron's initial comments about the project in late 2018 raised the specter of Europe having to defend itself against not only Russia and China, but possibly the United States (200). Whether a possible European Army has the potential to become an independent force or just an auxiliary for NATO remains to be seen.

Since the main post–Cold War thrust of expansion of both the EU and NATO has been aimed at the former Soviet satellite countries in Central and Eastern Europe, the goal has also been to prevent economic alliance with Russia. Indeed, Brzezinski stated in *The Grand Chessboard* that the "essential point regarding NATO expansion is that it is a process integrally connected with Europe's own expansion." He simultaneously makes it clear that Russia will not be considered for inclusion except perhaps at some point far into the future after they've been encircled and pass America's definition of democracy and free-market institutions—in other words, after they've accepted a subservient role (117).

Although many countries become NATO members first and then make their way into the EU, plans to reverse that sequence have been formulated with NATO membership not being far behind once EU membership has been established. There are various instruments that the EU utilizes under its European Neighborhood Policy (ENP) to expand EU membership. One is the European Neighborhood and Partnership Instrument (ENPI), which facilitates the conversion of economies to a privatized neoliberal capitalist system. After the privatization of state and public assets takes place in the target country, a Stabilization and Association Process (SAP) is implemented in which these assets are scooped up by French, British, German, Italian, Canadian, and American corporations, thereby preventing economic independence (116).

Recent recipients of the ENPI brand of political and economic manipulation are Ukraine, Georgia, and Moldova via the newfangled Eastern Partnership (EaP) instrument—a kind of preliminary SAP that opens up borders and mandates economic restructuring toward the privatized neocolonial process stated above, but makes no promises of EU membership or any of its reputed privileges. These same three countries have also been wooed by the Eurasian Union (116).

Analysts have recognized a disturbing pattern with countries that resist the ENPI program—they are usually targeted for military operations and attempts at regime change. Until the Ukraine crisis, this had been most apparent in the southern (MED) arm of the ENPI project, which has included Libya and Syria—an example of the fluid and opportunistic definition of European (116).

In 2006, the EU's Security Strategy was absorbed into NATO during its annual summit. The emphasis of that summit was on securing energy resources with the goal of "co-managing the resources of the EU's periphery from North Africa to the Caucasus." Also implied was the goal of redefining the EU's security borders in sync with both Franco-German and Anglo-American economic and geopolitical interests, indicating a rapprochement of the rift that temporarily cropped up between the axes as a result of the Iraq War. Around this time, the idea of ultimately creating a common economic union of Europe and North America was floated, along with the idea of one day totally integrating the EU with NATO (116).

In February 2007, then-Secretary of Defense Robert Gates admitted to Congress that Russia and China were officially viewed as threats. Several days later, the Chief of the Russian Armed Forces, General Yuri Baluyevsky, told the Russian public that they faced a threat from the United States and NATO greater than during the Cold War and urged commensurate preparations. Shortly thereafter, Putin complained during the Munich Conference on Security Policy that NATO was targeting Russia (116):

> I am convinced that the only mechanism that can make decisions about using military force as a last resort is the Charter of the United Nations. And in connection with this, either I did not understand what our colleague, the Italian Defence Minister, just said or what he said was inex-

act. In any case, I understood that the use of force can only
be legitimate when the decision is taken by NATO, the EU,
or the UN. If he really does think so, then we have different
points of view. Or I didn't hear correctly. The use of force
can only be considered legitimate if the decision is sanctioned by the UN. And we do not need to substitute NATO
or the EU for the UN. When the UN will truly unite the
forces of the international community and can really react
to events in various countries, when we will leave behind
this disdain for international law, then the situation will be
able to change. Otherwise the situation will simply result
in a dead end, and the number of serious mistakes will be
multiplied. Along with this, it is necessary to make sure
that international law has a universal character both in the
conception and application of its norms. . . .

I think it is obvious that NATO expansion does not have
any relation with the modernisation of the Alliance itself
or with ensuring security in Europe. On the contrary, it
represents a serious provocation that reduces the level of
mutual trust. And we have the right to ask: against whom
is this expansion intended? And what happened to the
assurances our western partners made after the dissolution of the Warsaw Pact? Where are those declarations
today? No one even remembers them. But I will allow
myself to remind this audience what was said. I would like
to quote the speech of NATO General Secretary Mr
Woerner in Brussels on 17 May 1990. He said at the time
that: "the fact that we are ready not to place a NATO army
outside of German territory gives the Soviet Union a firm
security guarantee." Where are these guarantees? (203)

The configuration of NATO currently reflects a Pan-European entity
ensconced in an Anglo-American security apparatus, but given the aforementioned dynamics and rivalries, it doesn't have to remain that way. Recent

events playing out in Eurasia reflect the strong engagement of Russia with the European Union over the past decade, much to the consternation of the Anglo-American axis, as Nazemroaya states:

> The alliance is increasingly being viewed as a geopolitical extension of America, an arm of the Pentagon, and a synonym for an evolving American Empire. . . . Ultimately NATO is slated to become an institutionalized military force. . . . Nevertheless for every action there is a reaction and NATO's actions have given rise to opposing trends. The Atlantic Alliance is increasingly coming into contact with a zone of Eurasia that is in the process of emerging with its own ideas and alliance. What this will lead to next is the question of the century (116).

With the Trump administration's unilateral withdrawal from the Paris Accord, the Iran Agreement, and the INF Treaty, European leaders may recognize that their interests are not served by being so tightly intertwined with Washington and may choose to accelerate their eventual disentanglement.

Chapter 8: Russia in the 1990s

> The result [of Boris Yeltsin's "shock therapy" program] was the worst economic and social catastrophe ever suffered by a major nation in peacetime. Russia sank into a corrosive economic depression greater than that of the American 1930s. Investment plunged by 80 percent, GDP by almost 50 percent; some two-thirds of Russians were impoverished; the life expectancy of men fell below 59 years; and the population began to decline annually by almost a million people. In 1998, with nothing left to sustain it, despite several large Western loans, the Russian financial system collapsed. State and private banks defaulted on their domestic and foreign obligations, causing still more poverty and widespread misery.
>
> —Stephen F. Cohen (38)

Ambassador Matlock further described conditions in the aftermath of the Soviet dissolution as follows: "In Russia, the Soviet collapse was followed by runaway inflation that destroyed all savings, even worse shortages of essential goods than existed under communism, a sudden rise in crime, and a government that, for several years was unable to pay even [its] miserable pensions on time. Conditions resembled anarchy much more than life in a modern democracy" (85).

When the communist command economy was dismantled, neoliberal economic advisors often insisted that Russians not rely on the state for any economic assistance during the transition, under the guise of leaving communism behind. One illustrative story relayed by Matlock involved a member of the Moscow city council who wanted to encourage small private businesses in his district. He had developed a plan to "offer long-term low-interest loans from the city budget to entrepreneurs. . . . When he explained his idea the Hoover (Institution) economists objected, saying that he must not involve the government. . . . If the government provided loans or subsidies, that would be perpetuating socialism" (85).

The city council member was taken aback and asked where entrepreneurs would get their seed capital. After being told that it would have to come from private sources, he inquired, "You mean from our criminals? If they provide the capital, they control the business. That's not what we want to happen" (85).

Unfortunately, that is what happened.

Exploitative conditions were foisted on Russia when economic advisors from the Harvard Institute for International Development and other advocates of the "Chicago School" of economics colluded with Russian predators like Anatoly Chubais, Mikhail Khodorkovsky, and others who would emerge as Russia's pack of oligarchs (204).

While some Russians were excited at the new possibilities of the democratic transformation they were undertaking, the dissolution of the Soviet Union, which had held together numerous republics that consisted of various ethnic groups and had provided a modest but stable livelihood for most, also resulted in destabilization and trauma. Russians tried to learn how to form and navigate democratic institutions and move toward a privatized economy, yet they had no meaningful experience with either in their long history of authoritarian rule, the last 70 years of which constituted a closed totalitarian state.

Sharon Tennison, American author, citizen diplomat, and founder of the Center for Citizen Initiatives, who has worked all throughout Russia (and the Soviet Union) since 1983, captured the hopes, fears, and confusion of Russians during this harrowing time when she relayed a conversation she had with a Russian scientist named Tatiana in 1991:

> We are not like Americans. We don't have the natural
> instincts your people have cultivated for generations. We
> have another set of instincts, another mentality. It will take

us a very long time . . . and it will be a very painful process for us to learn a new mentality. First, we will be flat on our stomachs for probably seven years, then we will have to hobble on our knees for probably seven more years, then maybe we will get on our feet in the next seven years. We don't know—we can't see what is ahead at the end of this black tunnel. It is a totally unknown future we are walking into (205).

Russians generally have a different ethic about the role of social and economic rights, a different geographic reality they are sensitive to, and a more conservative cultural view due to the closed nature of the Soviet Union, which is barely three decades into the past. Therefore, as Russians embarked on their journey toward democracy and a new economic order—a journey that is still in progress—they could not be expected to become a carbon copy of the United States or even of other European nations. They would need to find their own path consistent with their culture, geography, and history. This is part of the right of self-determination, a right that was not respected by international players in powerful positions who sought more profits, more markets, and more geopolitical power.

Gorbachev's Economic Vision

After overseeing a remarkable period of democratization that included the emergence of a free press, a parliament, an independent constitutional court, and the establishment of local councils and elections, Gorbachev's desire—to be implemented over a period of 10 to 15 years—was to create a mixed economy, similar to the Scandinavian social democracies, consisting of free markets balanced with robust social programs, including public control of certain essential industries (180).

But Gorbachev, recognized by the West to be in a weak position and in need of economic aid and guidance, received a very unsettling message from the leaders of the G7 nations when he attended their annual summit in 1991. They wanted Gorbachev to apply a "shock therapy" economic program like Poland had just undergone, only in an even more extreme form: on a shorter time frame and without any debt relief (180).

To reinforce the message and ratchet up the pressure to accept such a proposal, the International Monetary Fund (IMF)—at the behest of the U.S. Treasury Department—demanded harsh austerity measures in exchange for loans, and the World Bank followed by making similar demands (180).

Gorbachev knew that such a program would never be accepted by the Russian people. As post-Soviet polls indicated, 67 percent of Russians favored worker co-ops as the best way to facilitate privatization, and 79 percent believed the government should play an active role in promoting full employment (180). Consequently, Gorbachev faced a terrible choice. Mainstream media in the United States at the time, such as *The Economist* and *The Washington Post*, openly encouraged Gorbachev to adopt an authoritarian stance to implement what they deemed the necessary policies for creating their definition of a liberal market economy. In fact, they suggested that Russia exercise the "Pinochet Option"—a reference to the brutal Western-backed dictator who had overthrown the democratically elected socialist president of Chile, Salvador Allende, in 1973—if Gorbachev proved to be too squeamish to go along with the program (180).

U.S. economic advisors from the Chicago School, who followed Milton Friedman's scorched-earth philosophy of neoliberal economics that worshipped a mythical market that was unmoored from the needs of humanity, found their Russian Pinochet personified by Boris Yeltsin (180).

Yeltsin: The Russian Pinochet

Yeltsin wasted no time in appointing the Chicago School advisors from the United States, including Jeffrey Sachs, to comprise his economic team (180). Yeltsin, with the help of these advisors, was looking for a quick infusion of cash like that promised by the G7, the IMF, and the World Bank. Of course, the strings attached were well understood at that point. In order to pull this off without facing a backlash from the Russian populace, Yeltsin went to the parliament with an outrageous proposal: to be granted permission to circumvent parliament and rule by decree for one year on the pretext of solving the nation's economic mess. In recognition of the fact that they were desperate for aid, parliament agreed.

In the year that followed, parliament would come to regret their decision. After placing an authoritarian named Yury Skokov in charge of the military and security departments to control potential dissent, Yeltsin embarked quickly and ruthlessly on a plan of lifting price controls on food, cuts to various subsidies, and other policies, which resulted in an inflation rate of 2,500 percent at its height. With the ruble having lost its value, the life savings of millions disappeared, and workers went months with no pay. Many people were forced to sell their belongings on the sidewalk, farms were abandoned, food distribution networks collapsed, store shelves were empty, and the search for food often became the top priority as people spent hours in lines to obtain food imported from the outside (180) (204) (205).

During the first few years of this "shock therapy" program, Russia faced its greatest mortality crisis since WWII, as many middle-aged men drank themselves to death or met an early demise from other health problems related to neglect as well as suicide and homicide. All the sacrifices endured to emerge victorious in the Great Patriotic War, combined with rebuilding the Soviet Union, had suddenly come to nothing. The sense of being needed, particularly strong in Russian and Soviet culture, had evaporated for many of the men in this demographic, as their identity and sense of being needed were rooted in their role as economic provider for their families as well as guardian and beneficiary of the steadily improving "radiant future" under the Soviet state. Between 1993 and 1994 alone, around one million Russian men died prematurely (79).

A Mafia-style criminal group also emerged from the ruins, made up of disenfranchised police officers, KGB officials, and black-market operatives who soon formed protection rackets targeting the small- to mid-sized businesses that had started. The protection money that had to be paid, which increased anytime production went up, stunted the new entrepreneurial class (205).

By November 1992, Anatoly Chubais had been appointed as Yeltsin's economic tsar. He began working with the Harvard Institute for International

Development (HIID), which was funded by USAID and now headed by Jeffrey Sachs. One of HIID's cheerleaders in the Clinton administration was Lawrence Summers at Treasury. The HIID team and its enablers included former World Bank consultant Jonathan Hay, who had previously served as a senior legal advisor to the Russian state's privatization committee (GKI) and would now be serving as HIID's general director in Moscow (204).

In late 1991 and early 1992, the Chubais economic team concentrated the accumulation of property into a few well-connected hands in contravention of a privatization program previously passed in the country to prevent corruption. One of their projects was a voucher privatization plan paid for with $325 million in U.S. taxpayer money. It is reported that hundreds of investment funds simply resold the vouchers to domestic criminals, Western investment banks, and global money launderers. These schemes were the impetus for Yeltsin's rule by decree. Many of the decrees were written by Hay and his cronies (204) (206).

When the year was up in March 1993, with popular support, parliament attempted to rein in Yeltsin's abuses by repealing the decree powers they had granted him. In response, Yeltsin declared a state of emergency; however, the constitutional court ruled that Yeltsin's abuse of power violated the constitution on eight counts. A short time later, parliament passed a budget that would put the brakes on the austerity measures demanded by the IMF. Yeltsin, with the support of Washington—particularly, Lawrence Summers at the Treasury Department, who put additional pressure on the IMF to rescind a major loan to Russia—issued a decree dissolving parliament and abolishing the constitution. Parliamentarians then called a special session and voted to impeach Yeltsin (180).

With President Clinton continuing to support him, the U.S. Congress voting to provide $2.5 billion to his government, and the American mainstream media cheering him on while painting the parliamentarians in Orwellian terms as communist hangers-on and backwater anti-democrats, Yeltsin sent troops in to surround the parliament building and ordered all utilities cut. As Naomi Klein reported in her 2007 book, *The Shock Doctrine: The Rise of Disaster Capitalism,* Boris Kagarlitsky, director of the Institute of Global-

ization Studies in Moscow, and present at these events, told her that supporters of Russian democracy

> were coming in by the thousands trying to break the
> blockade. There were two weeks of peaceful demonstra-
> tions confronting the troops and police forces, which led
> to partial unblocking of the parliament building, with
> people able to bring food and water inside. Peaceful resis-
> tance was growing more popular and gaining broader
> support every day (180).

Word came out at this time that Polish citizens had just voted out the
party that had forced "shock therapy" on them. Consequently, Yeltsin's advisors saw early elections to break the standoff as too risky. Shortly thereafter,
Yeltsin's troops fired machine guns into a crowd of mostly unarmed demonstrators who had marched to a major television station to demand announcement of their heightened opposition to Yeltsin's rule. This was followed by
Yeltsin's orders to storm the parliament building and destroy it. As Klein sums
up the episode that killed around 500 people, wounded 1,000, and forever
changed the direction of Russia:

> Communism may have collapsed without the firing of a
> single shot, but Chicago-style capitalism, it turned out,
> required a great deal of gunfire to defend itself: Yeltsin
> called in five thousand soldiers, dozens of tanks and
> armored personnel carriers, helicopters and elite shock
> troops armed with automatic machine guns—all to
> defend Russia's new capitalist economy from the grave
> threat of democracy (180).

A sample of headlines from U.S. media outlets reporting on this turn
of events included "Victory Seen for Democracy" by *The Washington Post*
and "Russia Escapes a Return to the Dungeon of Its Past" in *The Boston Globe*.
Clinton even sent Secretary of State Warren Christopher to Moscow to con-
gratulate Yeltsin on keeping Russia safe for predatory capitalism (180).

By contrast, Putin has tended toward a soft form of authoritarianism when faced with certain problems. The West never tires of bemoaning and exaggerating these tendencies, with casual epithets of "thug," "gangster," and "Stalin" tossed about; however, he has never rolled tanks into the streets, ordered Russian troops to fire on their own people, or destroyed government buildings.

Yeltsin continued to steamroll over any last shreds of democracy by dissolving elected bodies, suspending the constitution and the court, ordering military patrol of the streets, and imposing censorship (some civil liberties were later reinstated). This turn of events, it should be noted, led to the 1993 Constitution, still in effect, that provides for a strong executive and a weak legislature—a political structure inherited by Putin but not initiated by him.

Meanwhile, freed from the constraints of parliament, the Chicago School devotees—led by the HIID team—ran amok, implementing deep budget cuts, removing more price controls, and privatizing faster and more broadly.

The HIID team facilitated Chubais's and other Russian predators' ability to create and fund private organizations whereby they could circumvent the Russian parliament and other regulatory agencies, or be considered Russian or American depending on what was advantageous in terms of attaining wealth and resources or avoiding penalties and taxes (204).

In 1995, Chubais also ran the notorious loans-for-shares program that auctioned off state-owned companies worth billions for token amounts to a select group of Russians; however, the Harvard Management Company (HMC), which manages the university's endowment, and George Soros—both non-Russian—were allowed to partake in the pillaging. Both HMC and Soros ended up with significant shares in one of Russia's largest steel mills as well as in Sidanko Oil. Soros was involved in other speculative ventures in Russia and was reportedly eyeing similar vulture opportunities in post-coup Ukraine (204) (207).

Western bankers enabled these kleptocrats to keep the proceeds in offshore accounts, thereby evading taxes. Klein describes the turn of events as follows:

> A clique of nouveaux billionaires, many of whom were to become part of the group universally known as the "oligarchs" for their imperial levels of wealth and power, teamed up with Yeltsin's Chicago Boys and stripped the country of nearly everything of value, moving the enormous profits offshore at a rate of $2 billion a month. Before shock therapy, Russia had no millionaires; by 2003, the number of Russian billionaires had risen to seventeen, according to *Forbes* list (180).

The oligarchs' wealth and power facilitated Yeltsin's reelection in 1996. In fact, two associates of Chubais were caught red-handed leaving a government building with $500,000 cash for Yeltsin's campaign. Tape recordings later emerged in which Chubais and his accomplices are heard discussing how to hide evidence of their illicit activities and how to use PR tactics to deflect accusations of wrongdoing in the political sphere (180) (207) (204).

Between 1992 and 1996, HIID alone received $57.7 million from U.S. taxpayers via USAID for their "economic development" of Russia. The vast majority of that money was granted absent any competitive bidding, all with the blessing of five different agencies of the U.S. government, including the Treasury Department and the National Security Council (204).

By now, the reader can probably deduce why Yeltsin—the hero of the West—was voted the least popular leader of the last 100 years by the Russian people. At the time of his departure from office, 90 percent of Russians polled did not trust him and 53 percent thought he should be put on trial (208) (38).

There were, no doubt, other options that would have been more fair and acceptable among the Russian people. As mentioned previously, a full two-thirds of Russians polled during the transition period preferred co-ops as a more equitable means of privatization. An even higher percentage advocated for a government role in support of economic justice. Similarly, there were programs in development by Russians that would have facilitated a more distributist approach to privatization. For example, there was the idea for modest government-subsidized loans for the start of small businesses in various localities that was put forth by the Moscow city council member and shot down by Western advisors. Another program was designed by a Russian free-market economist named Larisa Piasheva. Her program would have distributed property among average Russian citizens and would not have been dependent upon Western loans.

As Anne Williamson, a long-time American journalist who specialized in covering the Soviet Union and Russia, stated in her testimony before Congress on this topic in September 1999:

> When the administration says it had no choice but to rely upon the bad actors it did select for American largesse, Congress should call Larisa Piasheva. How different today's Russia might have been had only the Bush administration and the many Western advisors from the IMF, the World Bank, the International Finance Corporation, the European Bank for Reconstruction and Development and the Harvard Institute for International Development then on the ground in Moscow chosen to champion Ms. Piasheva's vision of a rapid disbursement of property to the people rather than to the "golden children" of the Soviet *nomenklatura* [elite bureaucrats].
>
> . . . Clearly, an equitable and transparent privatization that would have delivered property widely to Russia's many eager hands should have preceded the freeing of prices. And during privatization, native producers should have enjoyed some protectionism at least, as did developing American industry and manufacture in the 19th century.
>
> . . . Today the Clinton administration's chief defense for their hand in Russia's ruin is that somebody had to keep the communists at bay. But there were no communists in Russia by late 1991, only nascent investment bankers looking to nail down a stake any which way (206).

Chapter 9: The Putin and Medvedev Era in Russia

Economic Reforms of the Putin and Medvedev Era

The conditions described in the previous chapter constitute the mess that Vladimir Putin faced when he took over as president of the Russian Federation in 2000. It should be noted that Putin started his presidency having to navigate these crises amidst ruthless political clans within the Kremlin that were inherited from the Yeltsin era, without the support of a political party, and with the very real threat of being assassinated or overthrown if he trusted the wrong person or stepped too heavily on the wrong toes.

Some observers who were on the ground in Russia during this time believe that this was the reason Putin brought in trusted, dependable, and often lifelong friends and colleagues from St. Petersburg to comprise his political team (205). Western media, out of ignorance or malice, began referring to these new Putin appointees as the St. Petersburg "Chekists"—a derogatory reference to early Soviet-era secret police who carried out the "Red Terror."

Putin's team gradually implemented policies that stabilized the country, improved infrastructure and standards of living for many Russians, and led to a decrease in crime and chaos.

Sharon Tennison has visited different parts of Russia regularly over her three-decades-long career there. She describes the changes over the past two decades as follows:

During this time, I've traveled throughout Russia several times every year, and have watched the country slowly change under Putin's watch. Taxes were lowered, inflation lessened, and laws slowly put in place. Schools and hospitals began improving. Small businesses were growing, agriculture was showing improvement, and stores were becoming stocked with food.

Highways were being laid across the country, new rails and modern trains appeared even in far out places, and the banking industry was becoming dependable. Russia was beginning to look like a decent country—certainly not where Russians hoped it to be long term, but improving incrementally for the first time in their memories (209).

Tennison observed the same improvements starting to appear in areas farther away from the major cities of Moscow and St. Petersburg:

In September [2013] I traveled out to the Ural Mountains, spent time in Ekaterinburg, Chelyabinsk and Perm. We traveled between cities via autos and rail––the fields and forests look healthy, small towns sport new paint and construction. Old concrete Khrushchev block houses are giving way to new multi-story private residential complexes which are lovely. High-rise business centers, fine hotels and great restaurants are now common place––and ordinary Russians frequent these places. Two and three story private homes rim these Russian cities far from Moscow.

We visited new museums, municipal buildings and huge super markets. Streets are in good repair, highways are new and well-marked now, service stations look like those dotting American highways. In January [2014] I went to Novosibirsk out in Siberia where similar new architecture was noted. Streets were kept navigable with constant snowplowing, modern lighting kept the city bright all night, lots of new traffic lights have appeared. It is astounding to me how much progress Russia has made in the past 14 years since an unknown man with no experience walked into Russia's presidency and took over a country that was flat on its belly (209).

Moreover, those who didn't have an agenda of Russia-bashing acknowledged the impressive infrastructure at the Sochi Olympics, including "state-of-the-art bridges, roads and tunnels." The majority of this infrastructure was permanent for the city (210).

During my first visit to Russia in October 2015, I visited the city of Krasnodar near the Black Sea. Formerly a provincial town in a largely agricultural region, Krasnodar had recently evolved into a cosmopolitan city that was the eighth largest in the country. It saw such a high rate of civic construction in 2014 that it surpassed even Moscow. As a consequence of the challenges presented by this rapid development, Krasnodar's citizens started a successful initiative to force local officials to be more responsive to the public's needs when making development decisions.

During my travel throughout the city, including a guided tour, what was visible was a clean and orderly city with green spaces, a pedestrian thoroughfare with Western and Russian music piped in, well-groomed people dressed in attractive attire, families out shopping and partaking of various forms of entertainment, and couples walking hand in hand. The city also had an active Rotary Club with engineers, lawyers, educators, and small- to medium-business owners as members who were engaged with their community.

When Putin, at the outset of his first term as president, met with his circle of economic advisors to come up with a plan to restore stability and improvement, it is reported that, due to the fact that he was a novice, he spent a lot of the time at these meetings listening and asking questions. The one question he consistently asked when a policy was being considered was what its effect on social welfare would be (128).

As we have seen in the previous chapters exploring Russia's history, the concept of the "collective" interest was not merely a communist contrivance—it has deep roots in Russian culture. Putin himself mentioned this cultural difference with the United States, with its emphasis on the individual, when asked during a 2013 interview with Russian journalist Oksana Boyko (211).

Some Westerners eschew the idea that Russians have a distinct outlook that places less emphasis on individualism and is more interested in social connections and being needed, which provide a sense of meaning. However, as evidenced by surveys cited by ethnographer Michelle Parsons in her book *Dying Unneeded: The Cultural Context of the Russian Mortality Crisis*, there is a deep cultural interest in a meaningful life. This is crucial to understanding the consequences of having social relationships torn asunder via the various upheavals of the 20th century, particularly the dissolution of Soviet society in the 1990s. That dissolution produced a trauma that translated into millions of premature deaths, especially among Russian men. Women were also affected by the mortality crisis but on a smaller scale, as well as in a qualitatively different way (79).

Many older Russians have expressed nostalgia for the Soviet era because during that time they felt a relative sense of belonging and common identity as well as stability (38). And, according to a 2014 Levada poll, a majority of Russians would still rather live in a country that prioritizes social equality than one that prioritizes more personal achievement (212).

Putin understood that social welfare was something that had to be addressed, both in terms of creating long-term stability, increased living standards, and life expectancy, and in reflecting the values of the Russian people.

The economic team Putin put together included, among others, lawyer-businessman German Gref, Deputy Finance Minister Alexei Kudrin, and liberal economist Andrei Illarionov. One of the major problems to be addressed was solving Russia's revenue crisis, which was due to much of Russia's wealth leaving the country along with poor people refusing to pay high tax rates on meager incomes.

Subsequently, they came up with a plan to reduce the tax rate in the hopes that it would be paid. Personal income tax rates were decreased from as high as 30 percent to a flat rate of 13 percent. Corporate rates were dropped from 35 percent to 24 percent. It should be noted that the IMF did not like the plan. When the Russian government stated that it would stick with the plan regardless, the IMF left the country (128).

It was a gamble that paid off, as Russians started to pay their taxes and eventually the government had surpluses. Additionally, Putin had ordered the oligarchs to pay taxes and stay out of politics if they wanted to keep the loot they'd acquired from the Yeltsin years, which also added to the revenue stream.

A revolutionary land code was established, allowing for the buying and selling of residential property. A new legal code that sought to fight money laundering and to break up certain monopolies was implemented— though some monopolies remained, namely in the fossil fuel industry (128).

The Partnership and Cooperation Agreement (PCA) that went into effect in 1997 paved the way for increased trade relations between Russia and the EU. Prior to the Ukraine crisis and the post-sanctions recession, trade consisted mainly of mineral fuel products (77.3 percent) along with some manufactured goods, chemicals, and raw materials, worth 115 billion euros ($150.6 billion). EU exports to Russia were worth 65.6 billion euros ($86 billion). By 2012, overall trade between Russia and the EU totaled 325 billion euros ($426 billion), with the EU as Russia's largest trading partner at 41 percent. Trade between Russia and Germany alone in 2013 amounted to 76 billion euros ($100 billion) (213).

From 1999 to 2008, Russia's GDP increased by an average of 7 percent per year, and a stabilization or rainy day fund was established that included a $140 billion reserve fund and a $30 billion National Welfare Fund to ensure that pensions could be paid. The rate of Russians living in poverty decreased from 30 percent in 2000 to 14 percent in 2008, with average wages having quintupled. Moreover, Russia decreased its inflation rate from 20 percent to 9 percent (128) (214) (215).

By 2006, Russia had paid off most of its external debt, including all money owed to the IMF and the Paris Club (216) (217).

Financial Crisis of 2008

Russia refused to play the debt and austerity game and saw positive results. In response to the 2008 financial meltdown, Russia implemented a large stimulus package facilitated by the rainy day funds mentioned above. Public debt as of 2013 was 7.7 percent of GDP compared to 72.5 percent for the United States. The Russian government had a policy of not borrowing more than 1 percent of GDP and kept reserve funds at a 7 percent minimum and had been running virtually no budget deficit (128) (214).

From the post-crisis period of 2009 to 2013, all 10 of Russia's top exports (mineral oils [58%], iron and steel, pearls, gems and precious metals, fertilizers, machinery, wood, and aluminum) posted double-digit increases. These gains ranged from 24 percent for aluminum to 257 percent for non-industrial diamonds (218).

Furthermore, Russia's unemployment rate was 5.8 percent in 2013—which was lower at the time than both the United States (7.4 percent) and the EU (12 percent) (218) (219) (220).

In early September 2014, the World Economic Forum's Global Competitiveness Report showed that Russia had gained 11 points and was among 3 nations that had recorded increased values in all areas since 2010, representing Russia's biggest jump in that report's findings (221).

Economy Still a Work in Progress

Despite the phenomenal success enjoyed by Russia from 2000 to 2013 and the post-recession rebound since 2017—largely achieved by not following the neoliberal prescriptions of the West—Medvedev and Putin have both admitted that Russia's economy is still too dependent upon fossil fuels and raw materials exports.

Putin has also conceded on several occasions since 2013 that Russia's productivity has lagged behind other developed nations (214) (222).

And, of course, there is the continuing issue of corruption in government bureaucracy and in the business community, which erodes confidence and increases costs to those wanting to do business in Russia, whether they're Russians or foreigners. The Global Competitiveness Report cited above noted that a "major overhaul" was still needed to eradicate corruption and favoritism (221). In his December 2013 Annual Address to the Federal Assembly, Putin pushed for the Duma to draft a law streamlining an arbitration court system for resolution of economic conflicts. This law would also develop a federal portal that would provide transparent information on all inspections of businesses and the publication of a national rating of investment climate in the nation's various regions. The portal has since been implemented.

To grasp the possible significance of the portal, one must understand the background and nature of corruption in Russia. Ninety percent of all corruption throughout the country is estimated to be at the local level (205). Along with the powerful class of oligarchs that came to control the Kremlin in the 1990s were the 89 regional governors throughout the Russian Federation who ruled their respective fiefdoms, enriching themselves through massive bribery. Lower on the food chain were local officials who earned paltry salaries, bilked new entrepreneurs for bribes in exchange for signing off on official documents, and contrived inspections on charges of flimsy or nonexistent violations, requiring the payment of additional bribes for clearance.

Part of the reason this kind of corruption persists is due to the strong historical roots of getting essential things done via "connections" and its associated prestige rather than the rule of law as a foundation. As Jane Henderson notes in her contextual analysis of the Russian Constitution and law: "The dividing line between reciprocal assistance and corruption is difficult to draw, as the long-held tradition of mutual exchange of favors still holds sway, and personal trust and other informal relations are given higher priority than formal arrangements" (223). This was the case in tsarist Russia, as tributes were typically paid in the form of goods or money to officials.

As detailed in Chapter 1, due to Russia's sprawling geographic size and its lack of a developed transportation system, interaction with the outside world and the attendant exposure to new ideas was hindered until the 19th century. Russians' relationship with governmental authority was modeled on the administrative state system inherited from the Mongols. Consequently, their social contract had never been that of citizens with rights but as subjects that were granted varying amounts of social protection, and later some limited decision-making within autonomous peasant communities and then zemstvos, in exchange for submission to state authority. That submission was enforced by the harsh bureaucracy.

This arrangement of deference to authority and reliance on "connections" to obtain necessities continued under the Soviet system, with deference to authority demanded in exchange for security, stability, and a degree of social protection. The Communist Party bureaucracy also had party managers who lorded over their respective regions (205) (5).

A further step to address corruption has involved policies incentivizing the repatriation of Russian wealth that has been lost to offshoring. A key reason for these policies has been to keep money in Russia to provide internal financing to bring productive capacity online for import substitution and increased general industrial and technical buildup, which requires internal credit sources (224). As will be discussed later, import substitution was one of Russia's key responses to Western sanctions, along with increasing its economic relations with non-Western countries, particularly China.

While these repatriation policies have had only nominal success (225), financing for import substitution has been made available.

A common response in the Anglo-American media to Russia's post-sanctions retaliatory measure of banning most agricultural imports from the United States and EU was that Russians would go hungry and were, therefore, shooting themselves in the foot. Within a matter of days of the announcement, however, numerous Latin American countries, namely Argentina and Brazil, got in line to fill the gap, as well as China, which started selling produce directly to Russia (226) (227).

More importantly, according to the Food and Agriculture Organization, Russia ranked as one of the top three producers in the world for a range of agricultural products, from various fruits and vegetables to grains, potatoes, and poultry (226). As of 2018, it was the world's top exporter of wheat (228). The government has also had plans in place since 2013 to significantly boost the country's already respectable production of organic produce from small farms and gardens.

Natural Society reported in May 2014 that 35 million Russian families are growing an impressive percentage of Russia's fruits and vegetables on 20 million acres:

> According to some statistics, they grow 92% of the entire countries' potatoes, 77% of its vegetables, 87% of its fruit, and feed 71% of the entire population from privately owned organic farms or house gardens all across the country. These aren't huge Agro-farms run by pharmaceutical companies; these are small family farms and less-than-an-acre gardens (229).

By autumn 2017, Putin had publicly set a goal for Russia to become the world's top producer and exporter of organic agriculture. In summer 2018, the Russian president signed legislation creating official standards, labeling and certification procedures for organic products produced for commercial sale in Russia that went into effect in 2020. Government support will be available to organic farmers, and a public registry will be created listing certified producers (230).

The agricultural sanctions created some immediate problems, mainly temporary shortages of certain meat products and price increases due to the need to work out infrastructure issues to accommodate imports from countries at greater distances.

But Russians did not go hungry, as I witnessed plenty of food in markets, from street vendors, and in restaurants in all cities I visited during my trips in 2015 and 2017. There was, however, concern over price increases.

Sharon Tennison, during her trip to Moscow and St. Petersburg in September 2014, reported that the general attitude toward Western sanctions was as follows:

> The general outlook of Russians I spoke with is one of quiet confidence, saying that sanctions will turn out good for Russia in the long run--that Russia must become self-sufficient--remarking that Russia became infatuated with foreign products in the 1990s. At that time they felt Russia didn't need to manufacture high-end products, that they could purchase them from other countries. However, the situation has changed. Today production has become the "in" discussion wherever one goes. The sanctions have helped bring this about. Several Russians remarked that they hoped the sanctions lasted for three years or more, since that would give Russians sufficient time to learn to manufacture formerly imported items themselves. The Russian government is offering financial support to entrepreneurs who are ready to move into consumer production (231).

In order to provide the most accurate and comprehensive assessment of the effect of Western sanctions on Russia over the past five years, University of Birmingham professor Richard Connolly, in his 2018 book, *Russia's Response to Sanctions: How Western Economic Statecraft is Reshaping Political Economy in Russia*, describes how Russia's economy actually works in order to provide a contextual framework for understanding the success or failure of the West's policy. Consequently, he concluded that the ultimate effect of the sanctions is likely not what was intended by Washington policymakers.

Connolly explains that the Russian economy can be divided up into roughly four sectors.

Sector A generates revenue, or "rents," in the form of taxes, fees, and other benefits that support Sector B. Sector A is comprised largely of fossil fuel and mineral extraction industries but also includes large "agricultural conglomerates," manufacturers of nuclear power generation equipment, and some defense industry manufacturers. Economic actors in Sector A are highly profitable and competitive in the global market, which they are successfully integrated into. The state also plays a strong role in Sector A industries either through significant ownership stakes, as is the case with Gazprom, Rosneft, and Rosatom, or through strong personal ties between private owners and the political class, as is the case with Lukoil and Novatek (232).

Sector B is comprised of economic actors that are dependent upon the rents generated by Sector A. This includes companies that are generally not competitive globally and provide goods and services to the domestic market rather than for export. Despite state assistance, they do not always generate consistent profits. Examples include automotive manufacturing, shipbuilding, fossil fuel equipment, and some defense manufacturing. Other beneficiaries of Sector A include state bureaucracy workers and pensioners (232). It is estimated that Sectors A and B together comprise around 70 percent of the Russian economy (232).

Sector C is independent of Sectors A and B and includes large construction companies, retail and business services, and various small- to medium-sized enterprises (SMEs) in retail, transportation, business support, and communications technology. Because these businesses are outside of the Sector A and B relationship, they're dependent upon successful profit-making and tend to encourage more competition, innovation, and productivity, though they are vulnerable to various forms of outside corruption and unfair takeovers (232). One successful example of a Sector C industry that enjoys significant and growing export rates is computer software (232).

The last sector is the financial sector, which, as Connolly points out, developed virtually out of nothing over the past three decades into a system of numerous, largely state-owned or state-influenced banks that provide a wide range of services. However, Russia's overall financial sector is small in comparison with other middle-income countries, with Sector A and B entities getting preferential treatment in receipt of the limited credit that is available. There are few small banks or other financial institutions that can provide SMEs with credit, as is reflected in the fact that, as of 2016, two-thirds of assets and liabilities were owned by large state-controlled banks (232).

As Connolly notes, the obvious disadvantages of this system of political economy are hobbled competition, innovation, and productivity. It also limits the development of SMEs.

The advantages, however, include support of domestic employment and the funding of social programs. Perhaps most importantly, this system has also enabled the Russian state to cushion the country from the worst potential effects of Western sanctions and even encourage the stimulation of alternative economic investment, which has strengthened agriculture and some industry and finance.

In terms of how Russia responded to Western sanctions, Connolly provides the following summary:

> The Russian response was multifaceted and included the securitization of strategic areas of economic policy, a concerted effort to support import substitution in strategic sectors of the economy, and vigorous efforts to cultivate economic relations with non-Western countries, especially in Asia (232).

Securitization officially justified certain policies using national security and subordinating certain other objectives in the economic realm that might be prioritized under "normal" circumstances (232). In order to increase Russia's economic independence or sovereignty, policies of import substitution and "diversifying" its range of foreign economic partners and the extent of those relations were implemented.

Import substitution involved increasing the proportion of goods and services in Russia that were produced domestically. As an official policy, it was begun in earnest after the imposition of Western sanctions. By 2015, the government was providing federal budget funding, facilitation of loans, and access to state procurement funds as well as institutional support to specific sectors of the economy, which included the provision of legal and regulatory frameworks for such policies (232). In 2016, a plan was presented by Russia's minister for industry and trade that encompassed "2,000 projects across nineteen branches of the economy. These projects were to be carried out between 2016 and 2020" (232).

By early 2018, there were 2,500 projects worth $38 billion to be completed by 2020 (233). The areas of priority for industrial manufacturing included power equipment, oil and gas equipment, machine tool and civil aviation manufacturing, and agricultural machinery, all of which had import levels between 50 percent and 90 percent (233).

Gains in domestic food production were seen quickly as Russia became the world's number one supplier of wheat in early 2018 (228), now capturing over half of the world's market (234). Wheat exports continue to increase; sales to other nations increased by 80 percent during the first half of 2018 over the same period in 2017 (234).

Diversifying foreign economic relations is pretty self-explanatory, and in this case it focused heavily on countries in Asia such as China, India, Vietnam, and South Korea, as well as Turkey and Latin America (232). Connolly points out that Russia did not present this as a "zero-sum" action and still conducts most of its trade with various European countries (46 percent of exports and 38 percent of imports) (232). This fact should be considered when assessing the credibility of accusations against Putin that he wants to destroy the EU.

China, however, has now become Russia's single largest trading partner, accounting for 10 percent of Russia's exports and 22 percent of its imports (232). But this figure alone does not begin to provide the full picture of Russia's increasing partnership with Eurasia in general and China in particular.

According to *Asia Times* correspondent Pepe Escobar, who has been closely following the trend of Eurasian economic integration for several years, what's known in Russia as the "Greater Eurasia" project was presented to the Council of Ministers in Moscow in 2019 and is now largely accepted as an entrenched foreign policy guide for Russia's future.

After interviewing three top Russian academics and policymakers who have been championing the Greater Eurasia project for years, Escobar explained that the policy would not preclude continuing a relationship with Europe, recognizing that the Russian elite has been intimately influenced by

European culture and trade and technology since the time of Peter the Great, but is meant to be a rebalancing toward the inevitable economic center that will soon be led by Asia and to serve as a "civilizational bridge" between east and west.

Situated as it is geographically, Russia is in a perfect position to play this role, serving as a cultural connector between the Enlightenment and the Mongols and as a physical connector between Europe and Asia. In terms of the latter, Russia will play a pivotal role in connecting China's New Silk Road (aka Belt and Road Initiative, or BRI) through Russia and Central Asia and into Europe.

> Greater Eurasia and the Belt and Road Initiative are bound to merge. Eurasia is crisscrossed by mighty mountain ranges such as the Pamirs and deserts like the Taklamakan and the Karakum. The best land route runs via Russia or via Kazakhstan to Russia. In crucial soft power terms, Russia remains the lingua franca of Mongolia, Central Asia and the Caucasus.

> And that leads us to the utmost importance of an upgraded Trans-Siberian railway—Eurasia's current connectivity core. In parallel, the transportation systems of the Central Asia "stans" are closely integrated with the Russian network of roads; all that is bound to be enhanced in the near future by Chinese-built high-speed rail.

> . . . And all across the spectrum, Moscow aims at maximizing return[s] on the crown jewels of the Russian Far East: agriculture, water resources, minerals, lumber, oil and gas. Construction of liquefied natural gas (LNG) plants in Yamal vastly benefits China, Japan and South Korea (235).

Iran, Turkey, and India are all pivoting toward Eurasia as well, with a free trade agreement between Iran and the Russian-led Eurasian Economic Union having just been approved. Iran is also playing a role in the International North-South Transport Corridor (INSTC) to facilitate closer economic cooperation between Russia and India (235), who have enjoyed cordial relations and strong trade in defense for decades.

But Russia and China's "comprehensive strategic partnership"—as it is referred to officially by both countries—is much more than economic. In an unprecedented move, China sent 3,000 troops to join Russia in a 2018 military exercise to practice countering NATO in Eastern Europe (236). In July 2019, "Russian and Chinese bombers conducted their first long-range joint air patrol in the Asia-Pacific" (237). To reinforce the strategic importance of Russian-Chinese relations, the day after these maneuvers, the Chinese government published a "white paper" in which it promised to further increase military cooperation between the two countries, partly as a result of the United States's "undermining" of regional stability (238).

A former senior national security official in Russia described the relationship to *National Interest* correspondent Graham Allison as a "functional military alliance." Allison elaborated that "Russian and Chinese generals' staffs now have candid, detailed discussions about the threat US nuclear modernization and missile defense pose to each of their strategic deterrents" (236).

Allison also reiterated that Russia has lifted its decades-long withholding of advanced military technologies to its eastern neighbor, selling China the S-400 air defense system and partnering in research and development on rocket engines and drones. Furthermore, Russia and China vote the same on the UN Security Council 98 percent of the time, and Russia has supported all Chinese vetoes since 2007.

As evidence that the Russian public will likely support the Greater Eurasia project and Russia's diversifying of economic partnerships in an eastern direction, recent polling reveals that 69 percent of Russians hold a positive view of China—the exact same percentage that hold a negative view of the United States. Two-thirds of Russians identify the United States as their nemesis, while only 2 percent identify China that way (236).

Now that we've explored how Russia has actually responded to Western sanctions, we can turn to the question of how effective those sanctions have been in terms of what their presumed intent was. As Connolly enumerates, in addition to sending a symbolic message of disapproval of Russia's actions and to show a united front among Western allies, the intent among some policymakers was to cause significant economic harm to Russia—not just as a deterrent to further "bad behavior," but with the idea that this would encourage political revolt among targeted Russian elites that would endanger Putin's government and result in regime change with the installment of a new Russian leader that would be more amenable to Washington's desires.

The answer is that Washington has once again—in its hubris and ignorance—been hoisted on its own petard. As British scholar on Russia Paul Robinson sums up in his review of Connolly's book:

> First, it [sanctions] has created a system that "is less vulnerable to external pressure" than that which existed before, in that it is more independent from the West. Second, it has accelerated a shift in Russia's place in the global economy towards the East. This obviously has political ramifications which Connolly does not explore. Somewhat perversely, Western sanctions have reduced, not increased, Western leverage over Russia. This is probably permanent (239).

Moreover, since Russia has weathered the sanctions reasonably well, even using them to strengthen certain sectors of its economy in the long term, the sanctions have likely failed as a tool of deterrence. As Connolly states:

> How can policymakers expect sanctions to act as a credible deterrent to third countries when the target country in any given instance might appear to be coping or even flourishing under sanctions? In short, a significant and negative impact on the target economy is a necessary, although not sufficient, condition of sanctions to be effective (232).

For the policymakers implementing sanctions, it might have been worthwhile to have been briefed by real experts on what Russia's economy was actually like. If they'd done so, they might have realized that sanctions were likely to have a limited effect on a country that, as analyst Patrick Armstrong has pointed out, has a "full-service economy." In other words, Russia has demonstrated that it has both the natural and human resources to build sophisticated infrastructure, weapons and defense capabilities, a space station, military and commercial aircraft, heavy trucks and passenger cars, to provide energy and the attendant infrastructure, and to feed its people.

Therefore, beliefs that Russia is a "gas station posing as a country" or that it was still somehow frozen in the 1990s would not have underpinned policy decisions that ultimately failed.

Russia's current political economy reflects the fact that its present leadership, under Putin, prioritizes certain goals or values, such as stability, security, employment levels, and funding of social programs and infrastructure over economic efficiency for its own sake. In the short- to medium-term, that has not been a bad thing.

After two years of post-sanctions recession, Russia posted a growth rate of 1.5 percent in 2017, 2.3 percent in 2018, and was projected to grow at a rate of 1.2 percent in 2019 (240) (241).

As of 2017, Russia's debt was 12.6 percent of GDP (242) compared to 105.4 percent for the United States (243). Russia did run a budget deficit of 1.5 percent of GDP (244) for that year, but enjoyed a budget surplus for 2018 (245).

Currently, Russia's top exports are oil, natural gas, coal, aluminum, wheat, machinery (including computers), timber, gold, diamonds, and frozen fish (246).

Prior to the presidential election of 2018, the minimum wage was increased by 43 percent to match the subsistence level (247). By June 2019, Russia's unemployment rate was down to 4.5 percent (248).

Additionally, Russia advanced two more places to rank 43rd out of 198 countries in the Global Competitiveness Index, with high marks in the areas of "stable economics, a large market size, information and communications technology adoption and human capital" (240). Moreover, Russia advanced almost 100 places in seven years on the World Bank's ease of doing business index, to 28th place as of 2019. This ranking reflects how simple and convenient it is to start a business, obtain construction permits and credit, access utilities, and pay taxes in a given country (249). The World Bank also acknowledges that bureaucratic inspections are still problematic in Russia since they remain open to abuse rather than being used as a tool for enforcement of legitimate regulations (250).

However successful the government's stewardship of the economy has been in the face of multiple challenges, it must be acknowledged that the system is vulnerable in the sense that it is highly dependent upon the maneuverings of one person or a small group of people.

It should be considered that whoever comes after Putin may not be as judicious and conscientious of an arbiter of the various and powerful interests at play. What if Putin suddenly dies or doesn't groom an effective successor? Medvedev, who is now the least trusted politician in Russia (251), didn't turn out so well.

Although the Putin government has done a good job of turning lemons into lemonade in terms of the sanctions, recent polling from the end of 2018 reveals that a majority of Russians are still greatly concerned about high prices and overall economic well-being (252). That general economic concern has continued.

Putin's approval ratings dropped from his high of 89 percent to a still very respectable 66 percent in 2018, largely due to the government increasing the retirement age. Demographic pressure motivated the unpopular move, which resulted in some protests that summer that eventually petered out. But, despite the Russian public being largely resigned to the new reality, there is still widespread discontent with the decision (253).

After years of Russia making consistent headway on the demographic problem, recent statistics show a decline in the birth rate. However, gains in life expectancy seem to be holding steady, as death rates from homicide, suicide, and alcohol-related issues continue to be much lower than during the late Soviet era and the 1990s (254).

Putin is aware that more needs to be done to increase economic gains and standards of well-being. In his 2018 Address to the Federal Assembly, which Western media and commentators showered attention on due to Putin's unveiling of new high-tech weapons, he actually focused the first two-thirds of his speech on an ambitious social program.

In the speech, Putin set goals to be achieved by the end of his next term, or shortly thereafter, in the following areas: reducing the poverty rate by half, raising pensions, increasing per-capita GDP by 50 percent, increasing life expectancy from 73 to at least 80, increasing infrastructure development in small to medium cities farther out from the metropolises, increasing rural development, improving housing access for five million families a year by building more housing and lowering mortgage interest rates, improving regional and local roads, expanding the network of regional airports, expanding internet connection to all Russians, doubling investment in health care, increasing investment in science and technology education, reducing pollution and launching major conservation projects, building community cultural programs throughout the country, improving the business climate and support for SMEs, and continuing to develop the Eurasian Project (222).

Democracy and the Rule of Law in Russia

A 2015 poll by the independent Levada Center revealed that 66 percent of Russians feel free, and 68 percent don't believe it is likely that Russia will revert back to dictatorship (255). To understand why Russians may see themselves as fairly free, it is important to understand not only their history of authoritarian rule but also some facts and observations about Russia that run counter to the narrative often presented in our mainstream corporate media.

When I visited Russia for the first time, one of the first things I observed was that the police in both Moscow and St. Petersburg did not carry guns, only batons. I asked some Russians about this and was told that if an officer had a special assignment, he or she might carry a gun, but that generally they did not. This is not consistent with the characterization that most Americans have about Russia being a police state or autocracy.

Speaking of guns, Russian citizens have to abide by much stricter gun control laws than in the United States. These include the requirement for gun owners to obtain a five-year renewable license. Before the first license is issued, attendance in a firearms safety class and the passing of a federal safety exam is required, as well as a background check (256).

Russia has also had a moratorium on the death penalty since 1999, and its high court has upheld it, while Putin has publicly supported it, even in the face of popular sentiment for bringing back executions for certain crimes (257). As of 2018, Russia's murder rate was roughly equal to the United States (259), reflecting a pattern of major improvement since the Wild West days of the 1990s (258) when journalists who covered Russia, like Angus Roxburgh, acknowledged that people being gunned down in the streets of Moscow, reminiscent of an episode of *The Untouchables*, was a fairly regular occurrence (128).

During both of my visits to Russia, I traveled with one other woman and encountered no problems or threats, even when we walked from the Metro station to our hotel after dark in Moscow. A 2017 Thompson-Reuters Foundation survey found Moscow to be the fourth safest metropolis overall in the world for women, including safety from rape and sexual harassment (260).

Moreover, Russian citizens are guaranteed free universal health care in the constitution, enjoy one of the highest rates of education in the world (over half of Russians have a college degree) (261), and have 140 days of paid maternity leave for women (262).

Russians can travel freely as long as they can afford it. Orthodox Christians, Muslims, Jews, and Buddhists are generally free to worship as they please. There is little overt censorship, and all the Russians I spoke to said they had access to Western media through both satellite and the internet, although they all found it to be very distorted and inaccurate in its portrayal of their country and their leader. There is a variety of opinion represented in print media, and even on pro-government Russian TV, it is not unusual for a pro-Western viewpoint to be included on political talk shows (263).

Russia scholar Nicolai Petro, in his 2018 journal article "Are We Reading Russia Right?" goes into more detail about the current state of Russian
media:

> ... [S]everal of Russia's largest daily newspapers, like *Vedo-*
> *mosti*, *Kommersant*, and *Nezavisimaya gazeta*, are
> staunchly anti-Putin and reach tens of millions of readers.
> *Novaya gazeta's* website alone garners more than twenty
> million views a month. . . . Anti-Putinism has long been
> the norm on Russia's most popular radio station, *Ekho*
> *Moskvy*, and on opposition television channels like *Rain*
> *TV* and *RBC*. But these are not the only venues for oppo-
> sition voices. As presidential candidate Ksenia Sobchak's
> campaign advisor recently pointed out to *CNN*, opposition
> candidates now "speak freely on Kremlin-owned state tele-
> vision about Russia's internal problems and their ideas for
> how to fix entrenched systems of corruption . . ." (264).

Petro also points out that only three percent of the hundred thousand
Russian media outlets that are currently in existence are owned by the state,
and that the internet is the most common news source for people under the
age of thirty-four, not television (264).

The *Christian Science Monitor's* veteran Russia correspondent Fred
Weir recently reported increased media diversity—including a plethora of
independent internet sites—in a region farther away from Moscow and St.
Petersburg (265).

There is still considerable room for improvement for journalists in
Russia. However, according to the Committee to Protect Journalists, deaths
of journalists have actually gone down in the Putin era of governance compared to the Yeltsin era (266). One would be hard-pressed to know that judg-
ing by the way Western politicians and media have characterized Putin as an
"autocrat" but gushed that Yeltsin was a "democrat."

As for the fate of celebrated Russian journalist Anna Politkovskaya,
the idea that Putin was behind her murder has been promiscuously bandied

about in the West, but no evidence has ever been presented. Moreover, her employers at *Novaya Gazeta* believe the Chechen leadership was behind her death, not the Russian government (267). Those who carried out the murder have been convicted in Russian court and are now in prison, but it is troubling that whoever ordered it remains at large.

The development of civil society was set back by an amendment to the foreign agent law in 2014. While some civil society activists whom I spoke to in October 2015 acknowledged that Western provocateurs were a problem, there were many authentic NGOs that were being caught in the dragnet, and the law was consequently viewed among them as a mistake that needed to be rectified (268). The Russian population in general has been divided on this legislation. In response to some of the criticism, in May 2016, the Duma amended the law to exclude charities and cultural organizations (269).

However, there has been a significant amount of civil society work going on in Russia despite the law, as foreign funding only represented a total of 7 percent even at its height in 2009 (264). This means that Russians have found domestic sources, including both government and private businesses and individuals (264).

Though it may come as another surprise to many Westerners due to the extreme vilification of Putin in the media, some civil society advocates I spoke with in Krasnodar credit Putin with encouraging the development of civil society with the first Civic Forum in 2001. According to one activist, who sat at the same table with Putin at a subsequent Civic Forum, such an outreach to civil society never would have happened under Boris Yeltsin.

There was initially division among civil society activists in 2001, due to concerns that the government was trying to exert too much control over the conference and was potentially trying to co-opt the emerging civil society movement. However, citizen advocates successfully pressured the Kremlin into improving the organization of the conference, adding "a variety of round table discussions to incorporate a broad range of participants and topics," and the inclusion of previously uninvited human rights and environmental organizations.

According to Nicolai Petro:

Through what became known as "the Putin Plan," president Putin laid the groundwork for a dramatic expansion of civic initiative during his first two terms as president. During this period the number of non-governmental organizations expanded from 100,000 to more than 600,000, with at least another 600,000 active unofficially. The latest surveys suggest that more than ten million Russians are involved in some form [of] organized volunteer activity, roughly ten percent of the adult population (264).

One example of active civil society development is an independent organization of citizens called the Public Council that started in 2014 in Krasnodar. It has successfully worked to get the local authorities to start taking the needs and desires of citizens into account when making decisions regarding the rapid economic development of the city.

Among other things, they have stopped the destruction of old trees, buildings, and parks as well as networked with youth groups and infrastructure specialists, including foreign experts in urban planning, public arts, transportation, and city marketing. They have organized periodic cleanup and renovation days sponsored by local businesses that donate equipment, and they are working to connect the city's hiking trails and protect its 16 lakes.

Not only have they received no opposition from Russian authorities, they have begun to gain positive recognition as well as interest from other Russian cities looking to replicate their model (268).

Civil society development in Russia may not always follow the trajectory that Americans expect, with their strong libertarian cultural influence. As has been discussed earlier in this book, Russians have a history of a strong state and do not necessarily find state involvement to be problematic.

Putin, in his first Address to the Federal Assembly in July 2000, cited the need for a meaningful civil society but implied that the best chance for success was for the state and civil society to work together, stating that there was a "false conflict" between the two (270).

Another example of civil society development as alive and well is a civic education program to teach democracy skills to Russians designed by Charles Heberle, an independent American. The program has been under implementation in a province near St. Petersburg and has had the quiet backing of the Putin government since the early 2000s (271).

One very frequent criticism of Russia by the West is that the rule of law is weak, if it exists at all. Let's look at three important measures of the rule of law in Russia: the rights of the accused, judicial independence, and the confidence and participation of Russian citizens in the court system.

The 1993 constitution guarantees the presumption of innocence for criminal defendants as well as the right to counsel (223). During Putin's first two terms as president, he introduced or oversaw the implementation of the rights of habeas corpus and trial by jury, and increased rights to exculpatory evidence (264). After certain reforms made by Putin to the criminal code, acquittal rates in bench trials (only heard by a judge) doubled, and acquittal rates in jury trials tripled, contributing to a 40 percent drop in the overall incarceration rate and a 95 percent drop in the juvenile incarceration rate since 2001 (264).

He also introduced the role of bailiffs and justices of the peace (JPs) into the system (264).

JPs act as judges in the lowest tier of courts and preside over approximately 75 percent of civil cases and 45 percent of criminal cases—most of the latter are resolved through plea bargaining (272). University of Wisconsin Professor Kathryn Hendley concluded in her years-long study of Russia's court system, *Everyday Law in Russia*, that JPs demonstrate independence—in other words, they base their decisions on the written law—in the vast majority of cases before them. Exceptions involve the very small percentage of cases that are politically sensitive, particularly to the Kremlin. In these instances the JPs will often go along with power as a matter of being socialized into the system rather than being overtly told to do so.

JPs, who are primarily women and do not enjoy the same prestige as their counterparts in the United States, are not specialized and have very heavy caseloads that must be decided within statutory deadlines. Though they generally strive to be fair, they also tend to feel burdened by the work-load and diligently seek to avoid reversals on appeal, the ramifications of which can hurt them financially and professionally, though only a small per-centage of litigants ever exercise the right of appeal (272).

All JPs are required to be over the age of 25, have a law degree, and pass an exam and a strict security clearance. They are formally appointed by either regional governors or regional legislative bodies and are often former JP law clerks or prosecutors rather than attorneys in private practice, since, as some-one who has already served in a public position, their professional back-ground and propensities will be more readily ascertainable. They are then given three months of formal training before they are allowed to preside over cases (272).

Hendley also found that overall, in civil and administrative cases, the Russian government often loses.

> State agencies are frequent litigants in civil cases, both as plaintiffs and defendants. Both in JP courts and other courts, they are more likely to lose these cases than are private actors. Their victory in administrative cases involving private citizens, such as traffic violations and fines for noncompliance with various laws, is far from automatic. The same is true in the business setting. Eco-nomic actors' challenges to their treatment by the tax and other regulatory authorities are frequently successful (272).

Court rulings in civil cases favoring private plaintiffs over the govern-ment occur at a rate of approximately 70 percent (264).

Furthermore, during Putin's second term, courts ruled that individu-als arrested without merit must be compensated, and compensation limits for government negligence were struck down, making it more meaningful when the Russian government comes out on the losing end of such cases (264).

Foreign businesses operating in Russia have benefitted from the improved state of the legal system. Lawsuits on behalf of foreign businesses have tripled since 2014, and favorable judgments have increased from 59 percent to 83 percent (264).

Many Russians are reluctant to take a dispute to court, citing time, inconvenience, and "the difficulty of proving one's case." But as incomes increase and the traditional informal methods of resolving disputes become less relevant, more Russians are utilizing the court system, increasing from one million in 1998 to over 17 million in 2016 (264). Hendley found many of these Russians to be generally satisfied with their experiences, which largely take place in the JP system, regardless of whether they won or lost. Eighty percent of Russians find JPs to be "well trained and competent," with only 10 percent believing their JP was biased (272).

Russia's democracy is not as fully developed as many of those in the West, which have had hundreds of years to evolve as opposed to just barely over a generation. It still contains elements of authoritarianism—including a weak legislative branch, and local authorities who are often slow to implement reforms. The system that Putin has developed to keep oligarchs on a leash is also vulnerable to a successor president who is corrupt or has poor governing skills. Maintaining the oligarchic system of wealth concentration has contributed to what is still a major wealth disparity in the country, which is not conducive to democracy. Corruption is still a significant problem, though some gradual improvements are being seen.

Overall, compared to when he first took office, the Putin period of governance has seen dramatic improvements in most important areas of Russian life, including security, the economy, and the legal system. No doubt more work will need to be done once Putin leaves office, but he will be leaving his successor with a more stable foundation from which to build on if he or she is inclined to do so.

Western Criticisms of Putin's Policies

In an article for *Foreign Policy* in November 2013, "The Seduction of George W. Bush," author Peter Baker epitomizes the tone of most major Western media coverage of Russia in the post-2007 Putin era. Baker posits that Bush was naïve to consider trusting Putin as an international partner and that any problems leading to a rift in their relations were all due to Putin's endless character flaws. Whenever Putin doesn't want to do things the way the West wants, it is often characterized by the Washington political class as a throwback to his KGB mentality and/or a penchant for acting like a stubborn child who doesn't want to eat his brussels sprouts.

If the accounts in Baker's article are to be believed—and many of the events and conversations are presented with little to no historical or political context that may shed light on what shapes Russia's perspective and, hence, Putin's comments and actions—Putin told Bush that he believed centralization provided stability for Russia (273).

While somehow ignoring his own administration's centralizing of power with its unitary executive philosophy, Bush's reaction to Putin's comment—and the implicit attitude underlying it—was that it was the wrong path for Russia, regardless of whether post-Soviet Russia's conditions indicated that this course made some degree of sense in terms of bringing stability to a politically and economically chaotic nation that was on the brink of being a failed state. There was also no attempt to objectively analyze whether this course of action benefitted Russia and its people in any significant way and, therefore, may be valid for Russia, at least for a period of time.

One institution that attempted to objectively assess this policy in economic terms was the Institute for Economies in Transition, a project of Bank of Finland. In a 2008 discussion paper, the results of a comprehensive statistical analysis of corporate governance between the period of 2001 and 2004 in Russia revealed a positive correlation between state involvement and improved corporate governance, with the trend more marked in companies where the state owned a minority share as opposed to full ownership. Furthermore, Transparency International documented a steady increase in transparency and good corporate governance for state-owned companies Gazprom and Rosneft during this period. Indeed, the two Russian companies scored higher than American corporate giants Apple, Google, and ExxonMobil, which are notorious for having poor scores.

Since the idea of state involvement in business having positive effects is antithetical ideologically to the U.S.-led West, these reports got virtually no press coverage in the Western establishment media (274) (275).

But Bush, with little working knowledge of Russian history, culture, or nuances of policy, presumed that he knew what was best for Russia rather than the Russian president—another instance of the patronizing American attitude.

President Obama, for all the early suppositions that he was more enlightened and less arrogant than his shoot-from-the-hip predecessor, showed a similar lack of knowledge or understanding of Russia, as illustrated in his August 2014 remarks to *The Economist* that Russia didn't make anything and that immigrants didn't flock there. In actuality, Russia, after the United States, was the second most popular destination in the world for immigrants at the time (276). By 2017, Russia was third after Germany and Saudi Arabia, which were tied for second place (277). And, as discussed above, Russia does indeed make a few things, including the RD-180 rocket engine that gets U.S. satellites off the ground. The RD-180 is the most advanced such rocket engine in the world, and it is estimated it would take several years to bring an American alternative online (278). As of this writing, the United States is still reliant on Russian rockets.

Putin clearly spelled out his reasons for centralizing control in Russia in the first decade of the 21st century, stating in speeches that this policy was a necessary move to deal with a Russia that was in political and economic chaos.

Matthew Johnson, an academic specialist in Russian history and philosophy, wrote in the *Eurasia Review* that the United States has itself engaged in some of the same policies in times of crisis that it has criticized Putin for:

> During WWII, the federal government took over the economy for war production. This is not considered authoritarianism, but a response to an emergency. . . . As the Russian economy collapsed by 1995, Russians demanded action. The state was required to take action against organized crime, begin collecting taxes again and

reform the armed services. Only a fairly strong state could accomplish this (279).

Though Putin has made it clear in both words and actions that he believes in markets and global trade, he has also shown discernment in rejecting elements of neoliberal globalization and fundamentalist market theory that is anathema to long-term economic stability, independence, or social justice.

During a 2012 presidential campaign speech, Putin discussed how government support may still be needed in a focused manner, for example, to improve industrial policy in Russia:

> It is often argued that Russia does not need an industrial policy and that, when choosing priorities and creating preferences, the government often makes mistakes by supporting ineffective players and getting in the way of competition. It's hard to argue with such assertions, but they are valid only if all other conditions remain the same. We went through de-industrialization and the economic structure is severely deformed. Large private capital does not willingly flow into new sectors—in order to avoid higher risks. We will certainly use tax and customs incentives to encourage investors to allocate funds to innovative industries. But this could show its effects several years from now—or not if more attractive investment options emerge in the world. Capital, after all, does not have borders. Are we ready to put Russia's future at such great risk for the sake of purity of an economic theory? (280)

It is that "purity of an economic theory" as propagated by the disciples of Milton Friedman that is nonnegotiable to American elites; world leaders who seriously question it all too often end up in those American elites' crosshairs.

Johnson, in his insightful article "Globalization and Decline of the West: Eurasianism, the State and Rebirth of Ethnic-Socialism," analyzes the

West's preoccupation with "democracy" and "openness," especially in relation to criticisms of Russia. He deconstructs what the West, led by the United States, actually seems to mean by these terms with respect to their practical application:

> The ideas of "democracy" and "openness" are mere buzz-words that are explicitly connected to the economic inter-ests of those who created the globalization project. . . . The main focus of Western capital is that "openness" becomes universally conflated with cultural and ideological stan-dardization. "Democracy" can then become universally conflated with securing the maximum return on invest-ment (281).

What Johnson is touching on here is the fact that there is nothing that Western elites fear and disdain more than authentic and substantive democracy—not the perversion of the term that they have created in which it is conveniently equated with liberalized markets whereby they can exploit everyone's resources for their own benefit. This is combined with dog-and-pony-show elections where most of the candidates have been preapproved by the elites in order to provide a pretense of political democracy.

This is reflected in the United States's characterization of Yeltsin as a "democrat" on the one hand, and shrieks about or distortions of every little thing Putin does that they don't approve of—and the stated reasons for dis-approval are often not the actual ones—on the other hand. It is also tragically reflected in a review of post-WWII U.S. foreign policy in which democracy is reduced to a mere annoyance, as when Iranians freely elected Mohammad Mosadegh, but the United States and United Kingdom decided to overthrow him in 1953 for the crime of wanting to nationalize the fossil fuel industry so its proceeds could benefit the Iranian people rather than foreign corpo-rations. As a replacement, they installed the brutal Shah as dictator (282). A similar scenario played out the following year when the democratically elected leader of Guatemala, Jacobo Árbenz Guzmán, was overthrown in a CIA-backed coup after nationalizing agricultural land, including that owned by the American corporation United Fruit Company (283).

Johnson also points out that neoliberal capitalists implicitly believe that a country should have no "national interest" separate from those of Western capital, such as national independence, stability, or social justice.

By 2006, Putin had made it clear that foreign investment in Russia would have limitations and conditions placed upon it—namely, that such investment must be beneficial to the Russian people rather than exploitative, and that it must not undermine the security or independence of Russia. This was reflected in moves that year by the Russian government to regain control of oil and gas deposits that had been virtually given away by Yeltsin under Production Sharing Agreements to ExxonMobil and Royal Dutch Shell (195).

Putin had shown this inclination three years earlier when he had Mikhail Khodorkovsky arrested and jailed for tax evasion. However, tax evasion was merely the tip of the iceberg in terms of what this recalcitrant oligarch, who ran Yukos Oil, was in the midst of trying to pull off.

At the time of Khodorkovsky's arrest at Novosibirsk Airport in October 2003, he had succeeded in buying a huge number of votes in the Duma four weeks prior to elections. Having control of Russia's legislature would have allowed him to alter laws whereby he could effectively seize control of Russian oil and gas deposits and pipelines. Furthermore, he could have legislation passed that would position him for the Russian presidency (195).

Additionally, Khodorkovsky was colluding with Dick Cheney and other powerful players in the United States to sell a stake ranging from 25 to 40 percent in Yukos to ExxonMobil and Chevron, giving the United States major influence over decisions relating to Russian fossil fuel resources, the engine of the country's economic growth and recovery. The final details of the sale were set to be ironed out, when Putin intervened.

Of course, Khodorkovsky's cadre of friends in the West, like NATO enlargement cheerleader/war profiteer Bruce Jackson, George Soros, and Stuart Eizenstat—who had worked in the Treasury Department during the Clinton administration, representing the halcyon years for the oligarchs pillaging Russia's assets—immediately set up a PR campaign characterizing the Putin government as the bad guys bullying an innocent "dissident" oligarch who only yearned for Western-style democracy. A major lobbying effort to get Khodorkovsky freed was undertaken, but the Russians were not in a for-giving mood (195) (284). In 2011, the European Court of Human Rights essentially vindicated the Russian legal system with respect to its handling of the Khodorkovsky case by unanimously ruling that the government had not misused the legal process in breaking up Yukos and seizing its assets (264).

It appears that the concept of a Eurasian (Economic) Union represents Putin's attempt to integrate the benefits of global markets without compro-mising other important interests like the maintenance of sovereignty and regulation of economic relations to prevent or counter major imbalances that can lead to destabilization and dangerous levels of social inequality.

The common market space it encompasses, at least initially, was com-prised of two nations on Russia's borders, Belarus and Kazakhstan, which have long-standing historical, geographic, and ethno-cultural ties. It has gradually expanded to include other nearby nations, such as Armenia and Kyrgyzstan, with Tajikistan and Uzbekistan close to becoming members. This trend will only increase if it demonstrates a successful and appealing model. Russia had been in discussions with Ukraine regarding potential membership during Yanukovych's leadership—a move that Yanukovych was open to as long as it didn't preclude Ukraine's also being integrated with the EU (285).

The fact that Ukraine might have joined the Eurasian Union and that a successful Eurasian Union might one day link up to the EU had to have been an especially upsetting thought in the minds of U.S. elites.

Putin has consistently made the connection between stability and security with social justice and equitable development. For example, he said during his speech before the Munich Conference on Security Policy in 2007:

> And there is still one more important theme that directly
> affects global security. Today many talk about the struggle
> against poverty. What is actually happening in this sphere?
> On the one hand, financial resources are allocated for
> programmes to help the world's poorest countries—and
> at times substantial financial resources. But to be hon-

est—and many here also know this—linked with the development of that same donor country's companies. And on the other hand, developed countries simultaneously keep their agricultural subsidies and limit some countries' access to high-tech products.

And let's say things as they are—one hand distributes charitable help and the other hand not only preserves economic backwardness but also reaps the profits thereof. The increasing social tension in depressed regions inevitably results in the growth of radicalism, extremism, feeds terrorism and local conflicts. And if all this happens in, shall we say, a region such as the Middle East where there is increasingly the sense that the world at large is unfair, then there is the risk of global destabilisation (203).

At the Davos Economic Forum in 2009, when discussing various aspects of the financial crisis that had recently affected the world, Putin again addressed these interconnections by discussing the untenable levels of inequality the crisis had laid bare:

The benefits that were generated were distributed very disproportionately. In fact, such disproportions could be seen between layers of the population in individual countries and even in highly developed countries, as well as between different countries and regions of the world.

For a significant part of mankind, comfortable housing, education and qualit[y] medical care are still inaccessible. And the world upsurge of recent years has not radically changed this (286).

Putin has continued to encourage policies in Russia that acknowledge social responsibility. In his 2013 Address to the Federal Assembly, he outlined plans to raise salaries for teachers, professors, and doctors and for investment in affordable housing construction with the requisite social infrastructure for middle-income families (287). And, as discussed in the previous section, far more ambitious goals were laid out in his 2018 Address in order to cement his legacy as Russia's leader by the time he leaves office at the end of 2024.

Rebuffed by the West: Putin's Attempts at Negotiation and Reciprocity

Despite the image constantly portrayed in the West of Putin being an aggressor, he actually has a history of trying to achieve his goals using diplomacy and accommodation with the West that is meant to be reciprocal of each party's interests. As previously mentioned, Putin was the first world leader to call then-president George W. Bush to offer his condolences and support after the 9/11 attacks.

Putin's reasoning was twofold: 1) He saw the United States and Russia as having a mutual interest in fighting Islamist terrorism, and 2) He knew that he had a tall order in successfully addressing the many profound problems facing Russia at the time, which included a cratered economy, massive crime and corruption, and the worst mortality crisis since WWII. He would need to put as much time, energy, and resources as he could muster into the project of rehabilitating his country—which meant not wasting precious time, energy, and resources in unnecessary conflict with the world's lone superpower. Going against the advice of most of his security team, he provided logistical and intelligence support as well as access to temporary military bases on behalf of the U.S. operation in Afghanistan.

In return for this assistance, Putin received the equivalent of a slap in the face from the neoconservative Bush administration in the form of a unilateral withdrawal from the Anti-Ballistic Missile Treaty (ABM) in 2002 to pursue a "missile defense shield" and the accession of seven more nations of Eastern Europe into NATO in 2004.

Seemingly undeterred, in 2008, Putin ordered the Russian Foreign Ministry to draft a proposal that Dmitry Medvedev took to Brussels, outlining a security plan that would cover all of the Euro-Atlantic community and Russia, obviating the need for NATO's continued existence, much less its expansion (288).

The preamble states:

> The use of force or the threat of force against the territorial
> integrity or political independence of any state, or in any
> other way inconsistent with the goals and principles of the
> Charter of the United Nations is inadmissible in their
> mutual relations, as well as international relations in general.

It also reiterates the intent to cooperatively address any security concerns that may arise among members:

> Intending to build effective cooperation mechanisms that
> could be promptly activated with a view to solving issues
> or differences that might arise, addressing concerns and
> adequately responding to challenges and threats in the
> security sphere.

The body of the document contains mechanisms for how security concerns or breaches of security could be handled. This proposal was sent to the
leaders of relevant nations as well as to the heads of the EU, NATO, and
OSCE, emphasizing that Russia was open to suggestions and negotiation on
the plan (288).

Putin and Medvedev received no response to their proposal.

Not long afterward, Mikheil Saakashvili, egged on by figures in Washington, staged a military incursion into South Ossetia, killing Russian peace-
keepers and prompting a military response by Russia.

Although the subsequent Obama administration gave the appearance
of wanting to improve relations with the "reset," the project quickly fell apart,
largely due to the fact that it was not sincere, as Russia scholar Nicolai Petro
explains:

> From its inception, however, the reset rested on a flawed
> assumption—namely that there was a rift between the val-
> ues of the Kremlin and the Russian people that the United
> States could exploit. As Michael McFaul, the policy's archi-
> tect [and U.S. ambassador at the time] explained, the pur-

pose of the reset was "to establish a direct relationship with the Russian people" over the Kremlin's head. As a result, a golden opportunity to alter the course of Russian-American relations was lost to political expediency (264).

The Ukraine Crisis

In Jack Matlock's 2010 book, *Superpower Illusions*, he provides a description of modern Ukraine's complex political history and demographics that has proven prescient with respect to the post-coup problems we have witnessed: "Well over half of Ukrainian citizens oppose the country's entry into NATO. To understand why, one must bear in mind that Ukraine's biggest security problem is not Russian 'imperialism' but political, social, economic and linguistic divisions inside the country" (85). As touched on in Chapter 2, prior to WWI, the western area of modern-day Ukraine was part of the Austro-Hungarian Empire, with formerly Habsburg/Polish Galicia being annexed and incorporated into Ukraine by Stalin in 1945. The southeastern area of modern Ukraine, however, had historically been part of the Russian Empire (18).

Matlock concluded that any attempts to bring Ukraine into NATO would have dire consequences. Putin made this very argument to then-National Security Advisor Condoleezza Rice during an October 2006 meeting that became heated when the subject of Ukraine's potential future entry into NATO came up. According to Russian foreign minister Sergei Lavrov, who was present, Putin tried to impress upon Rice that efforts to bring Ukraine into NATO would be disastrous all the way around: "Putin explained what Ukraine was—at least a third of the population are ethnic Russians—and the negative consequences that could arise, not only for us but for all of Europe if Ukraine and Georgia were dragged into NATO."

American ambassador Bill Burns, who was with Rice at the meeting, stated that Rice responded by declaring that each sovereign nation had the right to decide for itself which institutions or alliances it wanted to join. Putin reportedly replied in what would turn out to be prophetic terms: "You do not understand what you are doing. You are playing with fire" (128).

To demonstrate the disingenuousness of Rice's argument, try to imagine the following: Russia convinces Mexico to join a military alliance hostile to the United States. In response, U.S. leaders proclaim that Mexico has the right to join any alliance it chooses and they have no concerns.

Of course, no one in their right mind believes that this is what would transpire.

In February 2008, Ambassador Burns sent a classified cable back to Washington, summing up a meeting with Foreign Minister Lavrov about Ukraine's intent to seek a NATO Membership Action Plan as "Nyet Means Nyet: Russia's NATO Enlargement Redlines." The Russians had reiterated again that Ukraine in NATO was unacceptable, citing among other concerns that the issue could precipitate division in the country, perhaps leading to civil war, which would put Russia in the difficult position of having to choose whether to intervene or not—a decision it was stressed that Russia did not want to be faced with (289).

Furthermore, Ukrainians themselves demonstrated their antipathy toward NATO membership from January to March 2005, when the Ukrainian parliament (Rada) was blocked from functioning by an opposition coalition that resulted from the "Orange Revolution" leaders Viktor Yushchenko and Yulia Tymoshenko trying to push the country into the alliance (290).

Despite all of this, it was declared at the 2008 NATO Summit in Bucharest that Ukraine and Georgia would eventually become NATO members, though no time frame or steps toward membership were undertaken (128).

The geopolitical reality was that Ukraine needed to be a buffer and a bridge between the West and Russia with the opportunity to have beneficial economic relations with both, since Russia had been Ukraine's largest trading partner, from which it received various subsidies, such as discounted gas. To ensure that buffer role, however, it was imperative for all parties that NATO membership was off the table.

Despite denials in some quarters, the Association Agreement with Europe, which deposed Ukrainian president Viktor Yanukovych refused to sign, included language that would lay the groundwork for NATO membership (291). This presented a serious problem in addition to the economic hardships it would have imposed on Ukraine.

The European Union, led by Germany, tried to pressure Yanukovych to sign the Association Agreement. Upon review of how the agreement would actually affect his country economically—the poorest in Europe at the time— including austerity measures, renunciation of their significant trade with Russia, and the supplanting of Ukraine's native oligarchs, Yanukovych balked and opted to go with a Russian deal comprised of a $15 billion loan and reduced gas rates (292). As it turns out, the West was not in fact offering Ukraine free trade or even visa-free travel at that time, but a self-serving deal that had little to no benefit to Ukraine. Most leaders in Yanukovych's place would have had the same inclination.

Several months before this, in September 2013, a large gathering of political and economic elites from the West, including Democratic Party heavyweights such as Bill and Hillary Clinton, had taken place in Yalta. During this gathering, they discussed how to pull Ukraine from the Russian sphere into the EU using an Association Agreement. Also in attendance at this conference, which was funded by one of Ukraine's wealthiest oligarchs, Victor Pinchuk, was Viktor Yanukovych, along with his eventual successor, Petro Poroshenko. One of the most interesting guests, however, was Sergey Glazyev, one of Putin's economic advisors. Glazyev explained that the economic promises from the West to Ukraine were illusory, as reflected in the fact that Ukraine had been running large deficits financed by foreign loans that would eventually require a major bailout or risk a default (293). According to journalist Diana Johnstone, who reported on this meeting for *CounterPunch*, further points were made in an attempt to get the Western elites to see the folly of their plans:

> As for the political impact, Glazyev pointed out that the Russian-speaking minority in Eastern Ukraine might move to split the country in protest against cutting ties with Russia, and that Russia would be legally entitled to support them, according to *The Times of London*.

In short, while planning to incorporate Ukraine into the
Western sphere, Western leaders were perfectly aware that
this move would entail serious problems with Rus-
sian-speaking Ukrainians, and with Russia itself. Rather
than seeking to work out a compromise, Western leaders
decided to forge ahead and to blame Russia for whatever
would go wrong (293).

Throughout the period of negotiating this agreement, Russia requested
three-way talks to avert problems. Of course, Russia wanted to protect its
own economic and trade interests, but as explained above, it also had an
interest in preventing friction or instability on its border. However, the West
refused Russia's requests.

An independent investigation was undertaken by Germany's *ARD TV*
into the events surrounding the subsequent ouster of the democratically
elected president after his decision to pull the plug on the Association Agreement—a decision that was not well-explained to the Ukrainian public. That
investigation focused specifically on the violence that occurred in the midst
of protests on Maidan Square in Kiev. It was concluded that sniper shots fired
on February 20, 2014, which resulted in almost 100 deaths, came primarily
from buildings controlled by the Maidan protesters, including members of
the neo-Nazi group Right Sector, not from Yanukovych's forces (294). A more
in-depth forensic investigation was conducted by Ukrainian-Canadian academic Ivan Katchanovski. His conclusions supported the *ARD* report (295).

This is all consistent with Estonian Foreign Minister Urmas Paet's
account to then-European High Commissioner Catherine Ashton in an
intercepted phone call posted to YouTube on February 26, 2014, wherein he
stated that his sources, including Dr. Olga Bolgomets—who was an ardent
supporter of the original Maidan protests—reported forensic evidence indicating that the snipers were Maidan protesters. Paet also reported that members of the Ukrainian parliament who supported Yanukovych had been
beaten and threatened during the period in question (120) (see Appendix
3).

Prior to the sniper violence and the ouster of Yanukovych, State Department official Victoria Nuland and U.S. ambassador Geoffrey Pyatt were caught planning the imminent coup in an intercepted phone call posted on February 6, 2014, in which they discuss how to "glue this thing" and who will be the best person to lead a post-Yanukovych Ukraine, declaring "Yats is the guy"—referring to Arseniy Yatsenyuk (119) (see Appendix 2). Yatsenyuk became prime minister after the coup, while oligarch and State Department asset Petro Poroshenko (296) became the president. Nuland also famously disparaged the EU's less aggressive approach to engineering a zero-sum position for Ukraine with respect to its relations with the West and Russia when she proclaimed, "Fuck the EU" (see Appendix 2).

The Kiev government that came after the overthrow of the corrupt but democratically elected Yanukovych oversaw, by all reasonable measures, a degeneration of the country into something far more sinister. Neo-Nazis were given posts in the Interior and Education Ministries and were elected to the Rada in small numbers, but they also became members of and gained significant influence in other parliamentary parties that won larger percentages (297). These neo-Nazis had allegedly threatened the Kiev government in the past with a coup if it didn't placate their desires (298). A Ministry of Truth was established, creating an atmosphere that allowed for the subsequent killing spree of journalists and opposition politicians (299). World War II–era Nazi collaborator Stepan Bandera, involved in the massacre of tens of thousands of Jews and Poles in western Ukraine, has become an openly celebrated hero, with streets named after him (300). A government that has such elements will not be inclined to reach a political compromise with the rebels in the southeast, although the Kiev government, as discussed in more detail below, is obligated by the Minsk 2.0 agreement to do so.

Ukraine's economy subsequently imploded, with its currency devalued by 40 percent in 2015 alone and an inflation rate of 272 percent at one point (301). The Kiev government has no money and has had to rely on EU and IMF loans.

Public polling from spring 2018 showed that 74 percent of Ukrainians thought Ukraine was heading in the wrong direction, Poroshenko's approval rate was 9 percent, his party's approval rate was 7.5 percent, and trust in politicians was the lowest it had been since 2014. "Ukrainians list the main barriers to the country's development as the Donbas conflict, the fact that economic reconstruction is taking too long, and the lack of visible progress in the fight against corruption" (302).

The West has typically characterized the Donbas rebels in southeastern Ukraine as puppets of Russia with no legitimate grievances or indigenous support. However, sociological surveys of Donbas residents from March, April, and May 2014 showed that majorities considered the Right Sector to be dangerous and influential and the Maidan protests to be illegal and representative of "an armed overthrow of the government, organized by the opposition, with the assistance of the West" (123).

Independent video journalist Patrick Lancaster, who has been reporting from the Donbas since spring 2014, stated that most of the fighters he has encountered on both sides are Ukrainian (303).

British scholar on Russia Paul Robinson has estimated that 90 percent of the fighters in the Donbas are Ukrainian (304). Furthermore, he states that the original rebellion was constituted of regular citizens who took control of local government buildings in response to the startling events coming out of post-coup Kiev, where laws were introduced seeking to delegitimize the Russian language, neo-Nazis were given posts in the Interior and Education Departments, and many acts of violence were committed against members of the Communist Party and the Party of Regions (Yanukovych's party). Moreover, many residents of the Donbas did not perceive the EU orientation of the coup government to be in their material interests, fearing austerity policies and loss of industrial trade with Russia and other EEU countries, which had provided thousands of jobs (305).

According to Assistant Professor of Political Science Serhiy Kudelia at Baylor University, in his 2016 scholarly analysis of the Donbas rebellion, there were numerous "miscalculations" by the Kiev regime that created conditions conducive to rebels consolidating their local power. Furthermore, Russia reacted to facts on the ground to support its own perceived interests but was not the cause.

> Russia exploited these developments, but did not play a
> determining role in them. . . . Kremlin and Russian agents
> did not act in a vacuum. The space for these events was
> largely created by events inside Ukraine, which were not
> only outside the direct control of Moscow, but often ran
> counter to the interests of the Russian leadership (306).

The events referenced above include the hijacking of the Maidan movement by the ultranationalist forces who utilized violence, beginning on February 18, 2014, with the march down Institutskaya Street in Kiev, which was initially billed as a "peaceful offensive" on the Rada; the inability or unwillingness of the rest of the Maidan movement to keep the protests peaceful; the rejection by those same violent extremists of the agreement negotiated on the eve of the coup by Poland, Germany, and France with the Yanukovych government, which called for early elections and a devolution of power; and the subsequent violence against the rebels by the new government of Kiev (306).

Kudelia states that the new Kiev government did make an attempt to negotiate with the rebels. However, one is left to wonder how seriously this was supposed to be taken by the rebels when one of the two men that Kiev sent for this purpose was neo-Nazi activist Andriy Parubiy (307), who participated in the violence of the Maidan (308) (the other was Deputy Prime Minister Vitaly Yarema). This attempt at negotiation occurred only after the Donbas cities of Donetsk and Luhansk had successfully held a referendum calling for self-determination, which was viewed as a bargaining chip to gain as much autonomy as possible.

These negotiations failed, and the newly installed Kiev government decided to use force against the Donbas rebels. Kudelia explains that Kiev's initial strategy of focusing its "Anti-Terrorist Operation" (ATO) on the city of Slavyansk also provided space for the development of what would become the Donetsk People's Republic (DPR) and the Luhansk People's Republic (LPR).

He also states that the rebellion originally called for federalization, with only a minority calling for an independent state known as Novorossiya.

These calls would understandably increase later on, after months of Kiev's ATO against the Donbas, which included shelling civilian neighborhoods and unleashing vicious neo-Nazi battalions to compensate for many Ukrainian army conscripts' lack of stomach for attacking their fellow Ukrainians:

> Rallies in support of federalizing Ukraine were held in most major cities in the Southeast. However, the Donbas was the only region where Kyiv was unable to regain control and prevent the outbreak of an armed movement to join Donetsk and Luhansk regions to Russia. This was facilitated by three factors. First, the Donbas was significantly different from other regions in terms of its politics and its level of integration into the Ukrainian state. In contrast to all other regions, the majority has traditionally supported the unification of Ukraine with Russia (66 percent) and regretted the collapse of the Soviet Union (61 percent). In April 2014, after Russia's annexation of Crimea, almost two-thirds of the region's residents continued to express a positive attitude toward Russian president Vladimir Putin, while in other regions the level of support was no higher than 20 percent. With the exception of Crimea, the Donbas was the only territory where a majority (57 percent in 2013) stated that it would not support the independence of Ukraine in the case of a second referendum (i.e., the 1991 referendum, when nearly 84 percent voted in favor of independence). While before the revolution few people supported separatism (8 percent in 2012), recognition of the Ukrainian government was conditional. This is evidenced by the prevalence among Donbas residents of a regional identity. In contrast to other Ukrainian regions, Donbas residents primarily identify themselves with their city or region, rather than with the state as a whole (306).

It is recognized that the historical ethnic ties of Donbas to Russia—since the 19th century, much of the area had been inhabited by Russian settlers after coal mining was established—fueled its having the highest "animosity toward Ukrainian nationalists," who are stridently, even violently, anti-Russian. This made the Donbas population particularly sensitive to news reports from Russia of the actions taking place during and after the Maidan protests.

When Robinson asked a Maidan protester why this political protest had led to a more violent and divisive result than the Orange Revolution in 2004, the protester admitted that this time they didn't care what the Crimeans or the residents of the Donbas wanted (304). So it seems the divisiveness was not initiated by Russia or the ethnic Russian population of Ukraine, but by a portion of the Maidan protesters who basically believed that the interests of a whole segment of their country should be dismissed.

Kiev also didn't factor in that the oligarchs of the Donbas region "hedged their bets" by trying to deal with the coup government in Kiev and its representatives as well as the rebels in Donbas. This was a contributing factor in how the Donbas rebels were able to establish their power, increasingly independent of Kiev's governance.

> After the Euromaidan victory, the Party of Regions' [Yanukovych's party] public statements were limited to demands that greater power be given to local authorities and that the rights of Russian-speaking people be protected. However, the sudden departure of Yanukovych and his supporters led the party to disintegrate into several factions associated with large business groups (e.g., Rinat Akhmetov, Dmitry Firtash, and Alexander Efremov). Each of these groups had its own interests in the Donbas; some were more insistent than others, and made tacit alliances with separatist leaders (306).

The fact that many government officers who had worked security on the Maidan during the violent protests lived in the Donbas also helped to cement support for resistance against what was perceived to be an illegitimate coup government in Kiev (306).

Although Russia provided some arms and equipment and allowed Russian volunteers to cross the border freely, it's unclear whether official Russian military forces intervened, as has been claimed by some. For example, an article published in March 2015 in the opposition Russian newspaper *Novaya Gazeta* (309) quotes at length a Buryat Russian soldier who says he was part of an operation involving hundreds of Russian troops and 31 tanks crossing into eastern Ukraine. According to the soldier's account, the Russian troops crossed over at night in February to prevent the Donbas rebels from being defeated by Kiev forces in the town of Debaltseve. However, the OSCE Special Monitoring Mission (SMM) to Ukraine, which has been stationed throughout the country since March 2014 (310), has never confirmed any such influx of Russian troops and tanks.

Professor Robinson points out that Moscow appears to have actually had a moderating influence on the rebels by facilitating the replacement of the original military leaders, Igor Strelkov and Alexander Borodai, who supported what was perceived as a quixotic quest for independence. An independent Donbas that would be economically unviable and would provide no counterweight to a hostile government in Kiev is not in Moscow's interests (304).

Unlike with the unique situation in Crimea, Putin has shown no interest in absorbing the Donbas into the Russian Federation. Setting aside the likely political repercussions and thornier issues of international law, if Putin were to absorb the Donbas, there would be no viable counterweight to an extremist government in Kiev that would be free to pursue NATO membership.

It is important to note that the Minsk 2.0 agreement (which did not define the final demarcation line) was never expected to fully resolve the crisis but did represent an important step forward in ending the violence and creating a diplomatic settlement (see Appendix 4).

In addition to the fact that German Chancellor Angela Merkel and then-President Hollande of France approached Moscow for another round of diplomacy that resulted in Minsk 2.0, there were significant political concessions Merkel made verbally during the negotiations, as reported in an in-depth article in *Der Spiegel* (311) and expounded upon by analyst and international law expert Alexander Mercouris:

> It was almost certainly in the talks with Putin in Moscow, where the Ukrainians were not present, that the broad outline of what was formally decided in Minsk was actually agreed. Merkel then flew to Washington to brief Obama and obtain his consent. Poroshenko was then presented in Minsk with what had previously been agreed, leaving him scope only to quibble over the technical details in a way that it is in Merkel's interests to highlight.
>
> *Der Spiegel* claims Merkel was able to extract one concession from Putin. *Der Spiegel* claims Putin agreed the forthcoming elections in the rebel regions will be limited to areas the rebel militia was to control in accordance with a ceasefire line agreed on 19th September 2014, and would not take place in territories the rebel militia has captured since the failure of the Ukrainian government's offensive in January (312).

Mercouris goes on to list Kiev's obligations and the timeline in which they were to be carried out: 1) pass a law granting the Donetsk People's Republic (DPR) and Luhansk People's Republic (LPR) special status within Ukraine by the end of March 2015, 2) work with the rebels toward an agreement of special status of their respective regions, and 3) agree to terms of a new constitution and enact it by the end of 2015.

Moreover, the agreement granted the DPR and LPR veto power over Ukraine's membership in NATO and the EU.

Mercouris emphasized that the above terms did not appear in the final draft of the Minsk 2.0 agreement (see Appendix 4), but with the *Der Spiegel* article obviously sourced from Merkel's office, the provisions were presumably agreed to verbally:

These provisions do not appear in writing in the Minsk agreements. If they exist (which, given that the *Der Spiegel* article is sourced from Merkel's office, they surely do) they must have been agreed verbally by Putin and Merkel, almost certainly during the talks in Moscow that preceded the ones in Minsk.

There would have been no point in asking Poroshenko to sign a document that contained these provisions since for political reasons he could never have signed it. However the Russians have obtained confirmation in writing that they may control Ukraine's border until the new Constitution is agreed. This gives them a powerful tool which they can use to enforce terms they dictated in Moscow and Minsk, even those that were only agreed verbally with Merkel, if or rather when the Ukrainians try to back out of them (312).

Events since the signing of Minsk 2.0 on February 12, 2015, have compromised the agreement. The Right Sector was officially incorporated into the Ukrainian Army under its neo-Nazi leader Dmytro Yarosh, who became Ukraine's Chief of General Staff.

In December 2017, the Trump administration sent its first (smaller) batch of arms to the Kiev government. As reported by Ted Galen Carpenter in *The American Conservative*, "That agreement included the export of Model M107A1 Sniper Systems, ammunition, and associated parts and accessories, a sale valued at $41.5 million" (313). But a more significant and potentially dangerous batch was sent in spring 2018:

A transaction in April 2018 was more serious. Not only was it larger ($47 million), it included far more lethal weaponry, particularly 210 Javelin anti-tank missiles—the kind of weapons that Barack Obama's administration had declined to give Kiev. Needless to say, the Kremlin was not pleased about either sale. Moreover, Congress soon passed legislation in May that authorized $250 million in military assistance, including lethal weaponry, to Ukraine in 2019. Congress had twice voted for military support on a similar scale during the last years of Obama's administration, but the White House blocked implementation. The Trump administration cleared that obstacle out of the way in December 2017 at the same time that it approved the initial small-weapons sale. The passage of the May 2018 legislation means that the path is now open for a dramatic escalation of U.S. military backing for Kiev (313).

Furthermore, Carpenter points out (313) a September 1, 2018, interview in *The Guardian* with Kurt Volker, the U.S. Ambassador to NATO, in which Volker acknowledges Washington's likely future weapons sales to Ukraine's navy and air force, which would represent an escalation.

Earlier in 2018, the U.S. army also sent soldiers to train Ukrainian military units, as announced publicly by then-Defense Secretary James Mattis (314). It should be noted that sending American troops to Ukraine would appear to be a violation of the Minsk 2.0 agreement, which requires the removal of all foreign fighters and mercenaries from that country (see Appendix 4).

Of course, the Minsk 2.0 agreement was being sabotaged by the Ukrainian government from the beginning, as the Kiev parliament demanded shortly after its signature that the rebels effectively surrender and allow Kiev to organize elections before any federalization would occur (315). The Minsk agreement reflected no such requirement from the rebels (see Appendix 4). Instead, Kiev was supposed to begin negotiating with representatives of the rebel republics toward a special status. As then-DPR official Denis Pushilin stated, "Chancellor Merkel and President Hollande have declared they would guarantee that Ukraine would carry out Minsk 2.0. Therefore, they now have to bring Poroshenko to heel as by his actions he is ripping up the Minsk agreements." (316).

Around the time the agreement was being negotiated, Germany was reportedly disgusted with shenanigans by American hawks like then-NATO commander Philip Breedlove and Victoria Nuland that thwarted work toward a settlement. As another *Der Spiegel* article detailed (317), Breedlove's constant assertions of Russia's military incursions at the time, which were contradicted by Germany's intelligence sources (as well as France's) (318), were particularly troubling:

> Sources in the Chancellery have referred to Breedlove's comments as "dangerous propaganda."

> "It is the tone of Breedlove's announcements that makes Berlin uneasy. False claims and exaggerated accounts, warned a top German official during a recent meeting on Ukraine, have put NATO—and, by extension, the entire West—in danger of losing its credibility."

> Berlin sources also say that it has become conspicuous that Breedlove's controversial statements are often made just as a step forward has been made in the difficult negotiations aimed at a political solution. Berlin sources say that Germany should be able to depend on its allies to support its efforts at peace (317).

The German media also exposed how Victoria Nuland, during secret meetings on the sidelines of the Munich Security Conference that year, pumped up her colleagues on how to "fight against the Europeans, fight against them rhetorically" in order to facilitate the arming of Kiev. This is where Breedlove and other officials were coached by Nuland on their warmongering propaganda: "While talking to the Europeans this weekend, you need to make the case that Russia is putting in more and more offensive stuff while we want to help the Ukrainians defend against these systems. It is defensive in nature although some of it has lethality" (317).

Despite Breedlove's and Nuland's machinations, the Obama administration vetoed sending such weapons to the Ukrainian coup government.

Crimea

In October 2015, I visited the three Crimean cities of Simferopol, Yalta, and Sevastopol, during which time I had conversations with a cross section of people, from cab drivers and bus riders to small business owners and participants in what is variously referred to by the locals as "The Crimean Spring" and "The Third Defense of Sevastopol." This culminated in a referendum in which 96 percent of voters chose to secede from post-coup Ukraine and rejoin Russia. After my visit, I came away with three conclusions.

The first is that Crimeans, who are mostly ethnic Russians who speak Russian, were genuinely alarmed by the ultranationalist rhetoric and violence coming out of Kiev, which resulted in what they viewed as an illegal coup by extremist elements of the Maidan movement, supported by Washington.

These extremists had attacked ethnic Russians from Crimea who had participated in anti-Maidan protests, and the attackers were reportedly on their way into the Crimean peninsula. As a result, Crimeans began to organize self-defense units to protect their communities (319).

Secondly, Crimeans did not necessarily think Russia would accept their requests for help (319). Crimea had been part of Russia from the time of Catherine the Great's reign in the 18th century. But in 1954, Nikita Khrushchev gifted Crimea to Ukraine as part of his campaign to consolidate power in the post-Stalin era.

Since both Russia and Ukraine were part of the Soviet Union at the time, this was not a problem. However, when the Soviet Union dissolved in 1991, Crimea remained in Ukraine as an autonomous region, while the naval base at Sevastopol was retained by Russia via a lease agreement with the Kiev government. Between 1991 and 2013, Crimeans had voted several times to be reunited with Russia, only to have their requests ignored by Moscow (319).

Putin, as any Russian leader would have, viewed the events of February 2014 as a threat to Russia's security. Sevastopol is a critical naval base that is the last "militarily defensible" barrier to an invasion into southern Russia (320). Indeed, Sevastopol has major historical importance for Russians due to the crucial battle against the Germans at Sevastopol in summer 1942 in which the Soviets ground down a portion of the German army for months, preventing their advance to Stalingrad, leaving a smaller and weaker German force that ultimately lost to the Red Army (320). Sevastopol is also Russia's only warm-water port. Since a hostile government in Kiev could unilaterally cancel the lease and allow NATO to de facto take control over the port, Putin had to act.

Knowing that the Crimean population had repeatedly expressed its desire to be part of Russia, Putin decided on an operation to assist the native Crimeans in blocking both marauding ultranationalists and representatives of the coup government from interfering in activities that would facilitate Crimea's quick reintegration into Russia.

Crimeans told me that they knew the so-called "little green men" were Russian soldiers legally stationed at the naval base who had donned unmarked uniforms. They also told me that they viewed them as protectors who allowed them to peacefully conduct their referendum, not as invaders. Suggestions that these Russian soldiers had pressured them to vote at gunpoint were dismissed as ridiculous (319).

Third, Crimeans were very happy to be part of Russia. Though they acknowledged that there was still a lot of work to be done, they viewed the future with hope. These sentiments have been borne out in several Western opinion polls (Gallup, Pew, GfK, and Levada-Open Democracy) over the past several years (319). Moreover, as many Crimeans told me, Kiev's violent response to the Donbas has only reinforced to them that their decision to secede from Ukraine and rejoin Russia was the right thing to do.

I conducted an email interview, via my fixer in Crimea, with two representatives of the Tatar community, an ethnic minority with a long history in the area that comprises about 12 percent of the population. The Tatar community at the time appeared to be split between a vocal opposition and a segment that was quietly waiting to see how things turned out under Russian governance (319).

Ukraine Today:
Still Corrupt, Still Poor, and Still a Potential Flash Point

Ukraine has made some progress from the economic disaster of 2014–2016, during which the GDP declined by 16.5 percent overall (321) and around 60 percent of Ukrainians were living below the poverty line (322). By early 2017, Ukraine's GDP had increased by 2 percent, and by the end of the year, due to a doubling of the minimum wage and increases in social welfare, the number of Ukrainians living in poverty decreased to around 39 percent (323).

However, given the context of the steep drop in GDP in the preceding years, a growth rate of 2 percent is very small. And despite the 15 percent decrease in the poverty rate, a very significant proportion of the population is still very poor and worried about their economic prospects, as the previously mentioned polling in 2018 reflects (302). Indeed, Ukraine was still the poorest country in Europe in 2018 (324).

Moreover, there was little incentive to implement meaningful reforms when the political leadership of Ukraine was still comprised of oligarchs like recently defeated president Petro Poroshenko.

Then there were the ultranationalist and neo-Nazi forces that the coup government used as the muscle to gain power. These forces are still alive and well and a source of trouble in the country. Although Western establishment media tried to deny or downplay their role in the aftermath of the coup, there has finally been some acknowledgment even in those quarters of how dangerous these reactionary forces are. According to a 2018 *Reuters* report, such groups have openly held marches in Kiev and other locations, violently attacked gays, media outlets, art exhibitions, anti-war activists, and gypsies, and stormed local government meetings and intimidated politicians to vote a particular way (325). Oftentimes, local police fail to arrest or punish these groups (325), either due to sympathy or fear of reprisal.

Fear of reprisal of these groups—most of them armed and experienced in combat against the rebels in the east—ensures that any president, including Volodoymyr Zelensky, will have a very difficult time reaching a settlement with the Donbas rebels, leaving the current conditions of a "frozen conflict," which still involves intermittent shooting and artillery exchanges that result in deaths of both combatants and civilians, in place indefinitely.

These reactionary groups have made it clear in the past that they are willing to intimidate the government. In October 2014, Right Sector and Svoboda participated in a violent protest in front of the Rada when the legislative body did not vote to officially recognize Stepan Bandera's anti-Soviet UPA militia, which had massacred Poles and Jews during WWII (326). In 2015, Right Sector engaged in bombings against police (327) when the president attempted to assert control over them. Later in the year, after the Rada voted to grant more autonomy to the Donbas rebels in Donetsk and Luhansk in compliance with the Minsk agreement, a member of Svoboda killed a national guard policeman and injured scores of others when he set off a grenade during riots in front of the parliament building (328).

This backdrop made Washington's decision to send more lethal arms to Kiev even more alarming, since it could embolden a government that was unwilling and/or unable to rein in such forces—and has even incorporated them into its national guard—to ratchet up fighting in the Donbas as a distraction from domestic problems.

Some have argued that the November 25, 2018, incident in which Ukrainian vessels were seized by Russia after attempting to enter the Sea of Azov from the Black Sea via the Kerch Strait was a possible provocation by the Poroshenko government to increase patriotic sentiment in the run-up to election season (329).

There have been different interpretations on the legality of Russia's actions during the incident in which the Russian Coast Guard intercepted and then fired shots at two Ukrainian naval vessels and a tugboat (330), injuring three Ukrainians. The boats were subsequently captured and confiscated by the Russians, and the crews were arrested and charged with illegally crossing Russian borders, which carries a sentence of up to six years in prison (331). (The crew members were later returned home as part of a prisoner exchange between Russia and Ukraine in September 2019.)

Legal interpretation largely depends on whether one accepts that an active state of conflict exists between Ukraine and Russia or not. If one does, then the Law of Naval Warfare supersedes the UN Convention on the Law of the Sea (UNCLOS), and Russia's actions can be construed as valid except for their treatment of the captured sailors as criminals rather than prisoners of war. International law expert James Kraska (who believes Russia to be the aggressor in the Ukraine crisis that started in late 2013) argues that such a state of conflict exists and may be recognized for legal purposes regardless of whether the parties involved officially recognize such a state existing between them. An excerpt from his legal assessment of the incident is as follows:

> The law of naval warfare largely displaces UNCLOS in this case since the law of the sea is a peacetime regime and Ukraine and Russia are engaged in an international armed conflict (IAC). . . . During international armed conflict, international humanitarian law applies, and at sea, the associated rules of the law of naval warfare. Thus, the rules governing the naval incident near the Kerch Strait derive from customary humanitarian law and The Hague Conventions and Geneva Conventions rather than UNCLOS. These rules are for the most part restated in the San Remo Manual on International Law Applicable to Armed Conflicts at Sea and permit targeting military objectives, such as enemy warships.
>
> . . . As part of the Ukrainian Navy, the artillery patrol boats are part of a belligerent force and may be targeted for capture, or attacked and destroyed without warning by Russian armed forces at any time during hostilities, unless they are hors de combat. The warships contribute to Ukraine's military action by their very nature, and their capture or destruction constitutes a military advantage for Russia. These rules also apply to auxiliary vessels, such as the Ukrainian tugboat, which is reportedly a Ukrainian Navy craft. During peacetime, Rules 6, 7 and 8 of the Convention on the International Regulations for Preventing

Collisions at Sea (COLREG) applies to the interception and collision of a tugboat by the Russian Coast Guard. During armed conflict, however, Russia's action to collide with the tugboat appears to be a proportionate use of force against either a Ukrainian military asset, or a civilian craft that was integrated into the Ukrainian order of battle and therefore without con-combatant immunity (330).

Others, however, argue that a state of armed conflict did not clearly exist between Russia and Ukraine at the time of the incident and that non-conflict maritime law is applicable. In that case, there are several articles under UNCLOS that govern innocent passage and transit in international waters that Russia would be in violation of. There is also the bilateral agreement of 2003 between Russia and Ukraine that allows merchant ships and warships of both states to pass through the Sea of Azov and the Kerch Strait unimpeded. However, that treaty is connected to the 1997 Friendship Treaty between the two countries, which Poroshenko unilaterally withdrew Ukraine from in September 2018, against warnings from some Ukrainian law experts (332).

People who make the argument that a state of war between Russia and Ukraine does not exist and that, therefore, Russia is in the wrong might be more credible if they were not often the same people who depict the rebels in Eastern Ukraine as Russian proxies and puppets (Russia-backed). If the rebels are Russian proxies and the Kiev government has engaged in military exchanges with them—as they have periodically since 2014, then that means that a conflict does indeed exist between Ukraine and Russia, albeit in a thinly veiled manner.

It should also be noted that an American journalist published an op-ed in the *Washington Examiner* in May 2018, just prior to the opening of the bridge that Russia built over the Kerch Strait to facilitate auto and rail traffic from the mainland to Crimea (333), encouraging Ukraine to destroy part of the structure. The Russian government is undoubtedly aware of this potential incitement and would understandably be concerned about security around the bridge.

The incident increased tensions, resulting in the Kiev government temporarily declaring martial law in areas bordering Russia, Russia announcing in mid-December 2018 that it was sending warplanes to Crimea based on intelligence regarding a potential Ukrainian provocation (334), and Ukraine then threatening to send warships back to the Sea of Azov (335). The U.S. Air Force also conducted a surveillance flight over Ukraine pursuant to the Open Skies Treaty to send its own message (336).

In conclusion, Ukraine remains a flash point between Russia and the West, is still a very poor country with intractable corruption, and exports little that the EU or the United States wants to buy. It has a smoldering conflict in the Donbas, which has officially claimed over 10,000 lives—although the toll is estimated to be much higher according to German intelligence (337). Moreover, the Kiev government has enabled the unleashing of a violent ultranationalist force that will not be easily placated. Consequently, it's difficult to assess the 2013 coup as a benefit to Ukrainians in general or the international community.

U.S.-Russia Relations in the Trump Era

Russia hasn't fared any better with the Trump administration. In Putin's first telephone call with the new president on January 28, 2017, Putin suggested that Washington and Moscow negotiate an extension to the New START Treaty, which limits each country's strategic nuclear warheads to 1,550 that can be deployed on no more than 700 ICBMS, SLBMS, and nuclear bombers (338).

After placing Putin on hold to ask his advisors to explain to him what the New START Treaty was, Trump said he was not interested, claiming that the treaty had been unfair to Washington. Putin tried again to encourage Trump to consider negotiations to extend the treaty at the Helsinki meeting in July 2018 (339). Not only did Trump not take Putin up on this offer, he later announced that Washington would unilaterally withdraw from the 1987 Intermediate Range Nuclear Forces (INF) Treaty, which removed a whole class of nuclear weapons from the two countries' arsenals.

Putin also proposed at the Helsinki meeting to add clauses to the joint declaration stating that both countries would refrain from interfering in each other's elections and would not attack each other's critical infrastructure. These proposed clauses were rejected by Washington (340).

Chapter 10: The U.S. Media Problem

The myth we're taught is that our democracy is underpinned by a media that serves as a watchdog on the government and other powerful institutions—a noble fourth estate.

But when it comes to issues of war and peace, the mainstream corporate media rarely—if ever—serves as a questioner of government claims, performing due diligence on matters of life, death, and destruction of societies.

We have seen the mainstream media's gross negligence with Iraq, Libya, and other examples stretching much further back. We are now seeing the same thing happen with the world's other nuclear superpower.

It's critical in a democracy to have an informed citizenry with a reasonable understanding of issues. This is especially true with issues most average Americans don't have practical experience with, such as international relations, our policies relating to other countries. As stated in the introduction to this book, in order to conduct a rational foreign policy, one must understand the other country's point of view.

Understanding that viewpoint means understanding the other side's history, geography, and culture. In other words, it means having context provided. The mainstream corporate media has not provided this crucial service or provided a platform for those who can with respect to Iraq, Libya, and many of the other nations with whom we've gone to war. The so-called experts the mainstream corporate media consult often have conflicts of interest, have nefarious agendas, and/or lack an objective understanding of the nation about which they are writing or talking. This has certainly been the case when it comes to reporting on Russia—a country with which the stakes are potentially much higher.

In order to understand what has gone wrong with our foreign policy in general and with our Russia policy specifically—and why it seems so impervious to course correction—it is necessary to understand how most of our media is not working in the public interest.

Edward Bernays and the Manipulation of the Public Mind

Edward Bernays was the nephew of pioneering Austrian psychiatrist Sigmund Freud. His parents settled in the United States and Bernays grew up American, but he came to be deeply influenced by his uncle's ideas about the unconscious, its role as the repository of repressed sexual and aggressive impulses, and its potential use as a means of manipulating the masses (341). Bernays was also influenced by social psychologist Wilfred Trotter's theories on crowd psychology and the "herd instinct" (342).

During WWI, which threw Freud into a deep depression because he saw it as confirmation of his worst fears about human behavior, Bernays was working as a press agent and was asked to assist the war effort by participating in the American government's committee on public information, known as the Creel Committee. His great contribution was effectively promoting President Woodrow Wilson's narrative of the war as a fight to spread democracy to Europe. During the Paris Peace Conference, Bernays saw firsthand the success of his propaganda efforts, as the Paris crowds greeted Wilson as "a liberator of the people. The man who would create a new world in which the individual would be free" (341).

Inspired by the achievements of propaganda during wartime, Bernays, looking to make his fortune, set to work on turning Americans from citizens into passive consumers who would be controlled by channeling their unconscious desires into a constant quest for goods and services that they would associate with their deepest yearnings for beauty, freedom, and fulfillment (341). Bernays would come up with tactics to bombard the public with messages that would cement this objective.

One of his first successes involved helping the tobacco industry expand its market by breaking the taboo against women smoking in public. After soliciting the advice of the top psychoanalyst in America, who told him that

cigarettes were a phallic symbol and represented male sexual power, he realized that if cigarettes could be associated with challenging men's power,
women would respond positively to smoking (341), as it would be connected
to the ideas of freedom and rebellion—two of the most common marketing
concepts to this day (343).

At the annual Easter Day Parade in New York City, Bernays staged a
memorable event in which a group of "rich debutantes" lit up cigarettes in
theatrical fashion at Bernays's prearranged signal. He had tipped off the
media that a group of "suffragettes" would be lighting up what they called
"torches of freedom" (341). As Bernays knew, who could argue against freedom in America? By associating cigarettes with freedom to women, Bernays
helped the tobacco companies hit the jackpot.

Bernays and his insights soon became indispensable to corporate
America, which was worried that consumer demand for products would
plateau, as mass production had been mastered and people at the time tended
to buy goods based on need and durability. Only a small group of wealthy
people could buy a significant number of luxury items. Consequently, to
continue growing their markets, they needed to "transform the way the
majority of Americans thought about products," as Paul Mazur, a Lehman
Brothers Wall Street banker, said. Mazur turned to Bernays for implementation of this transformation (341).

As Peter Solomon, investment banker for Lehman Brothers, said about
Mazur in the documentary film *The Century of the Self*:

> Prior to that time there was no American consumer, there
> was the American worker. And there was the American
> owner. And they manufactured and they saved and they
> ate what they had to and the people shopped for what they
> needed. And while the very rich may have bought things
> they didn't need, most people did not. And Mazur envi-
> sioned a break with that where you would have things that
> you didn't actually need, but you wanted as opposed to
> needed (341).

As the New York banks financed the spread of chain department stores across the country to serve as oases of consumerism, Bernays came up with many methods of product promotion that would become pervasive later on, such as linking products with movie stars who were also his clients, adorning those same movie stars in clothes and accessories made by other corporate clients during public events, and prominently placing products in films (341).

He also paid psychologists to issue reports claiming that certain products and services were good for people's well-being and celebrities to push the idea that clothes were not merely necessities but a means of self-expression (341). This became known as the "third-party technique" of conferring legitimacy by what appears to be a disinterested party or an authoritative source (344).

The dramatic growth in consumerism that Bernays actively facilitated contributed to the stock market boom. After it crashed in 1929, however, the idea that Americans were consumers rather than citizens was challenged, as the consumer boom could no longer be sustained and Franklin Roosevelt's administration actively lobbied against it as part of the New Deal program. Supreme Court justice Felix Frankfurter, in a letter to Roosevelt, described Bernays and his PR colleagues as "professional poisoners of the public mind, exploiters of foolishness, fanaticism, and self-interest" (341). Unlike Bernays, Roosevelt and his colleagues believed that people could be trusted to make rational decisions if their fears, desires, and insecurities were not manipulated in other directions, as reflected in Roosevelt's famous admonition, "The only thing we have to fear is fear itself."

Bernays eventually saw his ideas transferred into the realm of political philosophy (341) as renowned political writer and repentant former socialist Walter Lippmann, who had served with Bernays on the Creel Committee, began to apply Freud's ideas to a need to control the masses politically, viewing the Russian Revolution as an example of the dark forces of the rabble being unleashed. Bernays was intrigued by Lippmann's interpretation of his uncle's ideas contained in his books, which Bernays professionally promoted in the United States. Lippmann had begun to openly question the feasibility of democracy:

> The lesson is, I think, a fairly clear one. In the absence of institutions and education by which the environment is so successfully reported that the realities of public life stand out sharply against self-centered opinion, the common interests very largely elude public opinion entirely, and can be managed only by a specialized class whose personal interests reach beyond the locality (345).

In his 1922 book *The Phantom Public*, Lippmann states plainly: "The public must be put in its place [so that we may] live free of the trampling and the roar of a bewildered herd" (346).

In 1930s Germany, the Nazis also asserted that democracy was not feasible, and Joseph Goebbels, who emerged as the Nazis' preeminent propagandist, had taken note of Bernays's methods of public manipulation based on Freudian theory as a way to channel the desires of the population in a particular direction favored by the leaders. Goebbels reportedly admitted putting Bernays's book *Crystallizing Public Opinion* to use in the regime's genocidal campaign against the Jews in terms of creating a public environment of hatred and scapegoating (342).

Having honed his propaganda skills since WWI, Bernays would once again provide his services on behalf of the martial ambitions of the U.S. government. He served as an advisor to President Eisenhower and believed that the best way to deal with Americans' fear of Communism and the nuclear arms race was to manipulate those fears to support America's mobilization in the Cold War.

In 1954, Bernays assisted the CIA's overthrow of Guatemala's democratically elected leader Jacobo Árbenz, a democratic socialist with no ties to the Soviet Union. The CIA had a propaganda program in place called Operation Mockingbird, in which numerous journalists and editors—both paid and unpaid—published and broadcast stories sympathetic to the increasingly aggressive and unaccountable agency. Led by Frank Wisner, Operation Mockingbird was also used to suppress reporting that would expose the agency's nefarious covert activities or present them in a negative light (347).

Bernays's role was to create a narrative that portrayed the coup as the popular overthrow of a communist dictator and puppet of Moscow whose removal represented the spreading of democracy (344). In reality, Árbenz's ouster was to preserve the profits of United Fruit Company, a company that Bernays had worked for in a PR capacity since the 1940s. Meanwhile, the head of the CIA, Allen Dulles, had made investments in United Fruit in his earlier years as a lawyer at the Sullivan and Cromwell firm, which served as United Fruit's corporate counsel (348).

Bernays exploited the Red Scare of the McCarthy Era as well as the ignorance of most Americans in relation to foreign affairs. He did this by planting false stories in American newspapers and magazines, providing phony "intelligence" sources to the media, and bringing members of the press on a carefully orchestrated "fact-finding" mission to Guatemala paid for by the United Fruit Company (344).

As *PR Watch* noted in a 2010 article, "Bernays' carefully planned campaign successfully created an atmosphere of fear and suspicion in the U.S. about the Guatemalan government, compelling a U.S. intervention that advanced Chiquita's [then known as the United Fruit Company] interests and was internationally condemned" (344).

Bernays's biographer, Larry Tye, commented in *The Century of the Self*:

> [Bernays] totally understood that the coup would happen when conditions in the public and the press allowed for a coup to happen and he created those conditions. He was totally savvy in terms of just what he was helping create in terms of the overthrow. But ultimately he was reshaping reality, and reshaping public opinion in a way that's undemocratic and manipulative (341).

Bernays's propaganda narrative, combined with CIA Director Allen Dulles's ability to restrict the travel of independent journalists to Guatemala (347), ensured the success of the coup. Árbenz's overthrow led to a decades-long civil war that resulted in 200,000 dead and 100,000 disappeared (344).

Bernays rationalized his work at manipulating the masses—or "engineering consent," as he referred to it—as necessary to control what he saw as the dangerous and irrational forces that guided human behavior, particularly in large groups. Bernays's daughter, Ann, said the following about her father in *The Century of the Self*:

> What my father understood about groups is that they are malleable. And that you can tap into their deepest desires or fears and use that to your own purposes. I don't think he felt that all those publics [sic] out there had reliable judgment; that they may very easily vote for the wrong man or want the wrong thing. So they had to be guided from above (341).

Subsequent psychological studies as well as the observation of humans throughout history demonstrate that people are indeed malleable and capable of a wide range of behaviors, but there is nothing indicating that humans are doomed to act like brutal mobs or genocidal maniacs unless they are led in that direction by powerful social forces.

Bernays's work and the philosophy underpinning it have paved the way for the cynical use of grand ideas like freedom, democracy, and human rights to sell mindless consumption, wars, coups, and instability—all in the service of a small group of people who benefit.

The CIA, in fact, engaged in numerous covert actions in the decades following WWII to effect what is now referred to as regime change—assassinations, coups, civil wars, and destabilizations—throughout the third world, as historian and former State Department official William Blum documented in several books and essays, along with other researchers and CIA whistleblowers.

These actions involved killing, torture, destruction of infrastructure, delayed development, and impoverishment in target countries. In most cases, the victims were guilty only of supporting policies that were anathema to the American political class, such as socialism, economic populism, and national sovereignty in terms of control of natural resources and financial assets (143).

Congressional hearings in the 1970s led by Frank Church combined with a brief window of relative media openness exposed some of this ugly program to the American people. Rather than cease these kinds of actions, the American political establishment's response to the negative publicity was to create a separate entity that would take over for many of these covert operations. An entity that would obscure the nature of its activities under the guise of spreading democracy and would be funded by the U.S. Congress (110). In 1983, the National Endowment for Democracy (NED) was born, and Allen Weinstein, who helped write the legislation that brought it into existence, admitted in 1991, "A lot of what we do today was done covertly 25 years ago by the CIA" (110).

NED funds many innocuous-sounding groups, both domestic and foreign. One such domestic group is Freedom House. While receiving the majority of its funding from NED, Freedom House presents itself as an objective nonprofit interested in freedom, democracy, and human rights and publishes regular reports rating various countries on these supposed criteria (349). However, upon closer examination, the ratings tend to reflect well on those countries aligned with U.S. economic and geopolitical interests and poorly on countries that are rivals. Freedom House's assessment of the American media's coverage of the Tet Offensive during the Vietnam War (107) and its more recent assessment of post-coup Ukraine (350) are evidence of its lack of credibility in measuring a free and democratic media, among other issues.

In the international arena, NED has funded numerous "opposition" and "democracy" groups in Russia (before being booted out by the government), Venezuela, and pre-coup Ukraine. These groups are not funded out of the goodness of the U.S. government's heart to advance human rights and authentic democracy, but to create tension that is to be ratcheted up in the hopes of culminating in a coup, civil war, or other form of destabilization to remove or undermine governments that are viewed as a threat to the interests of the oligarchy that, according to a 2014 academic study, now officially governs the United States (351).

For all of Uncle Freud's faults—such as his stultifying preoccupation with sex and violence—he never intended for his theories to be used in this fashion, serving as the basis for justifying a never-ending sequence of actions that caused him so much worry for mankind: war. Freud, who did not like American culture, expressed disgust when Bernays encouraged him to write articles for clients in the popular media, which Freud perceived as a cheapening of his work.

Bernays, on the other hand, was a manipulative, arrogant, and self-aggrandizing man who essentially believed that humans were too stupid and too dangerous to be trusted with the truth or self-governance. He was an elitist who was right at home with the oligarchs and hawks of his day and their agenda of control, consumerism, militarism, and ignorance. What's more, he was paid handsomely for his work, in both money and stature.

It should be noted, of course, that fear of the rabble was articulated centuries prior to Freud, Trotter, and Bernays—although its underlying psychological dynamics may not have been clearly understood. This included a segment of the founding fathers, such as Alexander Hamilton and John Jay, whose ideas justified an effective rule by the elite (346).

Going back even further, one finds that David Hume made observations in the 17th century about the need to control the opinions of the masses to protect the rule of the few in light of the English political upheaval, which saw demands for universal education, democratization of the law, and social protections. Noam Chomsky has delineated the line of political thought stretching from Hume to John Locke to today:

> In the contemporary period, Hume's insight has been revived and elaborated, but with a crucial innovation: control of thought is *more* important for governments that are free and popular than for despotic and military states. The logic is straightforward. A despotic state can control its domestic enemy by force, but as the state loses this weapon, other devices are required to prevent the ignorant masses from interfering with public affairs, which are none of their business. These prominent fea-

tures of modern political and intellectual culture merit a
closer look (emphasis in original) (346).

The Mass Media: Whose Platform?

As alluded to earlier by Jean Bricmont, the secular priesthood, with its opinion makers, academics, and journalists, must have an effective and pervasive
platform through which to inculcate and constantly reinforce their message
on behalf of the oligarchy that now effectively controls all substantive public
policy in the United States, while the populace is reduced to participating in
theatrical elections at regular intervals.

Award-winning journalists Robert Parry (184) and Chris Hedges (352)
were marginalized by the corporate mass media after refusing to go along
with the false narratives presented in connection with foreign policy. They
each tell a similar story in terms of their exile after refusing to toe the line on
U.S. support for violent militias and destabilization in Central America in
the 1980s, and the run-up to the Iraq War in 2003, respectively. Their experiences indicate there are three things that a journalist who wants to have a
long-term and lucrative career will generally not report on: 1) stories that
will offend the corporate media owners, 2) stories that will offend the corporate media advertisers, and 3) stories that will jeopardize their relationships
with those in power.

Thanks to the 1996 Telecommunications Act, which enabled a major
deregulation of mergers in the media industry, 90 percent of what most people read, watch, or listen to in the United States comes from an entity that is
owned by one of six corporate conglomerates: Comcast, Disney Company,
AT&T, Viacom, 21st Century Fox, and CBS Corporation (353). Each of these
six conglomerates, in turn, has boards of directors who have financial ties to
other corporate interests, namely the Military-Industrial Complex (MIC),
Fossil Fuels, Banking, Big Ag, and Big Pharma (354).

A few examples: Disney has relations with Boeing and City National
Bank; NBC with Honeywell, Chase Manhattan, and the New York Stock
Exchange; Viacom with Honeywell, Bear Stearns, Chase Manhattan, JPMor-
gan Chase, and Pfizer; CNN/Time with Chevron, Citigroup, and Pfizer; News

Corporation with Philip Morris, Rothschild Investments, and the New York Stock Exchange; New York Times Company with Alcoa, Bristol-Myers Squibb, The Carlyle Group, Chase Manhattan, Lehman Brothers, and Texaco; The Wall Street Journal with Clear Channel, Pfizer, Texaco, and Royal Dutch Shell; Knight Ridder with Bank of America, Eli Lilly, GE, Raytheon, and Phillips Petroleum (354).

The Mass Media: Mechanisms of Control

The experiences of journalists like Parry and Hedges should come as no surprise according to the propaganda model outlined by analysts Noam Chomsky and Edward Herman in their seminal book *Manufacturing Consent: The Political Economy of the Mass Media*. Their model identifies five sets of filters that represent the methods by which a private and reputedly "free" media actually serve as the means by which the population is conditioned to believe what the elites who control American society want them to believe: that America is governed by a fair, democratic, and legitimate system, despite actual evidence to the contrary. I will focus on the first three filters below.

The first filter, already discussed, is the corporate ownership of the mass media. The corporate boards hire and/or approve editors who will enforce acceptable narratives based on their interests.

A second, less obvious filter of corporate control related to profit motive is the media's reliance on advertising to make money rather than on selling a quality news product. Newspapers, magazines, broadcasts, and internet programming make most of their money from selling space to corporate advertisers, which consequently drives the motivation to produce content that will grab people's attention in order to attract advertising dollars. Thus, the emphasis is on sensationalist stories focused on sex, violence, scandal, and celebrities. According to the Pew Research Center's Journalism & Media project, "69% of all domestic news revenue is derived from advertising" (355).

The third filter involves the reliance by journalists on representatives of the government and corporate elites as sources of inside information, along with "experts" who often represent elite interests in the tradition of those created by Edward Bernays. As Chomsky and Herman state:

> The mass media are drawn into a symbiotic relationship with powerful sources of information by economic necessity and reciprocity of interest. The media need a steady, reliable flow of the raw material of news. They have daily news demands and imperative news schedules that they must meet. They cannot afford to have reporters and cameras at all places where important stories may break. Economics dictates that they concentrate their resources where significant news often occurs, where important rumors and leaks abound, and where regular press conferences are held. The White House, the Pentagon, and the State Department, in Washington D.C., are central nodes of such news activity. On a local basis, city hall and the police department are the subject of regular news beats for reporters. Business corporations and trade groups are also regular and credible purveyors of stories deemed newsworthy (107).

Chomsky and Herman also point out that all of this reliance on elite sources and "experts" is cost-effective (107). Providing truthful and balanced journalism requires a large enough staff of full-time reporters who can perform due diligence. Over the last two decades, newsrooms have been starved of staff and resources as jobs decreased by 23 percent between 2008 and 2017 (356). The reliance on elite "experts" is also cost-effective in terms of the media protecting themselves from powerful moneyed interests who can afford to punish media outlets through libel litigation or government agencies that can suspend licenses and permits for broadcasters to operate. All of the aforementioned mechanisms contribute to perverting what journalistic "objectivity" means in practice.

Government Elites

With respect to government and military elites, numerous "news" shows allow a bevy of retired military leaders—many of whom have financial relationships with defense contractors—to provide commentary and analysis in connection with foreign policy, commentary and analysis that inevitably rationalizes a military solution of some sort with most "debate" turning on just how much military power or which military tactics to use. Very seldom are academics, activists, or journalists allowed to air alternatives to militarist policy, despite the availability of people who could articulate the benefits of such policies while providing historical, cultural, and geopolitical context that is often missing in a typical broadcast of shallow and self-serving sound bites.

Pundits and journalists will often sound articulate and provide a compelling narrative, but due to the fact that the average American doesn't know much about countries like Vietnam in the 1960s or today's Iran, Iraq, Libya, Syria, and Russia, they won't know enough to realize what they're being told is false or seriously distorted.

The Ukraine crisis and the civil war it touched off in early 2014 is a case in point. The American media narrative relied upon the repetition of two main ideas: 1) the portrayal of the coup instigated by the West—with neo-Nazis as the muscle and an Association Agreement from the EU filled with empty promises as the catalyst—as aggression by Russia; and 2) the demonization of Russian president Putin, mostly based upon distortions, exaggerations, innuendo, and outright falsehoods. Victoria Nuland and her NED cronies, who helped shape the narrative in western Ukraine during the coup and continued to shape it in the Western media afterward, have taken Bernays's playbook and refined it.

One of the mass media's favorite authorities on the topic of Russia and Ukraine is Anne Applebaum. By way of background, Applebaum is a widely published author and columnist, formerly with the neocon think tank American Enterprise Institute, and has worked with NED—an organization she describes as "independent" (357). She has also worked for the Legatum Institute in London (358), where she churned out anti-Russia propaganda with her neocon playmates Peter Pomerantsev and Michael Weiss. Legatum was founded by Christopher Chandler, who made billions off of the corrupt voucher program in Russia during the Yeltsin years (359). Applebaum is also the wife of Radoslaw Sikorski, who was the foreign minister of Poland until 2014. Sikorski gained notoriety when he told *Politico* reporter Ben Judah that he overheard a 2008 conversation between Putin and then-Prime Minister of Poland Donald Tusk in which Putin suggested that Ukraine be divided up between Russia and Poland. It didn't take long for Sikorski's story to fall apart, and he was forced to publicly retract the allegation and apologize to the Polish government.

As Moscow-based investigative journalist John Helmer has reported, there was controversy in Poland when Applebaum's income shot up from $20,000 in 2011 to $565,000 in 2013 with no details provided as to where the surge in income came from and whether it was related to her husband's political activities. Helmer's Polish sources express a suspicion that Applebaum is receiving money from revived U.S. government programs that have as their objective the dissemination of anti-Russia material. Helmer's attempts to find out from Applebaum's publishers and the Legatum Institute if the significant income increase was attributable to their compensation were stonewalled (360).

Notorious Russian oligarch Mikhail Khodorkovsky's family nonprofit, Institute of Modern Russia, has admitted that it was working with Applebaum through the Legatum Institute on a "series of studies" on Applebaum's persistent themes relating to Russia (360), including its "postmodern dictatorship." The papers were used as the foundation for public panels, including one in Washington, D.C., cosponsored by NED (359). Several scholars and writers who specialize in Russia and geopolitics have expressed concern about one of the papers that was hailed at these panels, "The Menace of Unreality," which attempts to legitimize what amounts to censorship of any reporting or analysis of Russia and related issues that does not adhere to the narrative outlined by government officials and their mass media lapdogs (359).

Applebaum flogged the same anti-Russia and Putin demonization themes during the Munk debates in Canada in April 2015. In arguing on behalf of the position that the West should continue to keep Russia in the naughty corner and eschew engagement, Applebaum turned reality on its head. In regards to Putin's relations with the West, notably the United States, she claimed that the West bent over backwards to welcome Putin and Russia into its paradise of peace, prosperity, and democracy only to have Putin cheat, steal, and aggress on his neighbors—accusations that take particular temerity given the enriching schemes by the Legatum Institute's founder in the 1990s, an era that Applebaum thinks was better for Russia. The truth, as documented by Stephen F. Cohen (one of her opponents in the Munk debate), Jack Matlock, Ben Aris, and Angus Roxburgh (among other academics and journalists), is that Putin made numerous attempts to have a mutually respectful and cooperative relationship with the United States and received little for his efforts except for several swift kicks to the shins in the form of NATO expansion, unilateral withdrawal from critical arms control treaties, provocations on his borders, and interference in Russia's internal affairs on a level that would never be tolerated by the United States, as demonstrated by the reactions of Americans who believed the (now largely debunked) Russiagate narrative. Despite Applebaum's gross distortions, her side swayed the audience and won the debate (361).

In addition to NED and its darlings like Applebaum, there is a possibility that the CIA revived or never really shut down its Operation Mockingbird program. A 2014 book by the late Dr. Udo Ulfkotte, former editor of major German newspaper *Frankfurter Allgemeine Zeitung*, stated that numerous journalists and editors in the German—as well as other European—mass media are on the payroll of the CIA. He describes how he put his name to and published articles that were actually penned by the CIA, articles that pushed whatever militarist narrative the U.S. political elites and security apparatus wanted (362). The book, *Bought Journalists*, has been a best seller in the original German language on Amazon, but the mass media in both the United States and Western Europe dummied up instead of reporting on the book or its allegations. One was left to look to the independent and non-Western media to even learn of its existence.

Americans' Growing Distrust of the Mass Media

Ironically, those bombarded constantly with propaganda, especially when it becomes more and more obvious—for example, in numerous reports originating from official government sources in the aftermath of the Ukraine crisis and subsequent civil war saying that Russia had invaded Ukraine, only to have the photographic evidence debunked within days or even hours—are bound to reach a point of distrust. According to a September 2014 Gallup poll, Americans' trust in the mass media was at an all-time low of 40 percent. Americans have also expressed a desire for a wider range of independent media sources (363).

An annual Gallup poll conducted in the latter part of 2016 revealed that trust in the American media had fallen even further, to 32 percent. A Harvard-Harris poll from May 2017 found that 65 percent of Americans believe the mainstream media publishes a significant amount of "fake news." The partisan breakdown was: 80 percent of Republicans, 60 percent of Independents, and 53 percent of Democrats (364).

A graphic from 2017 comparing polls of what issues Americans said they cared about most versus what issues the corporate media spent the most time covering illustrated the major disconnect between the two.

Health care and jobs were the top two issues of concern to Americans but received only 4 percent and 1 percent of total media coverage, respectively. Meanwhile, Russia was rated very low as an issue of concern but received 75 percent of media coverage (365).

So why does the media insist on giving a disproportionate amount of coverage to an issue for which the most important claims have largely been unsubstantiated at the expense of issues that the American people care far more about? *Rolling Stone* veteran journalist and media critic Matt Taibbi gave his perspective in a 2017 interview with the Real News Network:

> From the media standpoint, I think what people have to understand is that a lot of this is about money. The Russia story sells incredibly well and cable networks that traditionally have not made a lot of money are making a lot of

money with this story. So I understand that the relentless emphasis on the Russia story makes a lot of sense from the networks' point of view because it creates among viewers this impression that the fate of the nation may be decided any minute. This is like they're selling it as a kind of Watergate sequel, so you have to tune in every night. Not just on election night, you have to keep tuning in (366).

Media Coverage of Russiagate:
False and Exaggerated Claims. Rinse and Repeat

Well, there's no question that the national security establishment has grown and has become far more powerful than it ever was. But here's the change. We've shifted from the Industrial Age to the Information Age. And consequently, we've also shifted from the dominance of the military-industrial complex, if you will, to a much more insidious and much more difficult-to-diagnose information complex.

—William Arkin, journalist and analyst covering national security issues (367)

After reviewing a 2015 survey, Hillary Clinton's presidential campaign team discovered a disturbing weakness for their candidate. When people became aware of Clinton's role in facilitating the sale of 20 percent of U.S. uranium to Russian entities while she was secretary of state, their likeliness to vote for her declined significantly (368).

In order to not have to go on the defense about Clinton's actions, her campaign decided to go on the offense, taking her perceived weakness—subordinating American security interests to Russia—and projecting it onto her opponent, Donald Trump.

When Clinton lost the election, her campaign staff quickly huddled and within 24 hours decided to pursue a policy of blaming Russia for Trump's "illegitimate" victory (369), conveniently forgetting that they had wanted Trump as the Republican presidential nominee, assuming he'd be easy to defeat (370).

The political class, including organs of the national security state, was deeply unhappy with Trump's upset victory. Though a plutocrat, Trump is coarse and undisciplined, with an unpredictable temperament and an independent streak.

The majority of the corporate media, reflecting the views of the political class that owns it, has made no secret of its hatred for Trump and has been quick to publish virtually any story that paints Trump in a bad light, particularly in connection with the Russiagate scandal and the related investigation headed by Robert Mueller.

The most notable thing about the Mueller investigation to anyone who took a sober look at it was its constantly evolving purpose. First, the purpose of the investigation was to find any evidence to support the allegation that Russia had hacked into the DNC's emails. When no substantial evidence could be found to support that allegation, the purpose evolved into collusion between Trump and Russia to steal the election on behalf of Trump.

When no substantial evidence could be found to support that allegation, the purpose evolved yet again into Russia influencing the election on behalf of Trump, possibly without his knowledge or participation. When no substantial evidence could be found to support that allegation and all that could be found was a paltry number of social media ad buys—many of which were purchased after the election or advocated conflicting positions or didn't even have anything to do with the election (371), the purpose became "sowing discord."

As journalist Aaron Maté, who has provided in-depth analysis of the Russiagate story from the beginning, explained in response to the release of two Senate-commissioned reports at the end of 2018 that purported to provide evidence of election interference and how it was achieved through social media:

> Far from exposing a sophisticated propaganda campaign,
> the reports [from New Knowledge and the University of
> Oxford's Computational Propaganda Research Project]
> provide more evidence that the Russians were actually
> engaging in clickbait capitalism: targeting unique demo-
> graphics like African Americans or evangelicals in a bid
> to attract large audiences for commercial purposes (371).

The reports were being touted by both politicians and the establishment media as proof that Russia had manipulated a sliver of African Americans in Midwestern and Rust Belt states to not vote for Clinton, namely by
staying home. This, it was argued by some, was just enough to swing the
election in geographically relevant states.

Maté points out how this is not only insulting to the demographic of
voters in question, but is contradicted by the work of other reporters who
had the novel idea of actually asking people in this voting demographic why
they didn't vote:

> That it is even considered possible that the Russian cam-
> paign impacted the black vote displays a rather stunning
> paternalism and condescension. Would [David] Axelrod,
> [New York] *Times* reporters, or any of the others floating
> a similar scenario accept a suggestion that their own votes
> might be susceptible to silly social-media posts mostly
> unrelated to the election? If not, what does that tell us
> about their attitudes toward the people that they presume
> could be so vulnerable?
>
> . . . Rather than ruminating over whether they were duped
> by Russian clickbait, reporters who have actually spoken
> to black Midwest voters have found that political disillu-
> sionment amid stagnant wages, high inequality, and per-
> vasive police brutality led many to stay home (371).

Aside from charges against various individuals connected to Trump
for financial misdeeds and lying to authorities, the Mueller investigation only

yielded indictments against two sets of Russians. The first set consisted of 13 private individuals who worked for a St. Petersburg–based "troll farm" known as the Internet Research Agency, which had been exposed several years before and is run by a caterer with no proven orchestration by Putin or the Kremlin.

In fact, just prior to Mueller's testimony before Congress in July 2019, the judge hearing a case brought by the Internet Research Agency and its affiliated company issued an order enjoining Mueller from continuing to publicly assert—explicitly or implicitly—that the Internet Research Agency was connected to the Russian government, since such a connection had not been proven (372).

The second set consisted of 12 GRU agents who were indicted for hacking the DNC computers—the contents of which were obtained by WikiLeaks. There are several potential problems with this indictment. First, there is serious doubt among some analysts that the DNC emails obtained by WikiLeaks were the product of a hack at all. Forensic analysts hired by Veteran Intelligence Professionals for Sanity (VIPS)—a group of retired intelligence agents who first formed to warn of the false WMD claims prior to the Iraq invasion—concluded that the speed with which the DNC emails were downloaded was too fast for them to have been transferred across the internet at that time. The speed of download instead corresponded to that of a transfer to a thumb drive, which would indicate a leaker with physical access to the computer server, not a remote hacker (373).

Second, as military analyst and former weapons inspector Scott Ritter states, the indictment did not connect the technical details of the information transfer of the DNC emails to the GRU intelligence agency:

> There is one major problem with the indictment, however: It doesn't prove that which it asserts. True, it provides a compelling narrative that reads like a spy novel, and there is no doubt in my mind that many of the technical details related to the timing and functioning of the malware described within are accurate. But the leap of logic that takes the reader from the inner workings of the servers of the Democratic Party to the offices of Russian intelligence

officers in Moscow is not backed up by anything that demonstrates how these connections were made.

. . . [T]he Mueller indictment has taken detailed data related to hacking operations directed against various American political entities and shoehorned it into what amounts to little more than the organizational chart of a military intelligence unit assessed [by an NSA analyst]— but not known—to have overseen the operations described. This is a far cry from the kind of incontrovert-ible proof that Mueller's team suggests exists to support its indictment of the 12 named Russian intelligence offi-cers (374).

An indictment is not a conviction, but an accusation and a narrative of what the accuser is claiming happened. Most lawyers will tell you that it's not often difficult to obtain an indictment. That's far different from obtaining a conviction, for which evidence must be presented to prove the accusation beyond a reasonable doubt in open court. It must be kept in mind that Muel-ler knew there was an extremely low chance that any of the accused, partic-ularly the GRU agents, would appear in a U.S. court. Hence, he would never be forced to actually prove his case against them.

In terms of logic, it always seemed unlikely that the Kremlin autho-rized an operation to throw the election to Trump, through direct collusion or otherwise. First, why would Putin risk provoking further anger from a candidate (Clinton) with whom he'd already had tense relations and who was almost universally predicted to be the next U.S. president? What would be the benefit to Putin or Russia? Anyone who has objectively analyzed Putin and his actions over the years knows that he doesn't tend to take big risks with very low odds of a meaningful payoff. Second, if he were going to autho-rize such an operation, would it have been such a small and amateurish one with such inconsequential sums of money invested in it?

This scenario is possible, but it would be out of character for Putin in terms of cost-benefit analysis and sloppiness of execution. Its probability is therefore low.

As exaggerated as the Russiagate reporting was, the media frenzy spilled over from simply over-hyping this particular scandal to publishing any claims of Russian misdeeds, often having the claims fall apart under a modicum of scrutiny. As journalist Glenn Greenwald details, the sheer number of times that this has happened and the fact that the mistake was always in the same direction shows that the media was not just making a mistake here and there, but was engaged in a habit of publishing claims that fit a particular narrative when the claims had not been subjected to minimum standards of due diligence:

> The reality is that from the start of the Trump/Russia story, the US media has repeatedly and frequently—not rarely and periodically—gotten major stories completely wrong, always in the same direction: exaggerating the threat posed by Russia to the US, and concocting evidence of Trump/Russia collusion even when such evidence did not exist (375).

A list of Russia-related stories that were completely wrong and had to later be retracted—after they'd done damage by being widely disseminated—was compiled by Greenwald as of August 2018:

- Russia hacked into the U.S. electric grid to deprive Americans of heat during winter (*Washington Post*)

- An anonymous group (PropOrNot) documented how major U.S. political sites are Kremlin agents (*Washington Post*)

- WikiLeaks has a long, documented relationship with Putin (*Guardian*)

- A secret server between Trump and a Russian bank has been discovered (*Slate*)

- RT hacked C-SPAN and caused disruption in its broadcast (*Fortune*)

- Russians hacked into a Ukrainian artillery app (CrowdStrike)

- Russians attempted to hack elections systems in 21 states (multiple news outlets, echoing Homeland Security)

- Links have been found between Trump ally Anthony Scaramucci and a Russian investment fund under investigation (CNN) (375)

By January 2019, Greenwald had to add to the list the story that had been promoted since September 2017 by NBC and MSNBC that Russia was responsible for using "sophisticated microwaves"—so sophisticated that the U.S. government didn't yet understand how they worked—to cause brain injuries allegedly suffered by U.S. diplomatic personnel in Cuba.

Two scientists, Alexander Stubbs and Fernando Montealegre-Z, analyzed sound recordings of the noise supposedly causing the problem, and determined that it was the mating calls of a particular species of Caribbean cricket (376).

Perhaps equally as disturbing as the repeatedly bad reporting was the accepted vilification of not just the Russian president but Russians in general within our political, cultural, and media landscape.

Ruth Marcus, deputy editor of *The Washington Post*, sent out the following tweet in March 2017, squealing with delight at the thought of a new Cold War with the world's other nuclear superpower while referencing a television show about Soviet spies embedded deeply within a U.S. town during the 1980s: "So excited to be watching The Americans, throwback to a simpler time when everyone considered Russia the enemy. Even the president" (377).

Not only did Marcus's comment imply that it was great for the United States to have an enemy, but it specifically implied that there was something particularly great about that enemy being Russia.

The public discourse proceeded to get even nastier. Former Director of National Intelligence James Clapper—who notoriously perjured himself before Congress (378) about warrantless spying on Americans—stated on *Meet the Press* in May 2017 that Russians were uniquely and "genetically" predisposed toward manipulative political activities (379). If Clapper or anyone else in the public eye had made such a statement about Muslims, Arabs, Iranians, Jews, Israelis, Chinese, or just about any other group, there would have been some pushback about the prejudice that it reflected and how it didn't correspond with enlightened liberal values. But Clapper's comment passed with hardly a peep of protest.

John Sipher, a retired CIA station chief who reportedly spent years in Russia—although at what point in time is unclear—was interviewed in a *New Yorker* piece by Jane Mayer trying to spin the Steele dossier as somehow legitimate. On March 6, 2018, Sipher took to Twitter with the following comment: "How can one not be a Russophobe? Russia soft power is political warfare. Hard power is invading neighbors, hiding the death of civilians with chemical weapons and threatening with doomsday nuclear weapons. And they kill the opposition at home. Name something positive" (380).

In fairness to Sipher, he did backpedal somewhat after being challenged; however, the fact that his unfiltered blabbering reveals such a deep antipathy toward Russians ("How can one not be a Russophobe?") and an initial assumption that he could get away with saying it publicly is troubling.

Glenn Greenwald retweeted with a comment asking if Russians would soon acceptably be referred to as "rats and roaches." Another person replied with: "Because they are rats and roaches. What's the problem?" (381)

This is just a small sampling of the anti-Russian comments and attitudes that pass, largely unremarked upon, in our media.

There are, of course, the larger institutional influencers of culture doing their part to push anti-Russian bigotry in this already contentious atmosphere. *Red Sparrow*, both the book (382) and the movie (383), detail the escapades of a female Russian spy. The story propagates the continued fetishization of Russian women based on the stereotype that they're all hot and frisky. Furthermore, all those who work in Russian intelligence are evil and backwards rather than possibly being motivated by some kind of patriotism, while all the American intelligence agents are paragons of virtue and seem like they just stepped out of an ad for Nick at Nite's *How to be Swell*.

Similarly, *Loveless*, a 2018 film by Russian director Andrey Zvyagintsev (director of *Leviathan*), was largely reviewed—as British academic and film reviewer Catherine Brown points out—by writers from the mainstream American media in a predictably biased fashion. The film focuses on the disintegration of a married Moscow couple's relationship and the complicated web of factors involved, which have tragic ramifications for the couple's 12-year-old son (384).

American reviewers manage to paint the factors detailed in the film that are prevalent in most modern capitalist cities (e.g. being self-centered, materialistic, and preoccupied with technological gadgets) as somehow uniquely Russian sins. They also ignore a prominent character in the film that defies their negativity about modern Russia—a character that represents altruism and the growth of civil society in the country (384).

A common theme in all this is that Russia is a bad country and Russians can't help but be a bunch of good-for-nothings at best and dangerous deviants at worst. Indeed, according to media depictions, sometimes they manage to be both at the same time. But what they don't manage to be is positive, constructive, or even complicated. Sipher knows that the average American has been deluged with this anti-Russian prejudice, as reflected in the challenge at the end of his initial tweet about the largest country in the world: Name something positive.

Most people know, at least in the abstract, that few individuals or groups are purely good or bad. Most are a complex combination of both. But many—including those who normally consider themselves to be open-minded liberals—have allowed the primitive part of their brains to be triggered by the constant demonization of Russia in the hopes of taking down Trump, whom they deem to be a disproportionate threat to everything they hold dear. In the process, however, this particular group of anti-Trump liberals is ignoring Friedrich Nietzsche's warning that "Whoever fights monsters should see to it that in the process he does not become a monster."

For anyone who is able to think critically at all, this constant barrage of misreporting, exaggeration, and demonization will only further undermine the establishment media's credibility. In the long run that might provide space for a more vibrant independent media to fill the void, which would be a positive thing. But that doesn't mean that a lot of serious damage won't be done in the meantime, both in terms of domestic political debate and of U.S.-Russia relations, especially inasmuch as the former shapes the outlines of what is politically possible for the latter.

Afterword

As this book was going to press in January 2020, Vladimir Putin announced proposed amendments to the Russian Constitution. It kicked off with Putin's annual Address to the Federal Assembly, which usually happens in the spring, not in January. Among other topics, Putin discussed the changes he wanted made to the Russian Constitution, which he had telegraphed during his December 2019 Q&A. This was followed by Prime Minister Dmitry Medvedev's resignation (along with his cabinet) and the appointment of Mikhail Mishustin as his replacement.

This recent turn of events must be placed within the larger context of what Putin's priorities have been for Russia since he came to power. As I pointed out in Chapters 8 and 9, Russia was on the verge of being a failed state in 2000 when Putin took the helm. There were crises in every major area of state governance: the military was in shambles, the economy had collapsed, crime was rampant, massive poverty pervaded the country, and Russians were experiencing the worst mortality crisis since World War II.

Having studied Putin's governance and how Russia has fared over the two decades in which he has ruled, it's clear that he's had three main priorities for Russia, in the following order:

1. Ensuring Russia's national security and sovereignty as an independent nation;

2. Improving the economy and living standards for Russians; and,

3. The gradual democratization of the country.

These three priorities are reflected in Putin's 2020 Address to the Federal Assembly. Putin reiterated to his audience that the first priority of national security and state sovereignty had been secured:

> For the first time ever—I want to emphasise this—for the first time in the history of nuclear missile weapons, including the Soviet period and modern times, we are not catching up with anyone, but, on the contrary, other leading states have yet to create the weapons that Russia already possesses.
>
> The country's defence capability is ensured for decades to come, but we cannot rest on our laurels and do nothing. We must keep moving forward, carefully observing and analysing the developments in this area across the world, and create next-generation combat systems and complexes. This is what we are doing today.

Putin goes on to emphasize that success with this first priority enables Russia to focus even more seriously on the second priority:

> Reliable security creates the basis for Russia's progressive and peaceful development and allows us to do much more to overcome the most pressing internal challenges, to focus on the economic and social growth of all our regions in the interest of the people, because Russia's greatness is inseparable from dignified life of its every citizen. I see this harmony of a strong power and well-being of the people as a foundation of our future.

Despite the profound improvements in the economy and living conditions during Putin's earlier terms, comments from this address reflected mixed success, as economic conditions for Russians have stagnated over the past few years. One contributing factor has been the sanctions imposed by the West in response to Russia's reunification with Crimea as a result of the 2014 coup in Ukraine. As detailed in Chapter 9, Putin has done a respectable job of cushioning the Russian economy from the worst effects of the sanctions and even using them to advantage with respect to import substitution in the agricultural and industrial sectors. However, polls of the population have consistently shown over the past two to three years that Russians are losing patience with the lack of improvement in living standards.

Another problem that is limiting economic progress is the pattern of local bureaucrats not implementing Putin's edicts. For example, in his 2018 and 2019 addresses, Putin laid out an expensive plan for economic improvement based on infrastructure projects throughout the country as well as improving health and education. Budget allocations were made for these projects and the funds released, but many have only been partially realized. Confirming what has been reported in some quarters, Putin complained about the deficiencies in the rollout of these policies during his address.

I believe this is connected to the subsequent resignation of Medvedev as prime minister. Medvedev will now step into the newly created role of deputy chairman of the Security Council, while his cabinet remained in a caretaker capacity until a new government was formed the following week. Medvedev has not been particularly effective as prime minister and has been very unpopular over the past several years, as suspicions of corruption have swirled around him. He is also problematic ideologically, as he has always embraced neoliberal economic policy, which has no traction with most of the Russian people due to the experience of the 1990s, as discussed in Chapter 8. He also lacks the charisma and creative problem-solving skills of Putin.

But in all fairness, no prime minister will have an easy job in Russia if significant changes are needed or a transition is still in progress. Throughout Russia's history, whenever leaders wanted to reform the system, they've always encountered the problem of implementation in terms of the bureaucracy. Whether out of malevolence, fear of losing perceived benefits, inertia, or incompetence, bureaucrats lower down the chain don't always put the reforms effectively or consistently in place. Putin has complained at various times of local bureaucrats' intransigence and its negative effects on average citizens, whom they are supposed to be serving.

Not much is known about Medvedev's immediate replacement, Mikhail Mishustin, except that he is a former businessman and has served as head of Russia's Tax Service since 2010. In his capacity leading the tax agency, he has been held in positive regard, credited with modernizing and streamlining the historically onerous tax collection system.

The third priority of Putin has been gradual democratization of the country. Putin is often characterized in the West as an autocrat and a dictator. However, as I've detailed in Chapter 9, there are many democratic reforms that have been implemented under Putin's rule that are often ignored by Western media and analysts. It is not that democracy has not been a priority for Putin, it's that it was subordinate to the other two priorities. Putin, as well as many other Russians, has been nervous about possible instability. With Russia's history of constant upheaval over the past 120 years—two revolutions, two world wars, numerous famines, the Great Terror, and a national collapse—this is understandable.

Putin has used the constitutional system that he inherited from Yeltsin, which provides for a strong presidency and a weak parliament, effectively throughout his 20 years in power—16 of them as president—to try to solve the various crises mentioned earlier. Such strong, centralized power is necessary when a state is dealing with multiple existential emergencies.

At this point, Putin realizes that Russia, though it still has significant problems to be addressed, is no longer in a state of emergency. Therefore, it is no longer necessary to keep quite the same level of power concentrated in the office of the presidency, which is open to abuse by future occupants. Here is what Putin said about this:

> Russian society is becoming more mature, responsible and demanding. Despite the differences in the ways to address their tasks, the main political forces speak from the position of patriotism and reflect the interests of their followers and voters.

The constitutional reforms Putin goes on to discuss include giving the parliament the right to appoint the prime minister and his/her cabinet, restricting foreign citizenship or residency of major office holders at the federal level (president, prime minister, cabinet members, parliamentarians, national security agents, judges, etc.), expanding the authority of local governmental bodies, strengthening the Constitutional Court and the independence of judges, having proposed legislation reviewed by the Constitutional Court before passage, and declaring that the Russian Constitution overrules international law in cases of conflict between the two. He also mentioned codifying certain aspects of socioeconomic justice into the constitution:

> And lastly, the state must honour its social responsibility under any conditions throughout the country. Therefore, I believe that the Constitution should include a provision that the minimum wage in Russia must not be below the subsistence minimum of the economically active people. We have a law on this, but we should formalise this requirement in the Constitution along with the principles of decent pensions, which implies a regular adjustment of pensions according to inflation.

In other words, Putin realizes that the system as it is currently constructed has outlived its usefulness and some modest changes are needed to keep the country moving forward. Putin is no doubt aware of the citizen-led initiatives that have been occurring throughout the country to improve local communities, and it appears that he is ready to allow more space for this new participation of average Russians to solve problems for which the official bureaucracy seems to be stuck:

> Our society is clearly calling for change. People want development, and they strive to move forward in their careers and knowledge, in achieving prosperity, and they are ready to assume responsibility for specific work. Quite often, they have better knowledge of what, how and when should be changed where they live and work, that is, in cities, districts, villages and all across the nation.

The pace of change must be expedited every year and produce tangible results in attaining worthy living standards
that would be clearly perceived by the people. And, I
repeat, they must be actively involved in this process.

How these changes will actually be instituted and what the results will
be are, of course, unknown at this time. Putin suggested that the eventual
package of constitutional amendments will be voted on by the Russian people. As of this writing, it also appears that Putin is looking to step down at
the end of his presidential term in 2024, but it is still very likely that he will
remain in an active advisory role.

Unlike the knee-jerk malign motives that the Western political class
automatically attribute to anything Putin does, I see this as a calculated risk
that Putin is ready to take to make further progress on his second and third
priorities for Russia and to cement his legacy (385).

Appendix 1

Text of John F. Kennedy's American University Speech,
June 10, 1963

Courtesy of the John F. Kennedy Library

President Anderson, members of the faculty, board of trustees, distinguished guests, my old colleague, Senator Bob Byrd, who has earned his degree through many years of attending night law school, while I am earning mine in the next 30 minutes, distinguished guests, ladies and gentlemen:

It is with great pride that I participate in this ceremony of the American University, sponsored by the Methodist Church, founded by Bishop John Fletcher Hurst, and first opened by President Woodrow Wilson in 1914. This is a young and growing university, but it has already fulfilled Bishop Hurst's enlightened hope for the study of history and public affairs in a city devoted to the making of history and the conduct of the public's business. By sponsoring this institution of higher learning for all who wish to learn, whatever their color or their creed, the Methodists of this area and the Nation deserve the Nation's thanks, and I commend all those who are today graduating.

Professor Woodrow Wilson once said that every man sent out from a university should be a man of his nation as well as a man of his time, and I am confident that the men and women who carry the honor of graduating from this institution will continue to give from their lives, from their talents, a high measure of public service and public support.

"There are few earthly things more beautiful than a university," wrote John Masefield in his tribute to English universities--and his words are equally true today. He did not refer to spires and towers, to campus greens and ivied walls. He admired the splendid beauty of the university, he said, because it was "a place where those who hate ignorance may strive to know, where those who perceive truth may strive to make others see."

I have, therefore, chosen this time and this place to discuss a topic on which ignorance too often abounds and the truth is too rarely perceived--yet it is the most important topic on earth: world peace.

What kind of peace do I mean? What kind of peace do we seek? Not a Pax Americana enforced on the world by American weapons of war. Not the peace of the grave or the security of the slave. I am talking about genuine peace, the kind of peace that makes life on earth worth living, the kind that enables men and nations to grow and to hope and to build a better life for their children--not merely peace for Americans but peace for all men and women--not merely peace in our time but peace for all time.

I speak of peace because of the new face of war. Total war makes no sense in an age when great powers can maintain large and relatively invulnerable nuclear forces and refuse to surrender without resort to those forces. It makes no sense in an age when a single nuclear weapon contains almost ten times the explosive force delivered by all the allied air forces in the Second World War. It makes no sense in an age when the deadly poisons produced by a nuclear exchange would be carried by wind and water and soil and seed to the far corners of the globe and to generations yet unborn.

Today the expenditure of billions of dollars every year on weapons acquired for the purpose of making sure we never need to use them is essential to keeping the peace. But surely the acquisition of such idle stockpiles--which can only destroy and never create--is not the only, much less the most efficient, means of assuring peace.

I speak of peace, therefore, as the necessary rational end of rational men. I realize that the pursuit of peace is not as dramatic as the pursuit of war--and frequently the words of the pursuer fall on deaf ears. But we have no more urgent task.

Some say that it is useless to speak of world peace or world law or world disarmament--and that it will be useless until the leaders of the Soviet Union adopt a more enlightened attitude. I hope they do. I believe we can help them do it. But I also believe that we must reexamine our own attitude--as individuals and as a Nation--for our attitude is as essential as theirs. And every graduate of this school, every thoughtful citizen who despairs of war and wishes to bring peace, should begin by looking inward--by examining his own attitude toward the possibilities of peace, toward the Soviet Union, toward the course of the cold war and toward freedom and peace here at home.

First: Let us examine our attitude toward peace itself. Too many of us think it is impossible. Too many think it unreal. But that is a dangerous, defeatist belief. It leads to the conclusion that war is inevitable--that mankind is doomed--that we are gripped by forces we cannot control.

We need not accept that view. Our problems are manmade--therefore, they can be solved by man. And man can be as big as he wants. No problem of human destiny is beyond human beings. Man's reason and spirit have often solved the seemingly unsolvable--and we believe they can do it again.

I am not referring to the absolute, infinite concept of peace and good will of which some fantasies and fanatics dream. I do not deny the value of hopes and dreams but we merely invite discouragement and incredulity by making that our only and immediate goal.

Let us focus instead on a more practical, more attainable peace-- based not on a sudden revolution in human nature but on a gradual evolution in human institutions--on a series of concrete actions and effective agreements which are in the interest of all concerned. There is no single, simple key to this peace--no grand or magic formula to be adopted by one or two powers. Genuine peace must be the product of many nations, the sum of many acts. It must be dynamic, not static, changing to meet the challenge of each new generation. For peace is a process--a way of solving problems.

With such a peace, there will still be quarrels and conflicting interests, as there are within families and nations. World peace, like community peace, does not require that each man love his neighbor--it requires only that they live together in mutual tolerance, submitting their disputes to a just and peaceful settlement. And history teaches us that enmities between nations, as between individuals, do not last forever. However fixed our likes and dislikes may seem, the tide of time and events will often bring surprising changes in the relations between nations and neighbors.

So let us persevere. Peace need not be impracticable, and war need not be inevitable. By defining our goal more clearly, by making it seem more manageable and less remote, we can help all peoples to see it, to draw hope from it, and to move irresistibly toward it.

Second: Let us reexamine our attitude toward the Soviet Union. It is discouraging to think that their leaders may actually believe what their propagandists write. It is discouraging to read a recent authoritative Soviet text on Military Strategy and find, on page after page, wholly baseless and incredible claims--such as the allegation that "American imperialist circles are preparing to unleash different types of wars . . . that there is a very real threat of a preventive war being unleashed by American imperialists against the Soviet Union . . . [and that] the political aims of the American imperialists are to enslave economically and politically the European and other capitalist countries . . . [and] to achieve world domination . . . by means of aggressive wars."

Truly, as it was written long ago: "The wicked flee when no man pursueth." Yet it is sad to read these Soviet statements--to realize the extent of the gulf between us. But it is also a warning--a warning to the American people not to fall into the same trap as the Soviets, not to see only a distorted and desperate view of the other side, not to see conflict as inevitable, accommodation as impossible, and communication as nothing more than an exchange of threats.

No government or social system is so evil that its people must be considered as lacking in virtue. As Americans, we find communism profoundly repugnant as a negation of personal freedom and dignity. But we can still hail the Russian people for their many achievements--in science and space, in economic and industrial growth, in culture and in acts of courage.

Among the many traits the peoples of our two countries have in common, none is stronger than our mutual abhorrence of war. Almost unique among the major world powers, we have never been at war with each other. And no nation in the history of battle ever suffered more than the Soviet Union suffered in the course of the Second World War. At least 20 million lost their lives. Countless millions of homes and farms were burned or sacked. A third of the nation's territory, including nearly two thirds of its industrial base, was turned into a wasteland--a loss equivalent to the devastation of this country east of Chicago.

Today, should total war ever break out again--no matter how--our two countries would become the primary targets. It is an ironic but accurate fact that the two strongest powers are the two in the most danger of devastation. All we have built, all we have worked for, would be destroyed in the first 24 hours. And even in the cold war, which brings burdens and dangers to so many nations, including this Nation's closest allies--our two countries bear the heaviest burdens. For we are both devoting massive sums of money to weapons that could be better devoted to combating ignorance, poverty, and disease. We are both caught up in a vicious and dangerous cycle in which suspicion on one side breeds suspicion on the other, and new weapons beget counterweapons.

In short, both the United States and its allies, and the Soviet Union and its allies, have a mutually deep interest in a just and genuine peace and in halting the arms race. Agreements to this end are in the interests of the Soviet Union as well as ours--and even the most hostile nations can be relied upon to accept and keep those treaty obligations, and only those treaty obligations, which are in their own interest.

So, let us not be blind to our differences--but let us also direct attention to our common interests and to the means by which those differences can be resolved. And if we cannot end now our differences, at least we can help make the world safe for diversity. For, in the final analysis, our most basic common link is that we all inhabit this small planet. We all breathe the same air. We all cherish our children's future. And we are all mortal.

Third: Let us reexamine our attitude toward the cold war, remembering that we are not engaged in a debate, seeking to pile up debating points. We are not here distributing blame or pointing the finger of judgment. We must deal with the world as it is, and not as it might have been had the history of the last 18 years been different.

We must, therefore, persevere in the search for peace in the hope that constructive changes within the Communist bloc might bring within reach solutions which now seem beyond us. We must conduct our affairs in such a way that it becomes in the Communists' interest to agree on a genuine peace. Above all, while defending our own vital interests, nuclear powers must avert those confrontations which bring an adversary to a choice of either a humiliating retreat or a nuclear war. To adopt that kind of course in the nuclear age would be evidence only of the bankruptcy of our policy--or of a collective death-wish for the world.

To secure these ends, America's weapons are nonprovocative, carefully controlled, designed to deter, and capable of selective use. Our military forces are committed to peace and disciplined in self- restraint. Our diplomats are instructed to avoid unnecessary irritants and purely rhetorical hostility.

For we can seek a relaxation of tension without relaxing our guard. And, for our part, we do not need to use threats to prove that we are resolute. We do not need to jam foreign broadcasts out of fear our faith will be eroded. We are unwilling to impose our system on any unwilling people--but we are willing and able to engage in peaceful competition with any people on earth.

Meanwhile, we seek to strengthen the United Nations, to help solve its financial problems, to make it a more effective instrument for peace, to develop it into a genuine world security system--a system capable of resolving disputes on the basis of law, of insuring the security of the large and the small, and of creating conditions under which arms can finally be abolished.

At the same time we seek to keep peace inside the non-Communist world, where many nations, all of them our friends, are divided over issues which weaken Western unity, which invite Communist intervention or which threaten to erupt into war. Our efforts in West New Guinea, in the Congo, in the Middle East, and in the Indian subcontinent, have been persistent and patient despite criticism from both sides. We have also tried to set an example for others--by seeking to adjust small but significant differences with our own closest neighbors in Mexico and in Canada.

Speaking of other nations, I wish to make one point clear. We are bound to many nations by alliances. Those alliances exist because our concern and theirs substantially overlap. Our commitment to defend Western Europe and West Berlin, for example, stands undiminished because of the identity of our vital interests. The United States will make no deal with the Soviet Union at the expense of other nations and other peoples, not merely because they are our partners, but also because their interests and ours converge.

Our interests converge, however, not only in defending the frontiers of freedom, but in pursuing the paths of peace. It is our hope-- and the purpose of allied policies--to convince the Soviet Union that she, too, should let each nation choose its own future, so long as that choice does not interfere with the choices of others. The Communist drive to impose their political and economic system on others is the primary cause of world tension today. For there can be no doubt that, if all nations could refrain from interfering in the self-determination of others, the peace would be much more assured.

This will require a new effort to achieve world law--a new context for world discussions. It will require increased understanding between the Soviets and ourselves. And increased understanding will require increased contact and communication. One step in this direction is the proposed arrangement for a direct line between Moscow and Washington, to avoid on each side the dangerous delays, misunderstandings, and misreadings of the other's actions which might occur at a time of crisis.

We have also been talking in Geneva about the other first-step measures of arms control designed to limit the intensity of the arms race and to reduce the risks of accidental war. Our primary long range interest in Geneva, however, is general and complete disarmament-- designed to take place by stages, permitting parallel political developments to build the new institutions of peace which would take the place of arms. The pursuit of disarmament has been an effort of this Government since the 1920's. It has been urgently sought by the past three administrations. And however dim the prospects may be today, we intend to continue this effort--to continue it in order that all countries, including our own, can better grasp what the problems and possibilities of disarmament are.

The one major area of these negotiations where the end is in sight, yet where a fresh start is badly needed, is in a treaty to outlaw nuclear tests. The conclusion of such a treaty, so near and yet so far, would check the spiraling arms race in one of its most dangerous areas. It would place the nuclear powers in a position to deal more effectively with one of the greatest hazards which man faces in 1963, the further spread of nuclear arms. It would increase our security--it would decrease the prospects of war. Surely this goal is sufficiently important to require our steady pursuit, yielding neither to the temptation to give up the whole effort nor the temptation to give up our insistence on vital and responsible safeguards.

I am taking this opportunity, therefore, to announce two important decisions in this regard.

First: Chairman Khrushchev, Prime Minister Macmillan, and I have agreed that high-level discussions will shortly begin in Moscow looking toward early agreement on a comprehensive test ban treaty. Our hopes must be tempered with the caution of history--but with our hopes go the hopes of all mankind.

Second: To make clear our good faith and solemn convictions on the matter, I now declare that the United States does not propose to conduct nuclear tests in the atmosphere so long as other states do not do so. We will not be the first to resume. Such a declaration is no substitute for a formal binding treaty, but I hope it will help us achieve one. Nor would such a treaty be a substitute for disarmament, but I hope it will help us achieve it.

Finally, my fellow Americans, let us examine our attitude toward peace and freedom here at home. The quality and spirit of our own society must justify and support our efforts abroad. We must show it in the dedication of our own lives--as many of you who are graduating today will have a unique opportunity to do, by serving without pay in the Peace Corps abroad or in the proposed National Service Corps here at home.

But wherever we are, we must all, in our daily lives, live up to the age-old faith that peace and freedom walk together. In too many of our cities today, the peace is not secure because the freedom is incomplete.

It is the responsibility of the executive branch at all levels of government--local, State, and National--to provide and protect that freedom for all of our citizens by all means within their authority. It is the responsibility of the legislative branch at all levels, wherever that authority is not now adequate, to make it adequate. And it is the responsibility of all citizens in all sections of this country to respect the rights of all others and to respect the law of the land.

All this is not unrelated to world peace. "When a man's ways please the Lord," the Scriptures tell us, "he maketh even his enemies to be at peace with him." And is not peace, in the last analysis, basically a matter of human rights--the right to live out our lives without fear of devastation--the right to breathe air as nature provided it--the right of future generations to a healthy existence?

While we proceed to safeguard our national interests, let us also safeguard human interests. And the elimination of war and arms is clearly in the interest of both. No treaty, however much it may be to the advantage of all, however tightly it may be worded, can provide absolute security against the risks of deception and evasion. But it can--if it is sufficiently effective in its enforcement and if it is sufficiently in the interests of its signers--offer far more security and far fewer risks than an unabated, uncontrolled, unpredictable arms race.

The United States, as the world knows, will never start a war. We do not want a war. We do not now expect a war. This generation of Americans has already had enough--more than enough--of war and hate and oppression. We shall be prepared if others wish it. We shall be alert to try to stop it. But we shall also do our part to build a world of peace where the weak are safe and the strong are just. We are not helpless before that task or hopeless of its success. Confident and unafraid, we labor on--not toward a strategy of annihilation but toward a strategy of peace.

Appendix 2

Transcript of Telephone Conversation between Assistant Secretary of European & Eurasian Affairs Victoria Nuland and U.S. Ambassador to Ukraine Geoffrey Pyatt

February 2014

Nuland: What do you think?

Pyatt: I think we're in play . . . the [retired boxer Vitali] Klitsch[ko] piece is obviously the complicated electron here especially the announcement of him as deputy prime minister. Your argument to him which you'll need to make, I think the next phone call we want to set up is exactly the one you made to Yats [Yatsenyuk]. And I'm glad you sort of put him on the spot on where he fits in this scenario and I'm very glad he said what he said in response.

Nuland: I don't think Klitsch should go into government. I don't think it's necessary. I don't think it's a good idea.

Pyatt: Yeah . . . I mean, I guess. You think . . . what . . . in terms of him not going into the government, just let him sort of stay out and do his political homework and stuff. I'm just thinking in terms of the process moving ahead, we want to keep the moderate democrats together. The problem is going to be Tyahnybok [of neo-fascist group Svoboda] and his guys. I'm sure that's what Yanukoyvch is calculating on all this.

Nuland: I think Yats is the guy who's got the economic experience, the governing experience. What he needs is Klitsch and Tyahnybok on the outside and he needs to be talking to them four times a week, you know . . .

I think with Klitsch going in at that level, working for Yats, it's not going to work.

Nuland: My understanding is that the big three [Yatsenyuk, Klitsch, and Tyahnybok] were going in to their own meeting and that Yats was going to offer in that context a three plus one conversation with you.

Pyatt: That's what he proposed but knowing the dynamic that's been with them where Klitsch has been top dog; he's going to take a while to show up at a meeting, he's probably talking to his guys at this point so I think you reaching out to him will help with the personality management among the three and gives us a chance to move fast on all this stuff and put us behind it before they all sit down and he explains why he doesn't like it.

Nuland: When I talked to Jeff Feltman this morning, he had a new name for the UN guy . . . Robert Serry. He's now gotten both Serry and Ban ki-Moon to agree that Serry could come in Monday or Tuesday . . . so that would be great, I think, to help glue this thing and have the UN help glue it and, you know, fuck the EU.

Pyatt: Exactly. I think we've got to do something to make it stick together because you can be pretty sure the Russians will be working behind the scenes. . . . Let me work on Klitschko, and I think we want to get somebody with an international personality to come out here and help midwife this thing.

Nuland: Sullivan's come back to me saying you need [Vice President Joe] Biden and I said probably tomorrow for an 'atta boy' and get the deeds to stick, so Biden's willing.

Appendix 3

Transcript of Telephone Conversation between Estonian
Foreign Minister Urmas Paet and EU High Commissioner
Catherine Ashton

February 2014

Paet: Hello.

Ashton: Hello, how are you?

Paet: I am fine.

Ashton: Good.

Paet: And you?

Ashton: Good. I am good. I just wanted to catch up with you on what you thought when you were there.

Paet: Okay, yes. I returned last night already, so that was one day.

Ashton: Yeah. Impressions?

Paet: Impressions are sad.

Ashton: Um hum.

Paet: I met with representatives of Regions Party [Yanukovych's party], also new coalition representatives, and also civil society. There is this lady called Olga [Dr. Olga Bolgomets] who is head of the doctors. Yes, yes. You know her?

Ashton: I do.

Paet: Yes, so that, well, my impression is indeed sad that there is, well, no trust towards also these politicians who will return now to the coalition. Well, people from Maidan and from civil society, they say that they know everybody who will be in new government—all these guys have a dirty past.

Ashton: Yeah.

Paet: So that, well, they made some proposals to the same Olga and some others from civil society to join new government. But this Olga, for example, she says directly that she is ready to go to the government only in the case if she can take with her, her team of foreign experts to start real health care reforms.

Ashton: Yeah.

Paet: So that, well, basically, it is that the trust level is absolutely low. On the other hand, all the security problems, the integrity problems, Crimea, all this stuff. Regions Party was absolutely upset. They say that, well, they accept, they accept this that now there will be new government. And there will be external elections. But there is enormous pressure against members of parliament—that there are uninvited visitors during the night . . . to party members.

Well, journalists . . . some journalists who were with me, they saw during the day that one member of parliament was just beaten in front of the parliament building by these guys with the guns on the streets.

Ashton: Yeah.

Paet: So that all this mess is still there. And, of course, this Olga and others from civil society, they were absolutely sure that people will not leave the streets before they see that the real reforms will start. So that it's not enough that there is just change of government. So that that is the main impression.

So that, from EU's and also, well, Estonia's point of view, of course, we should be ready to put this financial package together. Also together with others. This very clear message is needed that it's not enough that there is change of government, but they say real reforms—you know, real action to increase the level of trust. Otherwise, it will end badly.

Because the Regions Party also said that, well, we will see that if the people from the eastern part of Ukraine will really wake up, and will start to demand their rights. Some people also with me, they were also in Donetsk. There people said that, well, we can't wait. How long still the occupation of Ukraine lasts in Donetsk. That it is real Russian city, and we would like now to see that, well, Russia will take over. So that well . . . short impressions.

Ashton: No, very, very interesting. I just had a big meeting here with Olli Rehn [EU Commissioner for Economic and Monetary Affairs] and the other commissioners about what we can do. I mean, we're working on financial packages—short, medium, long-term. Everything from how we get money in quickly. How we support the IMF. And how we get a kind of . . . investment packages and business leaders and so on.

On the political side, we've worked [inaudible] what resources we have got, and I offered to civil society, and to Yatsenyuk and Klitschko [retired boxer and mayor of Kiev], and everybody I met yesterday: "We can offer you people who know how to do political and economic reform. The countries that are closest to Ukraine have been going through dramatic changes and have done big political and economic reforms. So we have got loads of experience to give you, which we're happy to give."

I said to the people in Maidan, "Yes, you want real reforms, but you've got to get through the short-term first. So you need to find ways in which you can establish a process that will have anticorruption at its heart, that will have people working alongside until the elections, and that you could be confident in the process."

Then I said to Olga, "You may not be Health Minister now, but you need to think about becoming Health Minister in the future, because people like you are going to be needed to be able to get and make sure that reform happens."

I also said to them, "If you simply barricade the buildings now, and the government doesn't function, we cannot get money in, because we need a partner to partner with."

Paet: Absolutely.

Ashton: And I said to the opposition leaders, shortly to become government, "You need to reach out to Maidan. You need to be, you know, engage with them. You also need to get ordinary police officers back on the streets under a new sense of their roles, so that people feel safe."

I said to the Party of the Regions people, "You have to go and lay flowers for the people [who] died. You have to show that you understand what you have . . . what has happened here. Because what you were experiencing is anger of people who have seen the way that Yanukovych lived and the corruption. And they assume you are all the same."

And, also the people who have lost people and who feel that, you know, he ordered that to happen. There is quite a lot of shock I think in the city. A lot of sadness and shock, and that is going to come out in some very strange ways if they are not careful. I think all of us, we just have to work on this. We did a big meeting here today to try and get this in place.

But, yeah, very interesting, your observations.

Paet: It is. And, well, actually, the only politician the people from civil society mentioned positively was Poroshenko.

Ashton: Yeah, yeah.

Paet: So that he has some sort of, how to say, trust among all these Maidan people and civil society.

And, in fact, what was quite disturbing, the same Olga told that, well, all the evidence shows that people who were killed by snipers, from both sides, among policemen and then people from the streets, that they were the same snipers, killing people from both sides.

Ashton: Well, that's . . . yeah.

Paet: So that, then she also showed me some photos. She said that as medical doctor she can, you know, say that it is the same handwriting, the same type of bullets, and it's really disturbing that now the new coalition, that they don't want to investigate what exactly happened. So that there is now stronger and stronger understanding that behind [the] snipers, they were . . . it was not Yanukovych, but it was somebody from the new coalition.

Ashton: I think we do want to investigate. I mean, I didn't pick that up. It's interesting. Gosh.

Paet: Yeah. So that it was indeed disturbing that, if it starts now to live its own life very powerfully, that it already discredits from [the] very beginning also this new coalition.

Ashton: I mean this is what they have got to be careful of as well, that they need to demand great change, but they have got to let the Rada function. If the Rada doesn't function, then they have complete chaos. So that, it's all, you know, being an activist and a doctor is very, very important. But it means that you're not a politician. And somehow they've got to come to a kind of accommodation for the next few weeks, which is how the country is actually going to run. And then we get the elections and things can change. And that's, I think, going to be quite pop . . . I am planning to go back early next week, probably on Monday.

Paet: It's really important that now, well, people from Europe and also [the] West show up there so that it's absolutely . . .

Ashton: Well, [inaudible] is going with the Visegrad Group [Czech Republic, Hungary, Poland, and Slovakia] Friday. Friday, Saturday. William Hague (inaudible) on Sunday. I will be back again Monday.

Paet: Yes, I heard also that Canadian Minister is going on Friday. And yesterday also William Burns [American Deputy Secretary of State] was there, so we met . . .

Ashton: Yes, I saw Bill.

Paet: We met also with Burns there in Kiev yesterday.

Ashton: Yeah, good. Yeah, I didn't know that John Baird was going. I will get hold of him. Okay, my friend. It was great to talk to you.

Paet: Well, thanks for these comments, and wish you well. Nice Australia.

Ashton: Yeah. What?

Paet: Nice Australia. Enjoy!

Ashton: I am not going to go. I got to delay it because I'm going to do more Ukraine instead.

Paet: OK, good, good.

Ashton: All right, my friend . . .

Paet: OK. Thank you. Thank you. And all the best to you. Bye.

Ashton: Bye.

Appendix 4

Full Text of Minsk 2.0 Agreement

February 2015

1. Immediate and comprehensive ceasefire in certain areas of the Donetsk and Luhansk regions of Ukraine and its strict implementation as of 15 February 2015, 12am local time.

2. Withdrawal of all heavy weapons by both sides by equal distances in order to create a security zone of at least 50km wide from each other for the artillery systems of caliber of 100 and more, a security zone of 70km wide for MLRS and 140km wide for MLRS Tornado-S, Uragan, Smerch and Tactical Missile Systems (Tochka, Tochka U):

    -   for the Ukrainian troops: from the de facto line of contact;

    -   for the armed formations from certain areas of the Donetsk and Luhansk regions of Ukraine: from the line of contact according to the Minsk Memorandum of Sept. 19th, 2014;

    The withdrawal of the heavy weapons as specified above is to start on day 2 of the ceasefire at the latest and be completed within 14 days.

    The process shall be facilitated by the OSCE and supported by the Trilateral Contact Group.

3. Ensure effective monitoring and verification of the ceasefire regime and the withdrawal of heavy weapons by the OSCE from day 1 of the withdrawal, using all technical equipment necessary, including satellites, drones, radar equipment, etc.

4. Launch a dialogue, on day 1 of the withdrawal, on modalities of local elections in accordance with Ukrainian legislation and the Law of Ukraine "On interim local self-government order in certain areas of the Donetsk and Luhansk regions" as well as on the future regime of these areas based on this law.

   Adopt promptly, by no later than 30 days after the date of signing of this document a Resolution of the Parliament of Ukraine specifying the area enjoying a special regime, under the Law of Ukraine "On interim self-government order in certain areas of the Donetsk and Luhansk regions," based on the line of the Minsk Memorandum of September 19, 2014.

5. Ensure pardon and amnesty by enacting the law prohibiting the prosecution and punishment of persons in connection with the events that took place in certain areas of the Donetsk and Luhansk regions of Ukraine.

6. Ensure release and exchange of all hostages and unlawfully detained persons, based on the principle "all for all." This process is to be finished on the day 5 after the withdrawal at the latest.

7. Ensure safe access, delivery, storage, and distribution of humanitarian assistance to those in need, on the basis of an international mechanism.

8. Definition of modalities of full resumption of socio-economic ties, including social transfers such as pension payments and other payments (incomes and revenues, timely payments of all utility bills, reinstating taxation within the legal framework of Ukraine).

To this end, Ukraine shall reinstate control of the segment of its banking system in the conflict-affected areas and possibly an international mechanism to facilitate such transfers shall be established.

9. Reinstatement of full control of the state border by the government of Ukraine throughout the conflict area, starting on day 1 after the local elections and ending after the comprehensive political settlement (local elections in certain areas of the Donetsk and Luhansk regions on the basis of the Law of Ukraine and constitutional reform) to be finalized by the end of 2015, provided that paragraph 11 has been implemented in consultation with and upon agreement by representatives of certain areas of the Donetsk and Luhansk regions in the framework of the Trilateral Contact Group.

10. Withdrawal of all foreign armed formations, military equipment, as well as mercenaries from the territory of Ukraine under monitoring of the OSCE. Disarmament of all illegal groups.

11. Carrying out constitutional reform in Ukraine with a new constitution entering into force by the end of 2015 providing for decentralization as a key element (including a reference to the specificities of certain areas in the Donetsk and Luhansk regions, agreed with the representatives of these areas), as well as adopting permanent legislation on the special status of certain areas of the Donetsk and Luhansk regions in line with measures as set out in the footnote until the end of 2015.

12. Based on the Law of Ukraine "On interim local self-government order in certain areas of the Donetsk and Luhansk regions," questions related to local elections will be discussed and agreed upon with representatives of certain areas of the Donetsk and Luhansk regions in the framework of the Trilateral Contact Group. Elections will be held in accordance

with relevant OSCE standards and monitored by OSCE/ODIHR.

13. Intensify the work of the Trilateral Contact Group including through the establishment of working groups on the implementation of relevant aspects of the Minsk agreements. They will reflect the composition of the Trilateral Contact Group.

Participants of the Trilateral Contact Group:

-   Ambassador Heidi Tagliavini

-   Second President of Ukraine, L. D. Kuchma

-   Ambassador of the Russian Federation to Ukraine, M. Yu. Zurabov

-   A.W. Zakharchenko, Representative of Donetsk People's Republic

-   I.W. Plotnitski, Representative of Lugansk People's Republic

Bibliography

1. International Monetary Fund (IMF). "Largest Economies by PPP GDP in 2019." 2019.

2. Kristensen, Hans M. "Alert Status of Nuclear Weapons." Federation of American Scientists. April 21, 2017.

    https://fas.org/wp-content/uploads/2014/05/Brief2017_GWU_2s.pdf.

3. Billington, James R. *The Icon and the Axe: An Interpretive History of Russian Culture*. New York: Vintage Books, 1970.

4. Massie, Suzanne. *Land of the Firebird: The Beauty of Old Russia*. Blue Hill, ME: HeartTree Press, 1980.

5. Szamuely, Tibor. *The Russian Tradition*. London: Fontana Press, 1988.

6. Derbyshire, David. "Mercury Poisoned Ivan the Terrible's Wife and Mother." *The Telegraph*, March 14, 2001.

    https://www.telegraph.co.uk/news/worldnews/europe/russia/1326387/Mercury-poisoned-Ivan-the-Terribles-mother-and-wife.html.

7. Gerasimov, M. M. "Documentary Portrait of Ivan the Terrible." *Brief Communications Institute of Archeology of the USSR Academy of Sciences* 100 (1965): 139–42. (Accessed online in English using Google Translate.)

8. G. Maryamov "Kremlevskii tsenzor." Moscow, Moscow State University 1992, quoted in Seventeen Moments in Soviet History, "Stalin on the Film *Ivan the Terrible*."

    http://soviethistory.msu.edu/1943-2/the-cult-of-leadership/the-cult-of-leadership-texts/stalin-on-the-film-ivan-the-terrible/.

9. Popova, Natalia and Andrei Fedorov. *Saint Petersburg*. Medny Vsadnik Trading House Publishers, 2014.

10. Hays, Jeffrey. "Catherine the Great." Factsanddetails.com, updated May 2016. http://factsanddetails.com/russia/History/sub9_1b/entry-4938.html.

11. Doctorow, Gilbert. "'War and Peace': The Relevance of 1812 as Explained by Tolstoy to Current Global Affairs." Antiwar.com, January 31, 2019. https://original.antiwar.com/Gilbert_Doctorow/2019/01/30/war-and-peace-the-relevance-of-1812-as-explained-by-tolstoy-to-current-global-affairs/.

12. Gentes, Andrew A. "Other Decembrists: The Chizov Case and Lutskii Affair as Signifiers of the Decembrists in Siberia." *Slavonica* 13, no. 2 (2007): 140.

13. Mazour, Anatole G. *The First Russian Revolution, 1825*. Redwood City, CA: Stanford University Press, 1937.

14. Riggs, Robert. *Sofia Perovskaya, Terrorist Princess: The Plot to Kill Tsar Alexander II and the Woman who Led It*. Berkeley, CA: Global Harmony Press, 2017.

15. Salisbury, Harrison E. *Black Night, White Snow: Russia's Revolutions, 1905–1917*. New York: De Capo Press, 1977.

16. Ascher, Abraham. *P.A. Stolypin: The Search for Stability in Late Imperial Russia*. Redwood City, CA: Stanford University Press, 2001.

17. Nagorsky, Nikolai. *The Saviour on the Spilled Blood: Church of the Resurrection of Christ*. Medny Vsadnik Trading House Publishers, 2016.

18. Lieven, Dominic. *The End of Tsarist Russia: The March to World War I and Revolution*. New York: Viking, 2015.

19. Kotkin, Stephen. *Stalin: Paradoxes of Power, 1878–1928*. New York: Penguin Books, 2014.

20. Kevin, Tony. *Return to Moscow*. Perth: The University of Western Australia Press, 2017.

21. Krausz, Tamás. *Reconstructing Lenin: An Intellectual Biography*. New York: Monthly Review Press, 2015.

22. Deutscher, Isaac. "The Mensheviks: George Plekhanov." *The Listener*, April 30, 1964. Scanned and prepared for the Marxist Internet Archive by Paul Flewers.

https://www.marxists.org/archive/deutscher/1964/mensheviks-plekhanov.htm.

23. Cavendish, Richard. "The Bolshevik-Menshevik Split." *History Today*, November 11, 2003.

    https://www.historytoday.com/archive/months-past/bolshevik-menshevik-split.

24. Johnson, Keely. "The Identification of Weakness: A Psycho Historical Analysis of Tsar Nicholas II Using the NEO-Personality Inventory Revised Exam." McIntyre Library, University of Wisconsin Eau Claire, 2011.

25. Hall, Richard C. "Balkan Wars 1912–1913." International Encyclopedia of the First World War, October 8, 2014.

    https://encyclopedia.1914-1918-online.net/article/balkan_wars_1912-1913.

26. Sowards, Steven W. "Lecture 15: The Balkan Causes of World War I." Twenty-Five Lectures on Modern Balkan History, 1996.

    http://staff.lib.msu.edu/sowards/balkan/lect15.htm.

27. "Germany Gives Austria-Hungary 'Blank Check Assurance." History.com, July 28, 2019.

    https://www.history.com/this-day-in-history/germany-gives-austria-hungary-blank-check-assurance.

28. Liulevicius, Vejas Gabriel. "The Tactics of WWI: The Failure of the Schlieffen Plan." From the Lecture Series: World War I—The Great War. The Great Courses Daily, December 1, 2017.

    https://www.thegreatcoursesdaily.com/wwi-failure-schlieffen-plan.

29. Merridale, Catherine. *Lenin on the Train*. New York: Metropolitan Books, 2017.

30. Baldwin, Natylie. Visit to State Central Museum of Contemporary History of Russia, Moscow, May 2017.

31. Moss, Walter G. *A History of Russia Volume II: Since 1855*. 2nd ed. Anthem Press, 2005.

32. Stone, Oliver and Peter Kuznick. *The Untold History of the United States*. New York: Gallery Books, 2013.

33. "Where the Romanovs Were Murdered: Archived Images." Russia Beyond the Headlines (RBTH), April 17, 2014.

https://www.rbth.com/multimedia/pictures/2014/04/17/where_the_romanovs_were_murdered_archived_images_35985.

34. Timofeychev, Alexey. "How Many Lives Did the Red Terror Claim?" Russia Beyond the Headlines, September 7, 2018.

https://www.rbth.com/history/329091-how-many-lives-claimed-red-terror.

35. Kuzmarov, Jeremy and John Marciano. *The Russians are Coming, Again: The First Cold War as Tragedy, the Second as Farce.* New York: Monthly Review Press, 2018.

36. Rinke, Stefan and Michael Wildt. *Revolutions and Counter-Revolutions: 1917 and Its Aftermath from a Global Perspective.* Frankfurt: Campus Verlag, 2017.

37. Chapple, Amos. "Photo Galleries: The Horror of Russia's Civil War." Radio Free Europe/Radio Liberty, January 9, 2019.

https://www.rferl.org/a/the-horror-of-russias-civil-war-in-photos-from-red-cross-mission/29699442.html.

38. Cohen, Stephen F. *Soviet Fates and Lost Alternatives: From Stalinism to the New Cold War.* New York: Columbia University Press, 2009.

39. Siegelbaum, Lewis. "The New Economic Policy." Seventeen Moments in Soviet History. Moscow State University.

http://soviethistory.msu.edu/1921-2/the-new-economic-policy/.

40. Rozin, Igor. "Lenin May be Dead, But His Popularity is Alive and Kicking." Russia Beyond the Headlines, April 19, 2017.

https://www.rbth.com/politics_and_society/2017/04/19/lenin-may-be-dead-but-his-popularity-is-alive-and-kicking_746548.

41. "Stalin's Popularity in Russia Triples Since 1990." RT, April 5, 2017.

https://www.rt.com/russia/383597-stalins-popularity-in-russia-grows/.

42. Baldwin, Natylie. Interviews with Russians in Moscow and St. Petersburg. May 2017.

43. Weir, Fred. "A Revolution Forsaken? Why Russia is Ignoring its First Flirtation with Liberalism." The Christian Science Monitor, March 6, 2017.

     https://www.csmonitor.com/World/
     Europe/2017/0306/A-revolution-forsaken-Why-Russia-is-ig-
     noring-its-first-flirtation-with-liberalism.

44. "The Era of the New Economic Policy." Country Studies, U.S. Library of Congress.

     http://countrystudies.us/russia/9.htm.

45. Lenin, Vladimir. "'Last Testament': Letters to the Congress" by Vladimir Lenin. December 1922–January 1923. Retrieved from Marxists.org on March 8, 2019.

     https://www.marxists.org/archive/lenin/works/1922/dec/testamnt/index.htm.

46. Butler, Susan. *Roosevelt & Stalin: Portrait of a Partnership*. New York: Alfred A. Knopf, 2015.

47. Boyko, Oksana. "Stallin' History? Ft. Stephen F. Cohen, Professor of Russian Studies, New York University." RT, January 3, 2016.

     https://www.rt.com/shows/worlds-apart-oksana-boyko/320364-stalin-dra-
     matic-past-russia/.

48. Baldwin, Natylie. Visit to Gulag Museum. May 2017.

49. Harris, James. *The Great Fear: Stalin's Terror of the 1930s*. New York: Oxford University Press, 2016.

50. Grimes, William. "Robert Conquest, Historian Who Documented Soviet Horrors, Dies at 98." *The New York Times*, August 4, 2015.

     https://www.nytimes.com/2015/08/05/arts/international/robert-con-
     quest-historian-who-documented-soviet-horrors-dies-at-98.html?login=-
     google.

51. Fitzpatrick, Sheila. "People and Martians." London Review of Books, January 24, 2019.

     https://www.lrb.co.uk/v41/n02/sheila-fitzpatrick/people-and-martians.

52. Snyder, Timothy. "Hitler vs. Stalin: Who Was Worse?" New York Review of Books, January 27, 2011.

    https://www.nybooks.com/daily/2011/01/27/hitler-vs-stalin-who-was-worse/.

53. Tauger, Mark. "Review of Anne Applebaum's 'Red Famine: Stalin's War on Ukraine'" History News Network, July 1, 2018.

    https://historynewsnetwork.org/article/169438.

54. Tauger, Mark B. Review of "The Years of Hunger: Soviet Agriculture, 1931-1933" by R.W. Davies and Stephen G. Wheatcroft. EH.net, November 2004.

    https://eh.net/book_reviews/the-years-of-hunger-soviet-agriculture-1931-1933/.

55. Wheatcroft, Stephen G. "The Turn Away from Economic Explanations for Soviet Famines." Cambridge Core, July 23, 2018.

    https://www.cambridge.org/core/services/aop-cambridge-core/content/view/78C193C97E6C5383C37763CADA970644/S0960777318000358a.pdf/turn_away_from_economic_explanations_for_soviet_famines.pdf.

56. "The Kazakh Famine of the 1930s." Interview of Sarah Cameron by Jason Steinhauer. John W. Kluge Center Blog, Library of Congress, August 24, 2016.

    https://blogs.loc.gov/kluge/2016/08/the-kazakh-famine-of-the-1930s/.

57. Carley, Michael Jabara. "Justin Trudeau Needs a History Lesson." Voltaire.net, September 1, 2019.

    https://www.voltairenet.org/article207498.html.

58. Sykes, Tom. "How British High Society Fell in Love with the Nazis." The Daily Beast, updated April 14, 2017.

    https://www.thedailybeast.com/how-british-high-society-fell-in-love-with-the-nazis.

59. Carley, Michael Jabara. "History as Propaganda: Why the USSR Did Not 'Win' World War II: Part I." Strategic Culture Foundation, March 19, 2016.

    https://www.strategic-culture.org/news/2016/03/19/history-as-propaganda-why-the-ussr-did-not-win-world-war-ii-i/.

60. Freeman, Robert. "Re-Reflections on the Start of World War II." Common Dreams, September 1, 2019.

https://www.commondreams.org/views/2019/09/01/re-reflections-start-world-war-ii.

61. Andrews, Evan. "The Siege of Leningrad." History.com, August 29, 2018.
    https://www.history.com/news/the-siege-of-leningrad.

62. Carley, Michael Jabara. "History as Propaganda: Why the USSR Did Not 'Win' World War II: Part II." Strategic Culture Foundation, March 20, 2016.
    https://www.strategic-culture.org/news/2016/03/20/history-as-propaganda-why-the-ussr-did-not-win-world-war-ii-ii/.

63. Tharoor, Ishaan. "Don't Forget How the Soviet Union Saved the World from Hitler." *The Washington Post,* May 8, 2015.

64. Armstrong, Patrick. "D-Day More Difficult Than You Think." Strategic Culture Foundation, June 26, 2019.
    https://www.strategic-culture.org/news/2019/06/26/d-day-more-difficult-than-you-think/.

65. Polk, William R. "What's Behind the Conflict between Russia and Ukraine?" History News Network, December 21, 2014.
    https://historynewsnetwork.org/article/157941.

66. Margoulis, Eric. "Stalin's Soviet Union Defeated Germany—We Should Not Forget." Ericmargolis.com, May 9, 2015.
    https://ericmargolis.com/2015/05/stalins-soviet-union-defeated-germany-we-should-not-forget/.

67. Kuznick, Peter. "The Decision to Risk the Future: Harry Truman, the Atomic Bomb and the Apocalyptic Narrative." *The Asia Pacific Journal* 5, no. 7 (2007).
    https://apjjf.org/-Peter-J.-Kuznick/2479/article.html.

68. "Stalin's Popularity in Russia Reaches 16 Year High." *The Moscow Times,* February 15, 2017.
    https://www.themoscowtimes.com/2017/02/15/stalins-popularity-in-russia-reaches-16-year-high-a57152.

69. White, Adam. "The Death of Stalin: What Really Happened on the Night that Forever Changed Soviet History?" *The Telegraph,* October 19, 2017.

https://www.telegraph.co.uk/films/0/truth-death-stalin-really-happened-night-forever-changed-soviet/.

70. Cavendish, Richard. "Lavrenti Beria Executed." *History Today*, December 23, 2003.

    https://www.historytoday.com/archive/months-past/lavrenti-beria-executed.

71. Mansky, Jackie. "The True Story of the Death of Stalin." *Smithsonian Magazine*, October 10, 2017.

    https://www.smithsonianmag.com/history/true-story-death-stalin-180965119/.

72. Khrushchev, Nikita. "The Crimes of the Stalin Era: Special Report to the 20th Congress of the Communist Party of the Soviet Union" (aka "The Secret Speech"), February 1956.

    https://archive.org/details/TheCrimesOfTheStalinEraSpecialReportToThe20thCongressOfTheCommunistPartyOfTheSovietUnion.

73. Taubman, William. *Khrushchev: The Man and His Era*. New York: W. W. Norton, 2004.

74. Sakwa, Richard. *The Rise and Fall of the Soviet Union: 1917–1991*. New York: Routledge, 1999.

75. Douglass, James W. *JFK and the Unspeakable: Why He Died and Why it Matters*. Maryknoll, NY: Orbis Books, 2010.

76. Blight, James G. and Janet M. Lang. *Dark Beyond Darkness: The Cuban Missile Crisis as History, Warning, and Catalyst*. Lanham, MD: Rowman & Littlefield, 2018.

77. "Russians' Opinions of Past and Current Leaders." Levada Center, February 15, 2017.

    https://www.levada.ru/2017/02/15/lyubov-rossiyan-k-stalinu-dostigla-maksimuma/attachment/754871360185521/.

78. Sakwa, Richard. *Soviet Politics in Perspective*, 2nd ed. New York: Routledge, 1998.

79. Parsons, Michelle A. *Dying Unneeded: The Cultural Context of the Russian Mortality Crisis*. Nashville: Vanderbilt University Press, 2014.

80. Gerson, Michael S. "The Sino-Soviet Border Conflict: Deterrence, Escalation, and the Threat of Nuclear War in 1969." CNA, November 2010.

   https://www.cna.org/CNA_files/PDF/D0022974.A2.pdf.

81. Farley, Robert. "In 1969, Russia and China Fought a Brief Border War. It Could Have Started World War III." *The National Interest*, June 13, 2018.

   https://nationalinterest.org/blog/the-buzz/1969-russia-china-fought-brief-border-war-it-could-have-26240.

82. "Soviet Report to East German Leadership on Sino-Soviet Border Clashes." Wilson Center Digital Archive, March 2, 1969.

   https://digitalarchive.wilsoncenter.org/document/116975.

83. "Strategic Arms Limitations Talks/Treaty (SALT) I and II." U.S. State Department Office of the Historian. Viewed on July 9, 2019.

   https://history.state.gov/milestones/1969-1976/salt.

84. Taubman, William. *Gorbachev: His Life and Times*. New York: W. W. Norton, 2017.

85. Matlock, Jack. *Superpower Illusions: How Myths and False Ideologies Led America Astray—and How to Return to Reality*. New Haven, CT: Yale University Press, 2010.

86. Reynolds, Douglas B. "Peak Oil and the Fall of the Soviet Union: Lessons on the 20th Anniversary of the Collapse." The Oil Drum, May 27, 2011.

   http://theoildrum.com/node/7878.

87. Cooper, Julian. *The Soviet Defence Industry: Conversion and Economic Reform*. The Royal Institute of International Affairs on Foreign Relations Press, 1991.

88. CIA Intelligence Memorandum. "The Impending Soviet Oil Crisis." March 1977.

89. Schweitzer, Peter. *Victory: The Reagan Administration's Secret Strategy That Hastened the Collapse of the Soviet Union*. New York: Atlantic Monthly Press, 1994.

90. Sakwa, Richard. "The Soviet Collapse: Contradictions and Neo-Modernisation." *Journal of Eurasian Studies* 4, no: 1 (2012).

   https://journals.sagepub.com/doi/10.1016/j.euras.2012.07.003.

91. Krasnov, George W. "Suzanne Massie's Advice to President Obama: Revive Reagan's Policy toward Russia." Russia Other Points of View, December 5, 2008.

92. Malinkin, Mary Elizabeth. "Reagan's Evolving Views of Russians and Their Relevance Today." Kennan Institute, December 1, 2008.

   https://www.wilsoncenter.org/publication/reagans-evolving-views-russians-and-their-relevance-today.

93. Roberts, Paul Craig. "Telling the Truth Has Become an Anti-American Act." Paulcraigroberts.org, October 30, 2019.

   https://www.paulcraigroberts.org/2019/10/30/telling-the-truth-has-become-an-anti-american-act/.

94. Sarotte, Mary Elise. "Not One Inch Eastward? Bush, Baker, Kohl, Genscher, Gorbachev, and the Origin of Russian Resentment Toward NATO Enlargement in February 1990." *Diplomatic History* 34, no. 1 (2010).

   https://academic.oup.com/dh/article-abstract/34/1/119/379802.

95. Melman, Seymour. "The Economic Conversion Imperative: Eleven Propositions." August 1990. Available at Economic Reconstruction.org.

   http://economicreconstruction.org/sites/economicreconstruction.com/static/SeymourMelman/archive/ec/econ_conversion_imperative.pdf.

96. "Discretionary Spending Breakdown." Peter G. Peterson Foundation, May 2, 2018.

   https://www.pgpf.org/Chart-Archive/0070_Discretionary-Breakdown.

97. Amadeo, Kimberly. "Current U.S. Discretionary Spending: FY 2020 Budget Request." *The Balance*, May 12, 2019.

98. Keck, Zachary. "Russian Military Spending Soars." *The Diplomat*, April 18, 2014.

   https://thediplomat.com/2014/04/russian-military-spending-soars/.

99. "Russian Military Spending Falls, Could Affect Operations: Think-Tank." *Reuters*, May 1, 2018.

https://www.reuters.com/article/us-military-spending/russian-military-spending-falls-could-affect-operations-think-tank-idUSKBN1I24H8.

100. American Society of Civil Engineers. "America's Infrastructure Scores a D+." Infrastructure Report Card, 2017.

https://www.infrastructurereportcard.org/.

101. Broad, William J. and David Sanger. "U.S. Ramping Up Major Renewal in Nuclear Arms." *The New York Times*, September 21, 2014.

https://www.nytimes.com/2014/09/22/us/us-ramping-up-major-renewal-in-nuclear-arms.html.

102. Melman, Seymour. *After Capitalism: From Managerialism to Workplace Democracy*. New York: Alfred A. Knopf, 2001.

103. Lepic, Arthur. "The Outrageous Strategy to Destroy Russia." Voltaire.net, October 22, 2004.

https://www.voltairenet.org/article30038.html.

104. Brinkley, Douglas. "The Lives They Lived; Out of the Loop." *The New York Times*, December 29, 2002.

https://www.nytimes.com/2002/12/29/magazine/the-lives-they-lived-out-of-the-loop.html.

105. Cohen, Jeff. "Internet Samizdat Releases Suppressed Voices, History." Common Dreams, November 30, 2001.

https://www.commondreams.org/views/2001/11/30/internet-samizdat-releases-suppressed-voices-history.

106. Khalidi, N. A. "Afghanistan: Demographic Consequences of War, 1978–1987." *Central Asian Survey* 10, no. 3 (1991): 101–126.

107. Chomsky, Noam and Edward S. Herman. *Manufacturing Consent: The Political Economy of the Mass Media*. New York: Pantheon, 2002.

108. "American Committee for Peace in Chechnya." Sourcewatch. Updated April 23, 2009.

https://www.sourcewatch.org/index.php?title=American_Committee_for_
Peace_in_Chechnya.

109. Laughland, John. "The Chechens' American Friends." *The Guardian*, September 8, 2004.

https://www.theguardian.com/world/2004/sep/08/usa.russia.

110. Blum, William. *Rogue State: A Guide to the World's Only Superpower*. Monroe, ME: Common Courage Press, 2005.

111. Brzezinski, Zbigniew. "After Putin's Aggression in Ukraine, the West Must Be Ready to Respond." *The Washington Post*, March 3, 2014.

https://www.washingtonpost.com/opinions/zbigniew-brzezinski-after-putins-aggression-in-ukraine-the-west-must-be-ready-to-respond/2014/03/03/25b3f928-a2f5-11e3-84d4-e59b1709222c_story.html.

112. Baldwin, Natylie. Telephone Interview with Col. Lawrence Wilkerson, August 7, 2014.

113. Brzezinski, Zbigniew. "What Obama Should Tell Americans About Ukraine." *Politico*, May 2, 2014.

https://www.politico.com/magazine/story/2014/05/what-obama-should-tell-americans-about-ukraine-106277.

114. Fry, Douglas. *The Human Potential for Peace: An Anthropological Challenge to Assumptions about War and Violence*. New York: Oxford University Press, 2006.

115. Sloan, Geoffrey. *Geopolitics in United States Strategic Policy, 1890–1987*. Harvester Wheatsheaf, 1988.

116. Nazemroaya, Mahdi Darius. *The Globalization of NATO*. Atlanta: Clarity Press, 2012.

117. Brzezinski, Zbigniew. *The Grand Chessboard: American Primacy and Its Geostrategic Imperatives*. New York: Basic Books, 1997.

118. Brzezinski, Zbigniew. "Confronting Russian Chauvinism." Transcript of Speech at Wilson Center June 16, 2014. The American Interest.

https://www.the-american-interest.com/2014/06/27/confronting-russian-chauvinism/.

119. "Telephone Conversation between Assistant Secretary of State for European and Eurasian Affairs Victoria Nuland and U.S. Ambassador to Ukraine Geoffrey Pyatt." February 4, 2014.

https://www.youtube.com/watch?v=WV9J6sxCs5k.

120. "Telephone Conversation between Estonian Foreign Minister Urmas Paet and EU High Commissioner Catherine Ashton." February 2014.

https://www.youtube.com/watch?v=kkC4Z67QuC0&t=10s.

121. Luhn, Alec. "Protesters in Ukraine Guard Biggest Weapons Cache in Eastern Europe" by Alec Luhn. *The Guardian*, April 24, 2014.

https://www.theguardian.com/world/2014/apr/24/protesters-ukraine-weapons-cache-mine.

122. "East Ukraine Militias Seize Large Amount of Ukrainian Armor—Kiev's Hacked Data." TASS Russian News Agency, August 28, 2014.

https://tass.com/world/747032.

123. Petro, Nicolai. "Eastern Ukraine: The Neverending Crisis." *The National Interest*, September 3, 2014.

https://nationalinterest.org/feature/eastern-ukraine-the-neverending-crisis-11181.

124. Brzezinski, Zbigniew. Testimony Before Senate Foreign Relations Committee, July 7, 2014.

125. Zakaria, Fareed. Interview with Zbigniew Brzezinski on CNN, July 20, 2014.

126. Gardels, Nathan. "Brzezinski: Russia's Invasion of Georgia is Reminiscent of Stalin's Attack on Finland." *HuffPost*, September 10, 2008.

https://www.huffpost.com/entry/brzezinski-russias-invasi_b_118029

127. "Independent International Fact-Finding Mission on the Conflict in Georgia." Official Journal of the European Union, September 2009.

128. Roxburgh, Angus. *The Strongman: Vladimir Putin and the Struggle for Russia*. London: I.B. Tauris, 2013.

129. Armstrong, Patrick. "The EU Report: Little and Late." Abkhaz World, October 8, 2009.

https://abkhazworld.com/aw/analysis/881-the-eu-report-little-and-late-by-patrick-armstrong.

130. Graham, Thomas. "A Russia Problem, Not a Putin Problem." Perspectives on Peace & Security, Carnegie Corporation of New York, August 20, 2014.

    https://perspectives.carnegie.org/
    us-russia/a-russia-problem-not-a-putin-problem/.

131. Putin, Vladimir. Annual Address to the Federal Assembly of the Russian Federation, April 25, 2005.

132. Drake, Bruce. "In Germany, U.S., Polls Find Little Support for Military Aid to Ukraine." Pew Research Center, May 1, 2014.

    https://www.pewresearch.org/fact-tank/2014/05/01/in-germany-u-s-polls-find-little-support-for-military-aid-to-ukraine/.

133. Kall, Rob. Interview with Col. Lawrence Wilkerson. *OpEd News*, May 28, 2014.

134. Curtis, Adam (director). *The Power of Nightmares (Parts 1–3)*. BBC. Originally aired October and November 2004.

135. Zuckert, Michael and Catherine Zuckert. *Leo Strauss and the Problem of Political Philosophy*. Chicago: University of Chicago Press, 2014.

136. Frachon, Alain and Daniel Vernet. "The Strategist and the Philosopher." Translated by Norman Madarasz. *CounterPunch,* May 29, 2003.

    http://blog.lege.net/content/frachon06022003.html

    https://www.counterpunch.org/2003/05/29/the-strategist-and-the-philosopher/.

137. Burr, William. "Prevent the Reemergence of a New Rival." The National Security Archive, The George Washington University, February 26, 2008.

    https://nsarchive2.gwu.edu/nukevault/ebb245/index.htm.

138. Wolfowitz, Paul. "FY 94–99 Defense Planning Guidance Sections for Comment" (aka Wolfowitz Doctrine), 1992. Available at The National Security Archive, George Washington University.

    https://nsarchive2.gwu.edu/nukevault/ebb245/doc03_extract_nytedit.pdf.

139. Parry, Robert. "The Human Price of Neocon Havoc." *Consortium News*, July 17, 2014.

https://consortiumnews.com/2014/07/17/the-human-price-of-neocon-havoc/.

140. Christison, Bill and Kathleen Christison. "A Rose by Another Name: The Bush Administration's Dual Loyalties" CounterPunch, December 13, 2002.

https://ifamericansknew.org/us_ints/nc-christisons1.html.

141. Beaumont, Peter. "A Neocon by Any Other Name." *The Guardian*, April 26, 2008.

https://www.theguardian.com/world/2008/apr/27/usa.

142. Militarist Monitor. "Robert Kagan." Updated November 30, 2018.

https://militarist-monitor.org/profile/robert-kagan/.

143. Blum, William. *Killing Hope: U.S. Military and C.I.A. Interventions Since World War II*. Monroe, ME: Common Courage Press, 2000.

144. Lobe, Jim. "Neocons Shaken, But Not Deterred." Inter Press Service, January 25, 2008.

https://original.antiwar.com/lobe/2008/01/25/neocons-shaken-but-not-deterred/.

145. Taylor, Adam. "John McCain Went to Ukraine and Stood on Stage with a Man Accused of Being an Anti-Semitic Neo-Nazi." *Business Insider*, December 17, 2013.

https://www.businessinsider.in/John-McCain-Went-To-Ukraine-And-Stood-On-Stage-With-A-Man-Accused-Of-Being-An-Anti-Semitic-Neo-Nazi/articleshow/27490942.cms.

146. Horgan, John. *The End of War*. San Francisco: McSweeney's Publishing, 2012.

147. Jacobson, Brad. "Why War Isn't Inevitable: A Scientist Studies the Secret to Peaceful Societies." AlterNet, March 18, 2012.

https://readersupportednews.org/opinion2/26632/10537whywarisntinevitable.

148. Grossman, Lt. Col. David. *On Killing: The Psychological Cost of Learning to Kill in War and Society*. New York: Back Bay Books, 1996.

149. Zinn, Howard. *Terrorism and War*. New York: Seven Stories Press, 2002.

150. Bricmont, Jean. *Humanitarian Imperialism: Using Human Rights to Sell War*. Translated by Diana Johnstone. New York: Monthly Review Press, 2006.

151. Johnstone, Diana. "The Good Intentions That Pave the Road to War." CounterPunch, February 1, 2013.

https://www.counterpunch.org/2013/02/01/the-good-intentions-that-pave-the-road-to-war/.

152. Boyle, Francis. *Destroying Libya and World Order: The Three-Decade U.S. Campaign to Terminate the Qaddafi Revolution*. Atlanta: Clarity Press, 2013.

153. Williamson, Clint. "Statement by the Chief Prosecutor of the Special Investigative Task Force (SITF) on Investigative Findings." Special Investigative Task Force, July 29, 2014.

http://www.hlc-rdc.org/wp-content/uploads/2014/07/Press_release_EN.pdf.

154. Queally, Jon. "Obama Bombs Iraq 'In Order to Save It.'" Common Dreams, August 8, 2014.

https://www.commondreams.org/news/2014/08/08/obama-bombs-iraq-or-der-save-it.

155. "Obama: US Intervening to Protect American Personnel." Democracy Now! Headlines for August 11, 2014.

156. Leverett, Flynt and Hillary Mann Leverett. "Neocons Double-Down on Iraq/ Syria." *Consortium News*, June 13, 2014.

https://consortiumnews.com/2014/06/13/neocons-double-down-on-iraq-syria/.

157. Greppi, Edoardo. "The Responsibility to Protect: An Introduction." University of Torino, 2009.

158. Cohn, Marjorie. "The Responsibility to Protect—the Cases of Libya and Ivory Coast" by Marjorie Cohn. Truthout, May 16, 2011.

https://truthout.org/articles/the-responsibility-to-protect-the-cases-of-libya-and-ivory-coast/.

159. Obama, Barack, David Cameron, and Nicolas Sarkozy. "Libya's Pathway to Peace." *The New York Times*, April 14, 2011.

https://www.nytimes.com/2011/04/15/opinion/15iht-edlibya15.html.

160. "Clinton on Qaddafi: We Came, We Saw, He Died."

https://www.youtube.com/watch?v=mlz3-OzcExI.

161. Quackenbush, Casey. "The Libyan Slave Trade Has Shocked the World: Here's What You Should Know." *Time*, December 1, 2017.

https://time.com/5042560/libya-slave-trade/.

162. Parry, Robert. "The Dangerous Neocon-R2P Alliance." *Consortium News*, April 18, 2014.

https://consortiumnews.com/2014/04/18/the-dangerous-neocon-r2p-alliance/.

163. Kuperman, Alan. "Lessons from Libya: How Not to Intervene." Belfer Center for Science and International Affairs, September 2013.

https://www.belfercenter.org/publication/lessons-libya-how-not-intervene.

164. Norton, Ben. "U.K. Parliament Report Details How NATO's 2011 War in Libya was Based on Lies." *Salon*, September 16, 2016.

https://www.salon.com/2016/09/16/u-k-parliament-report-details-how-natos-2011-war-in-libya-was-based-on-lies/.

165. Hersh, Seymour. "The Red Line and the Rat Line." London Review of Books, April 2014.

https://www.lrb.co.uk/v36/n08/seymour-m-hersh/the-red-line-and-the-rat-line.

166. Lloyd, Richard. "Possible Implications of Faulty US Technical Intelligence in the Damascus Nerve Agent Attack of August 21, 2013." MIT Science, Technology and Global Security Working Group, January 14, 2014.

https://www.voltairenet.org/IMG/pdf/possible-implications-of-bad-intelligence.pdf.

167. "Statement to International Press Regarding UN Resolution on Libya." RT, August 2011.

https://www.youtube.com/watch?v=BvP3BW21VWU.

168. "What Does Russia Want?" Slavyangrad, September 3, 2014.

https://slavyangrad.org/2014/09/03/what-does-russia-want/.

169. Kennan, George. "A Fateful Error." *The New York Times*, February 5, 1997. https://www.nytimes.com/1997/02/05/opinion/a-fateful-error.html.

170. "Gorbachev Blasts NATO Eastward Expansion." Sputnik News, April 2, 2009. https://sputniknews.com/russia/20090402120879153/.

171. McGovern, Ray. "Rebuilding the Obama-Putin Trust." *Consortium News*, January 3, 2015.

    https://consortiumnews.com/2015/01/03/rebuilding-the-obama-putin-trust/.

172. Sarotte, Mary Elise. "Not One Inch Eastward? Bush, Baker, Kohl, Genscher, Gorbachev, and the Origin of Russian Resentment toward NATO Enlargement in February 1990." Diplomatic History Journal. 1/6/10.

173. Savranskaya, Svetlana and Tom Blanton. "NATO Expansion: What Gorbachev Heard." National Security Archive, George Washington University, December 12, 2017.

    https://nsarchive.gwu.edu/briefing-book/russia-programs/2017-12-12/nato-expansion-what-gorbachev-heard-western-leaders-early.

174. Pushkov, Alexey. "Broken Promises." *The National Interest*, April 16, 2007.

    https://nationalinterest.org/commentary/broken-promises-1535.

175. Hartung, William. "The Hidden Costs of NATO Expansion." Arms Trade Resource Center, World Policy, March 1998.

    https://worldpolicy.org/2009/11/13/report-the-hidden-costs-of-nato-expansion-world-policy-institute-research-project/.

176. *Chicago Tribune*. "Clinton and Dole and the Polish Vote," May 20, 1996.

    https://www.chicagotribune.com/news/ct-xpm-1996-05-20-9605200029-story.html.

177. Beebe, George S. *The Russia Trap: How Our Shadow War with Russia Could Spiral into Nuclear Catastrophe*. New York: Thomas Dunne Books, 2019.

178. Rice, Condoleezza. *No Higher Honor: A Memoir of My Years in Washington*. New York: Crown Publishers, 2011.

179. Rohde, David and Arshad Mohammed. "Special Report: How U.S. Made Its Putin Problem Worse." *Reuters*, April 19, 2014.

https://www.reuters.com/article/us-ukraine-putin-diplomacy-special-repor/ special-report-how-the-u-s-made-its-putin-problem-worse-idUS-BREA3H0OQ20140419.

180. Klein, Naomi. *The Shock Doctrine: The Rise of Disaster Capitalism*. New York: Picador, 2007.

181. Hounshell, Blake. "Salzburg Diary: 'Here's Some More [Expletive] for Your Face." *Foreign Policy*. 4/8/08.

https://foreignpolicy.com/2008/04/08/salzburg-diary-heres-some-more-ex-pletive-for-your-face/.

182. Rozoff, Rick. "NATO Expansion, Missile Deployments and Russia's New Military Doctrine." Voltaire.net, February 15, 2010.

https://www.voltairenet.org/article164065.html.

183. "Central and Eastern European Security Concerns." Federation of American Scientists.

https://fas.org/man/eprint/aurora_29/part03.htm.

184. Parry, Robert. "The Victory of 'Perception Management.'" *Consortium News*, December 28, 2014.

https://consortiumnews.com/2014/12/28/the-victory-of-perception-man-agement/.

185. "Review of the Role of the Polish American Congress in Bringing Poland into NATO (Timeline)." Polish American Congress.

http://polishamericans.org/nato-enlargement/ -background/.

186. Gati, Charles. *Zbig: The Strategy and Statecraft of Zbigniew Brzezinski*. Baltimore, MD: John Hopkins University Press, 2013.

187. Łukasiewicz, Sławomir. "Jan Nowak-Jeziorański: A Sketch for a Portrait." New Eastern Europe, October 2, 2014.

http://neweasterneurope.eu/old_site/articles-and-commentary/1345-jan-nowak-jezioranski-a-sketch-for-a-portrait.

188. Asmus, Ronald. *Opening NATO's Door*. New York: Columbia University Press, 2002.

189. "Poland NATO Report." Center for International Relations, Warsaw: Euro-Atlantic Association, 1994.

190. Laughland, John. "The Prague Racket." *The Guardian*, November 21, 2002.
    https://www.theguardian.com/world/2002/nov/22/nato.comment.

191. "U.S. Committee on NATO." Militarist Monitor, May 10, 2012.
    https://militarist-monitor.org/profile/us_committee_on_nato/.

192. Gerth, Jeff and Tim Weiner. "Arms Makers See Bonanza in Selling NATO Expansion." *The New York Times,* June 29, 1997.
    https://www.nytimes.com/1997/06/29/world/arms-makers-see-bonanza-in-selling-nato-expansion.html.

193. Brzezinski, Zbigniew. "Hearings before the Committee on Foreign Relations." United States Senate, October 1997.
    https://www.govinfo.gov/content/pkg/CHRG-105shrg46832/html/CHRG-105shrg46832.htm.

194. Tarifa, Fatos. *To Albania, with Love*. Lanham, MD: University Press of America, 2007.

195. Engdahl, William. "The Emerging Russian Giant Plays its Cards Strategically." Global Research, October 7, 2006.
    https://www.globalresearch.ca/the-emerging-russian-giant-plays-its-cards-strategically/3408.

196. Jackson, Bruce. Testimony Before Senate Foreign Relations Committee, April 1, 2003.

197. Von Sponeck, Hans. "The UN and NATO: Which Security and for Whom?" Nuclear Age Peace Foundation, April 14, 2009.

198. Lekic, Slobodan. "Despite Cuts, NATO Still Accounts for Most of World's Military Spending." *Stars and Stripes*, February 25, 2014.
    https://www.stripes.com/news/despite-cuts-nato-still-accounts-for-most-of-world-s-military-spending-1.269882.

199. Link, Gregor. "'Defender 2020': NATO Powers Threaten War Against Russia." World Socialist Web Site, October 8, 2019.

https://www.wsws.org/en/articles/2019/10/08/nato-o08.html.

200. Meixler, Eli. "French President Emmanuel Macron Calls for a 'European Army' to Defend Against China, Russia and the U.S." *Time,* November 6, 2018.

https://time.com/5446975/emmanuel-macron-european-army-russia-us/.

201. de la Baume, Maïa and Herszenhorn, David M. "Merkel Joins Macron in Calling for EU Army to Complement NATO." *Politico*, November 14, 2018.

https://www.politico.eu/article/angela-merkel-emmanuel-macron-eu-army-to-complement-nato/.

202. "Franco-German Treaty A Step Toward 'European Army': Merkel." AFP, January 22, 2019.

http://english.ahram.org.eg/NewsContent/2/9/322219/World/International/FrancoGerman-treaty-a-step-toward-European-army-Me.aspx.

203. Putin, Vladimir. "Speech and the Following Discussion at the Munich Conference on Security Policy." February 10, 2007.

http://en.kremlin.ru/events/president/transcripts/24034.

204. Wedel, Janine. "The Harvard Boys Do Russia." *The Nation*, May 14, 1998.

https://www.thenation.com/article/harvard-boys-do-russia/.

205. Tennison, Sharon. *The Power of Impossible Ideas: Ordinary Citizens' Extraordinary Efforts to Avert International Crises.* Odenwald Press, 2012.

206. Williamson, Anne. Testimony Before House of Representatives. September 21, 1999.

207. Hudson, Michael. "The New Cold War's Ukraine Gambit." Michael-Hudson.com, May 13, 2014.

208. Wahlberg, Eric. "Vladimir Putin and Russia's 'White Revolution.'" Global Research, February 9, 2012.

https://www.globalresearch.ca/vladimir-putin-and-russia-s-white-revolution/29177.

209. Tennison, Sharon. "Who Is Vladimir Putin? Why Does the U.S. Government Hate Him?" Global Research, May 8, 2014.

https://www.globalresearch.ca/who-is-vladimir-putin-why-does-the-us-government-hate-him/5381205.

210. Kovacevic, Dejan. "The Winter Olympics in Sochi Are a Success . . . But Don't Tell Russia." Triblive, February 23, 2014.

https://archive.triblive.com/news/the-winter-olympics-in-sochi-are-a-success-but-dont-tell-russia/.

211. "Putin on Ideology—Difference Between Americans and Russians." RT, 2013.

https://www.youtube.com/watch?v=3JVR0zAiyw0&feature=youtu.be.

212. "68% of Russian Citizens Consider Russia a Superpower." Levada-Center poll, December 23, 2014.

https://www.levada.ru/en/2014/12/23/68-of-russian-citizens-consider-russia-a-superpower/.

213. Euronews. "Ties that Bind: The Economics of the EU-Russia Relationship." March 18, 2014.

https://www.euronews.com/2014/03/18/the-ties-that-bind-the-economics-of-the-eu-russia-relationship.

214. Mellow, Craig. "Balanced Budgets, Managed Debt: What the U.S. Could Learn from Russia." Minyanville, October 10, 2013.

http://www.minyanville.com/sectors/global-markets/articles/russia-Vladimir-Putin-russian-government-russian/10/10/2013/id/52186.

215. "Russia's Economy Under Vladimir Putin." RIA Novosti, January 3, 2008.

216. Conway, Edmund. "Reborn Russia Clears Soviet Debt." *The Telegraph*, August 22, 2006.

https://www.telegraph.co.uk/finance/2945924/Reborn-Russia-clears-Soviet-debt.html.

217. "Russia Has Paid Off IMF Debts." UPI, February 2, 2005.

https://www.upi.com/Russia-has-paid-off-IMF-debts/66111107283700/.

218. "Russia's Top 10 Exports." World's Top Exports, 2013.

219. "Regional and State Unemployment—2013 Annual Averages." Bureau of Labor Statistics, U.S. Department of Labor, February 28, 2014.

220. "December 2013: Euro Area Unemployment Rate at 12%." Eurostat—News Release, Euro Indicators, January 31, 2014.

221. "Russia Gains 11 Points in Global Competitiveness Report 2014." RT, September 3, 2014.

https://www.rt.com/news/184720-russia-global-competitiveness-rises/.

222. Putin, Vladimir. "Presidential Address to the Federal Assembly" March 1, 2018.

http://en.kremlin.ru/events/president/news/56957.

223. Henderson, Jane. *The Constitution of the Russian Federation: A Contextual Analysis.* London: Hart Publishing, 2011.

224. bne IntelliNews. "Russia to Crack Down on Tax Evasion." October 17, 2014.

https://www.intellinews.com/russia-to-crack-down-on-tax-evasion-500432561/?archive=bne.

225. Bershidsky, Leonid. "Putin Baits the West to Bring Russian Money Home." *Bloomberg*, October 10, 2018.

https://www.bloomberg.com/opinion/articles/2018-10-11/putin-baits-the-west-to-bring-russian-money-home.

226. Brown, Jeff. "Operation Rescue Russia and a Big 'F.U.'" OpEd News, August 25, 2014.

https://www.opednews.com/articles/2/Operation-Rescue-Russia-an-by-Jeff-J-Brown-Agriculture_America_Boycott_Brics-140825-518.html?p=2&f=Operation-Rescue-Russia-an-by-Jeff-J-Brown-Agriculture_America_Boycott_Brics-140825-518.html.

227. "Russia's Import Ban Means Big Business for Latin America." RT, August 7, 2014.

https://www.rt.com/business/178664-latin-america-benefits-russia-ban/.

228. McMillan, D'Arce. "Russia's Wheat Dominance Set to Get Bigger in the Future." *The Western Producer*, January 25, 2018.

https://www.producer.com/2018/01/russias-wheat-dominance-set-to-get-bigger-in-the-future/.

229. Sarich, Christina. "Russians Prove Small-Scale Organic Can Feed the World." The Cornucopia Institute, May 29, 2013.

    https://www.cornucopia.org/2013/06/russians-prove-small-scale-organic-can-feed-the-world/.

230. "Here's How Russia Is Planning to Shake Up Organic Agriculture." Yugagro, August 29, 2018.

    https://www.yugagro.org/en-GB/press/news/Russia-organic-agriculture.aspx.

231. Tennison, Sharon. "Russia Sanctions Report and India's Perspective." Email report dated September 19, 2014.

232. Connolly, Richard. *Russia's Response to Sanctions: How Western Economic Statecraft is Reshaping Political Economy in Russia*. Cambridge, UK: Cambridge University Press, 2018.

233. Goncharoff, Paul. "Russian Food Production Booming Thanks to Import Substitutions, Western Sanctions." The Duran, April 5, 2018.

    http://russiafeed.com/russian-food-production-booming-thanks-to-import-substitutions-western-sanctions/.

234. "From Russia with Wheat: Exports by Global Grain Superpower Soar 80%." RT, September 7, 2018.

    https://www.rt.com/business/437886-russian-wheat-exports-increase/.

235. Escobar, Pepe. "How the New Silk Roads are Merging into Greater Eurasia." *Asia Times*, December 13, 2018.

    https://www.globalresearch.ca/how-the-new-silk-roads-are-merging-into-greater-eurasia/5663036.

236. Allison, Graham. "China and Russia: A Strategic Alliance in the Making" by Graham Allison. *The National Interest*, December 14, 2018.

    https://nationalinterest.org/feature/china-and-russia-strategic-alliance-making-38727?page=0%2C1.

237. "Russia-China Bomber Patrol Shows Stronger Alignment Between the Two." Russia Matters, July 26, 2019.

https://www.russiamatters.org/analysis/russia-china-bomber-patrol-shows-stronger-alignment-between-two

238. Page, Jeremy. "China Promises Further Military Cooperation with Russia." *The Wall Street Journal*, July 24, 2019.

https://www.wsj.com/articles/china-promises-further-military-coopera-tion-with-russia-11563973937.

239. Robinson, Paul. "Book Review: Russia's Response to Sanctions." Irrussianal-ity, August 16, 2018.

https://irrussianality.wordpress.com/2018/08/16/book-review-russias-re-sponse-to-sanctions/.

240. "Russia Climbs in Global Competitiveness Index." *The Moscow Times*, October 17, 2018.

https://themoscowtimes.com/news/russia-climbs-global-competitive-ness-index-63211.

241. "Russia Economic Report: Modest Growth; Focus on Informality." The World Bank, June 6, 2019.

https://roscongress.org/en/materials/doklad-ob-ekonomike-ros-sii-41-umerennye-tempy-rosta-ekonomiki-v-tsentre-vnimaniya-neformal-nyy-sektor/

242. "Russia Government Debt to GDP." TradingEconomics.com. Retrieved on December 21, 2018.

https://tradingeconomics.com/russia/government-debt-to-gdp.

243. "United States Gross Federal Debt to GDP. TradingEconomics.com. Retrieved on December 21, 2018.

https://tradingeconomics.com/united-states/government-debt-to-gdp.

244. "Russia Government Budget." TradingEconomics.com. Retrieved on Decem-ber 21, 2018.

https://tradingeconomics.com/russia/government-budget.

245. Foy, Henry. "Russia 2018 Budget Surplus to be Close to 3% of GDP—Minis-ter." *Financial Times*, December 12, 2018.

https://www.ft.com/content/9b20ad82-fde5-11e8-aebf-99e208d3e521.

246. "Russia's Top 5 Imports & Exports: Do You Believe They're the World's Biggest Wheat Exporter?" Commodity.com. Retrieved on December 20, 2018.

    https://commodity.com/russia/

247. "Russia Raises Minimum Wage 43% Ahead of Presidential Elections." *The Moscow Times*, February 16, 2018.

    https://themoscowtimes.com/news/russia-raises-minimum-wage-43-percent-ahead-presidential-elections-60535.

248. "Russia Unemployment Rate." CEIC Data. Retrieved on November 3, 2019.

    https://www.ceicdata.com/en/indicator/russia/unemployment-rate.

249. "Knocking Out the Competition! Russia Moves Up 100 Ranks in 7 Years Along Business Ratings!" Vesti News, October 25, 2019.

    https://www.vesti.ru/doc.html?id=3203443&cid=4441.

250. "Vedomosti: 'Doing business' isn't everything in Russia." Meduza, October 24, 2019. Republished on Johnson's Russia List, October 25, 2019.

251. "Trust in Putin Drops to 39% as Russians Face Later Retirement, Poll Says." *The Moscow Times*, October 8, 2018.

    https://www.themoscowtimes.com/2018/10/08/trust-putin-drops-39-percent-russians-face-later-retirement-poll-says-a63110.

252. "Social Problems." Levada-Center Poll, December 2018.

    https://www.levada.ru/en/2018/10/12/the-social-problems-which-most-concern-the-public/.

253. "Russians are Much Less Willing to Protest Retirement Age Hike, Poll Says." *The Moscow Times*, September 27, 2018.

    https://www.themoscowtimes.com/2018/09/27/russians-are-much-less-willing-to-protest-retirement-age-hike-poll-says-a63006

254. Karlin, Anatoly. "Russian Demographics in 2018." *The Unz Review*, January 29, 2018.

    http://www.unz.com/akarlin/russian-demographics-in-2018/.

255. Sharkov, Damien. "Poll: The Majority of Russians See Themselves as Free." *Newsweek,* December 8, 2015.

https://www.newsweek.com/majority-russians-see-themselves-free-poll-402513.

256. "Firearms-Control Legislation and Policy: Russian Federation." Library of Congress. Viewed on September 7, 2019.

http://www.loc.gov/law/help/firearms-control/russia.php.

257. "Putin Says He Is Against Lifting Death Penalty Moratorium." TASS Russian News Agency, April 25, 2013.

https://tass.com/old-the-direct-line-with-vladimir-putin/692749.

258. Weiler, Jonathan Daniel. *Human Rights in Russia: A Darker Side of Reform.* Boulder, CO: Lynne Rienner Publishers, 2004.

259. Karlin, Anatoly. "A Short History of Russian Homicides." Unz Review. December 4, 2018.

https://www.unz.com/akarlin/russia-homicides/

260. "Moscow Named World's Fourth Safest Megacity for Women." *The Moscow Times*, October 27, 2017.

https://themoscowtimes.com/news/moscow-named-worlds-fourth-safest-megacity-for-women-59295.

261. "Population with Tertiary Education." OECD, 2014–2017. Accessed on January 6, 2019.

https://data.oecd.org/eduatt/population-with-tertiary-education.htm.

262. "Maternity Leave Around the World: Russia." Mom.me., July 2, 2014.
https://mom.com/pregnancy/5336-maternity-leave-around-world

263. Hahn, Gordon. "Putin: A Russian Neo-Traditionalist, Not a Western Conservative." December 8, 2015.

https://gordonhahn.com/2015/12/08/putin-a-russian-neo-traditionalist-not-a-western-conservative/.

264. Petro, Nicolai N. "Are We Reading Russia Right?" *The Fletcher Forum of World Affairs* 42, no. 2 (2018): 131–54.

265. Weir, Fred. "Russia's Media Scene: Not Just a State Affair." Christian Science Monitor, February 6, 2018.

https://www.csmonitor.com/World/Europe/2018/0206/Russia-s-media-scene-not-just-a-state-affair.

266. "58 Journalists Killed in Russia Between 1992 and 2019." Committee to Protect Journalists. Accessed on January 6, 2018.

https://cpj.org/data/killed/europe/russia/?status=Killed&motiveConfirmed%5B%5D=Confirmed&type%5B%5D=Journalist&cc_fips%5B%5D=RS&start_year=1992&end_year=2019&group_by=location.

267. Cohen, Stephen F. "Stop the Pointless Demonization of Putin." Reuters, May 7, 2012.

http://blogs.reuters.com/great-debate/2012/05/07/stop-the-pointless-demonization-of-putin/.

268. Baldwin, Natylie. "Building Civil Society in Russia—An Example from Krasnodar." Russia Insider, March 17, 2016.

https://russia-insider.com/en/culture/citizen-initiative-krasnodar-takes/ri13407.

269. "Russian Charities to be Exempt from 'Foreign Agent' Label." The Moscow Times, May 17, 2016.

https://themoscowtimes.com/articles/russian-charities-to-be-exempt-from-foreign-agent-label-52901.

270. Putin, Vladimir. "Annual Address to the Federal Assembly of the Russian Federation." July 8, 2000.

http://en.kremlin.ru/events/president/transcripts/21480.

271. Email Correspondence between Natylie Baldwin and Charles Heberle. February 4–5, 2016.

272. Hendley, Kathryn. Everyday Law in Russia. Ithaca, NY: Cornell University Press, 2017.

273. Baker, Peter. "The Seduction of George W. Bush." Foreign Policy, November 6, 2013.

https://foreignpolicy.com/2013/11/06/the-seduction-of-george-w-bush/.

274. Yakovlev, Andrei. "State-Business Relations and Improvement of Corporate Governance in Russia." Bank of Finland, 2008.

275. "Rosneft and Gazprom Overtake Google and Apple in Corporate Transparency." Russia Beyond the Headlines, November 12, 2014.

https://www.rbth.com/business/2014/11/11/rosneft_and_gazprom_overtake_google_and_apple_in_corporate_transpare_41307.html.

276. Adomanis, Mark. "Three Things Obama Got Wrong About Russia." *Forbes*, August 4, 2014.

277. "International Migration Report." United Nations, 2017. Page 6.

http://www.un.org/en/development/desa/population/migration/publications/migrationreport/docs/MigrationReport2017_Highlights.pdf.

278. Howell, Elizabeth. "US Too Dependent on Russian Rocket Engines, Experts Tell Lawmakers." Space.com, July 17, 2014.

https://www.space.com/26551-us-military-launches-russian-rocket-engines.html.

279. Johnson, Matthew. "Dealing with the 'Authoritarian' Label: Putin and the Fraud of American Exceptionalism—Analysis." Eurasian Review, May 13, 2014.

280. Putin, Vladimir. "We Need a New Economy." RT, January 30, 2012.

https://www.rt.com/russia/official-word/putin-article-economy-competitiveness-011/.

281. Johnson, Matthew. "Globalization and Decline of the West: Eurasianism, the State and the Rebirth of Ethnic Socialism." Eurasian Review, May 2, 2014.

282. Risen, James. "Secrets of History: The C.I.A. in Iran." *The New York Times*, April 16, 2000.

https://www.nytimes.com/2000/04/16/world/secrets-history-cia-iran-special-report-plot-convulsed-iran-53-79.html.

283. Kornbluh, Peter and Kate Doyle. "CIA and Assassinations: The Guatemala 1954 Documents." The National Security Archive, George Washington University.

https://nsarchive2.gwu.edu/NSAEBB/NSAEBB4/.

284. Clark, Neil. "A Funny Sort of Democracy." *New Statesman*, November 17, 2003.

285. Bespalova, Natalia. "Ukraine: Straddling Between the EU and the Customs Union." Russia Beyond the Headlines, March 12, 2013.

   https://www.rbth.com/international/2013/03/12/ukraine_straddling_ between_the_eu_and_the_customs_union_23739.html

286. Putin, Vladimir. "Prepared Remarks at the Davos World Economic Forum" January 28, 2009.

287. Putin, Vladimir. "Annual Address to the Federal Assembly of the Russian Federation." December 12, 2013.

   http://en.kremlin.ru/events/president/transcripts/messages/19825.

288. Aris, Ben. "It's Time for a New Pan-European Security Treaty." bne IntelliNews, January 13, 2015.

   http://www.intellinews.com/perspective-it-s-time-for-a-new-pan-european-security-treaty-500442961/?archive=bne

289. "Nyet Means Nyet: Russia's NATO Enlargement Red Lines." WikiLeaks, February 2008.

290. Rozoff, Rick. "NATO's Incremental Absorption of Ukraine." Voltaire.net, April 26, 2014.

   https://www.voltairenet.org/article183470.html.

291. Stea, Carla. "The UN Says the Ukrainian People Must Decide Their Fate, NATO Wants Something Else." Global Research, December 29, 2013.

   https://www.globalresearch.ca/the-un-says-the-ukrainian-people-must-decide-their-fate-nato-wants-something-else/5362936.

292. "How the EU Lost Russia over Ukraine." *Der Spiegel,* November 24, 2014.

   https://www.spiegel.de/international/europe/war-in-ukraine-a-result-of-misunderstandings-between-europe-and-russia-a-1004706-2.html.

293. Johnstone, Diana. "Washington's Iron Curtain in Ukraine." CounterPunch, June 6, 2014.

   https://www.counterpunch.org/2014/06/06/washingtons-iron-curtain-in-ukraine/.

294. Hudson, Michael. "Investigation Finds Former Ukraine President Not Responsible for Sniper Attack on Protestors." Dandelion Salad, April 17, 2014.

https://dandelionsalad.wordpress.com/2014/04/17/michael-hudson-investigation-finds-former-ukraine-president-not-responsible-for-sniper-attack-on-protestors/.

295. Katchanovski, Ivan. "The Snipers' Massacre on the Maidan in Ukraine." Academia, 2015.

https://www.academia.edu/8776021/The_Snipers_Massacre_on_the_Maidan_in_Ukraine.

296. "Ukraine: Our Ukraine Insider Poroshenko on Rada Majority Coalition Talks, Tymoshenko" WikiLeaks, April 28, 2006.

https://wikileaks.org/plusd/cables/06KIEV1706_a.html.

297. Hahn, Gordon. "Maidan Reforms or Maidan Meltdown?" GordonHahn.com, April 6, 2015.

https://gordonhahn.com/2015/04/06/maidan-reforms-or-maidan-meltdown/.

298. Raimondo, Justin. "The Murderers of Kiev." Antiwar.com, April 17, 2015.

http://original.antiwar.com/justin/2015/04/16/the-murderers-of-kiev/.

299. "Ukraine's 'Ministry of Truth' Wants 15-Year Prison Terms for Journalists." Sputnik News, March 22, 2015.

https://sputniknews.com/europe/201503221019858686/.

300. Brendle, Frank. "A Visit to Ukraine, Where the Holocaust Becomes a Negligible Detail." Defending History, December 14, 2014.

http://defendinghistory.com/visit-ukraine-holocaust-negligible-detail/70186.

301. O'Brien, Matt. "Ukraine Unofficially Has 272 Percent Inflation." *The Washington Post*, March 1, 2015.

https://www.newcoldwar.org/ukraine-unofficially-has-272-percent-inflation/.

302. "Poroshenko Stands Alone: Ukraine Politics in a Pre-Election Year." Centre for Eastern Studies (OSW), May 21, 2018.

https://www.osw.waw.pl/en/publikacje/osw-commentary/2018-05-21/poroshenko-stands-alone-ukraine-politics-a-pre-election-year-0#_ftn1.

303. Lancaster, Patrick (@PLnewstoday). "Ukraine is in Civil war almost all soldiers I have met on both sides seem to be from Ukraine." Twitter, August 2, 2014, 10:35 a.m.

https://twitter.com/PLnewstoday/status/495623963406774272

304. Kelly, Alexander Reed. "Vladimir Putin Not Responsible for Ukrainian Civil War, Expert Says." Truthdig, March 21, 2015.

https://www.truthdig.com/articles/vladimir-putin-not-responsible-for-ukrainian-civil-war-expert-says/.

305. Giuliano, Elise. "The Origins of Separatism: Popular Grievances in Donetsk and Luhansk." PONARS Eurasia Policy Memo no. 396. October 2015.

306. Kudelia, Serhiy. "The Donbas Rift." *Russian Politics and Law Journal* 54, no. 1 (2016).

307. Hellevig, Jon. "Meet Andriy Parubiy, the Neo-Nazi Leader Turned Speaker of Ukraine's Parliament." Global Research, April 17, 2016.

https://www.globalresearch.ca/meet-andriy-parubiy-the-former-neo-nazi-leader-turned-speaker-of-ukraines-parliament/5520502.

308. Hahn, Gordon. "The Real Ukrainian 'Snipers' Massacre.'" GordonHahn.com, March 9, 2016.

https://gordonhahn.com/2016/03/09/the-real-snipers-massacre-ukraine-february-2014-updatedrevised-working-paper/.

309. Kostychenko, Elena. "The Story of a Russian Soldier's War in Ukraine." *Novaya Gazeta*, March 2, 2015. English translation at:

http://euromaidanpress.com/2015/03/02/the-story-of-a-russian-soldiers-war-in-ukraine-we-all-knew-what-we-had-to-do-and-what-could-happen/.

310. "OSCE Special Monitoring Mission to Ukraine." OSCE, March 21, 2014.

https://www.osce.org/special-monitoring-mission-to-ukraine.

311. "Can Merkel's Diplomacy Save Europe?" *Der Spiegel*, February 14, 2015.

https://www.spiegel.de/international/europe/minsk-deal-represents-and-fragile-opportunity-for-peace-in-ukraine-a-1018326.html.

312. Mercouris, Alexander. "Merkel in Moscow and Minsk: Der Spiegel Says Putin Has Won." Russia Insider, February 18, 2015.

https://russia-insider.com/en/opinion/2015/02/18/3599.

313. Carpenter, Ted Galen. "Washington Quietly Increases Lethal Weapons to Ukraine." The American Conservative, September 10, 2018.

https://www.cato.org/publications/commentary/washington-quietly-increases-lethal-weapons-ukraine.

314. Cronk, Terri Moon. "U.S. Troops Training Ukrainian Soldiers, Mattis Says." Department of Defense, February 2, 2018.

https://www.defense.gov/Explore/News/Article/Article/1431947/us-troops-training-ukrainian-soldiers-mattis-says/.

315. Parry, Robert. "Ukraine's Poison Pill for Peace Talks." *Consortium News*, March 19, 2015.

https://consortiumnews.com/2015/03/19/ukraines-poison-pill-for-peace-talks/.

316. "'Foreign Troops Stay Out of Ukraine,' Says Donetsk Republic Leader." DAN News, April 21, 2015. Translation on New Cold War:

https://www.newcoldwar.org/foreign-troops-stay-out-of-ukraine-says-donetsk-republic-leader/.

317. "Berlin Alarmed by Aggressive NATO Stance on Ukraine." *Der Spiegel*, March 6, 2015.

https://www.spiegel.de/international/world/germany-concerned-about-aggressive-nato-stance-on-ukraine-a-1022193.html.

318. "French Military Intelligence Rules Out 'Russian Invasion Plans' for Ukraine." RT, April 11, 2015.

https://www.rt.com/news/248877-france-ukraine-russian-military/.

319. Baldwin, Natylie. "How Crimeans See Ukraine Crisis." *Consortium News*, February 11, 2016.

https://consortiumnews.com/2016/02/11/how-crimeans-see-ukraine-crisis/.

320. Caroll, Richard E. "Russia and the West: How the West Won the Cold War but Lost the Peace." International Policy Digest, September 1, 2019.

https://intpolicydigest.org/2019/09/01/russia-and-the-west-how-the-west-won-the-cold-war-but-lost-the-peace/.

321. "The Stable Crisis. Ukraine's Economy Three Years after the Euromaidan." Centre for Eastern Studies, April 5, 2017.

    https://www.osw.waw.pl/en/publikacje/osw-commentary/2017-04-05/stable-crisis-ukraines-economy-three-years-after-euromaidan.

322. "Understanding Poverty in Ukraine." The Borgen Project, August 26, 2017.

    https://borgenproject.org/understanding-poverty-ukraine/.

323. "Poverty in Ukraine Sharply Down in 2017 Due to Higher Incomes: Minister." Xinhua, December 29, 2017.

    http://www.xinhuanet.com/english/2017-12/29/c_136858440.htm.

324. "IMF Ranks Ukraine as Europe's Poorest Country." bne IntelliNews, October 16, 2018.

    https://www.intellinews.com/imf-ranks-ukraine-as-europe-s-poorest-country-150301/.

325. Cohen, Josh. "Commentary: Ukraine's Neo-Nazi Problem." *Reuters*, March 19, 2018.

    https://www.reuters.com/article/us-cohen-ukraine-commentary/commentary-ukraines-neo-nazi-problem-idUSKBN1GV2TY.

326. "Ukraine Far Right Battles Police at Parliament in Kiev." BBC, October 14, 2014.

    https://www.bbc.com/news/world-europe-29611588.

327. Luhn, Alec. "Tensions Rising in Ukraine as Far-Right Militia's Boobytraps Injure Two Police." *The Guardian,* July 14, 2015.

    https://www.theguardian.com/world/2015/jul/14/tensions-rising-in-ukraine-as-far-right-militias-boobytraps-injure-two-police.

328. Miller, James. "Ukraine's Anti-Terrorist Terror." *The Daily Beast*, September 1, 2015.

    https://www.thedailybeast.com/ukraines-anti-terrorist-terror.

329. Nichols, Michelle. "At UN, US Warns Russia over 'Outrageous Violation' of Ukraine Sovereignty." *Reuters*, November 26, 2018.

https://www.reuters.com/article/us-ukraine-crisis-russia-un/
at-un-us-warns-russia-over-outrageous-violation-of-ukraine-sovereign-
ty-idUSKCN1NV26C.

330. Kraska, James. "The Kerch Strait Incident: Law of the Sea or Law of Naval
Warfare?" *European Journal of International Law*, December 3, 2018.

https://www.ejiltalk.org/the-kerch-strait-incident-law-of-the-sea-or-law-of-
naval-warfare/.

331. Roth, Andrew. "Ukraine President Warns Russia Tensions Could Lead to
'Full-Scale War.'" *The Guardian*, November 27, 2018.

https://www.theguardian.com/world/2018/nov/27/russia-to-charge-
ukrainian-sailors-as-kerch-crisis-deepens.

332. Petro, Nicolai. "Ukraine's Pinochet Scenario." *The Nation*, November 28,
2018.

https://www.thenation.com/article/ukraines-pinochet-scenario/.

333. Rogan, Tom. "Ukraine Should Blow Up Putin's Crimea Bridge." *Washington
Examiner*, May 15, 2018.

https://www.washingtonexaminer.com/opinion/ukraine-should-blow-up-
putins-crimea-bridge.

334. "Russia to Deploy Warplanes to Crimea Amid Ukraine Standoff." Deutsche
Welle (DW), December 17, 2018.

https://www.dw.com/en/russia-to-deploy-warplanes-to-crimea-amid-
ukraine-standoff/a-46775626.

335. Zinets, Natalia. "Ukraine to Send Warships Back to Azov Despite Russian
Capture." *Reuters,* December 19, 2018.

https://www.reuters.com/article/us-ukraine-crisis-russia/ukraine-to-send-
warships-back-to-azov-despite-russian-capture-idUSKCN1OI2C8.

336. Vandiver, John. "US Military Conducts Open Skies Observation Flight Over
Ukraine." *Stars and Stripes*, December 6, 2018.

https://www.stripes.com/news/us-military-conducts-open-skies-observa-
tion-flight-over-ukraine-1.559536.

337. "50,000 Casualties in Ukraine? German Intel Calls Kiev's 6K Toll 'Not
Credible.'" RT, February 8, 2015.

https://www.rt.com/news/230363-ukraine-real-losses-german-intelligence/.

338. Pifer, Steven. "The Problem with President Trump's Hasty Denunciation of New START." The Brookings Institution, February 10, 2017.

https://www.brookings.edu/blog/order-from-chaos/2017/02/10/the-problem-with-president-trumps-hasty-denunciation-of-new-start/.

339. Bender, Bryan. "Leaked Document: Putin Lobbied Trump on Arms Control." *Politico*, August 7, 2018.

https://www.politico.com/story/2018/08/07/putin-trump-arms-control-russia-724718.

340. "US Dropped Mutual Assurances of Non-Meddling from Helsinki Declaration—Reports." Sputnik News, August 9, 2018.

https://sputniknews.com/us/201808091067062332-usa-drops-helsinki-mutual-assurances/?eType=EmailBlastContent&eId=56cb3140-e7ff-4208-929e-49dfce86efd3.

341. Curtis, Adam (director). *The Century of the Self*. BBC Two, 2005.

342. "Edward Bernays." Sourcewatch.org.

https://www.sourcewatch.org/index.php/Edward_Bernays.

343. Heath, Joseph and Andrew Potter. *Nation of Rebels: Why Counterculture Became Consumer Culture*. New York: Harper Business, 2004.

344. Fischer, Brendan. "A Banana Republic Once Again?" PR Watch, December 27, 2010.

https://www.prwatch.org/news/2010/12/9834/banana-republic-once-again.

345. "Walter Lippmann." Sourcewatch.org.

https://www.sourcewatch.org/index.php/Walter_Lippmann.

346. Chomsky, Noam. "Force and Opinion." *Z Magazine*, July/August 1991.

https://chomsky.info/199107__/.

347. "MOCKINGBIRD, Project." Encyclopedia of Intelligence and Counterintelligence (1st ed.). Armonk, NY: Routledge, 2004.

348. Kinzer, Stephen. *The Brothers: John Foster Dulles, Allen Dulles, and Their Secret World War.* New York: Times Books, 2013.

349. "Freedom House." Sourcewatch.org.

https://www.sourcewatch.org/index.php?title=Freedom_House

350. Karlin, Anatoly. "Freedom House on Ukraine." Unz Review, April 29, 2015.

http://www.unz.com/akarlin/freedom-house-on-ukraine/.

351. Gilens, Martin and Benjamin Page. "Testing Theories of American Politics: Elites, Interest Groups, and Average Citizens." Cambridge, UK: Cambridge University Press, 2014.

https://scholar.princeton.edu/sites/default/files/mgilens/files/gilens_and_page_2014_-testing_theories_of_american_politics.doc.pdf.

352. Interview with Chris Hedges. Sophie Co. RT, April 28, 2014.

https://www.rt.com/shows/sophieco/155268-ukraine-crisis-cold-war/.

353. Rapp, Nicholas and Aric Jenkins. "Chart: These 6 Companies Control Much of U.S. Media." *Fortune*, July 24, 2018.

http://fortune.com/longform/media-company-ownership-consolidation/.

354. "Interlocking Directorates." FAIR.org.

https://fair.org/interlocking-directorates/.

355. Mitchell, Amy and Jesse Holcomb. "Revenue Sources: A Heavy Dependence on Advertising." Pew Research Center, Journalism and Media, March 26, 2014.

http://www.journalism.org/2014/03/26/revenue-sources-a-heavy-dependence-on-advertising/.

356. Robinson, Paul. "It Lies Within." Irrussianality, January 10, 2019.

https://irrussianality.wordpress.com/2019/01/10/it-lies-within/.

357. Applebaum, Anne. "The Arab World Isn't Clamoring for Our Help." *The Washington Post*, March 7, 2011.

358. Ames, Mark. "Neocons 2.0: The Problem with Peter Pomerantsev." Pando, May 17, 2015.

https://pando.com/2015/05/17/neocons-2-0-the-problem-with-peter-pomerantsev/.

359. Carden, James. "Neo-McCarthyism and the US Media: The Crusade to Ban Russia Policy Critics." *The Nation*, May 19, 2015.

https://www.thenation.com/article/neo-mccarthyism-and-us-media/.

360. Helmer, John. "Anne Applebaum Is Not a War Profiteer, but Her Husband Reveals That She Was Paid More Than $800,000 in 2013—And That Was Before the Shooting Started in Ukraine." Dances with Bears, November 5, 2014.

http://johnhelmer.net/anne-applebaum-is-not-a-war-profiteer-but-her-hus-band-reveals-that-she-was-paid-more-than-800000-in-2013-and-that-was-before-the-shooting-started-in-ukraine/.

361. The West vs. Russia. Munk Debates. 2015.

https://munkdebates.com/debates/the-west-vs-russia

362. Lopez, Ralph. "Editor of Major German Newspaper Says He Planted Stories for the CIA." Global Research, February 4, 2015.

https://www.globalresearch.ca/editor-of-major-german-newspaper-says-he-planted-stories-for-the-cia/5429324.

363. "Americans, Europeans Want Non-MSM Coverage of International News—Poll." RT, May 19, 2015.

https://www.rt.com/news/259921-us-europe-alternative-media/.

364. Easley, Jonathan. "Poll: Majority Says Mainstream Media Publishes Fake News." *The Hill*, May 24, 2017.

https://thehill.com/homenews/campaign/334897-poll-majority-says-main-stream-media-publishes-fake-news.

365. Gabriel, Jon. "What Americans Care About vs. What the Media Cares About." Ricochet.com, July 18, 2017.

https://ricochet.com/442941/archives/americans-care-vs-media-cares/.

366. "Russiagate: Kooky Characters, Cold War Liberals." Interview with Matt Taibbi. The Real News Network, July 20, 2017.

https://therealnews.com/stories/mtaibbi0720russia.

367. "Longtime Reporter Leaves NBC Saying Media Is 'Trump Circus' That Encourages Perpetual War." Interview with William Arkin. Democracy Now! January 9, 2019.

https://www.democracynow.org/2019/1/9/longtime_reporter_leaves_nbc_saying_media?utm_source=Democracy+Now%21&utm_campaign=85e9891a21-Daily_Digest_COPY_01&utm_medium=email&utm_term=0_fa2346a853-85e9891a21-191485825.

368. Podesta Emails: Re: Topline Results. WikiLeaks, June 27, 2015.

https://wikileaks.org/podesta-emails/emailid/277.

369. Allen, Jonathan and Amie Parnes. *Shattered: Inside Hillary Clinton's Doomed Campaign.* New York: Crown Publishers, 2017.

370. Debenedetti, Gabriel. "They Always Wanted Trump." *Politico*, November 7, 2016.

https://www.politico.com/magazine/story/2016/11/hillary-clinton-2016-donald-trump-214428.

371. Mate, Aaron. "New Studies Show Pundits Are Wrong About Russian Social-Media Involvement in US Politics." *The Nation*, December 28, 2018.

https://www.thenation.com/article/archive/russiagate-elections-interference/

372. *United States of America v. Concord Management and Consulting, LLC.* Case No. No. 18-cr-32-2 (DLF). Memorandum Opinion and Order signed by Judge Dabney L. Friedrich. July 1, 2019.

https://assets.documentcloud.org/documents/6185644/Sealed-Order.pdf.

373. VIPS. "Intel Vets Challenge 'Russia Hack' Evidence." *Consortium News*, July 24, 2017.

https://consortiumnews.com/2017/07/24/intel-vets-challenge-russia-hack-evidence/.

374. Ritter, Scott. "Indictment of 12 Russians: Under the Shiny Wrapping, a Political Act." Truthdig, July 15, 2018.

https://www.truthdig.com/articles/indictment-of-12-russians-under-the-shiny-wrapping-a-political-act/.

375. Greenwald, Glenn. "Beyond Buzzfeed: The 10 Worst, Most Embarrassing U.S. Media Failures on the Trump-Russia Story." The Intercept, January 20, 2019.

https://theintercept.com/2019/01/20/beyond-buzzfeed-the-10-worst-most-embarrassing-u-s-media-failures-on-the-trumprussia-story/.

376. Stubbs, Alexander and Fernando Montealegre-Z. "Recording of 'Sonic Attacks' on U.S. Diplomats in Cuba Spectrally Matches the Echoing Call of a Caribbean Cricket." BioRxiv, January 4, 2019.
https://www.biorxiv.org/content/early/2019/01/04/510834.

377. Marcus, Ruth (@RuthMarcus). "So excited to be watching The Americans, throwback to a simpler time when everyone considered Russia the enemy. Even the president." Twitter. March 7, 2017, 10:09 p.m.
https://twitter.com/ruthmarcus/status/839312156780818432?lang=en.

378. **378.** Nelson, Steven. "Lock Him Up? Lawmakers Renew Calls for James Clapper Perjury Charges." U.S. News & World Report, November 17, 2016.
https://www.usnews.com/news/articles/2016-11-17/lawmakers-resume-calls-for-james-clapper-perjury-charges.

379. James Clapper Appearance on Meet the Press. May 28, 2017.
https://www.nbcnews.com/meet-the-press/meet-press-may-28-2017-n765626.

380. Sipher, John (@john_sipher). "I'm getting a lot of pushback for using 'Russophobe'. My intent is to focus on Putin's Kremlin. The Russian people and the world deserve better. Think where Russia could be without a corrupt leadership who is at war with much of the world." Twitter, March 6, 2018, 11:48 a.m.
https://twitter.com/john_sipher/status/971065012382035969.

381. Berliner, Martin (@MartinBerliner). "Because they ARE rats and roaches. What's the problem?" Twitter, March 6, 2018, 2:59 p.m.
https://twitter.com/martinberliner/status/971113099616014337.

382. "Review: Red Sparrow." Russia Reviewed, March 1, 2018.
https://russiareviewed.wordpress.com/2018/03/01/review-red-sparrow/?c=2265#comment-2265.

383. Mercouris, Alexander. "Red Sparrow: Yet Another Racist Russophobe Film from Hollywood." The Duran's Russia Feed, March 5, 2018.
http://russiafeed.com/red-sparrow-yet-another-russophobe-film/.

384. Review of Loveless. Catherine Brown. February 25, 2018.
https://catherinebrown.org/loveless/.

385. Baldwin, Natylie. "Putin Proposes Changes to Constitution, Medvedev Resigns: What's Going On?" *Consortium News*, January 29, 2020.

https://consortiumnews.com/2020/01/19/putin-proposes-changes-to-constitution-medvedev-resigns-whats-going-on/.